New Jersey
GARDENER'S
GUIDE

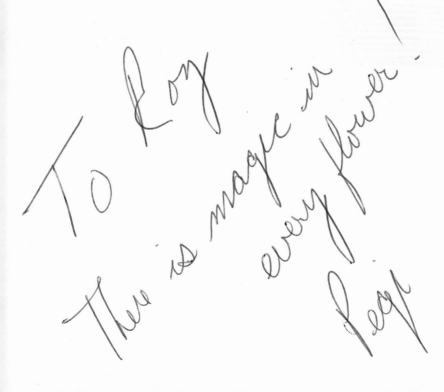

To Roy
This is magic in
every flower!
Peg

The What, Where, When, How & Why
Of Gardening In New Jersey

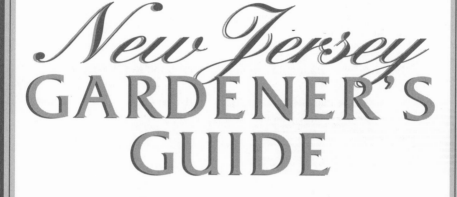

PEGI BALLISTER-HOWELLS

COOL
SPRINGS
PRESS

Ballister-Howells, Pegi
    New Jersey Gardener's Guide: the what, where, when, how & why of gardening in New Jersey / Pegi Ballister-Howells

    p.   cm.
    Includes bibliographical references (p.   ) and index.
    ISBN 1-888608-47-1
    1. Landscape plants -- New Jersey 2. Landscape gardening -- New Jersey
    3. Gardening -- New Jersey I. Title
635.9--dc20
Bal

Cool Springs Press, Inc.
206 Bridge Street
Franklin, Tennessee 37064

First printing 1998
Printed in the United States of America
10 9 8 7 6 5 4 3 2 1

Horticultural Nomenclature Editor: Robert F. Polomski, Extension Consumer Horticulturist, Clemson University

On the cover (clockwise from top left): Lilac, Columbine, Zinnia, Peonies

Map (on last page of color insert) provided by Agricultural Research Service, USDA

Color photographs provided courtesy of the author.

Visit the Cool Springs Press website at: www.coolspringspress.com

DEDICATION

TO SPENCER H. DAVIS JR. AND WARNER H. THURLOW. They gave me the guidance I needed to find my way on the path I had chosen.

ACKNOWLEDGMENTS

I COULD NOT POSSIBLY HAVE WRITTEN THIS BOOK without the wonderful, all-encompassing love and support of my husband, Tom Costantino. Our normally very full life with two small children, careers, and the demands of Blooming Acres was packed full to the point of bursting as page after page was churned through the computer. It is his accomplishment as much as my own, and his assistance with children and home, and keeping me always with a hot cup of coffee, allowed me to fulfill a lifelong dream. My love and appreciation are yours, Tommy, forever and a day.

On the technical level, Mel Moss of Livingston Park Nursery in North Brunswick tolerated many an inquiring phone call about everything from flower petals to fall color on trees. You were wonderful, Mel. Mr. and Mrs. Frank Benardella provided great insight on rose selections. Dr. Bruce Hamilton and his staff at Rutgers University made themselves available on several occasions. Drs. Reed Funk and William Meyer, both of Rutgers University, provided invaluable information on turfgrass varieties.

Nancy Quarella did an outstanding job helping me with the manuscript.

On a personal level, Patti Ferriola and Laurie Berman gave me time to breathe by taking care of the kids. Both Ellen Fox and Cindy O'Connor listened patiently when I needed to vent. Alan Danser called regularly to give moral support. Jim Quarella took care of business so I could devote the necessary time to writing. Holly, my border collie, never left my side. I could not have gotten through the process without the tremendous support of these friends. In the garden of life, I think friends must be the zinnias: bright, cheerful, and dependable. My sincere thanks, appreciation, and love to all.

CONTENTS

INTRODUCTION

New Jersey Gardening

*I*F YOUR HOME IS YOUR CASTLE, THEN THINK OF YOUR YARD AS YOUR KINGDOM. *You* decide if you want formal gardens or meadows of wildflowers, if you prefer low-maintenance evergreens or blasts of color. Plant the flowers that bring you joy and the shrubs that make you smile. Your yard is an extension of your personality and must fit your own concept of beauty and function. It must also fit with your lifestyle. Lots of shade trees do not make an area good for touch football games, but large areas of open ground do need to be mowed. Delicate flowers in the back yard where toddlers play is asking for disaster, but to share a love of growing things with children is a gift for both teacher and pupil.

As ruler of your kingdom, you need to decide what you want and need from your yard. You should have a plan. It doesn't have to be a plan that has every tree and blade of grass outlined on a diagram, but a general plan of open areas and private nooks. A major part of the plan should be a consideration of how much effort you intend to expend on maintenance.

Consider planting shade trees on the south side for summer shade and winter sun. Plant hardy evergreens on the north side to give protection from winter wind. Border plantings and flowering hedges can create privacy. You will need a focal point or two, and be sure to consider plantings that unfold their own brand of majesty in the dead of winter. A snow-covered scene will make even a compost pile gorgeous, but a well-planned winter landscape will have a stark and regal beauty in the absence of snow.

If you were starting from scratch, you might consider planting some groups of plants in a particular order—the order that they are presented in this book.

SHADE TREES AND LARGE EVERGREENS
Start by planting shade trees and large evergreens. These create the basic structure on which you will build your empire. Choose both plants and planting locations carefully. It is not easy to change your mind once these cornerstones become established. To reduce the risk of insects and/or disease wiping out an entire planting, avoid

Introduction

planting monocultures. Mixed evergreens add subtle variations to the landscape. It is like combining velvet with velveteen and suede; the textures are rich and cry out to be touched.

Think about what you are planting. A blue spruce outside the front door is a big mistake. It can reach 100 feet! Maple trees have tenacious roots that will wreak havoc on your septic system if planted too close to it. The beautiful native dogwood needs shade. These are all fine trees, but in the wrong spot they can make you miserable.

SMALL FLOWERING TREES

Next it will be time to select small flowering trees, which is a little like choosing chairs for your living room. They can be similar in style to what is already there, or completely different. Maybe just one will make a perfect focal point in a small space, or scatter several about to fill a larger area. Use all the same plants for impact or add diversity with plants that have different key features.

The joy of small flowering trees is their return engagements every year: same time, same place. It can take a while before small trees bloom to full capacity, so plan carefully to have trees that behave according to the blooming needs of your landscape. But even if they do not thrive, or have pest problems, or encounter some other disaster, it is not difficult to remove them and start over.

Mixing small flowering trees with evergreens can create a wonderful effect. Crape myrtles are only borderline-hardy in New Jersey, but when protected by a clump of evergreens, they may endure and present their midsummer frills with enthusiasm. Dogwoods will be happier nestled into the shady boughs of evergreens and will brighten the evergreens' shadowy skirts with spring color. Plant one or two little beauties and see how they do. One or two may be just enough; or you may decide you need another one over here, and another over there. You do not just plant a garden and walk away. You mold it, watch it grow, shape it, sculpt it, and grow with it. The planting of small flowering trees is one of the most satisfying of planting projects. These plants offer years of quiet joy.

9

Introduction

SHRUBS

Shrubs can be small or almost treelike. They may hold their leaves
or shed their summer raiment. In a small yard, a single shrub may
take center stage. On sprawling grounds, plant in clusters or rows
for impact. You need to know a lot about the particular plant you
are considering; before you plant, be sure to ask the right questions.
Some yews grow straight up. Some spread out low and wide like a
hovering pterodactyl. A pterodactyl in a three-foot space is destined
for extinction! Euonymus get scale like an ice cream cone dipped in
chocolate jimmies. Wisteria growing on a wooden porch will eventually crush the porch wood. Asking questions about size, habit, rate
of growth, and pests *before* you encounter them as problems will
help you have a peaceful co-existence with your landscape plants.

Most shrubs can be moved or pruned or replaced without
destroying a long-term investment. It is not a good idea to move
shrubs around like checkers on a checkerboard, but if you have a
change of heart, or find that a plant is not doing what you had
hoped in a particular spot, get out your shovel and move it. If you
follow reasonable planting procedures at an acceptable time of year,
transplanting can be accomplished without too much trauma to
yourself or the plant.

VINES AND GROUNDCOVERS

After planting shrubs, you can fine-tune your grounds with vines
and groundcovers. Vines can create vertical interest and sometimes
a truly dramatic focus. When planted in the wrong spot, some vines
can get other plants all tangled up as if they were caught in a spider
web. Ask, read, investigate, and observe before you plant anything
creeping, climbing, twining, or spreading.

Groundcovers are great work-savers that offer their own brand of
beauty. The "Big Three" are English ivy, pachysandra, and periwinkle. These will all get the job done, but a little creativity in this arena
will be most rewarding.

Introduction

✣

Roses, Perennials, Bulbs, and Annuals

The leap to planting roses, perennials, bulbs, and annuals is like moving from building to decorating. The first major steps of landscaping (or creating a home) should create harmony and personal satisfaction, but adding the trimmings can be rollicking good fun. Go for bold colors or delicate pastels. Be daring and experimental or elegant and refined. Plant, move, divide, change. Plan a color theme or a riot of brilliance. Express yourself and have as much fun as possible doing it. Nothing is permanent, and everything generates new ideas for next year.

In this kingdom of yours, you need to spend time with your subjects. Your yard is full of wondrous delights, but you have to take the time to see them. If you wander about your kingdom only when trudging behind a lawn mower, you will not notice the new shoots on the weeping Norway spruce which are so bright they look like they have tiny lights inside, nor will you see the red anthers on the black pussy willows as the fuzzy buds begin to mature.

Although there is much satisfaction and true pleasure in taking time to appreciate what you have, there is more to spending time in the yard than simply appreciating its charms. If you do not know what your plant kingdom should look like when it is healthy, you will not recognize the subtle signs when all is not well. At some point, the leaves will yellow or the limbs become bare and you may notice something is wrong as you dash from the car to the kitchen door. If you spot a problem at a run, it may be too late to solve it.

Look at the leaves. Turn a leaf over and look at its underside. Sometimes it is the same color as the top of the leaf, but on some leaves the two surfaces are different. Look for bumps and ridges on the stems, look at the shape of buds, notice whether the flowers grow at the tips of the branches or further back. The new growth often emerges one color and then matures to another shade. Flowers, fruits, and seeds come in an almost infinite variety of sizes and shapes. A novice Christmas tree grower once called me in a panic. There were horrible growths all over his trees. He was sure the

Introduction

growths were certain death for the trees and no one knew what they were. It was a new disease and no one cared! He could lose everything and no one cared! The poor man was borderline hysterical. Instead of heading to the beach for the weekend, I rushed out to his farm armed with reference books, magnifying glass, sampling bags, and spray recommendations to stop the onslaught of the unknown enemy. His tree-destroying growths turned out to be the male cones. If he had taken the time to know his plants, there would have been no panic.

Time spent in quiet observation is time well spent. By being prepared to "nip it in the bud," you can keep a problem from becoming overwhelming. The occasional few minutes spent mingling with foliage and flowers can save you hours of pruning, battling bugs, and even replacing damaged plants.

CHOOSING THE PLANT AND CHOOSING THE RIGHT SPOT

The plant and its spot have to be considered at the same time. Whether you want to plant a tree, a shrub, or even a herbaceous plant, first take a good look at the planting spot. Is there standing water? Sandy soil? Clay? Sun? Shade? Root competition? Air pollution? A septic system? If the spot receives blazing sun, a flowering dogwood will fry. You may have to tuck the dogwood into a shady nook and plant a sun-loving flowering cherry in the sunny front yard.

If the magnetism of a particular plant makes it irresistible, take the opposite approach. You might be able to find a spot in your landscape that has conditions suited for the plant. Find out if the plant needs sun or shade, learn its ultimate size and rate of growth, and learn about potential pest problems and soil and water requirements. There may also be a few unique characteristics such as fall color or your own preference for male or female plants that could affect your planting decision. A female holly has berries and might be a perfect choice for center stage, but without a male somewhere close by to provide pollen, you will be berryless.

Introduction

⚘

The right plant in the right location will have the best chance for an uneventful, successful life. Anything less than a good match will become a maintenance nightmare.

The United States Department of Agriculture (USDA) Plant Hardiness Zone map divides our country into minimum-temperature zones. We have listed the zones in which each plant in this book can survive winter conditions. You will notice that the zone list in most of the plant entries includes zones that are not New Jersey zones (the New Jersey zones, 5, 6, and 7, are printed in boldface type to differentiate them from those in other states). We have listed *all* the zones a particular plant is hardy in because this is useful information for the gardener who is making decisions on how to handle a particular plant (is it likely to thrive in a harsh location in the landscape? does it need winter protection?). Remember that it is not only zone hardiness that determines whether a plant will survive the winter in your area. Other factors include wind, sunlight, rain, humidity, soil, drainage, and exposure.

We have also provided symbols for the amount of light suitable for each plant's growing requirements. The following symbols indicate full sun, partial shade, and shade.

Full Sun   Partial   Shade
           Shade

PREPARING THE HOLE

Dig a big hole. Make it much bigger than you need. Then make it a little bigger than that.

Look into the hole. Is it wet? Try filling it with water to see if it drains. If the water just sits, you may have a drainage problem. You can compensate for this by digging up a large area several feet down and incorporating organic matter and sand throughout the area. If drainage is a serious problem, you can install drainage pipe.

Introduction

If it is minor, large rocks well beneath the rootball will provide a well for the water to collect away from the roots. You can also plant with the rootball slightly above ground level to keep the roots out of the soggy soil.

Just about all New Jersey soils will benefit from the addition of organic matter: peat moss, well-rotted manures, or compost. Leaf compost is commonly available in large quantities from local composting facilities. Some towns make it available to residents for free; check with your department of public works or parks. You can always make compost yourself. It is neither difficult nor time consuming. If you mix your leaves and grass clippings, you can produce a fine-quality compost that will improve your soils and reduce the waste management burden on your community. Compost is not a substitute for fertilizer, but because nutrients cling to the organic matter particles, the plants have more opportunity to make use of existing nutrients. Check with your County Extension Office for details on backyard composting. They can also provide information on testing your soil; a good practice prior to planting as well as for maintaining your landscape.

Organic matter improves both sand and clay soils. In sand, organic matter helps hold on to soil moisture and nutrients. In clay, it opens air spaces and allows water to drain more effectively. The organic matter will hold on to residual moisture longer and so delay or prevent that rock-hard, water-repelling condition that occurs when clay soils get overly dry.

It is possible to add both organic matter and sand to heavy clay soils to open up the soil even more. *Never* add sand to clay without also adding organic matter. Clay and sand makes something very similar to concrete, which is not something you want to encourage in your yard. If you add a 2:1 mixture of organic matter and sand, you will enjoy significant improvement in tilth, moisture content, and nutrient levels.

There is no exact rule for the amount of organic matter you should add. If you add one shovelful of organic matter for every one to two shovelsful of soil, you will be doing well. Mix the soil amendments with the soil you put back into the hole and the soil you will use to fill in around the plant. Then you are ready to plant.

PLACING THE PLANT

Unless you are attempting to compensate for a drainage problem, place the plant at the same height it was in the ground or container. You may want to slightly mound up very loose soil since the soil will tend to settle, but experience with your own soils will give you the best guidance.

Do not throw fertilizer into the hole; this will burn the roots. Don't even mix fertilizer into the soil you use to fill the hole. Wait until the plant has been established for at least one year before fertilizing with anything.

Be very careful not to damage any roots in the planting process. When clumps of dirt fall away from the ball, tiny hair roots go with them. It is these tiny roots that are responsible for most of the plant's water uptake. Treat the rootball gently and shift it as little as possible once the plant is out of its pot.

It is not necessary to remove burlap from around the roots of a balled tree or shrub if it is a natural burlap. The roots grow right through the weave. By the time the roots get large enough to feel any restrictions from the fabric, it will have rotted away. New, plastic burlaps must be removed.

Always remove any wires, cords, or strings that encircle the trunk. Even those made of natural materials may not deteriorate quickly enough to avoid damaging the trunk. If the trunk should become girdled, the tree is dead. This is not an "if" or a "maybe." It is a fact. It happens surprisingly suddenly. The trunk continually expands, but at some point the restriction goes from letting small amounts of moisture through to completely cutting off moisture. It is often a very clean, uniform death without spots or gaping wounds, but the tree is still dead. Remove the tags and strings.

Introduction

Fill the hole with the amended soil. Tamp it down firmly, but do not hard-pack. You may want to stake trees or large shrubs, especially if you are planting in the fall. Winter winds can wreak havoc on newly planted material.

Water thoroughly.

MAINTENANCE

Each of the plant entries in this book has a section on care and maintenance, but there are a few general rules that are worth noting right away. To begin, throw away your electric hedge shears. They are the most destructive piece of noise-making, plant-ruining equipment ever made. You *think* they save you time. What they really do is make such a mess of a plant you get trapped into using them over and over. Eventually the plant is worthless and you have to start all over again, or you must perform several years of meticulous hand pruning to allow the plant to recover.

A pair of long-handled loppers (with a ratchet mechanism for extra power if you need it) and good hand pruners are the best tools. *Selective* pruning, where you remove the offending branches at a joint or major V, maintains the natural shape and beauty of a plant. If you have a plant that requires that half be removed once or even twice a year so that it will fit in its space, you have the wrong plant for that space. Move it or get rid of it and plant something more appropriate.

When you prune depends on the species. Never prune spring-blooming plants in early spring or you will remove all the flowers. Shade trees can have major limbs removed any time, but such removal is best performed during winter dormancy or in the middle of summer. If you cannot remove a branch while standing on the ground with a pole pruner, *hire a professional.* Climbing large trees and swinging from ropes is not for the inexperienced.

The need to control insects and diseases can be kept to a minimum with careful plant selection. If and when you have a problem, the window for effective control is often very limited. Early spring,

Introduction

when buds are just starting to open, is a critical time for the prevention of many diseases. Controlling insects while the pests are in juvenile stages or in smaller numbers is much more satisfactory than at any other time. Knowing your plants and being able to spot a problem early can make a big difference in effecting its solution.

Transplanting woody ornamentals is best done in the early spring, but many are easily moved in the early fall as well. As for perennials, there is a general rule that spring-blooming species are divided in the fall and fall bloomers can be moved or propagated in the spring.

Watering can be critical, especially for newly planted material or when drought makes living in the garden difficult. It is always better to water in the early morning than at night; this reduces the risk of disease. If at all possible, keep the water on the ground rather than on the leaves; this will also help minimize disease.

When watering is necessary, water deeply and thoroughly. Make sure the entire root system has a good drink. Shallow watering encourages shallow roots, which will dry out more quickly in the long run. One inch of water per week, put down all at once, is good for most plants. Measure by using several tunafish cans under the sprinklers. Shade trees may need more water, but not as often. Newly planted trees and shrubs should be watered more frequently in really hot weather, especially the first year or two.

How much maintenance your yard requires is largely a result of the plants you have chosen and where they are growing. It is also a mindset. A soft, natural look is a lot easier than carefully groomed shrubs forced into the shape of meatballs and hockey pucks. It is your home, your yard, your kingdom. Rule it wisely.

Shade Trees

HEN JOYCE KILMER WROTE "I THINK THAT I SHALL NEVER SEE A POEM LOVELY AS A TREE," he was referring to a white oak growing on Cook College campus in New Brunswick. A mature shade tree is a thing of beauty that has tremendous impact on a property with both appearance and function.

When there is new home construction on wooded lots, there is often an effort to save existing trees. When the effort is successful, these older trees give a feeling of maturity and dignity that can take years to achieve with newly planted trees. Unfortunately, even when trees are protected during construction, the constant moving of heavy machinery across their roots causes a compaction that can take its toll. A change in grade six inches up or down can eventually kill a tree; so can changes in the flow of water. Within five years of new construction, many established trees often begin to die. It is very expensive to remove large dying trees from around buildings, so carefully choose the trees you intend to save.

Whether you start out with a wooded lot or have a yard that is a "blank canvas," plant shade trees in key locations as your first step in making your grounds all you want them to be. The newly planted shade trees in a wooded lot will have gotten fairly large if and when you lose what was already growing there.

Adding a shade tree to an established landscape requires even more consideration than when starting with a blank canvas. Established plants that thrive in the sun may suffer as your shade tree grows. If the lawn is your pride and joy, remember that many shade trees compete with lawngrasses and make growing grass difficult, if not impossible.

It is important to think about why you want a shade tree. A nice shady tree or two in the backyard is greatly appreciated in summer. They are terrific on the south side of a property, where they block

Chapter One

intense sunlight in the summer but allow warm rays through in the winter. If you are planting trees in the front yard, decide whether you want to *frame* the house or *hide* it for privacy. Keep in mind the location of sewer and water lines, since roots may grow to seek water and cause problems down the road.

Think carefully about how the rooms in your home will be affected by the trees you plant. Do you want the east-facing bedroom to be sunny in the morning? Will a west-facing dining room have magnificent sunsets—or would that be too hot? Will a shade tree block your view of incoming cars? Once a tree becomes established, it will be a heartbreaker to remove it.

A vegetable or flower garden needs full sun to thrive. Be sure to leave an open area on the grounds if you intend to grow an annual garden.

There are many trees from which to choose. It is hard to go wrong with the sturdy tap-rooted oak. Pin oaks have been very popular in recent years, but the mature trees retain unsightly dead branches at the bottom, requiring professional pruning. Sweet gum is hardy with very attractive leaves, but many object to the gumballs that drop every fall. Sycamores and London planetrees are similar in appearance, with lovely peeling bark, but you should avoid these two as well if you don't like trees that "drop things" like bark, gumballs, and leaves. Gray birch is a graceful tree, but the birch leaf miner and the bronze birch borer are serious pests.

Maples are classic shade trees, and for good reason. Their shape and dense masses of leaves produce terrific shade. Most maples have excellent fall color, but the roots of these trees stay close to the surface, making wicked competition for lawngrasses. Many maples have trouble with wilt disease, for which there is no control. Silver maple may be the tree most plagued by this disease; the common Norway also struggles with severe wilt.

Planting a shade tree is an investment in the future. It will mark the passage of time and store memories as it grows with you. Choose and plant your trees with care.

Ginkgo

Ginkgo biloba

Other Name: Maidenhair Tree	**Light Requirement:**
Height: Up to 80 ft.	
Spread: Usually 30 to 40 ft. but possibly as much as 100 ft.	
Zones: 3, 4, **5, 6, 7,** 8	

The ginkgo is a wonderful tree that has a fascinating history. It is one of the oldest trees known to humankind, dating as far back as 150 million years. Like many needled evergreens, the ginkgo is a "gymnosperm," which means "naked seeds"—the plants in this primitive class produce seeds that develop without being inside an ovary. The ginkgo is a rare exception, as most deciduous trees belong to the "angiosperm" class of plants—plants in this more advanced angiosperm class grow seeds that are enclosed in an ovary. In simple terms, angiosperms have flowers and gymnosperms do not. There was a time when ginkgoes grew worldwide, but they are now native only to China, and it is possible that they exist in China only in cultivation. The ginkgo's wide-spreading branches and moderately leaved limbs provide extensive light shade, which can be more desirable than the heavy shade associated with more traditional shade trees. The winter appearance of this tree has its own appeal; the open habit and the spurred branches create an unusual but attractive silhouette. The leaves themselves are works of art, with interesting fan shapes and lovely golden-yellow fall color. The leaf pattern is often used in fabric design and in jewelry. Ginkgo leaves are currently in demand as an herbal treatment for a variety of ills, including use to dilate blood vessels with the hope of enhancing memory. The seed is considered a delicacy in Japanese cuisine, but ginkgo fruit can be a problem. The female trees produce a plumlike fruit that has slimy, smelly flesh. Many experts recommend planting only male specimens. Since sex determination is impossible until the trees bloom, and as they often do not mature until they are 20 years old, you must take care to purchase a named male variety that has been asexually propagated. Ginkgoes are extremely hardy and suffer few, if any, insect or disease problems. They tolerate air pollution and also withstand some salty soil conditions.

When to Plant

Plant ginkgoes in late March or early April. Spring planting is generally preferred, but since they establish without much difficulty, these trees may also do well in September.

Where to Plant

Choose a sunny location. A ginkgo will spread far; be sure to allow plenty of room for it to grow. The tree will tolerate streetside planting, though the wide spread makes this inappropriate for most ginkgoes. Ginkgoes are not particular about soil type but prefer moderately moist soil conditions.

How to Plant

Ginkgoes are often used as specimen trees. Since they spread so far, one tree is usually enough for most yards. Do not fertilize at planting time. If planting the tree in the fall, be sure to stake it securely so that it will be better able to withstand winter winds.

Care and Maintenance

The ginkgo is a low-maintenance tree. Any necessary pruning can be done in the spring before bud-break.

Additional Information

Ginkgoes are not fast-growing trees, but if watered and fertilized appropriately (*not* to excess!), they will grow at a much faster rate.

Additional Species, Cultivars, or Varieties

There is only one species, but there are several named cultivars. The names are important if you are seeking a male tree. 'Santa Cruz' and 'Autumn Gold' are two male varieties. 'Sentry' is a male variety with an upright growth habit that makes it an excellent selection for a street tree.

Heritage River Birch

Betula nigra 'Heritage'

Other Names: River Birch, Red Birch **Height:** 40 to 70 ft. **Spread:** 40 to 60 ft. **Zones:** 4, **5**, **6**, **7**, 8, 9	**Light Requirement:**

*E*ach species of birch has a certain appeal. The gray is favored for its clump habit and graceful branches, and the white is majestic in both color and stature. The black and yellow birches are the least popular kinds, but they are perhaps underappreciated. Both have a wonderful, strong oil-of-wintergreen smell under the bark and in the twigs; and black birch is resistant to the bronze birch borer, a pest that can devastate white and gray birches. Of all the birch species, the river birch may be the best choice for New Jersey gardens. The white does best further north and the gray, though amazingly pliable, often snaps under the weight of snow and ice. River birch are ideal for wet spots where many other trees do not survive. They can even tolerate short periods of standing water. One of the river birch's greatest attractions is its peeling bark. The bark of the colorful 'Heritage' peels back to reveal many shades of pink, peach, and cream. Bark begins peeling at an early age; larger scrolls fall away as the tree matures. This adds winter interest as well as color, which is always in short supply during cold weather. 'Heritage' is available as a single trunk or clumping specimen. It is very dense when in full leaf; its spreading habit will require room to grow. In winter, its multi-colored bark and delicate, thin branches give 'Heritage' river birch a special place in the landscape. It is particularly resistant to both the birch leaf miner and the bronze birch borer.

WHEN TO PLANT

Birches are not good choices for fall planting. Late March or early April is the ideal time to plant.

WHERE TO PLANT

Since river birch is tolerant of wet ground, it is ideal for planting along streams or in places where the ground is wet for part of the year. It requires a pH of 6.5 or below, but New Jersey soils are notorious for being acidic so that should be no problem. River birch is very effective as a specimen tree or in groups. In its clump form, its branches reach down almost to the ground, adding privacy in summer.

HOW TO PLANT

River birch is not a difficult tree to get established. Selective pruning at the time of planting may be particularly helpful, especially for balled trees. River birch requires high soil moisture to do its best; take care to keep the tree well watered during its first summer.

CARE AND MAINTENANCE

The persistent birch leaf miner plagues most birches, especially the gray. Larvae feed between the leaf layers, turning the leaves brown. Miners may weaken gray and white birches, making them more susceptible to the devastating bronze birch borer. But river birch is resistant to these major pests, so you should not have to spray it. Expect some minor damage from birch leaf miners; there is usually not enough to be problematic. Occasional removal of crossing sucker branches from clump forms of river birch may be necessary.

ADDITIONAL SPECIES, CULTIVARS, OR VARIETIES

'Heritage' is a patented variety introduced by Mr. Earl Cully of Illinois. This variety's many advantages over the species make it worth seeking out. Don't be fooled by tags that have a designation such as "clump river birch." True 'Heritage' specimens will be marketed with that name.

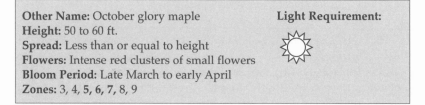

October Glory Red Maple

Acer rubrum 'October Glory'

Other Name: October glory maple
Height: 50 to 60 ft.
Spread: Less than or equal to height
Flowers: Intense red clusters of small flowers
Bloom Period: Late March to early April
Zones: 3, 4, **5, 6, 7,** 8, 9

Light Requirement:

With their dense foliage and beautiful fall color, maples are the classic shade tree. As many species are native to eastern forests, it is reasonable to expect them to do well in our environment. Red maples get their common name not from the color of the leaves, but from the color of the flowers. Many maple trees do turn red in the fall, but the color can vary from tree to tree, and foliage can be colored from yellow to dark red. Red maples have a large range and can be found from Maine to Florida. Seedlings selected from locally grown trees will do best. This is one reason October Glory is such a good choice for New Jersey landscapes. It was developed right in the center of the state at Princeton Nursery in Plainsboro, New Jersey. In general, maples have a shallow, fibrous root system that can present problems; it may lift sidewalks or extend its roots into water lines. Because the leaves are relatively free of disease and the wood is strong, red maple is one of the best maple species.

WHEN TO PLANT

All red maples do best when planted in spring. Late March to early April, while the tree is still dormant, is the best time to plant.

WHERE TO PLANT

Choose a sunny location where you will be able to appreciate red maple's fall color. It will tolerate wet ground. This tree will not thrive in areas where pollution is heavy. Soil with a high pH can cause chlorosis of the leaves, though this should not be a problem in our acidic Jersey soils.

How to Plant

Red maple is not a difficult plant to get established. Very young trees can be moved bare-rooted, but you will most likely find 'October Glory' balled and waiting for you at your nursery in the spring. Fall planting is risky.

Care and Maintenance

Maples may be attacked by cankerworms (commonly called "inch-worms") in the spring. Spray if necessary with carbaryl or BT (*Bacillus thuringiensis*). Maples also drop their fruits, or "samaras" ("whirlybirds," if you're under ten years old), sometimes in large numbers.

Additional Information

'October Glory' is a patented variety. The intense red fall color is outstanding, and the tree holds its leaves longer than most other red maples. If you have your heart set on a particular look for your grounds, be sure to plant a named variety with the fall coloration you desire.

Additional Species, Cultivars, or Varieties

'Armstrong' red maple is a columnar form that works well in confined streetside plantings. 'Red Sunset' is an excellent cultivar whose brilliant orange-red fall color appears about 3 weeks earlier than that of 'October Glory'. *Acer saccharum*, the sugar maple, is a beautiful, hardy, long-lived tree that has dense foliage and a pleasing shape. It is famed for its fall color but does best in the more northern part of its range. Sugar maple does not tolerate air pollution or crowded situations. While it will do well in much of the state, specimens planted in the mountainous northwest will produce the best fall color. Often mistaken for a red maple, the red-leaved 'Crimson King' is a variety of *A. platanoides*, the Norway maple. It makes quite a statement in the landscape. Norways are one of the more pollution-tolerant shade trees; this has unfortunately resulted in their rampant overuse. They are particularly shallow-rooted, making for serious competition in the lawn and producing roots that come to the surface. Norway maples are highly subject to maple wilt, a disease for which there is no cure. With its delicate leaves, the silver maple, *Acer saccharinum*, is a true beauty. But it is also weak-wooded, shallow-rooted, and subject to many insect pests and leaf diseases. Avoid any temptation to plant a silver maple! Stick with one of the other maple species, which in the long run will be far superior in performance.

Purple Beech

Fagus sylvatica 'Riversii'

Other Name: Rivers Purple Beech
Height: Usually 50 to 60 ft. but can
    reach 100 ft.
Spread: 35 to 40 ft.
Zones: 4, 5, 6, 7

Light Requirement:

The beech is a magnificent tree. The American beech, *Fagus grandiflora*, is easily identified in the forest by its smooth, gray bark. It is interesting to note that few if any varieties or cultivars have been developed. The European beech, *F. sylvatica*, has received the most horticultural attention. It has long been cultivated in Europe, with many named varieties dating back to the 1800s. The purple beech has all the majesty of the species. Its rich maroon-colored leaves add focus as well as beauty to the summer landscape. Be patient; this tree is not a fast grower. Do not overlook the many other varieties. Mature weeping beeches create magical havens under which one can hide. There are variegated leaves as well as cutleaf varieties, upright growth forms as well as weeping. Each one is more beautiful than the next.

WHEN TO PLANT

It is recommended that you plant beech trees in spring (late March to early April), but there are no serious objections to fall planting in September if you have a container-grown tree or a balled specimen that was dug in the spring. Digging a beech in the fall is not recommended.

WHERE TO PLANT

Avoid wet sites and compacted soil. Do not plant a beech where its root system will receive heavy foot or vehicle traffic as the tree matures. Beeches are true beauties that are generally under-appreciated in the landscape. The purple beech in particular makes an excellent specimen tree. Plant it where you can enjoy watching it grow.

How to Plant

Beeches require oxygen in the soil; prepare the soil thoroughly. Dig a hole at least 3 times the diameter of the rootball. Heavy clay soils will benefit from the addition of both organic matter and sand to open up air spaces. Always mix 2 parts organic matter to 1 part sand before adding it to the soil.

Care and Maintenance

Beech trees can tolerate severe pruning if necessary. It is best to prune in late summer or early fall. Their dense foliage and low branching growth habit makes it difficult to grow grass beneath these trees. Beech is not particularly subject to any insects or diseases, but bagworms may be a problem. An even bigger problem is the tendency tree-ignorant people have to carve their initials in the bark. Any wound to a tree's bark makes it more susceptible to disease.

Additional Information

The species and most of the named varieties have dark-green leaves that turn a beautiful golden-bronze in the fall. Some purple varieties fade to green in the summer, but 'Riversii' holds its dark maroon color well. The slender, 1 in. long, brown, pointed buds on a beech are easily identified. The edible nuts are an important food source for wildlife, especially for squirrels, chipmunks, and bears.

Additional Species, Cultivars, or Varieties

The native beech, *Fagus grandiflora*, makes a fine shade tree. In a beech forest, the roots can send up many suckers, creating a spectacular grove of beech trees that is especially striking in the fall. For a focal point, consider one of the other varieties of European beech. 'Asplenifolia' is the best of the cutleaf varieties. 'Cuprea' is supposed to refer to the copper beech, but watch out for a lot of confusion with this variety. The copper beech is a pale-purple-leafed variety, though there is little consistency among specimens. Even so, most are lovely. 'Fastigata' and 'Dawyckii' have upright growth habits, and 'Pendula' is the weeping beech. A mature weeping beech may be the most beautiful of all trees. The sight of one can take your breath away.

Red Oak

Quercus rubra

Other Name: *Q. borealis*
Height: 75 ft., but up to 100 ft. in the wild
Spread: 40 to 50 ft.
Zones: 4, 5, 6, 7, 8

Light Requirement:

*I*t is hard to go wrong with the mighty oak. Oak species are, in general, fine trees. The red oak is the state tree of New Jersey, and with good reason. It is native to our forests, where deer, bears, raccoons, squirrels, turkeys, and bluejays feast on its acorns. Deer also feed on the twigs of low-growing branches. This lovely native transplants well to the city; it is tolerant of air pollution and grows more rapidly than other oaks: about 2 ft. per year when it is young. Red oak prefers an acidic pH; most New Jersey soils are acidic. As the tree matures, flat, white surfaces resembling "ski trails" develop on the bark. These marks are one of the red oak's identifying characteristics. The rich red wood of this oak is important in the lumber industry. The deeply lobed leaves sport bristles at the ends of pointed leaf tips. Summer foliage color is dark green, turning to rich, deep red in the fall.

WHEN TO PLANT

This is another tree that does best with spring planting. Late March or early April is the best time.

WHERE TO PLANT

The red oak has been successfully used as a street tree, but it will be happier in a location where it has more room to grow. It is an excellent choice for parks, golf courses, or lawn areas. It prefers well-drained, sandy loam soils, so avoid wet sites. Since squirrels love the red oak's acorns, you may not want to plant the tree so close to the house that it will eventually touch the building. This may encourage squirrels to take up residence in your attic.

How to Plant

Because it doesn't have a significant tap root, red oak is easier to establish than many other oaks. Tap-rooted trees are often difficult to transplant. When you plant it as a specimen, expect red oak to produce a wider spread than you see in the wild.

Care and Maintenance

Oaks are susceptible to a variety of insects and diseases, but they are usually not serious enough to be of concern. You do have to watch out for gypsy moth caterpillars. In a bad year they can completely defoliate an oak tree. One year of defoliation may not kill a well-established oak, but two years will put even an old established tree at risk. Major limbs can be removed at any time. Pruning and shaping is best done while the tree is dormant in winter, or in midsummer during summer dormancy.

Additional Information

Because oaks in the wild often hybridize, proper identification can be difficult. To grow your own red oak seedlings, keep the seeds at 40 degrees Fahrenheit for 30 to 45 days. It will take 20 to 25 years before the tree begins to flower, and as many as 25 more years before it produces much in the way of a crop. At that time, you can expect a large production of acorns every 2 to 5 years.

Additional Species, Cultivars, or Varieties

Though there are not many cultivars of red oak, there are several related species. The black oak, *Q. velutina*, is the most similar to the red oak, but its major tap root makes it more difficult to establish. The pin oak, *Q. palustris*, is probably the most popular oak used for landscaping, but for uncertain reasons. Though the fibrous root system makes for easy establishment, and pin oak tolerates wet ground better than some oak species. Its lower branches become pendulous and die as the tree matures. This is perfectly natural, but it gives the tree an unhealthy appearance. The willow oak, *Q. phellos*, may be considered as an alternative selection for wet sites.

Tulip Tree

Liriodendron tulipifera

Other Names: Tulip Magnolia, Tulip Poplar,
Yellow Poplar, Whitewood
Height: Usually 90 ft. but can reach
150 ft. or more
Spread: 35 to 40 ft.
Flowers: Beautiful pale greenish yellow
petals with orange centers; similar in
shape to a tulip
Bloom Period: June
Zones: 4, 5, 6, 7, 8, 9

Light Requirement:

The straight, majestic trunk of the tulip tree is dramatic, but it requires space to be appreciated. It is one of the few shade trees which also contributes significant bloom to the landscape, although the trees are quite tall by the time they are ready to flower. Bees love the flowers; the honey they produce from them has a reputation for excellent quality. Even the tulip tree's foliage is interesting. The unusually shaped leaves are large and bright green. Fall color is a rich yellow. Though fast-growing trees are generally less desirable due to weak wood and pest problems, tulip trees may be the best of the fast-growing shade trees. They are one of our tallest native deciduous trees and have been known to reach 200 ft.

WHEN TO PLANT

Plant the tulip tree in late March or early April. This is the only good time for planting.

WHERE TO PLANT

Plant tulip tree in wide open spaces. The tall, straight trunk will eventually be bare for 70 to 80 percent of its height, so plan to utilize the space below it. Avoid wet sites or very dry, sandy soil. Tulip tree grows quickly. Its annual rings can be as much as one centimeter wide.

How to Plant

Tulip tree prefers a deep loam soil, so be sure to add plenty of organic matter to existing soil. Prepare the soil deeply and take extra care to keep the tree well watered while it is getting established. Tulip tree's fleshy roots do not usually branch very much, and they need a little extra attention while being established.

Care and Maintenance

The tulip tree is slightly weak wooded, but this weakness varies greatly among individual specimens. You may have to tend to occasional storm damage. Winter pruning is best. Tulip tree is subject to tulip tree scale, but this is usually not a serious problem. You can control tulip tree scale when it appears by applying a dormant oil in April and carbaryl or malathion in late August. Treating the tops of large trees for tulip tree scale may require professional services.

Additional Information

The wood of the tulip tree is important in the lumber industry. It is used for furniture, for the interior finishes of buildings, and in general construction. Tulip tree seeds feed many birds and small mammals. Young seedlings are nibbled by rabbits and deer.

Additional Species, Cultivars, or Varieties

The Chinese tulip tree bears smaller flowers; it is not often planted. A few cultivars of our native tulip tree exist. They are available but not common. 'Aureo-marginatum' has a yellow margin around the edge of each leaf. 'Fastigatum' is an extremely upright form. It has received significant praise and is used in European gardens. A few other cultivars exist, but they are not produced commercially on a large scale.

Evergreen Trees

*E*VERGREEN TREES PLAY ANOTHER CRITICAL ROLE IN THE LANDSCAPE. They do much to define spaces and can set the tone for either a formal or a more natural setting. In summer they provide the backdrop for seasonal display, but they must be selected and arranged with enough character and interest to carry the burden of being the focus in winter.

Traditionally, landscape designers have frowned upon mixing deciduous material with evergreens. Perhaps it is time to break some of these rules and make your yard a personal statement. What could be lovelier than dogwood flowers peeking out from between the branches of a cluster of spruce and pines? The dogwood will benefit from the shade, and the dark-green needles will make the flowers visually jump out like a Van Gogh painting. Shade-loving oak-leaf hydrangeas thrive beneath mature white pines, bringing midsummer color to otherwise shadowy nooks.

A common problem is planting young evergreens in places where they will not have sufficient room to grow. Many a blue spruce has outgrown the spot outside the front door just when it starts to be large enough to have some character. It can't be pruned down to size, so the only option is to cut it down and start over.

A second common problem is the tendency to plant monocultures. A long, straight row of a single species of evergreen creates a very formal look, like a row of marching soldiers. That is great if you happen to like marching soldiers; but you will have a problem if a single tree—or one here and there—should die. New, short trees will draw the eye to notice the irregularity instead of the original line. In general, it looks patched and incongruous.

A more serious problem with monocultures occurs with the appearance of insects or disease. Once a pest has a foothold, it will spread through a monoculture like wildfire. It can wipe out, or at

Chapter Two

least severely damage, the entire planting even before you know you have a problem. Bagworms on arborvitae will take out a border planting in no time.

A staggered planting of different-size trees eliminates the soldier look and the replacement problem. A staggered row will fill in the gaps in short order and so establish privacy much more quickly. If you use different species, you eliminate the risk of losing everything with a single blow. Where space is a limiting factor, work with columnar varieties that have a very narrow span. 'Skyrocket' juniper and 'Flushing' yew are two of these, and there are many others. Think past planting a row of boring arborvitae. A mixed planting will not only be softer on the eye, it will perform better in the long run.

Choosing locations for evergreens requires serious thought. You will have to live with them where they are planted for a long time. While they create privacy year-round, they can also block your view, which can be desirable or not.

When planted on the north side of a house, evergreens will block the wind and protect the house during winter weather. They can make a remarkable difference in heat loss. Planted on the south side, they are great for summer shade, but you may prefer deciduous trees which will let in winter rays.

Don't plant evergreens too close to the house. You need to allow room to get behind the plantings to do routine maintenance. Don't plant them too close together either. Whatever species you choose, find out their rate of growth as well as their expected height at maturity so you can plan accordingly.

There are a few species that you may want to avoid. Norway spruce gets spruce canker badly; this is a disease which is ultimately fatal. Austrian pine has struggled with tip blight for the last fifteen years and no longer should be planted. Hemlocks are beautiful, but the woolly adelgid has become a plague in recent years; the coats protecting the insects within make chemical control difficult.

If your deciduous shade trees form the foundation of your yard, the evergreens build the walls. Later you will get to decorate.

American Holly

Ilex opaca

Height: 40 to 50 ft. **Spread:** 18 to 40 ft. **Flowers:** Very small white flowers **Bloom Period:** Late May to early June **Zones:** 5, 6, 7, 8, 9	**Light Requirement:**

The American holly is native to New Jersey and so can be expected to do well throughout most of the state. In the wild it is more often found in the south, in both the Pine Barrens and the shore area where it tolerates sandy soil and salty conditions. In the woods it tends to be an open, almost spindly tree. When planted in full sun, American holly is a much more full and rich looking tree. A little protection from wind and afternoon sun in the winter is beneficial. The rich-green or variegated leaves do much for the winter landscape—and the holidays would seem incomplete without holly's brightly colored berries. Flowers and fruit both appear on the current year's growth. This means that trees can be pruned in December, making the prunings available for indoor use without preventing the following year's fruit set. It is important to know that berries appear only on female trees. This can be a problem when you are attempting to grow seedlings. There is no way to know a seedling's sex until it matures. For specimen plants or groupings in key locations it is especially important to grow named varieties. This will ensure berries where you want them.

WHEN TO PLANT

Plant American holly in late March or early April. It can be planted in early fall if you provide winter protection.

WHERE TO PLANT

American holly prefers acidic soil. Hollies hate wet feet and prefer sandy soil, though any well-drained soil will do. While sun is necessary to produce full specimens, be sure to choose a site that is out of the winter wind. Avoid western exposures. American holly is a good choice for planting at the shore.

How to Plant

If planting American holly in the northern part of the state, be sure to add both organic matter and sand to heavy clay soils. Water settled around the base during the winter will kill your holly. Pruning at the time of planting is desirable, especially if you are planting at a less-than-ideal time of year. Containerized material is less likely to wilt and may not need pruning. You can take off as much as one-third if wilting occurs.

Care and Maintenance

Wait until your holly has reached 6 to 7 ft. before doing any holiday pruning. Fertilize in March or early April with 1/2 cup of 10-10-10 fertilizer. Never fertilize after early July. Leaf miners can do damage by burrowing between leaf layers; control these pests in mid-May. Leaf spines may sometimes puncture other leaves, causing the holly to appear spotted. There is no control for this.

Additional Information

Hollies propagate readily from cuttings you take in December. They grow slowly. Expect to see older leaves yellow and drop in April and May. Hollies are so much a part of New Jersey history that Millville was once known as "Holly City of America."

Additional Species, Cultivars, or Varieties

English holly, *Ilex aquifolium,* is not reliably hardy in most of New Jersey. Unless you are willing to provide winter protection and still risk loss in a severe winter, stick with the native. New Jersey residents are very lucky when it comes to the holly. Dr. Elwin Orton of Rutgers University has spent much of his illustrious career breeding and selecting this beautiful species. Two of his prize varieties are 'Jersey Princess' (female) and 'Jersey Knight' (male). Dr. Orton's holly collection can be seen at the Rutgers Gardens in New Brunswick. Many of the over 1,000 cultivars of American holly were developed at Rutgers University. 'Boyce Thompson Xanthocarpa' is particularly hardy and produces yellow berries. 'Dan Fenton' is a 1986 Rutgers release. 'Wyetta' has a conical form.

Colorado Blue Spruce

Picea pungens

Height: 30 to 60 ft. in cultivation; up to 135 ft. in the wild **Spread:** 10 to 20 ft. in cultivation; up to 30 ft. in the wild **Zones:** 2, 3, 4, **5, 6, 7**	**Light Requirement:**

The Colorado blue spruce is a beautiful tree. Its color stands out whether it is planted as part of a group or as a single specimen tree. It is magnificent with a dusting of snow and provides a haven for birds in the winter as well as a place to nest in the summer. Its biggest drawback is its overuse in the landscape. In a small yard, it can be an overwhelming focal point year round that overshadows the rest of the yard. Blue spruce are popular as Christmas trees. If you purchase a balled tree for the holidays, it will usually do well when planted outside. These trees have sharply pointed needles, but their color and scent make up for it.

WHEN TO PLANT

These lovely evergreens will tolerate spring or fall planting. If you purchase a balled tree for holiday use, dig the planting hole well in advance. Keep the tree inside for no more than 10 days in a cool room. Move to an intermediate temperature location for a few days and then plant the tree outside. It will stand a better chance of survival if planted immediately than if you try to keep it above ground all winter.

WHERE TO PLANT

Choose a location with plenty of sun. Spruce prefer a moist-type soil but blues will tolerate drier conditions than most. Do *not* plant blue spruce by the front door. It will soon outgrow that space. Mixed in with other evergreens for a border planting or privacy screen, blue spruce adds color and character. In the center of your front yard, it will be the dominant feature year-round.

How to Plant

Blue spruce is a very adaptable tree. Good planting practices should easily result in a healthy tree. Because it is so dense, blue spruce will carry much weight in ice and snow. It will also be subject to our brutal winter winds. Stake blue spruce when newly planted to keep them upright until establishment.

Care and Maintenance

Do not let a blue spruce get so tall that major pruning is required to keep it in line. It can be pruned slightly each spring by snipping the new growth (called "candles") back halfway. This will force side shoots to grow and will maintain a fuller, more compact tree. If you must prune, be sure to leave some green shoots on the branch or you will have removed all the dormant buds. Spruce can suffer from severe mite infestation. Mites are best controlled in May and then again in September. Do *not* use oil sprays, which remove the needles' blue color. Spruce gall aphids look like miniature pineapples on the tips of the branches. Spray in April or early May and repeat in early fall. Remove the galls by August. Check with your County Extension Agent for current pesticide recommendations.

Additional Information

In its native Rocky Mountains, this tree can live to be 800 years old. It grows very slowly but produces large crops of seeds every 2 to 3 years. Blue spruce readily reproduces from seeds, which require no pretreatment. Seedlings will vary in the degree of blue color their needles possess.

Additional Species, Cultivars, or Varieties

There are many varieties available. They are produced from cuttings which are then grafted onto seedling understock. 'Hoopsii' is given great praise in the trade for color and dense habit. 'Glauca Pendula' weeps so abundantly that it can grow as a groundcover, or simply train it as an upright weeper. 'Glauca Globosa' is a bush form that reaches only 3 ft. in height at maturity and grows wider than it is tall. 'Mission Blue' grows in the more classic form, as does 'Fat Albert', although 'Fat Albert' has a "more plump" shape.

Cryptomeria

Cryptomeria japonica

Other Name: Japanese Cedar
Height: Usually up to 60 ft. but has
    reached 180 ft. in Japan
Spread: 20 to 30 ft.
Zones: 5, 6, 7, 8, 9

Light Requirement:

---

his evergreen has an unusual but graceful appearance. Its reddish brown bark is its greatest claim to beauty. The rich color is particularly evident during winter, and is enhanced by the bark's habit of peeling away in long, thin strips. Cryptomeria's tiny needles are only 1/4 in. long. They persist for 4 or 5 years and turn bronze in the winter, or brown if the tree is subject to winter wind. The round cones appear at the branch tips and grow about 1 in. in diameter. They are attractive both on the tree and in wreaths and dried arrangements.

WHEN TO PLANT

Plant cryptomeria in early spring or early fall.

WHERE TO PLANT

Plant cryptomeria in a sunny location where it will be protected from high winds. Its upright but relatively narrow habit makes it a good choice for smaller yards and urban settings. The closeness of buildings in these areas make finding a spot where the wind is blocked relatively easy. When protected from wind, cryptomeria makes an attractive, interesting evergreen specimen.

HOW TO PLANT

Because cryptomeria is so sensitive to wind, trees planted in fall may require winter protection for at least the first year. Do not overcrowd this tree; it needs room to grow. Cryptomeria prefers rich but not heavy, and moist but not wet soil with a slightly acidic pH. It is not a difficult tree to grow.

CARE AND MAINTENANCE
Cryptomeria is an easy-care tree. It should need little or no pruning. Leaf diseases show up on occasion but are not usually significant.

ADDITIONAL INFORMATION
A mature cryptomeria specimen is striking. There are several examples in the New Brunswick area; they were once a favorite of landscape designers at Rutgers University.

ADDITIONAL SPECIES, CULTIVARS, OR VARIETIES
There are many varieties of cryptomeria. 'Lobbii' is similar to the species but is a little more compact and hardy. It is supposed to hold its color in the winter, but it is listed in Princeton Nursery's catalog as "having rich bronze winter color." Princeton suggests 'Yoshino' maintains its green color through the winter, but Forest Farm in Oregon calls the same variety "bronzy green" in winter. There must be inconsistency among cultivars. 'Knaptonensis' is a mounded dwarf propagated from a "witches'-broom" discovered in Italy in 1930. 'Globosa Nana' is a dwarf reaching 3 ft. It turns slightly blue in winter. There are also many contorted and severely dwarfed forms that are suitable for bonsai. 'Spiralis' Granny's Ringlets is one; 'Tansu' is another.

Douglas Fir

Pseudotsuga menziesii

Other Names: *P. douglasii, P. taxifolia*
Height: 40 to 80 ft. in cultivation in NJ;
   200 ft. in its native Northwest
Spread: 12 to 20 ft. under cultivation
Zones: 4, 5, 6, 7

Light Requirement:

The Douglas fir is native to both the Pacific Northwest and the Rocky Mountains, with significant differences in hardiness. Selections have been created that do well in the East, and nurseries throughout New Jersey grow Douglas fir commercially. Be sure to purchase a locally grown tree. This will prevent problems with regional variations. Careful selection is well worth the effort. Douglas fir is an elegant tree that works well in groups or as a specimen. Give it plenty of room to grow. Douglas fir dislikes windy sites and is inappropriate for use as a windbreak. It is a popular Christmas tree, but again, be sure to purchase an eastern tree. These trees hold their needles exceptionally well indoors; western varieties subjected to cold in transit, however, often experience a drastic needle drop when exposed to room temperatures. Locally grown trees can be purchased balled and then can be planted out after the holidays. Douglas fir trees are slow growing when young, but they begin to grow more quickly as they age. Seeds are produced in interesting cones that have "bracts" resembling feathery wings; the cones can be used decoratively. Seed production does not begin until the tree is 25 to 30 years old. Maximum production is not reached for 200 to 300 years. Individual specimens can live 1,000 years if they are not cut down for their valuable lumber.

WHEN TO PLANT

Plant Douglas fir in early spring or fall. Holiday trees should be kept indoors for no more than 10 days. After a few days on an unheated porch or breezeway, plant outside.

WHERE TO PLANT

Choose a location that is sunny but not windy. Douglas fir trees do best with well drained but moist soil. Avoid dry, poor soils. The soil pH can be neutral to slightly acidic.

HOW TO PLANT

Be sure to add organic matter to sandy soils. Add a 2:1 mixture of organic matter and sand to heavy clay soils. Douglas fir trees are often sold balled and burlapped. If plastic burlap is used, it must be removed prior to planting; natural fiber can be left in place. In either case, be sure to remove any wire or string that was used to secure the burlap to the tree trunk.

CARE AND MAINTENANCE

Pinch the new growth back halfway when the tree is young to maintain a bushier, more compact shape. Remove dead or damaged branches as needed. Douglas fir is subject to some needle diseases. The most common in New Jersey is needle cast, which can be controlled in the spring when new growth is $1/2$ in. long.

ADDITIONAL INFORMATION

It should be pointed out that despite its common name, Douglas fir is not a true fir. In their native temperate rain forest, these trees are spectacular, reaching a height of 300 ft. Without the high atmospheric and soil moisture of that region, trees do not come close to that size or stature. The lumber is exceptionally valuable for both its strength and beauty. Deer, birds, and small mammals rely heavily on the seeds for food.

ADDITIONAL SPECIES, CULTIVARS, OR VARIETIES

A related species, *P. macrocarpa*, the big-coned Douglas fir, is hardy only to Zone 7. It may do well in southern New Jersey, but it is not cultivated much there and is restricted mostly to its native southern California. Professor Richard West of Rutgers University conducted a study of how different strains of Douglas fir grew in New Jersey. He determined that the Arizona strain did the best. Most New Jersey trees have arisen from that project. There are several named varieties that weep or have a conical habit. Like the species, there is confusion about their hardiness, so proceed with caution.

Fraser Fir

Abies Fraseri

Other Names: Southern Balsam Fir, Southern Fir, She Balsam **Height:** 30 to 40 ft. **Spread:** 20 to 25 ft. **Zones:** 4, 5, 6, 7	**Light Requirement:**

*F*raser fir is an absolutely beautiful tree with a terrific scent. Its almost perfect pyramid shape requires little pruning to maintain. The dark-green color is rich and lustrous. Fraser fir is very popular as a Christmas tree and gains in popularity every year; the horizontal branches are perfect for hanging ornaments. This tree is native to the Appalachian Mountains in Virginia, West Virginia, North Carolina, and Tennessee. It is slow growing and is smaller than many other ever-greens, so it is a good choice for suburban yards. It struggles in hot, dry weather.

WHEN TO PLANT

Plant Fraser fir in early spring or early fall. It does well as a balled-and-burlapped Christmas tree. Plant immediately after the holiday; do not wait till spring to plant.

WHERE TO PLANT

Fraser fir prefers sun but will tolerate a little shade. It may even benefit from some protection in dry, sandy soil, where summer stress is one of its few problems. This tree is an excellent choice for the smaller yard.

HOW TO PLANT

If you are transplanting a specimen, root pruning will make the transition easier. Fraser fir prefers moist soil conditions; the addition of organic matter to sandy soils will be beneficial.

CARE AND MAINTENANCE

Fraser fir is a low maintenance tree that requires little pruning or shaping. In hot, dry, summer weather, occasional deep watering is recommended.

ADDITIONAL INFORMATION

In its native environment, Fraser fir can be found at elevations as high as 6,900 ft. There it is mixed with red spruce and a few yellow birch. These deep, shady woods are acclaimed for their beauty. Red squirrels are the primary consumers of the seeds. Fraser fir is one of my personal favorites.

ADDITIONAL SPECIES, CULTIVARS, OR VARIETIES

There are no cultivars commonly cultivated commercially but Donald Wyman lists 'Prostrata' as a groundcover form.

Himalayan Pine

Pinus wallichiana

Other Names: Bhutan Pine, *P. griffithii*, *P. excelsa*
Height: Usually 50 to 80 ft., but can grow up to 150 ft.
Spread: 1/2 to 2/3 the height
Zones: 5, 6, 7

Light Requirement:

One should plant a Himalayan pine only if there is plenty of room for it to spread out. These pines can eventually reach 50 ft. across, although growing is a slow process. If you do have the room, this is a magical tree. Its enormous bulk is softened by the 5 to 8 in. long needles that droop down, creating a delicate, feathery appearance. The needles are clustered together in groups of five and are so soft looking that you will want to stroke them. The light brown cones are up to 12 in. in length. There is a wonderful old specimen of Himalayan pine at the Rutgers Gardens in New Brunswick.

WHEN TO PLANT

Plant Himalayan pine in early spring or early fall.

WHERE TO PLANT

Choose a location with plenty of room in full sun that provides some protection from winter wind. Himalayan pine tolerates air pollution better than most pines, but it is too large for most urban settings. Acidic sandy loam soil, which is easy to find in New Jersey, is the best soil for this tree.

HOW TO PLANT

Be sure to plant a young tree. Plant it in its permanent location. A container grown tree will suffer very little root disruption in the planting process and may be preferred to a balled and burlapped specimen. In heavy soils, add a 2:1 mixture of organic matter and sand to ensure good drainage. Prepare a big area since Himalayan pine is a large, spreading tree.

CARE AND MAINTENANCE

Himalayan pine does not suffer any particular problems. Its needles will brown if temperatures drop to -15 degrees Fahrenheit. In a windy setting the top of the tree may thin out and become weak.

ADDITIONAL INFORMATION

This tree is native to the Himalayan mountains where it is found at elevations of up to 12,500 ft. In its place of origin, the lumber is used for construction.

ADDITIONAL SPECIES, CULTIVARS, OR VARIETIES

'Zebrina' has variegated needles with yellow bands. There is a breathtaking specimen at the National Arboretum. A variety called 'Frosty' with white bands is available from Forest Farm in Oregon, though I have never seen one.

Serbian Spruce

Picea omorika

Height: Up to 100 ft. **Spread:** 25 ft. **Zones:** 4, 5, 6, 7	**Light Requirement:**

By all accounts, the Serbian spruce one of the best ornamental spruces. Its narrow growth habit makes it a good choice for smaller yards or for border plantings where space is a problem. It is even considered tolerant of city air and is worth considering as an evergreen street tree. The leaves are dark green on the surface but have white stripes underneath. The Norway spruce has been overused—why not try something a little different? This tree has an exceptionally narrow trunk and grows into a slender pyramid with gracefully cascading branches. Some references report Serbian spruce is difficult to locate, but it is carried by the wholesale grower, Princeton Nursery, in Allentown, New Jersey, and should be readily available at the retail level.

WHEN TO PLANT

Plant Serbian spruce in early spring or early fall.

WHERE TO PLANT

This tree prefers a bit of shade and rich, deep, well-drained soil. It does best in a moist location. Protect specimens from severe winter winds. Open rolling lawns may not be the best place to plant Serbian spruce, but it is a great choice for urban spots where buildings block the wind and space is limited.

HOW TO PLANT

This tree requires moist but well-drained soil; both heavy clay and sandy soils will benefit from the addition of organic matter. When planting in a border for privacy, make sure you mix Serbian spruce with more wind tolerant evergreens, placing it on the more protected side of a staggered row.

CARE AND MAINTENANCE

Serbian spruce is a low maintenance tree. Its narrow habit eliminates the need for pruning. It can have trouble with aphids, spruce bud-worm, and borers, but there is no indication that such problems are pervasive.

ADDITIONAL INFORMATION

Serbian spruce is native to Yugoslavia but could be found through-out Europe before the Ice Age. A unique characteristic of this tree is that its needles are flat (like the hemlock's), not 4-sided as are the needles of most spruces.

ADDITIONAL SPECIES, CULTIVARS, OR VARIETIES

There are several named varieties. 'Pendula' is the most common; it has drooping and slightly twisted branches.

Swiss Stone Pine

Pinus cembra

Other Name: Arolla Pine
Height: Usually 30 to 40 ft. but up to 100 ft.
Spread: 15 to 25 ft.
Zones: 4, 5, 6, 7

Light Requirement:

---

*S*wiss stone pine is a narrow columnar species. Its shape and its slow rate of growth make it ideal for suburban and urban yards. If you use one of these trees to frame your home, you will not have to worry about cutting it down in 10 years. There are five needles per cluster; though they are usually 2 to 3 in. long, they can reach up to 5 in. Needles persist for 4 to 5 years. The habit of the Swiss stone pine opens up as it matures, though not as much as most other pines.

WHEN TO PLANT

Plant Swiss stone pine in early spring or early fall.

WHERE TO PLANT

Plant Swiss stone pine in a sunny, open area in well-drained, slightly acidic soil. It is considered very hardy and tolerates windy, exposed conditions better than the Serbian spruce does, although both work well in smaller yards. According to Donald Wyman, it is being grown as far north as Manitoba, Canada.

HOW TO PLANT

Swiss stone pine transplants relatively easily. It prefers well-drained soil; heavy clay soils will benefit from the addition of organic matter and sand (2 parts organic matter to 1 part sand).

CARE AND MAINTENANCE

A variety of insects and diseases can affect pines. None are of particular danger to the Swiss stone pine. Its narrow growth habit generally makes pruning unnecessary. Where a particularly compact plant is desirable, the candles (new growth) can be pinched back halfway to force lateral bud formation. When more pruning is necessary, take care to prune back to a side branch or shoot and not beyond. If you cut all the way to bare wood, the needles will not resprout.

ADDITIONAL INFORMATION

Swiss stone pine is native to the Alps and grows at an elevation of 10,000 ft. Very old trees become open and flat at the top. The large seeds are edible.

ADDITIONAL SPECIES, CULTIVARS, OR VARIETIES

P. pumila or dwarf stone pine is a shrubby species that can reach 9 ft. and is hardy to Zone 5. Native to Siberia and Japan, it is sometimes considered a regional variation of the Swiss stone pine.

Umbrella Pine

Sciadopitys verticillata

Other Name: Japanese Umbrella Pine
Height: Usually 30 ft. in cultivation but
occasionally 70 ft.; can reach 120 ft.
in Japan
Spread: A 30 ft. tall tree spreads about
20 ft. wide
Zones: 4, **5, 6, 7,** 8

Light Requirement:

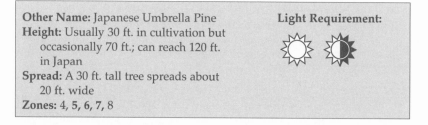

This tree makes you want to touch it. At first glance it looks like just another evergreen; then you realize it's different, and you want to touch it to see why. Most people have this reaction. Once you see an umbrella pine up close, you never forget it. The needles are arranged in whorls that resemble umbrellas that have had their fabric blown away. The long needles are up to five in. long; there are also scalelike needles on the branches. The texture is mesmerizing. The dark-green needles are thick, almost succulent in appearance. They retain their color year-round. Though the habit is described as "broadly pyramidal," the term "chubby" probably gives a better visual image. Umbrella pine's overall shape is that of a pyramid with the sides bowed out. This tree opens as it ages but grows so slowly that the person who plants an umbrella pine may never get to see it.

WHEN TO PLANT

Plant umbrella pine in early spring or early fall.

WHERE TO PLANT

Umbrella pine makes a great specimen tree. It can also add interest to a border planting. Since it does best with a little protection from hot afternoon sun and winter wind, planting this tree in a staggered row with other pines may create the perfect spot.

HOW TO PLANT

Umbrella pine is not particularly fussy about getting established. (We transplanted a 5 ft. tree in late spring without difficulty.) It requires good drainage; amend clay soils with a mixture of 2 parts organic matter and 1 part sand. Dig a very large hole for the rootball. Stake this tree, especially during the first winter, since umbrella pine's full shape and thick branches will catch the wind.

CARE AND MAINTENANCE
Umbrella pine's slow rate of growth makes major pruning unwarranted if the tree is located properly. Occasional pruning to shape is all that will be necessary. Those few branches you do remove can be used as greens in flower arrangements. They last for weeks and provide an exotic look. The umbrella pine has no serious pest problems.

ADDITIONAL INFORMATION
The umbrella pine is not really a pine at all. It is in the family *Taxodiaceae*, which makes it a closer relative of yew bushes and the giant redwood of California than a true pine. Propagation of this tree is difficult. Cuttings taken in winter are expected to root, though they continually give nursery professionals a hard time. Seeds require extensive stratification for germination. This is a major reason there are not more umbrella pines in the trade. Even so, they are available without the need for an extensive search.

ADDITIONAL SPECIES, CULTIVARS, OR VARIETIES
The umbrella pine is a one-of-a-kind!

White Fir

Abies concolor

Other Names: Concolor Fir, Colorado Fir
Height: Usually 30 to 50 ft. but can reach 120 ft.
Spread: Usually 15 to 30 ft.
Zones: 3, 4, **5, 6, 7**

Light Requirement:

The white fir is not planted nearly as often as one would expect. The 2 in. long needles usually have a subtle blue tint, though the degree of blueness varies among seedlings. The needle texture is slightly flattened but somewhat stout. White fir is a more flexible tree than other firs and even some spruce. It is accepting of an urban environment and will grow in spite of heat, drought, and rocky, barren soil. It does not like heavy clay soil and does best in deep, sandy loam soils. White fir's fullness and color soften the appearance of its stiff shape. Bluer specimens of white fir provide strong competition for the Colorado blue spruce. White fir trees grow fairly rapidly when young, but slow down as they age. It takes about 40 years before a tree is mature enough to produce cones, and the average life span is about 350 years. White fir holds its needles longer than other firs.

WHEN TO PLANT

Balled and burlapped trees do best when planted in late March or early April. Container material can be planted in early fall.

WHERE TO PLANT

White fir is an excellent choice for the not-too-small suburban yard or city location. Do not plant this tree in a tight spot; white fir does not tolerate pruning.

HOW TO PLANT

White fir is considered a very cooperative evergreen, yet transplanting is not always easy. Trees should do well with good soil preparation if they are not planted in heavy clay soil. Make sure the location is well drained.

CARE AND MAINTENANCE

White fir should not be significantly pruned—severely pruned limbs will probably not resprout. Insects and diseases pose no major problems. Stake a white fir until you are certain it is established.

ADDITIONAL INFORMATION

White fir is occasionally used as a Christmas tree, but not as often as it could be. It has a very pleasant citrusy odor. While the blue spruce's sharp points make it less desirable for indoor use (especially with small children decorating the tree), white fir gives a comparable look without the tendency to stab the decorators. (I enjoy a white fir as a Christmas tree. We alternate between Fraser fir and white from year to year. Our trees are always balled and burlapped, so we choose them not only for their beauty and scent, but also because they make interesting additions to the landscape.) White fir wood is soft and so is not much used in construction. It was at one time the wood of choice for making butter tubs because it imparted no additional flavor to the butter.

ADDITIONAL SPECIES, CULTIVARS, OR VARIETIES

'Violacea' is one of the bluest of the blue needled types. 'Conica' is a dwarf that is more slow growing than the species. 'Pendula' is a weeping form. These have a bit more character than the species, which is in its own right one of the more interesting evergreens.

White Pine

Pinus strobus

Other Name: Eastern White Pine
Height: Usually 80 ft. but up to 150 ft.
Spread: 20 to 40 ft.
Zones: 3, 4, **5, 6, 7,** 8

Light Requirement:

The white pine is an extremely important native tree. It is the largest of the eastern evergreens and its wood was at one time claimed by the British throne for use as ship masts. This royal greed was one of the factors that contributed to the Colonial rebellion and, ultimately, the American Revolution. It is still an important species used for lumber, but there are few giant white pines left in the east. Its adaptability, tolerance for pruning, ease of transplanting, and graceful appearance has made it one of the most popular landscaping trees. White pine has the natural ability to reseed itself in abandoned fields and so is useful in land reclamation projects. It is also an important species in the Christmas tree industry. Following a dry summer, the needles on some trees may yellow, but in most years white pine retains its bluish green color. The 5 in. long needles grow 5 to a cluster. Young trees are considered pyramidal in shape, but they are another of the "chubby" pyramids. White pine's general appearance is soft and rather huggable. (At our farm, Blooming Acres, we always have 2 Christmas trees. One is balled and burlapped and one is cut. Tommy, my husband, prefers a "poofy" cut tree to match childhood memories. "Poofy" has turned out to mean a white pine, but watch out! Ornaments tend to slide off its long, slippery needles.)

WHEN TO PLANT

Plant white pine in early spring or early fall, or immediately after the holidays for balled Christmas trees.

WHERE TO PLANT

White pine prefers well-drained, moist, fertile soils, but it is one of the most adaptable evergreens. It can even be used as a hedge as long as it is not overpruned. This tree is not a good choice for the shore—it is intolerant of salt. It is also intolerant of pollutants and does not make a good city tree. Severe wind can cause limb breakage.

How to Plant

White pine is easily established; there is little need for special attention. As always, thorough soil preparation gives the tree its best chance for success. Fall or winterplanted trees will benefit from staking their first year to keep them upright until their roots take hold.

Care and Maintenance

Snipping the candles in spring will keep white pine full and compact. This type of pruning, if performed consistently every spring, will allow white pines to make a very effective hedge. Keep the top rounded to shed snow since the weight on a flat-topped hedge may break branches. Once the branches all reach the surface of the hedge, the candles can be pruned with a machete or (if you *must*) an electric hedge pruner. White pine weevil can be a problem. It is more serious in forest situations where the damaged leader renders the lumber far less valuable. At home, remove the leader below the dead section in early summer when you see it. Spray in early to mid-April to prevent this injury.

Additional Information

If you are planting a group of white pines, uniformity may be a desired part of the design. Since seedling variation is the nature of the beast, choose carefully to ensure consistent color. Also note that white pine's mature habit differs significantly from that of the young tree. Its height and habit are as identifiable as a name tag. It has horizontal branches that float above the other trees, so it is easy to spot a tall white pine in the distance.

Additional Species, Cultivars, or Varieties

There are many varieties available. Some dwarf varieties grow as bushes. The two most common varieties are 'Fastigata', a columnar type that is considered very beautiful, and 'Pendula', which weeps down to the ground. Many cultivars can be quite interesting if placed in the right spot.

Small Flowering Trees

*A*FTER PLANTING LARGE EVERGREENS AND SHADE TREES, IT IS TIME TO ADD SMALL FLOWERING TREES. This is very exciting! Flowering trees add color and personality. Their inclusion is a major step in making your yard an everchanging garden of delight. Flowers can appear from very early spring into the fall. They draw the focus from a single spot to all around the grounds like a roving spotlight. Once established, flowering trees bloom year after year with just routine maintenance.

It is important to choose your flowering trees as carefully as you choose any other tree. A major consideration is light. Since the shade trees and evergreens are probably already in place, they will affect the amount of light any given location will receive. A classic gardening mistake is locating native flowering dogwood in the sun-drenched center of the front yard. Because dogwoods are native to New Jersey, many gardeners assume they will thrive anywhere they put down roots. When growing naturally in the woods, they are "understory" trees. This means they live in the shade of their larger neighbors. Center stage, in hot July sun, the leaves will crisp. A lilac, on the other hand, will not bloom in the shade.

Another consideration is the time of bloom. If your flowering plants are all dogwoods, it makes for a spectacular spring display, but that doesn't leave much for the rest of the year. With the right mix of small flowering trees and flowering shrubs it is possible to have something in bloom or bearing decorative fruit for nine or even ten months of the year.

It is also a lot of fun to be the only person on the block to have something unusual. Plant all the dogwoods your heart desires, then add a stewartia for large white flowers in July. Goldenraintree (*Koelreuteria paniculata*) also blooms in July, with fountains of yellow flowers; as a bonus, the large lantern-like seed capsules are exceptionally interesting in the fall.

Chapter Three

The mixing of evergreen material with deciduous plants also requires some thought. Evergreen trees have a majestic beauty all their own, but "ever green" is all you get. Add a cherry tree to the sunny side of a cluster or row of evergreens; the shady side may be the perfect spot for all those dogwoods.

If you worry about trees dropping things, be sure to find out about flower, fruit, and seed development before you plant *anything*. It should not surprise anyone that flowering crab apples produce crab apples. Some gardeners want to spray a crab apple to prevent fruit development. Does this make sense? It happens often.

If you have a small yard, it may be important to get more than one season of interest from a flowering tree. Stewartia blooms in July and has magnificent peely bark for a winter show. Franklinia blooms even later, often until frost; the rich red fall color of its large leaves is its second act.

Find out if flower production is on new wood or old. Trees where the flower buds are set the previous year should not be pruned until after bloom, unless you want to force the branches indoors. Trees that bloom on current season's growth can be pruned in early spring. Pruning at the wrong time could prevent flowering and, after all, you grow these trees for their flowers.

Flowering Crab Apple

Malus species

Height: 15 to 25 ft. **Flowers:** White, pink, red **Bloom Period:** Ranges from late April to early June **Zones:** 2, 3, 4, **5, 6, 7,** 8, depending on variety	**Light Requirement:**

*T*he difference between a crab apple and an apple is only the size of the fruit. Fruit 2 in. or smaller is a crab apple; larger fruit is an apple. Larger crab apples are considered edible, but even the smaller varieties or the bitter-tasting fruits can be used for jams and jellies—it depends on how badly you want to eat them! The world of flowering crab apples can be very confusing. There are 700 named cultivars, and new ones are being developed all the time. If you have your heart set on a particular cultivar, you may not be able to find it in the trade. Some crab apple trees are propagated from cuttings and others are grafted. Since crab apples (and apples) require cross pollination, seedlings are very diverse. The flower display is one of this tree's most beautiful characteristics, while disease problems are one of its most frustrating. Many a crab apple tree is leafless by midsummer. The literature indicates that many disease-resistant cultivars exist, but they are not necessarily the trees being grown commercially. If the flowers are particularly magnificent, a cultivar stays in the trade even though it gets ugly later in the season. Unless you are willing to battle leaf diseases on an annual basis, buy only crab apples that are listed as highly resistant to disease. Even then, it's a good idea to check with your nursery professional regarding his or her experience with that particular cultivar.

WHEN TO PLANT

Plant flowering crab apple in early spring or early fall.

WHERE TO PLANT

All are hardy in Zones 5, 6, 7 in New Jersey. Some are hardy to Zone 4 or 3 or 2; some will do well as far south as 8. Plant in a sunny location where you can enjoy the flowers. Soil should be well drained although crabs are flexible in regard to soil type. A slightly acidic pH is desirable and should not be difficult to locate in New Jersey.

How to Plant

Follow good planting practices. Crabs are easy to establish and require no special attention.

Care and Maintenance

Flowering crab apple generally requires little pruning, but be sure to remove any suckers. To enjoy maximum bloom, prune the tree after it has finished flowering but before early June. It sets next year's flower buds very early in the season. Disease control can be difficult with susceptible cultivars. Rust and scab are the two primary problems. To control both you must start spraying at budbreak and continue at 10 to 14 day intervals until 2 weeks after the petals fall off. Chlorothalonil will control both diseases. Cleaning up the leaves will minimize the chances of disease for the following year.

Additional Information

Some cultivars will bear flowers and fruit in alternate years. There is not much that can be done to change this. If you have to choose between abundant flowers every year on trees that are seriously susceptible to disease and cyclical bloom without disease, you may be willing to sacrifice the flowers.

Additional Species, Cultivars, or Varieties

In his *Manual of Woody Landscape Plants*, Michael Dirr lists the following varieties as being very or highly resistant to disease: 'Adams', 'Ames White', 'Autumn Glory', 'Baskatong', 'Beauty', 'Centurion', 'Coral Cascade', 'Evelyn', 'Gibbs Golden Gage', 'Gwendolyn', 'Harvest Gold', 'Henningi', 'Molten Lava', 'Mount Arbor Special', 'Professor Sprenger', 'Red Snow', 'Robinson', 'Tina', and 'Weis'. They are worth searching for but there is no guarantee you will find them. Of all these, only 'Centurion', a columnar variety with rose-red flowers, is readily available. 'Harvest Gold' is available through Forest Farm in Oregon. The following are locally grown in New Jersey with claims of disease resistance: 'Donald Wyman', 'Louisa' (a weeping form), 'Madonna', 'Prairie Fire', and 'Winter Gem'.

Franklinia

Franklinia alatamaha

Other Name: Franklin Tree **Height:** 10 to 20 ft. **Spread:** 6 to 15 ft. **Flowers:** 3 in. white flowers **Bloom Period:** Late July until frost **Zones:** 5, 6, 7, 8	**Light Requirement:**

Franklinia is an underappreciated small tree. Its large, beautiful, simple flowers arrive at a time when other woody ornamentals are not doing much flowering. Its deep red fall color is a bonus. In addition to its beauty, the history of this native tree makes it a featured attraction in any American garden. It was discovered in 1770 along the Alatamaha River in Georgia. John Bartram collected samples, but when he returned, the original grove had disappeared. It is unclear as to whether natural disaster killed it off or whether trees were collected by others until the source was finally depleted. This small treasure was named after Ben Franklin. No wild populations exist today. Mystery always adds to beauty. In spite of its relative obscurity, however, it is not difficult to find locally.

WHEN TO PLANT
Plant in late March or early April.

WHERE TO PLANT
Plant in a sunny location in well-drained soil. Franklin tree prefers acidic soil, which is easily supplied in New Jersey.

HOW TO PLANT
Franklinia does not transplant easily, so is best to begin with a small tree. Improve the soil by adding organic matter such as leaf compost. Franklinia can be grown as either a small tree or a shrub.

CARE AND MAINTENANCE
Phytophthora wilt can be a problem during propagation and in containers. This is all the more reason to be sure that you plant the tree in a place with good drainage. It should not need major

pruning, but if slight pruning is necessary, early spring is the best time. Franklinia blooms on new wood.

ADDITIONAL INFORMATION
Franklinia will occasionally still be in bloom when its leaves turn red. This is a particularly lovely sight.

ADDITIONAL SPECIES, CULTIVARS, OR VARIETIES
Franklinia is unique, although its 3 in. white flowers are similar to those of the stewartia.

Fringetree

Chionanthus virginicus

Other Names: White Fringetree, American
Fringetree, Grancy Gray-beard,
Old Man's Beard
Height: Up to 30 ft.
Spread: Up to 30 ft.
Flowers: Large, fluffy panicles of small
white fragrant blooms
Bloom Period: May
Zones: 3, 4, **5, 6, 7,** 8, 9

Light Requirement:

*T*his large shrub or small tree is native to New Jersey but can
be found as far south as Florida. There is a significant movement
supporting the use of native plant material. Native trees are well
adapted to their environment, making them tolerant of most endemic
diseases and insect infestations. This reduces the need for pesticides.
This sensible approach applies to fringetree, since it has no serious
pests (though it may occasionally be bothered by scale). These trees
are either male or female, and you need both to produce the almost-
black fruits. Because they are mostly hidden by foliage, the fleshy
fruits are not particularly showy, but they are a favorite of our feath-
ered friends. If feeding the birds is one of your interests, this tree is a
good choice. In the trade, trees are not often sexed prior to sale, so
you may have to take your chances. If you purchase the plants while
in bloom, you may be able to distinguish between male and female
trees by comparing their flowers. Male flowers have significantly
longer petals.

WHEN TO PLANT

Because it can be fussy about being transplanted, fringetree does
best when planted in early spring.

WHERE TO PLANT

Fringetree prefers a sunny location but is a good choice for
moderately wet sites. In the wild, it is usually found growing
along streams or the edges of swamps. Fringetree is also credited

with being more tolerant of air pollution than many other trees, so it is a good choice for urban locations.

HOW TO PLANT
Fringetree does best in moist soil. Add organic matter to help maintain soil moisture. The tree will need extra attention during its first hot, dry summer. It can be persnickety about being moved, and it doesn't like dry soil. If you intend to grow it as a small tree, be sure to do some selective pruning at the time of planting to establish a trunk and to keep it from growing into a bush.

CARE AND MAINTENANCE
Fringetree requires little pruning and has few pest problems, so little maintenance is necessary. If you grow a specimen with multiple trunks, you may need to prune out any crossing branches while they are young. Remove suckers if you are cultivating a tree form. Since the flowers are borne on the previous year's growth, do your pruning after fringetree blooms or you will deflower it.

ADDITIONAL INFORMATION
Fringetree is very slow growing and very late to leaf out in the spring. Fall color ranges from brownish yellow to a yellow that is quite bright. Cuttings of this plant are extremely difficult to root. Most fringetrees are grown from seed, which accounts for the lack of gender-identified young trees, as well as for the variation in fall color.

ADDITIONAL SPECIES, CULTIVARS, OR VARIETIES
Fringetree's only close relative is *C. retusus*, the Chinese fringetree, which is hardy to Zone 5. Its overall habit is smaller, but it produces similar fruits and flowers. Because it blooms on the current year's growth, fruits are more exposed and therefore more ornamental. The peely gray bark is also interesting. This species blooms with enthusiasm.

Japanese Snowbell

Styrax japonicus

Other Name: Japanese Styrax
Height: 30 ft.
Spread: 30 ft.
Flowers: White, bell shaped, slightly fragrant,
$^3/_4$ in. wide
Bloom Period: June
Zones: 5, 6, 7

Light Requirement:

apanese snowbell is a lovely tree that extends the bloom of spring into early summer. It should be planted where its enormous number of small flowers can be appreciated up close. The tree appears to be covered with delicate bells peeking out from beneath its leaves. They ring a gentle fragrance that is music to the senses. Young trees are pyramidal in shape; their growth habit becomes more open and spreading as they mature. The bark of Japanese snowbell is smooth and grayish brown with patches and streaks of orange that add a bit of winter interest. This tree is not easily established, but you will be rewarded for your effort. Its lovely white blooms make a stunning combination with richly colored rhododendrons and late-blooming azaleas. Their bloom periods overlap for a breathtaking display. Japanese snowbell is virtually pest-free.

WHEN TO PLANT

Plant Japanese snowbell only in early spring. This tree can be a bit fussy and you will have the easiest time getting it established if you start in late March or early April.

WHERE TO PLANT

Japanese snowbell likes full sun but is happy in partial shade. In the northwest part of the state, it will benefit from a site with a little protection from harsh winter weather.

HOW TO PLANT

Start with a small plant. It will have a much greater tolerance for transplanting than will a larger tree. If the tree is container-grown, there will be even less stress to the roots during the planting process. Add copious amounts of organic matter to the soil. This will be helpful in getting the finicky root system established.

CARE AND MAINTENANCE
Japanese snowbell is practically pest free. Perform any necessary minor pruning in winter when the temperature is above freezing.

ADDITIONAL INFORMATION
The leaves of Japanese snowbell appear lightly poised on its branches, exposing the dangling flowers that hang below them. If the tree is planted so that you can look up into the branches while it is in bloom, you will get a spectacular view. The common practice of using berms in today's landscapes, or locating the tree partway up on a slope, may create the perfect setting.

ADDITIONAL SPECIES, CULTIVARS, OR VARIETIES
The variety 'Pendula' is a graceful weeping form. 'Carillon' also weeps but is hardy only to Zone 7. 'Rosea' is pink with an upright habit.

Kousa Dogwood

Cornus kousa

Other Names: Chinese Dogwood, Japanese Dogwood
Height: 20 to 30 ft.
Spread: 20 to 30 ft.
Flowers: Inconspicuous, surrounded by 2 to 3 in. wide creamy white pointed bracts
Bloom Period: Early June
Zones: 5, 6, 7, 8

Light Requirement:

*K*ousa dogwood is the ideal substitute for the struggling native *Cornus florida*, the flowering dogwood. Though the flowering dogwood can be found in our own local forests, it is in a state of decline in many locations. This is not due to a particular disease or insect; even trees growing in the woods are showing signs of stress. Kousa dogwood blooms in very early June in New Jersey, about one month later than *C. florida*. The creamy white bracts are pointed at the tips, not notched like the bracts of the flowering dogwood, but the overall effect is similar. Some trees produce so many of these bracts that they resemble a snowdrift. The display can last for up to 6 weeks. Since many homeowners choose dogwood to be the focal point of the front yard; the sun-loving Kousa is a better choice than the native. It is resistant to the multiple problems that are leading to the flowering dogwood's decline, and it produces a profusion of the white flowerlike bracts. These are followed by bright red fruits that resemble pudgy raspberries and grow up to 1 in. in diameter. Birds love them. Kousa dogwood's red fall color lasts for up to 5 weeks. Exfoliating bark adds a little winter zing.

WHEN TO PLANT

All dogwoods fare better with spring planting. Late March or early April is ideal.

WHERE TO PLANT

Plant Kousa dogwood where its flowers can be appreciated. These trees tend to spread, so give them a little room. Kousa prefers more sun than the flowering dogwood, but light shade is fine. It does best in acidic, well-drained soil.

HOW TO PLANT
Add plenty of organic matter and start with a young tree. Keep it well watered during the first summer. Since many problems with dogwood begin with injury to the trunk, be sure to leave a grassless area around the base that will eliminate the need for mowers to get too close. Groundcover is a good alternative to grass in that area.

CARE AND MAINTENANCE
Kousa dogwood has few pest problems. It does not like to be pruned, though you should remove suckers if any appear.

ADDITIONAL INFORMATION
Since the branches and the flower bracts both grow horizontally, you may want to locate this tree where you can look down on it, such as beneath a bedroom window. The flowers are equally magnificent by morning sun or moonlight.

ADDITIONAL SPECIES, CULTIVARS, OR VARIETIES
'Milky Way' produces a prodigious number of blooms. 'Rosabella' and 'Radiant Rose' have pink flowers. The bracts on 'Moonbeam' are up to 8 in. across. 'Gold Star' has variegated foliage and 'Elizabeth Lustgarten' weeps. I recommend getting one of each. It is hard to choose among them.

Kwanzan Cherry

Prunus serrulata 'Kwanzan'

Other Names: 'Kanzan', 'Sekiyama',
  'Hisakura'
Height: 20 to 25 ft. if grafted; taller on its
  own roots
Spread: 20 ft.
Flowers: Fragrant, double pink, up
  to 2$^1/_2$ in. across
Bloom Period: Late April to early May
Zones: 5, 6, 7, 8, 9

Light Requirement:

The Kwanzan cherry is available in two distinct forms: grafted trees and those grown on their own roots. Grafted trees are all very uniform in size and shape. The graft is high on the trunk so the branches start 5 or 6 ft. off the ground. This makes them popular street trees. Even so, the "cloned" look of these trees is so consistent that more free spirited landscapers shy away from them. Specimens grown on their own roots have a more interesting form and reach up to 40 ft. in height. The growth habit is upright but the tree opens up with age. Kwanzan cherry is one of the varieties responsible for the fabulous display each spring in Washington, D.C. Its profusion of flowers is really quite spectacular. Each blossom has 30 petals. These trees bloom later than flowering plums, which are in the same genus. Leaves appear with the flowers or just after. They emerge bronze and retain their color for some time. As it matures, the foliage turns green. Fall color is an attractive orange bronze. Unfortunately, the Kwanzan cherry is a short lived tree that will last only 15 to 25 years.

WHEN TO PLANT
Plant Kwanzan cherry in early spring. Late March or early April is the best time to plant.

WHERE TO PLANT
Plant Kwanzan cherry in a sunny location where its abundant flowers can be appreciated. Grafted trees are popular for use as street trees. Avoid heavy or wet soils, but keep the soil moist.

How to Plant

Follow thorough soil preparation practices. In heavy soils, raise the ball slightly to avoid root rot. The addition of a 2:1 mixture of organic matter and sand will be beneficial.

Care and Maintenance

Prune only the occasional rebellious branch. If you prune during bloom, the flowers can be used indoors. Branches pruned during the tree's dormant season can be forced into bloom, bringing a bit of spring ahead of the season. Tent caterpillars can be a problem in May; spray as soon as you see the tents forming. Control with B.T. (*Bacillus thuringiensis*). If you learn to recognize the egg masses, you will be able to remove them before they even get started. Tent caterpillar eggs resemble a wad of granular charcoal stuck on the branch.

Additional Information

The name 'Kwanzan' comes from the Chinese character that represents a sacred mountain. The tree may produce very small fruits, but they are inconspicuous and neither add to nor detract from the appearance. Birds enjoy them.

Additional Species, Cultivars, or Varieties

'Shirofugen' has pink buds and white double flowers that bloom late but last a long time. The white flowers against the bronze juvenile foliage is particularly lovely. 'Royal Burgundy' has double pink flowers and purple red foliage. 'Amanogawa' is columnar with fragrant, pale pink, semi-double blooms. There are many others.

Purple Leaf Plum

Prunus cerasifera 'Atropurpurea'

Other Names: Cherry Plum, Myrobalan Plum, Pissard Plum, *P. cerasifera* 'Pissardii' **Height:** 15 to 30 ft. **Spread:** 15 to 25 ft. **Flowers:** Very fragrant, light pink; grow to ³/4 in. across **Bloom Period:** Late April **Zones:** 5, 6, 7, 8	**Light Requirement:**

The small pale pink blossoms of purple leaf plum are not long lasting, but they are still very pretty against the emerging cherry red foliage. Foliage continues to darken until it is a deep wine purple. It retains this color throughout the summer. Purple leaf plum's 1 in. dark purple fruits develop in July and August; they are edible but taste awful, so it is probably best to eat them only if you are starving. The birds are not quite as picky and will appreciate the fruit. In his respected book *Manual of Woody Landscape Plants*, Michael Dirr speaks rather harshly about this tree. It is true that ornamental plums are short lived, and they are often bothered by pests; but the purple leaves are striking in the landscape, especially against a green background. If you grow a purple leaf plum, you will have to maintain the philosophy that you can enjoy it while it is beautiful and then replace it with something else. These trees last up to 20 years.

WHEN TO PLANT

Plant purple leaf plum in late March or early April.

WHERE TO PLANT

Purple leaf plum requires full sun to produce the best foliage color. It is not overly fussy about soil, but the soil does need to be well drained. Plums do not tolerate pollution and may not be suitable in some urban settings.

How to Plant

Raise the ball slightly in heavy soils. Add a 2:1 mixture of organic matter and sand to improve clay soils. If you order your plum tree from a catalog, you may receive a bare-root specimen. Plant the tree as soon as possible after its arrival. Soak the roots for several hours in a bucket of water prior to planting. Dig your hole and put a mound of soil in the bottom. This will support the roots as you carefully spread them out. Plant at the same depth the plant was growing previously. Gently work the soil in around the roots. Water when the hole is half filled and again when it is full.

Care and Maintenance

During their first year, pay extra attention to the watering of bare-root trees. The little hair roots responsible for water uptake are seriously traumatized during digging and planting. You can prune purple leaf plum in late winter and force the branches indoors. You can also prune during bloom or just after. Heavy winter pruning will reduce or eliminate flowers. Pruning during or after bloom will reduce or eliminate fruit. A fungus disease, black knot, prefers plum trees to all others. The black thickened areas this disease creates on the branches are easy to identify. They should be pruned off 4 in. behind the swelling. Be sure to dip your pruners in a 10 percent bleach solution in-between cuts. Control black knot by spraying the following spring before the buds open. Spray 3 times at 7 day intervals with a product containing benomyl. Aphids, tent cater-pillars, scale, and borers can all be problems.

Additional Information

This tree was discovered in Persia (Iran) by Mr. Pissard, gardener to the Shah. It was a sport which was introduced into France in 1880. Other varieties have resulted from the selection and hybridization of the original.

Additional Species, Cultivars, or Varieties

'Thundercloud' is another purple leaf plum. Some sources prefer it over 'Atropurpurea', while others claim it is not quite as hardy. 'Vesuvius' is the darkest purple of the purple varieties. 'Hollywood' leaves emerge green and then turn deep purple.

Stellar Series Hybrid Dogwoods

Cornus kousa × *C. florida*

Other Names: Rutgers Dogwoods,
   Cornus × *rutgersensis*
Height: 25 ft.
Spread: 25 ft.
Flowers: White or pink showy four petaled
   bracts
Bloom Period: May
Zones: 5, 6, 7, 8

Light Requirement:

The Stellar Series dogwoods have a wonderful history, one that makes these beautiful trees even more special for New Jersey gardens than for anywhere else in the world. They were developed by Dr. Elwin Orton at Rutgers University. The hybrid is a cross between the native dogwood, *C. florida*, and the Kousa dogwood, *C. kousa*. Because the two are distinct species that evolved on two different continents, the likelihood of successful hybridization was slim. To make things more difficult, the flowering dogwood finishes blooming completely before the Kousa even gets started. That made it necessary to save pollen from *C. florida* for hand pollination when *C. kousa* came into bloom. It took 25 years of patient waiting, testing, and selecting to finally choose and release the six varieties that survived the stringent evaluation period. The hybrids' bloom time is between the parents' bloom times. If you have all the hybrids and both the parents, the blooming season can last up to two full months. It is interesting to note that the two hybrids, whose bloom period is closer to that of the native dogwood, also have its spreading habit. The other four hybrids grow more upright, like the Kousa. The hybrids' only disadvantage is that as a result of the parents being so distantly related, they are sterile. There is no fruit to add winter interest, but the hybrids' lovely red fall foliage still provides a great late-season display.

WHEN TO PLANT

Plant dogwoods in early spring. Late March or early April is the best time to plant.

WHERE TO PLANT

Unlike the flowering dogwood, these hybrids prefer full sun. Choose a place where they will not be subject to lawn mower damage or other bark injury. These trees will spread, so plant them at least 20 ft. apart.

HOW TO PLANT

Rutgers dogwoods require well-drained acidic soil. Add a 2:1 mixture of organic matter and sand to heavy clay soil. Sandy soils in the southern part of New Jersey can be improved with a copious amount of organic matter such as leaf compost. Provide a 2 ft. wide grass free area around the trunk; cover this area with an organic mulch.

CARE AND MAINTENANCE

Rutgers dogwoods prefer not to be pruned, so remove only suckers and crossing branches as necessary. These hardy trees are resistant to the problems that plague *C. florida*.

ADDITIONAL INFORMATION

There are still quite a few Rutgers dogwood hybrids on display at the Rutgers Gardens in New Brunswick. They are now available through many local nurseries. All are patented and cannot be propagated without permission from Rutgers University.

ADDITIONAL SPECIES, CULTIVARS, OR VARIETIES

'Rutlan' Ruth Ellen® blooms just as the flowering dogwood finishes. It is followed by 'Rutfan' Star Dust® and slightly later by 'Rutcan' Constellation®. 'Rutdan' Celestial® and 'Rutban' Aurora® come next. The final hybrid to bloom is 'Rutgan' Stellar Pink®, the only pink-flowering variety in the group. Finally, the Kousa dogwood blooms for three more weeks. The full complement of trees is magnificent; they are a New Jersey treasure.

Saucer Magnolia

Magnolia × soulangiana

Other Names: Chinese Magnolia, Tulip Tree
Height: 20 to 30 ft.
Spread: 20 to 30 ft.
Flowers: 5 to 10 in. diameter; pink to purple on the outside, white on the inside
Bloom Period: March to April
Zones: 5, 6, 7, 8, 9

Light Requirement:

Saucer magnolia trees have the classic look associated with magnolias. Their enormous dark buds open up to spectacular white flowers. The tree branches close to the ground and spreads. While in bloom it resembles a soft white cloud at rest. The large petals are silky smooth. When they float down from the tree, it seems as though the ground is covered in a sea of large pearls. This hybrid is a cross between *M. denudata*, a Chinese species, and *M. liliiflora* from Japan. According to Donald Wyman, the hybridizer was a retired soldier from Napoleon's army. The cross was made in 1820; the hybrid first flowered in 1826 in Fromont, France. Flowering is initiated when the tree is only 2 to 4 ft. tall. Trees will occasionally produce a pineapplelike aggregate of bright-red fruits. A serious problem with the species is its susceptibility to late spring frosts. Once every three or four years, the entire crop is killed back due to weather.

WHEN TO PLANT

Early spring planting of balled and burlapped trees should be done in late March or early April. If a fall planting is desired, plant only in early September.

WHERE TO PLANT

Saucer magnolia prefers full sun. Avoid warm, protected south-facing locations. Planting it in a sunny south facing sheltered site may cause the tree to warm up and bloom prematurely, only to have its flowers killed by a late frost.

How to Plant

Add plenty of organic matter to the soil. Take care not to plant saucer magnolia too deep. In most cases you should not use lime, since magnolias prefers a soil pH of 5.0 to 6.5. Be sure to plant before new growth begins in the spring.

Care and Maintenance

Prune after flowering if necessary. Check at the base for crossing or rubbing branches that may cause trouble later on. Saucer magnolia may, on occasion, put out a flower or two in the summertime.

Additional Information

A personal note: This is the first tree I learned to identify as a very young child. I rubbed the velvety petals on my cheek and was enchanted by the sensation. It seemed all was well with the world. That magical feeling returns whenever I see a magnolia in bloom.

Additional Species, Cultivars, or Varieties

'Lennei' has darker petals and blooms after the last frost. 'Brozzonii' has 10 in. blooms in profusion and is one of the last to flower. *M. stellata* has 3 in. flowers with 18 petals on each one; it grows to 20 ft. tall. This cultivar may be particularly susceptible to late-season frosts. The variety 'Betty' is a cross between *M. stellata* and *M. lili-iflora*. It reaches only 10 ft. in height, has dark-purple buds which open to white, and blooms after frost. 'Elizabeth' is a hybrid that reaches 35 ft. tall. Its yellow blooms also arrive after danger of frost has passed.

Scholartree

Sophora japonica

Other Names: Pagoda Tree, Japanese Pagoda Tree, Chinese Scholartree
Height: 50 to 75 ft.
Spread: 50 ft.
Flowers: Slightly fragrant, creamy-white pealike flowers in panicles up to 12 in. long at the branch tips
Bloom Period: July and August
Zones: 4, 5, 6, 7, 8

Light Requirement:

Its profusion of flowers in August provides so much appeal that this tree doesn't need much else. The attractive, compound leaves have 7 to 17 leaflets each; leaflets can be either rounded or pointed. The 3 in. long green seedpods turn brown in winter. As the seeds within the pod grow, it begins to resemble an exaggerated string bean. Seedpods hang from the tree throughout the winter. Once established, scholartree will tolerate heat and drought. It is also exceptionally tolerant of urban conditions, including pollution. Scholartree grows at a medium rate but does not produce flowers until it is 10 to 14 years old; some trees can take up to 25 years to bloom. The trunk on older trees often becomes wonderfully contorted and twisted, adding character to scholartree's other attributes. The flowers and fruits are a little messy. They may discolor pavement and parked cars with a yellow stain, but they do fine in a lawn area. The foliage has no fall color change, but the tree's dark-green branches provide some winter appeal.

WHEN TO PLANT
Plant scholartree in early spring or early fall.

WHERE TO PLANT
This tree prefers a sunny location. It does best with a little winter protection until it gets a little larger. Choose a well-drained site with loam soil.

How to Plant
Plant a young tree to make establishment easier. Add organic matter to the soil. Wrap with burlap in winter for the first few years, and hope for a mild winter.

Care and Maintenance
Prune scholartree in the fall. Extra attention to pruning may be required to ensure that the tree develops a strong leader and a nice shape. Powdery mildew and leaf hoppers can be problems, though occurrences are not usually serious.

Additional Information
A natural yellow dye can be made from the flowers. Bake the flowers until they are brown and then boil to extract the colorant.

Additional Species, Cultivars, or Varieties
'Regent' grows rapidly and bears flowers earlier than the species. It has a more upright habit and will bloom in 6 to 8 years. It was developed and patented at Princeton Nurseries here in New Jersey. 'Pendula' is a weeping form.

SMALL FLOWERING TREES

Stewartia

Stewartia pseudocamellia

Other Name: Japanese Stewartia **Height:** 30 to 40 ft. Up to 60 ft. in the wild **Spread:** 20 ft. **Flowers:** 2¹/₂ in. white flowers with orange anthers; similar to a camellia **Bloom Period:** July **Zones:** 5, 6, 7, 8	**Light Requirement:**

I once met a landscaper who said he wished he could find an abandoned grove of old stewartias: it would make his fortune. It is certainly true that these fabulous garden plants become more wonderful with age. The peeling bark with patches of red becomes increasingly intricate and interesting as the tree matures. Stewartia's large summer flowers are truly elegant in both purity and simplicity. Fall color is brilliant and comes in shades from bronze to red to purple.

WHEN TO PLANT

Plant stewartia in late March or early April.

WHERE TO PLANT

Stewartia likes sun but a little shelter from the hottest part of the day is advisable. Locate it as a specimen plant to enjoy its multi-season attributes. This tree does well as part of a woodland garden.

HOW TO PLANT

Despite the landscaper's fantasy, transplanting larger trees is difficult. Even young trees are finicky. It is best to start small and plant a tree in its permanent location. A container grown stewartia will have the best chance of good establishment. This will minimize root disturbance. Add large amounts of compost or other organic matter to enrich the soil. Stewartia does best in acidic soil.

CARE AND MAINTENANCE

Stewartia is virtually pest-free and requires little or no pruning. Be sure to keep it especially well watered in the first year and during hot, dry summers.

Additional Information

Stewartias are slow growing and pyramidal in shape. They make an excellent choice for a small yard. Plant this tree where you can appreciate it up close.

Additional Species, Cultivars, or Varieties

There are a total of 7 species of stewartia. Virginia or silky stewartia, *S. malacodendron*, reaches 18 ft. and is hardy to the southeastern United States. It is hardy only to Zone 7, so it will not do well in the northern half of New Jersey. Korean stewartia, *S. koreana*, is slightly smaller, but its flowers are slightly larger. Its bark color is not quite as vivid. It is hardy to Zone 5. *S. sinensis* is the Chinese stewartia. It has a more bushlike habit, with smaller flowers, and makes a lovely addition to the garden. It is hardy to Zone 5. *S. ovata* var. *grandiflora*, showy stewartia, is less common in the industry but may be worth a search. It is only 15 ft. tall but has 4-in. white flowers with purple stamens. This Georgia native is hardy to Zone 5. *S. ovata*, mountain stewartia, is also 15 ft. tall and hardy to Zone 5. Tall stewartia, *S. monadelpha*, reaches up to 75 ft. but is only hardy to Zone 6. Fairweather Gardens, a mail-order nursery located in Greenwich, New Jersey carries an excellent selection of all these species.

Weeping Japanese Cherry

Prunus subhirtella 'Pendula'

Other Names: Weeping Higan Cherry, Single Weeping Cherry
Height: Usually 15 ft., but up to 30 ft.
Spread: Usually 15 ft., but up to 30 ft.
Flowers: Lots of small, pale pink single flowers
Bloom Period: Late April
Zones: 4, 5, 6, 7, 8

Light Requirement:

All flowering cherries are beautiful, and all struggle with a variety of pests. The blizzard of flowers in early spring and its ground-sweeping branches make the weeping Japanese cherry irresistible despite its shortcomings. Most trees are grown on tall, straight trunks called "standards." The weeping part is grafted onto the trunk about 6 ft. up. Some plant people grow them on their own roots. These trees are small and compact, which makes them a natural for smaller yards and courtyards. 'Pendula' produces small black fruits that are tucked away under the leaves and therefore not very apparent, though the birds can always find them. Weeping Japanese cherries are not considered long-lived trees, but 30 to 50 years is a reasonable expectation. Weepers do well as specimen trees where their graceful habit can be fully appreciated. Foliage turns an attractive yellow to bronze in the autumn. In winter the arching branches, devoid of leaves, are like a work of modern art; their strong lines are woven together to create a compelling effect.

WHEN TO PLANT

Plant weeping Japanese cherry in early spring; late March or early April is the best time.

WHERE TO PLANT

Choose a sunny location with good drainage where you will be able to enjoy the blossoms to their fullest.

HOW TO PLANT

Provide good drainage. This may require the addition of organic matter, such as leaf compost, during the soil preparation process. Add a 2:1 mixture of compost and sand to keep the soil aerated. Since root rot is an occasional problem, thorough soil preparation, especially in heavy clay soils, can keep the roots fat and happy.

CARE AND MAINTENANCE

Making a few snips in the spring may be motivated more by wanting to enjoy the branches indoors than by necessity. Little pruning is required, but do remove the occasional offending branch. Watch out for tent caterpillars (see Kwanzan cherry for details). Other pests include leaf spots, fall webworm, and peach scale.

ADDITIONAL INFORMATION

This variety was introduced from Japan in 1862. It is far more popular than the species. Why anyone would prune the branches straight across like a Cleopatra haircut is a mystery, though it is often done. This creates a very artificial look. If you must shorten the branches, vary the heights so that the tree retains a natural air. (I once knew a family that was short on cash when it came time for their daughter's wedding. The date coincided with the blooming of the cherry trees. To decorate the tables, they pruned the cherry trees and arranged the branches as the centerpieces. It was stunning.)

ADDITIONAL SPECIES, CULTIVARS, OR VARIETIES

There are two other popular varieties. 'Autumnalis' is more upright like the species, but many of its flowers open in November and December. The remaining blooms open in the spring. 'Yae-shidare-higan' is also a weeping variety, but it has double flowers. From these varieties, selections have been made which include 'Rosy Cloud' and 'Pink Cloud'.

*L*ANDSCAPING PROJECTS BEGIN TO BE A LOT OF FUN WHEN YOU START TO SELECT GARDEN SHRUBS. The options are almost limitless. If new gardeners are uncertain about where to begin, it may be worthwhile to have some professional direction. At least take the time to learn which plants will do well in your area and what constraints your soil type and sun exposure may offer. The shrubs we have selected in this chapter are a good start.

After you have gathered some basic information, let the games begin. Your yard and garden areas need to be places you enjoy. If you want a low-maintenance yard, you will have to select shrubs that thrive with just a minimum of attention. Avoid formal plantings—they often require rigid pruning schedules and constant attention to detail. You should also acquire a taste for the natural growth habit of the plants you choose. Nothing is uglier than a butchered forsythia, massacred with an electric hedge shears. The natural arched branches are breathtaking while in bloom, yet people work so hard to keep them ugly.

Foundation plantings are important spots for shrubs. Take care to choose plants that will be pleasing but will also stay in bounds. All too often gardeners will overplant shrubs in an attempt to get a mature look right at the time of planting. There is not much room to grow in the confines of foundation beds, so overplanted shrubs will all grow together. Some will get too large. Others will become such a mess they cannot be salvaged. It is better to plant smaller, slow-growing varieties and fill in with perennials, ornamental grasses, and annual flowers until the bed matures. Starting with smaller sizes gives the plants a better chance to become established and the bed will be more attractive for a longer period of time. In the long run it will probably be much less work.

Chapter Four

If you are a flower fancier, the use of flowering shrubs can supply a blast of seasonal color without the need to replant every year. Witch hazel will bloom as early as February. Cornelian cherry, related to the dogwood, is another early bloomer. *Caryopteris* species produce blue flowers from August until frost. The large panicles of PeeGee hydrangea stay dry on the bush into late fall. *Lespedeza thunbergii* has panicles of rosy purple pealike flowers in September and October.

Don't forget the old favorites: azaleas, rhododendrons, mountain laurel, and many others. Summer bloomers include the rose-of-Sharon, St. Johnswort, potentilla, and *Itea*. Fall berries can be just as fascinating as flowers. The white berries of *Symphoricarpos* are so abundant they can weigh the branches down. Winterberry holly is covered in red fruits which last well into winter.

There are shrubs for shade, shrubs to add winter interest, others for flowers, and some that are delightful for their ability to attract butterflies. Choose a few old friends, and mass-plant something colorful for a dramatic impact. Create privacy with a hedge, but make it informal to cut down on maintenance chores.

Then get a bit daring. Plant something odd or new or twisted. Try some variegated foliage, or purple, or maybe a cutleaf variety. Add a weeper or a creeper or a dwarf. Do something dramatic or silly or elegant. This is *your* garden and needs to be an extension of *your* personality. You will want your shrubs to be successful, but planting shrubs does not require the same commitment as planting a mighty oak. If you don't like a shrub, you can change it or move it or prune it; but first, you have to plant it.

Andromeda

Pieris japonica

Other Names: Japanese Pieris, Lily-of-the-Valley Bush **Height:** 9 to 12 ft. **Spread:** 6 to 8 ft. **Flowers:** 3 to 5 in. clusters of small, white elliptical flowers **Bloom Period:** Early April **Zones:** 5, 6, 7, 8	**Light Requirement:**

Its bronze to bright red (sometimes even pink!) new growth combined with its long lasting white flowers have earned andromeda a place in many gardens. The 3 to 5 in. flower clusters are very similar to those of lily-of-the-valley, but there are more flowers per cluster and they are slightly more pendulous. The evergreen leaves mature to a rich dark green. They are arranged in whorls with the abundant leaves packed in around the stem. The plants continue to put out new growth during much of the summer, so the splashes of color keep the bush interesting. The flower buds are set by fall, and the beady-looking clusters add a touch of winter drama as they wait for their chance to perform. The plant is shade tolerant and mixes well with azaleas, rhododendrons, and mountain laurel, but it needs some sun to flower with enthusiasm. The plants stay compact; they tolerate containers on the deck or patio, but they will have to be protected from the freezing and thawing of winter. Andromeda is native to Japan.

WHEN TO PLANT
Plant in early spring or early fall.

WHERE TO PLANT
This plant will benefit from a little protection from winter wind. Avoid western exposures where in the winter it may be warmed prematurely in the afternoon sun. Andromeda prefers light shade during hot summer afternoons, but it needs some direct sun to bloom at its best. Avoid wet spots. It is often used near the house; check carefully for the location of downspouts before picking a planting site.

How to Plant

Andromeda needs an acid soil, so planting right up against a foundation wall can sometimes present difficulties. Most New Jersey soils are fine, as long as you do not add lime. Adding lots of organic matter at planting time is the best thing you can do to help this plant get started.

Care and Maintenance

If you prune any time after midsummer before the flowers open, you will remove the flower buds. The little pruning this shrub may need should be done after blooming. An organic mulch is beneficial. Do not use the white marble chips as a mulch; they are a form of limestone which will make the pH skyrocket. Since andromeda requires an acid pH (4.0 to 5.0), this could be deadly. (Besides, marble chips are really ugly!) You will have to watch out for lacebug; whenever you see them, control with carbaryl.

Additional Information

Andromeda is a member of the family *Ericaceae*. This is the "acid-loving" family which includes rhododendrons and azaleas. The use of acid fertilizer is fine but not strictly necessary. The use of *any* fertilizer renders the soil slightly more acidic, and most New Jersey soils are acidic without any help. Just don't add lime unless a soil test tells you it is necessary.

Additional Species, Cultivars, or Varieties

P. floribunda, mountain pieris, is slightly small, with upright panicles of white flowers in April. It is native to Virginia and Georgia. It is not as common as andromeda, but it is just as hardy if not hardier. As a bonus, it has no lacebug problem to battle. This supports the concept that native plant material is better adapted to its environment. *P. japonica* comes in a plethora of varieties. 'Flamingo' has rose-red flowers; 'Christmas Cheer' has pink. 'White Cascade' produces long panicles of pure-white flowers in large numbers. There are many more varieties.

Arborvitae

Thuja occidentalis

Other Names: Eastern Arborvitae, American Arborvitae, White Cedar
Height: Usually to 25 ft., may grow up to 60 ft.
Spread: 10 to 15 ft.
Zones: 3, 4, **5, 6, 7**

Light Requirement:

The arborvitae is native to the east and can be found wild in many areas of New Jersey. This fact alone has appeal for those that stress the environmental advantages of planting material which evolved under local conditions. In addition, arborvitae is far more tolerant of marshy soil conditions than are many landscape plants. From a design perspective, the narrow pyramidal habit is very useful in smaller residential properties and for foundation plantings. As a border planting, arborvitae make a formal straight row without taking up an excessive amount of room. While they have only a moderate rate of growth, the dense branches create privacy fairly quickly. If planted in a staggered row, they will get the job done even more rapidly. While it is effective and attractively green in summer, there is nothing very exciting about this plant. It is included in this list because, for some reason, it is still in demand. It does work well as a backdrop for more colorful plantings. On the down side, most varieties turn a rather pitiful brown in winter. Arborvitae can be sheared lightly in April and again in June if necessary, but please do this with a pair of hand pruners to maintain a natural shape. They *cannot* be severely pruned if they get overgrown. If the bottom branches die back, they will not fill in. Once the branches are taken back to bare wood, either by dieback or pruning, there are no buds to resprout.

WHEN TO PLANT
Early spring or early fall.

WHERE TO PLANT
Arborvitae prefers a sunny location where it will be quite full and dense. Although it will tolerate some shade, it will have a more

open, leggy habit. It requires abundant soil moisture, so avoid excessively sandy soil. Arborvitae tolerates limestone soils.

HOW TO PLANT
Add copious amounts of organic matter to sandy soil. Do this to the entire bed before planting if possible. Take extra care to make sure the rootball is moist prior to planting since drying out can be a big problem. Arborvitae usually establish easily if you don't let them dry out; a thick layer of organic mulch will help.

CARE AND MAINTENANCE
Since arborvitae thrive under moist soil conditions, water them deeply when you water, especially during hot, dry summers. Keep the mulch in good condition to reduce water evaporation from the soil. The biggest problem with arborvitae may be winter damage. Branches have a tendency to bend or snap under the weight of ice and snow; because they don't resprout, the damage can be permanent. Try to shake off the snow while it is still light and fluffy or before it accumulates excessively. Bagworms can be a serious problem. The pointed "bags" are made of bits of twigs and leaves, so they look like part of the tree. The hungry critters within are very destructive. Remove the bags when you see them and spray in mid-June and late June with B.T. (*Bacillus thuringiensis*).

ADDITIONAL INFORMATION
The leaves smell like apples when crushed. Early settlers made a tea from the twigs.

ADDITIONAL SPECIES, CULTIVARS, OR VARIETIES
Western arborvitae, *T. plicata*, can get up to 75 ft., much taller than its eastern cousin. It is considered a more beautiful tree, and more valuable for lumber. It has not received as much attention from the industry, perhaps because it is hardy only to Zone 5, but it should do quite well throughout New Jersey. Its strong wood was once used for totem poles and its roots for fish hooks. There are many cultivars of *T. occidentalis* available. 'Nigra' and 'Emerald Green' both offer good winter color. 'Wansdyke Silver' is a dwarf columnar form that reaches only 4 ft. 'Aurea' has yellow foliage. 'Hetz Midget' is a globe shaped dwarf that also stays at only 4 ft.

Azalea

Rhododendron hybrids

Height: 4 to 5 ft.
Spread: 4 to 5 ft.
Flowers: Many shades of white, pink,
   coral, red, burgundy, lilac
Bloom Period: Usually spring
Zones: Tremendous variation among varieties;
   many are hardy only to Zone 7 but quite a
   few to Zone 5; locally grown varieties
   are the best bet

Light Requirement:

*A*ll azaleas are rhododendrons, but not all rhododendrons are azaleas. There are over 900 species which hybridize freely. This is one of the most confusing groups of plants to try to organize in a way that makes sense. Most people have a very clear image of a rhododendron, with its large leathery leaves and softball-sized clusters of flowers. Azaleas are smaller plants with smaller leaves and a more evenly dispersed array of flowers. There is a gray area between these two categories in which the differences in appearance are not so clearcut. It is best to use cultivar names that have been developed and commercially grown locally to be sure of having suitable varieties.

WHEN TO PLANT

Plant in early spring; late March or early April is best.

WHERE TO PLANT

Azaleas all need some shade and almost all need acidic soil. Avoid wet ground. Before planting, check for downspouts, which may create waterlogged soil in your beds. It is especially important to avoid locating your azaleas facing west where they will receive afternoon winter sun. This can force them out of dormancy and cause subsequent winter injury.

HOW TO PLANT

Improve the soil with the addition of organic matter. In heavy clay soils it is particularly important to prepare a large area prior to planting—in clay soil, a small hole with improved soil can become a "bucket" of water where water will flow as it follows the path of least resistance. Do not lime.

CARE AND MAINTENANCE

Prune after azaleas finish blooming in the spring. Be sure to use hand pruners and selectively remove the branches to maintain a natural shape. Never use electric hedge shears on an azalea. Keep an eye out for lacebugs and spray with carbaryl when you see them. Water thoroughly during hot, dry weather and use an organic mulch. Acid fertilizer is fine, but any fertilizer renders the soil more acidic over time. Most New Jersey soils are acidic on their own and don't need the extra help.

ADDITIONAL INFORMATION

Remember that an azalea's cultural requirements, regardless of zone, demand a protected spot in the landscape. While it might be risky to locate a variety of questionable hardiness around the mailbox by the open road at a Zone 5 property, the same variety may thrive if tucked into a nook by the front door. New varieties are being constantly introduced. Contact the New Jersey Rhododendron Society for the most current information on new offerings and sources.

ADDITIONAL SPECIES, CULTIVARS, OR VARIETIES

'Delaware Valley White' is derived from *R. mucronatum*, the snow azalea, which is hardy to Zone 5. 'Hino-Crimson' has crimson-red flowers. It is from *R. obtusum* and is one of the most popular varieties in the state, but it may be hardy only to Zone 6. 'Amoenum' is of the same group but hardy to Zone 5. R. × *arnoldianum* is derived from 'Amoenum' and is hardy to Zone 4. It has pink flowers. Some of the deciduous azaleas are more hardy than the evergreen. The royal azaleas, 'R. schlippenbachii', can reach 15 ft. and are hardy to Zone 4. The Exbury hybrids are probably all hardy to Zone 5, but a few may make it in Zone 4. They come in wonderful colors, including almost white, yellow, orange, pink, rose, and red. The Robin Hill series has some of the prettiest late-blooming evergreen azaleas you would ever want to see. Many varieties are claimed to be hardy to Zone 5. In many cases, the only way to be absolutely sure is to try them in your own garden.

Bumald Spirea

Spirea × bumalda

Height: 3 to 4 ft. **Spread:** Up to 5 ft. **Flowers:** Flat clusters, up to 6 in. across, of tiny pink to white flowers **Bloom Period:** June through August **Zones:** 3, 4, **5, 6, 7,** 8	**Light Requirement:**

'Anthony Waterer' is the variety most plant people think of when you mention this hybrid. It may be close to the truth to say it is the only one. It has been around for over 70 years. Flowers in midsummer always get a gold star, but this plant also has pink leaves when new growth first emerges. Its low, rounded habit is easy to maintain. It can take severe pruning since it blooms on new growth. (Mine was accidentally mowed one year and it still bloomed beautifully.) There are many other varieties that should receive more attention than they are currently getting. It seems the horticulture industry occasionally gets into a rut, and it needs a tractor-trailer to pull it out. The Bumald hybrids are a cross between *S. albiflora* and *S. japonica*. The first is quite small, reaching only 1 1/2 ft. in height, and has white flowers. Japonica can reach 5 ft. and has white to pink flowers. The hybrid is a combination of the best characteristics of both.

WHEN TO PLANT

Planting in early spring or early fall is best. Container plants are often available while the plant is in bloom in midsummer. They can be planted at that time and do very well if you take extra precautions both at the time of planting and when watering during hot weather.

WHERE TO PLANT

Plant in full sun in an open area. These plants are tolerant of many soil types, but be sure to avoid really soggy ground. Since they are small they can be used in a lot of places to create variation in height as well as seasonal interest; they are a great choice for tiny yards.

SHRUBS

HOW TO PLANT

Bumald spirea is not very fussy and transplants quite easily. If you can't resist popping in a container-grown plant in the heat of summer, take a few precautions to protect your new friend. Water the bed (not just the spot) thoroughly the day before you intend to plant. Make sure the pot is well watered several hours before transplanting. Do the planting on a rainy or at least cloudy day; the end of the day is best. Water thoroughly and mulch with an organic mulch. If it is really sunny the next few days, provide some light shade. Keep the plant well watered and it should do great.

CARE AND MAINTENANCE

Bumald spirea plants can have a few problems, but these are tough little plants. There may be some winterkill of branches, but prune the plants in early spring and they will flourish.

ADDITIONAL INFORMATION

The Bumald spireas are easily rooted from cuttings, but they also make suckers and so can be propagated by division. If you have one, you can easily make more.

ADDITIONAL SPECIES, CULTIVARS, OR VARIETIES

There are other species of spirea addressed in this book. Keep your eyes open for varieties of Bumald hybrids. 'Crispa' has twisted leaves. 'Gold Flame' has orange new growth that turns yellow-green for the summer and orange again in the fall. It has given rise to 'Fire Light', which has deep red-orange new growth. 'Norman' hits full size at 10 in. 'Shibori' is the peppermint spirea with red, white, and pink flower clusters. You may be able to find others. All of these make interesting choices for the small condo yard or for tight, almost urban places. They can be tucked into a rock garden or massed together in open spaces.

Doublefile Viburnum

Viburnum plicatum var. tomentosum

Other Names: *V. tomentosum, V. tomentosum plicatum, V. tomentosum sterile*
Height: 8 to 10 ft.
Spread: 10 to 12 ft. or more
Flowers: Flat clusters of white flowers up to 4 in. across
Bloom Period: May
Zones: 4, **5, 6, 7,** 8

Light Requirement:

---

*W*hen covered in its horizontal double clusters of white flowers, this plant is breathtaking. The arrangement appears as if each cluster were being served up for your personal inspection. The flower clusters themselves are very interesting. The center is so delicate it could be made by an industrious spider. The tiny fertile flowers in the center are surrounded by a circle of showy white sterile flowers, giving the overall appearance of a pretty hat from the 1940s. The tiny center flowers are followed by red fruits in July and August that will eventually turn black if the birds don't get to them first. The leaves are "opposite" (arranged in pairs along the stem) and dangle down slightly as if moving out of the way to show off the flowers. The fall foliage color is a red purple. In winter, the naked spreading branches have an interesting effect, especially when covered in snow. The beauty of the doublefile viburnum has been compared to the beauty of the dogwood. Plant them both. Then you can compare them yourself . . . every spring.

WHEN TO PLANT
Plant in early spring or early fall.

WHERE TO PLANT
Plant in a sunny location in New Jersey. Some references indicate partial shade is fine, but that is really more for viburnums down south. Avoid wet, heavy clay soils. Since they can get wider than tall, make sure these plants have enough room to spread. After all, that is one of their most beautiful features.

HOW TO PLANT

This plant is not fussy. Add organic matter to heavy clay soils. (We once stuck 12 rooted cuttings in the ground in late fall, in an open, windy location. Ten of the 12 survived the winter and are now thriving.)

CARE AND MAINTENANCE

This plant doesn't need much care. Prune it after it blooms so you will be able to fully enjoy its blossoms. Insects and diseases are generally not a problem. Water thoroughly in the heat of summer.

ADDITIONAL INFORMATION

Doublefile viburnum is one of the easiest plants to propagate by cuttings. They can be taken almost any time of year, but late June is probably the best time. Use a rooting hormone to help them get started.

ADDITIONAL SPECIES, CULTIVARS, OR VARIETIES

There are several cultivars available. 'Lanarth' is strongly horizontal and its showy perimeter flowers are each up to 2 in. across. 'Mariesii' is a very old variety and may be more readily available; its flowers are almost as large. 'Shasta' was introduced by Dr. Donald Egolf at the National Arboretum in 1979. It is slightly smaller than the traditional doublefile; its flowers clusters are up to 6 in. across with a few showy flowers scattered among the tiny fertile ones in the center. 'Summer Snowflake' blooms all summer. 'Pink Beauty' has pink flowers in colder climates.

Dwarf Alberta Spruce

Picea glauca 'Conica'

Other Names: Dwarf White Spruce,
 P. albertiana
Height: 12 ft.
Spread: 5 to 10 ft.
Zones: 2, 3, 4, **5, 6, 7,** 8

Light Requirement:

The dwarf Alberta spruce is one of the most widely used dwarfs, readily available in the trade. It grows very slowly: a 40 year old shrub may be only 10 ft. tall. It has an almost-perfect cone shape. The light green color and the dense, short needles have a soft appearance. It looks "huggable." While the new growth is very soft, it stiffens up as it matures. Sometimes plants of unusual form are unusual because they have been growing under stress, but that is not always the case. Dwarf Alberta spruce is thought to be the result of a witches'-broom. Even in the absence of stress, the phenomenon of a "witches'-broom" can cause all the dormant buds on a plant to grow at once. The result is a very dense, compact shoot. These can be rooted and subsequent cuttings usually retain the habit. The resulting shrubs are almost always dwarfs, like dwarf Alberta spruce; on rare occasion, one of these dwarfs will get a witches'-broom, which is even more compact to the point of being tiny. Witches'-brooms are thought to be the result of a mite and a fungus, but no laboratory has been able to force a witches' broom by presenting this combination of pests. It is something of a mystery. Dwarf Alberta spruce was discovered in 1904 by J. G. Jack and Alfred Rehder at Lake Laggan, Alberta, Canada. These gentlemen were botanists from the Arnold Arboretum of Harvard University. While waiting for their train home, they happened to discover this unusual plant at the base of the Canadian Rocky Mountains.

WHEN TO PLANT
Plant in early spring or early fall.

WHERE TO PLANT
It is best to plant in a sunny spot, but dwarf Alberta spruce will tolerate a bit of shade. Since it is so small and grows so slowly, this dwarf makes a terrific foundation plant. It can also be successfully

used in containers but will need winter protection. It works well in rock gardens, in planters, and around condos.

How to Plant

The dwarf Alberta spruce is not too difficult to get established. It likes moist, well-drained soil so be sure to add lots of organic matter such as leaf compost and keep it well watered. As is true of most plants, it will appreciate an organic mulch.

Care and Maintenance

Since its rate of growth is about 1 in. per year and it grows in an almost perfect conical shape, pruning would be totally super-fluous. The only time you may need to use the hand pruners is if the plant throws out a reversion-type branch. In that case, remove the offending shoot immediately. One problem that often pops up is an infestation of mites. The plant may begin to lose color, and in the morning, especially when it is covered in dew, you will see webbing that resembles not-very-artistic spiderwebs within the branches. If you shake a branch onto a white paper towel, you will shake off a few mites. The dust-sized insects are much easier to see on the paper towel. Infestations are more likely to appear in hot, dry weather and are worse on drought-stressed plants. The first defense is to hose them off with a hard stream of water, which will also give the plant a thorough drink. This treatment may be sufficient. Mites reproduce rapidly, so you should hose them off every few days until you are sure you have them under control. If this does not give adequate control, contact your County Extension office for current pesticide recommendations.

Additional Information

On an extremely rare occasion, dwarf Alberta spruce will send up a shoot that has reverted back to normal. This should be removed immediately or it will rapidly dominate the plant and look very strange. These trees are very popular for use as container Christmas trees. They will do well, but try to keep them in a cool location, and don't keep them indoors any longer than absolutely necessary. From a decorating point of view, they are really too compact for the grace-ful hanging of ornaments.

Additional Species, Cultivars, or Varieties

'Densata' is sometimes called the black hills spruce. Don't plant it if you are in a hurry; it reaches 20 to 40 ft. in 40 to 80 years. *P. abies* 'Little Gem' is a witches'-broom from the witches'-broom 'Nidiformis'.

Eastern Redcedar

Juniperus virginiana

Other Name: Pencil Cedar
Height: 40 to 50 ft.
Spread: 8 to 20 ft.
Zones: 2,3, 4, **5, 6, 7,** 8, 9

Light Requirement:

One of the fine personality traits of the redcedar is that it is one of the first trees to reforest an abandoned field. That is an important job. Since it is also tolerant of soil conditions that would make many plants choke, it is an essential plant for land reclamation projects. In addition to being a workhorse in the plant world, it is an attractive, easy care, practical landscape plant. Root pruned plants will transplant easily. It is extremely drought resistant and will live a respectable 200 to 350 years. Most of these plants are grown from seed, so there is significant variation in color and shape. They can be pyramid-shaped or almost tubular. For uniformity, choose young plants carefully or use named varieties. If you are using them in a mixed evergreen grouping, you may enjoy the natural variation. Eastern redcedar is the most widespread native evergreen in North America. The young seedlings can pop up almost anywhere, with a little help from bird friends. The beautiful cedar waxwing is particularly fond of the fruits. It is a thrill to see a migrating flock stopping for a snack. The young plants have a very soft, fluffy appearance which differs from the adult foliage. If you find one, transplant it carefully while it is still quite small. On the down side, it is not the most interesting plant for specimen planting, and many turn an unattractive brown in the winter. The named cultivars will have the best of the characteristics; plants grown from seed will not. Redcedars are great for grouping, borders, or backgrounds. They are among the better choices for use as a windbreak and in other difficult situations.

WHEN TO PLANT
Plant in early spring or early fall.

WHERE TO PLANT
Redcedar prefers sun but you may find seedlings popping up in shade. Very young plants tolerate light shade. The soil of choice is

deep, moist, and well-drained, but this plant will tolerate a wide range of conditions.

How to Plant

Redcedar is not fussy, but transplanting will be more successful if you root-prune first.

Care and Maintenance

You can prune lightly in April and again in June if necessary. Avoid the use of electric hedge shears; a light touch with hand pruners will maintain a natural shape. Remember that constant major pruning is a poor substitute for proper plant selection. Bagworms are the most destructive problem. The bags are made from bits and snips of twigs and leaves. They dangle from the branch tips as if they belong there. These critters come out and devour your tree when you aren't looking. Remove the bags whenever you see them and spray in mid-June and late June with *Bacillus thuringiensis* (B.T.). Cedar apple rust is more of a problem for apple trees, but if you see bright orange Medusa like growths on the branches of redcedar, it is in the "teliospore" stage of the disease. The disease will dry up shortly on a redcedar, but any nearby apples are in trouble.

Additional Information

This is the cedar of cedar closets and chests. It has a lovely scent which is effective in keeping away clothes moths. The wood is also important in the production of pencils. The berries are used in making gin, and they smell like gin if crushed. Redcedar is also considered a good choice for bonsai.

Additional Species, Cultivars, or Varieties

'Burkii' is popular because of its bluish gray foliage and almost-purple winter color. 'Canaertii' has yellow green new growth, but it stays dark green all winter. It has an attractive shape as an older tree. 'Nova' is very narrow and upright, while 'Pendula' has both spreading and hanging branches. There are many varieties of red-cedar from which to choose.

Forsythia

Forsythia × intermedia

Other Name: Golden Bells
Height: 8 to 10 ft.
Spread: 10 to 12 ft., sometimes up to 15 ft.
Flowers: Many bright yellow, 1 in.,
    trumpet shaped flowers
Bloom Period: April
Zones: 5, 6, 7, 8

Light Requirement:

A gracefully arching forsythia covered in masses of yellow flowers is a spectacular show even when there is one on every corner. These are easy care, fast growing shrubs that need little attention when properly sited, and are horrid beasts when shoved into the wrong spot. When used as a border planting in tight quarters or as a foundation plant, they need constant pruning to keep them in line. This results in lots of short, twiggy growth with little flower production and a total loss of natural elegance. The absolute worst is when they are pruned repeatedly with an electric hedge shears and then pruned again just before they bloom. All you will see is old bare trunks with a few specks of pitiful yellow drips inside. Why? Why? Why? This type of pruning makes no sense what-so-ever! It is an enormous amount of work to fight forsythia's programmed growth habit. Let it be itself or grow something else! Long handled loppers will take out the old trunks to encourage young shoots. Hand pruners can shorten up the longest shoots, but take them way back to the trunk to resprout inside. A few snips in late winter can provide branches to be forced inside for early spring color. Most pruning should be done right after it blooms or you will cut off all the flowers. Appreciate this shrub for the beauty it is. It will be easier on you, easier on the plant, and easier on anyone who has to look at it.

WHEN TO PLANT
Plant in early spring or early fall.

WHERE TO PLANT

Forsythia needs full sun to flower brilliantly. It tolerates a wide range of soil conditions and will even do well in an urban setting. Just be sure to pick a place where it has enough room to spread.

HOW TO PLANT

Forsythia makes an excellent specimen plant and can be incredibly dramatic when planted en masse. For a border planting, consider mixing it with weigela and/or spirea; then your planting will have more than one season of bloom. If you plant a staggered row, you can have all the front row bloom yellow and the back bloom white. Balled and burlapped, container grown, even bare-root plants all transplant easily. Sometimes branches forced to bloom indoors will root in the vase. Even they can get established with relative ease.

CARE AND MAINTENANCE

Prune properly. The first step is to retire your electric hedge shears for everything but hedges (maybe even for hedges). Forsythia can be pruned severely after bloom, but start by taking the oldest wood out at the base. That step will remove much top growth. Selective pruning of the rest with hand pruners will be easy. The young growth you keep will continue to bloom while the rest of the shrub fills in. Forsythia can get a variety of insects and diseases, but they rarely amount to much.

ADDITIONAL INFORMATION

If you inherit a really overgrown or overpruned forsythia, it can be salvaged. Right after it blooms, cut it down to the ground. Give it a dose of fertilizer and it should regrow more to your liking. With a small amount of annual pruning each spring you should be able to maintain an attractive shrub for many years.

ADDITIONAL SPECIES, CULTIVARS, OR VARIETIES

'Spectabilis' was introduced in 1906. It is still readily available in the trade and is the industry standard. 'Lynwood' has paler flowers that are more uniformly distributed. It originated as a sport (or unusual shoot) from 'Spectabilis' in 1935. 'Tremonia' is a cutleaf form. 'Fiesta' is small, reaching only about 3 ft., and its leaves are variegated with yellow. There is another species, *Forsythia suspensa*, called weeping forsythia, but it is not as floriferous as *F.* × *intermedia*. The variety 'Sieboldii' has larger flowers than *F.* × *intermedia*, is hardy in New Jersey, and is available in the trade.

Junipers

Juniperus scopulorum, J. chinensis

Height: Variety dependent	**Light Requirement:**
Spread: Variety dependent	
Zones: 3, 4, **5, 6, 7**	

These two species have been grouped together because between them they have given rise to some of the most well-known and popular juniper varieties in the landscape industry. Their care is similar, but their growth habits vary as much between varieties within the same species as between the species themselves. There are tall junipers, fat ones, creepers, and weepers. For better or worse, junipers in general and these two species specifically are among the most commonly planted landscape plants in the business. Junipers transplant easily and are adaptable to a wide range of conditions. They are sometimes used to the point of total monotony and boredom, but as screens, hedges, and windbreaks they have no equal. As specimen plants and for foundation plantings they are ho-hum at best and an overgrown tangle most of the time. Junipers can handle some pruning to keep things in line, but when they get severely overgrown, they cannot be pruned back to bare wood. A branch will not resprout if all the green is removed, so you might as well pull out the plants and start over with something more appropriate for that particular spot. Annual pruning of new growth will help keep plants more compact. Michael Dirr offers the following general rule in his book: "If you cannot grow junipers, then do not bother planting anything else." I offer a parallel word of advice: "If you must grow junipers, less is better than more."

WHEN TO PLANT
Plant in early spring or early fall.

WHERE TO PLANT
Junipers prefer a sunny location; they will get loose and ratty in too much shade. Their tolerance for a range of soil types and pH contributes to their popularity. They are also tolerant of urban

conditions, can be used as windbreaks and a few varieties exhibit salt tolerance.

HOW TO PLANT

They are easy to get established. Follow good planting practices and watch them grow.

CARE AND MAINTENANCE

Light pruning of new growth can be done in April. A second pruning of rebellious branches or thinning of crowded spots can be done in June. Prune back to a side shoot. Bagworms affect these junipers just as they do the eastern redcedar. The bags are constructed so that they look like part of the plant. The worms can completely strip a plant of its foliage. The biggest problem is that the damage is often severe before you notice it. Remove the bags whenever you see them and spray in mid-June and late June with *Bacillus thuringiensis* (B.T.). Junipers are susceptible to a number of diseases. When pruning to remove diseased branches, be sure to dip your pruners in a solution of chlorine bleach to prevent contamination.

ADDITIONAL INFORMATION

The word "gin" is derived from the Dutch "jenever," which means juniper, and we can credit the Dutch for inventing it. All juniper berries can be used to make gin. Only females produce the small bluish fruits. After the grain is distilled, juniper and sometimes coriander can be added. After a second distillation, you will have gin. There is a legend that says a juniper planted by the front door will keep witches away. The only way they can pass through the door is to correctly count all the needles. (Finally! An explanation for why these plants are so popular!)

ADDITIONAL SPECIES, CULTIVARS, OR VARIETIES

There are an enormous number of varieties. *J. chinensis* varieties include the well-known pfitzer juniper, 'Pfitzeriana', which can grow at least 5 ft. tall and 10 ft. wide. 'Hetzii' grows to be 15 ft. by 15 ft. 'San Joseé is a creeper that stops at a maximum of 24 in. but can grow 8 ft. wide. *J. scopulorum* claims the popular 'Skyrocket', which is a very narrow columnar form, and 'Moonglow', a globe-shaped variety. 'Tolleson's Weeping Juniper' has interesting dangling foliage on arched branches; it is very hardy. Whatever variety piques your interest, be sure to gather all the information you can about its height, spread, and rate of growth. If you locate the plant with this information in mind, you will get more enjoyment from it.

Lilac

Syringa vulgaris

Other Name: Common Lilac
Height: 8 to 15 ft.
Spread: 6 to 12 ft.
Flowers: Upright panicles of white, pale yellow, pink, blue, lilac, wine, and purple flowers; very fragrant
Bloom Period: May
Zones: 3, 4, ,5, 6, 7, 8

Light Requirement:

Lilacs are romantic flowers. Their scent is full of spring fever and warm sunshine. Common lilac is not native to North America but was brought over with the early settlers and has been here ever since. If you visit Colonial homes, you can often find original plantings. Buccleuch Mansion in New Brunswick, New Jersey, dates back to 1739. Its lilac hedge is at least 200 years old. There are many varieties, and new ones are still being introduced. The biggest problem is powdery mildew, so resistant varieties are advantageous. Some of the earliest to bloom can get nipped by late frosts, especially in the northwest part of the state which is in Zone 5. Most bloom late enough to avoid damage. By planting a variety of lilacs you can extend the bloom to a full 5 weeks. If that tickles your fancy, plant a whole bunch and enjoy them. There is not much to recommend lilacs other than their flowers; they get no fall color, and their habit tends to be a little leggy. If you get swept away to a magical place with each whiff, then it doesn't matter. Practical gardeners may prefer something else.

WHEN TO PLANT
Plant in early spring. Late March or early April is best.

WHERE TO PLANT
Plant in a sunny spot. You may not want it front and center in your yard, since it doesn't have much to offer when not in bloom. Try it in view of a kitchen or family-room window. There you will see it while in bloom, but it can blend into the background at other times.

How to Plant

Lilacs are not too particular about soil type, but they are fussy about pH, which needs to be neutral. In New Jersey that means most soils will require a thorough lime application at planting time. A soil test will tell you the exact amount needed.

Care and Maintenance

Prune lilacs while they are in bloom and you will get to enjoy the blossoms indoors. Pruning at that time will also help the plants fill in. If you wait until all the flowers have faded to prune, you will be removing much of the new growth. It is better to have that plant energy go into new growth further back on the plant where you want it. While pruning, you should take some of the old wood out at the base. Older wood does not produce much in the way of flowers, and removing it will trigger new shoots that will be more productive. If too many suckers shoot up, thin them out. If they are coming up far enough away from the main trunk, you can take a division and propagate the variety easily. Even if you are not doing major pruning, remove the dead flowers. You should also check regularly for borers. They should be controlled in early May and mid-June. Powdery mildew is often sarcastically referred to as "fall color." Most lilacs get it to some degree. Resistant varieties will help with this problem. Use an appropriate fungicide when you see the first signs of white specks on the leaves, usually in July or August. Lime regularly.

Additional Information

There is a lilac grove at the Rutgers Gardens in New Brunswick. It is very old and was neglected, but it recently began to undergo renovation. Some of its varieties have been discovered to be very rare.

Additional Species, Cultivars, or Varieties

Japanese tree lilac (*S. reticulata*) can reach 30 ft. It is not as common as *S. vulgaris*, and its scent is not as wonderful, but it does warrant more attention. Its flowers arrive in mid-June, extending the lilac flowering season. There are many varieties of lilac; some are hybrids. 'Ludwig Spaeth' is a beautiful dark purple. 'Charles Joly' is a stunning magenta. 'Primrose' is a slow grower, but the pale-yellow buds open to creamy-white flowers, which make it unique. 'Sensation' is red-violet with a distinct white edge on the petals; it is a show stopper. (It is my personal favorite.)

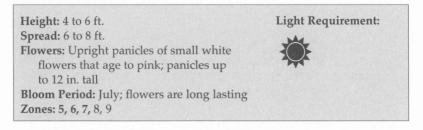

Oak Leaf Hydrangea

Hydrangea quercifolia

Height: 4 to 6 ft.
Spread: 6 to 8 ft.
Flowers: Upright panicles of small white flowers that age to pink; panicles up to 12 in. tall
Bloom Period: July; flowers are long lasting
Zones: 5, 6, 7, 8, 9

Light Requirement:

The oak leaf hydrangea is a plant for all seasons. The 8 in. leaves look like oversized red oak leaves in a bright shade of green. Their bold shape stands out among the delicate ferns that share its tolerance for a shady spot. The appearance also contrasts wonderfully with needled evergreens when these hydrangeas are planted beneath the branches of mature trees. In summertime, when many flowering shrubs have already finished their big show, oak leaf hydrangeas burst out in large panicles of white flowers. This display is particularly appreciated in shady nooks where flower options are more limited. As the flowers age, they develop a rose cast which deepens over time. Fall leaf color is a deep red to an almost bronze with possible hints of purple. This may be their most beautiful time of year. As the leaves drop, an exfoliating bark with a deep rich brown color is exposed. The skeletal shape is coarse with little side branching. The silhouette, bark texture, and color make for a bit of winter drama.

WHEN TO PLANT
Plant in early spring or early fall.

WHERE TO PLANT
Oak leaf hydrangea prefers some shade and can tolerate deep shade. It will endure full sun, but it will require a heavy organic mulch to keep its roots cool and moist. It is an excellent choice for the edge of woods and under mature evergreens.

HOW TO PLANT
This plant requires moist, well-drained soil. The addition of organic matter during soil preparation is beneficial, as is the use of an

organic mulch. Young plants are slightly delicate and may need winter protection until they are established, especially in Zone 5.

CARE AND MAINTENANCE

Oak leaf hydrangea has no serious pest problems. Pruning is best done right after blooming to avoid removing flower buds for the following year. Since these plants have a somewhat coarse habit, commercial growers pinch the new growth repeatedly to keep them full in containers. You can do the same, but it is easier in the long run to let them be themselves. Overgrown oak leaf hydrangeas can be rejuvenated by severe pruning in the early spring. They can be cut back to about 6 in., but you will probably not get flowers that year. They occasionally show the ability to generate flowers on current year's growth, but most flower production is set the previous fall. Oak leaf hydrangea can be propagated by division of the suckers; this is best done in early spring. The long, upright branches do sometimes snap at the base as the result of winter ice and snow. This is not great for the overall shape, but the plants generally resprout at the base and suffer no long term consequences.

ADDITIONAL INFORMATION

A native of Georgia, Florida, and Mississippi, this plant can fill a niche in New Jersey gardens. The combination of shade tolerance and summer bloom make it a real pick-me-up for difficult spots at a difficult time of year. Don't try to force it into a sunny location where there are many more suitable choices. You can treasure it all year long when it is properly situated.

ADDITIONAL SPECIES, CULTIVARS, OR VARIETIES

'Snow Queen' was selected at Princeton Nurseries. It is slightly more compact than the species. 'Harmony' has enormous panicles that can weigh down the branches. 'Snow Flake' has extra sepals, so has the appearance of having double flowers. 'Sikes Dwarf' gets only 2 ft. tall and is great for tight spots.

Old Fashioned Weigela

Weigela florida

Other Name: *W. rosea*
Height: 6 to 10 ft.
Spread: 9 to 12 ft.
Flowers: Many pink, rose, ruby, or
    purplish pink 1 in. flowers
Bloom Period: Late May and June; sporadic
    summer repeat-blooming
Zones: 5, 6, 7, 8
	Light Requirement:

*F*ull, tangled, and exuberant is the best way to describe weigela. This is not a plant for tight places or places where you will view it up close. The explosion of flowers in the spring is a riot of color and even more dramatic when planted en masse or as a border. The arching branches will sweep the ground while covered in blossoms for major "drive-by" impact. Don't bother trying to force it into a formal hedge. The rigid pruning would destroy the wild elegance and you would be left with just the tangled messy part. Weigela is tolerant of pollution, but its habit makes it tough to squeeze into most urban settings. The winter look is a little sad, so "up close and personal" is not a great choice of locations. Pruning should be done right after bloom. It can take significant pruning, but do not use electric hedge shears. Take out some of the old growth at the base or close to it; that will take away a lot of the fullness at the same time. Then just shape with hand pruners to keep it looking natural. While getting the job done, you may come across branches that have rooted where they hit the ground. These can be transplanted if you are interested in having more, or they can be potted for sharing with a friend.

WHEN TO PLANT
Plant in early spring or early fall.

WHERE TO PLANT
Plant in full sun where there will be some room to spread out. Do not plant too close to the house, and do not use as a foundation plant. This is not a great choice for a formal garden, but is a wonderful, easy care, free-spirited plant that can be used as a specimen or

border plant. It gets so thick it is a good privacy planting. Even when leafless it is massive.

How to Plant

This is one of the easiest plants to get started. It is very adaptable to a wide range of conditions. It can be started bare root, balled, or from a container-grown plant.

Care and Maintenance

Insects and disease are not serious. Pruning is the biggest job, but it is not so bad if the plant is sited properly. Some annual removal of excessive growth right after it blooms will keep it under control. Some branches die back occasionally and can be removed any time. The worst thing you can do is try to squeeze this plant into a confined space. You will be unhappy with the result and the plant will be miserable.

Additional Information

For many years the idea of mixing a border planting of weigela, spirea, and forsythia has been very appealing. With this combination you can enjoy early yellow flowers, mid-season white, and late-spring red or pink. All three have similar growth habits, but the combination allows you to eliminate the problems sometimes incurred with monocultures, and you will have a much longer flowering season. Since the blooms do not quite overlap, there is no conflict between the flowers themselves.

Additional Species, Cultivars, or Varieties

'Bristol Ruby' has dark red flowers that repeat throughout the summer. 'Variegata' has green and white leaves with pink flowers. 'Rumba' reaches only 3 ft. and has wine red flowers with yellow throats. 'Versicolor' has both creamy white and rose blooms on the same plant. There are many more.

PeeGee Hydrangea

Hydrangea paniculata 'Grandiflora'

Height: 10 to 25 ft.	**Light Requirement:**
Spread: 10 to 20 ft.	
Flowers: Enormous panicles of sterile white flowers that fade to pink and then tan	
Bloom Period: August; flowers are long lasting	
Zones: 4, 5, 6, 7, 8, 9	

*T*his is an old-fashioned faithful bloomer. For some reason it is maligned in some of the literature as "overused." Perhaps it was at one time, but there is hardly one in every backyard now. Even if there were, big showy flower clusters in August are not exactly a hardship. The problem with PeeGee is it is a little difficult to blend in with other plants. Its unrefined habit makes it stand out when planted as part of a bed or design. It looks better as a specimen plant or maybe a border planting. You may even consider tucking one here and there in an informal evergreen border planting. PeeGee can take a little shade and will break up the green with a splash of summer blooms. PeeGee hydrangea normally grows as a large shrub, but you can force a tree form by selecting a trunk at the time of planting and removing the suckers. Since it blooms on new wood, pruning can be done in early spring without shortchanging yourself in flower production. If you want really enormous flower heads, prune away everything but about 10 primary branches. These will then produce panicles up to 18 in. in length; they will be so massive they can weigh the branches down.

WHEN TO PLANT
Plant in early spring or early fall.

WHERE TO PLANT
This is not a great choice for a small yard but is tolerant of urban conditions. It will do fine in full sun as a specimen plant, but will do just as well tucked into the shade of a few evergreens. It is also adaptable to different soil conditions but prefers moist, sandy loam soil that is well drained.

HOW TO PLANT

This is an easy plant to get established. If you prefer a tree form, it is important to choose your trunk at the time of planting. The use of an organic mulch will help retain soil moisture, which will keep PeeGee fat and happy.

CARE AND MAINTENANCE

Prune hard in the spring to control flower size or to keep it contained. Remove flower heads in late fall or they will get brown and unattractive. The flower clusters can be cut and dried. PeeGee can get a few insects and diseases, as can other hydrangeas, but they are not usually serious. This is a tough plant.

ADDITIONAL INFORMATION

These plants will last for years. There is a lovely specimen on Main Street in Hightstown. This PeeGee is very large and appears very old. It is on the property of a building registered with the Historical Society. The flowers are magnificent every summer. It is impossible to see this beauty and not wish there were more around just like it.

ADDITIONAL SPECIES, CULTIVARS, OR VARIETIES

The variety 'Praecox' is similar to PeeGee and blooms 3 weeks earlier. 'Tardiva' is sometimes called the compact PeeGee hydrangea; it blooms in September. There are other species of *Hydrangea* that are certainly worth noting. *Hydrangea macrophylla* is the big-leaf hydrangea which has round flower heads of pink to blue flowers. It blooms on old wood, so it can only be pruned right after it blooms. There are many varieties and flower color is often dependent on soil pH. *H. arborescens* flowers on new wood and produces white flower clusters after PeeGee. There are several varieties; 'Grandiflora' may be the best.

Rhododendron

Rhododendron catawbiense

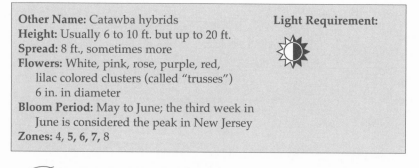

Other Name: Catawba hybrids
Height: Usually 6 to 10 ft. but up to 20 ft.
Spread: 8 ft., sometimes more
Flowers: White, pink, rose, purple, red,
　　lilac colored clusters (called "trusses")
　　6 in. in diameter
Bloom Period: May to June; the third week in
　　June is considered the peak in New Jersey
Zones: 4, **5, 6, 7,** 8

Light Requirement:

hododendrons are such an important garden shrub it is hard to imagine a yard without one. The genus is very complex, with over 900 species that hybridize readily. Catawba hybrids are among the hardiest and best for New Jersey. They are native to the Allegheny Mountains down to Georgia and Alabama. They have large leathery leaves that are almost exotic in appearance. There is a theory that one can tell the temperature in winter by the degree of curling on the leaves. This method may not be precise, but if the leaves are all curled up, it is probably very cold. There are many flower colors available and many cultivars in different sizes—and there are new ones coming out all the time. Most yellows and oranges are not hardy, but hybridizers in California are currently working to cross these tender varieties with those that are more cold tolerant.

WHEN TO PLANT

Plant in early spring or early fall. Late March or early April is best, but early September is a close second.

WHERE TO PLANT

Choose a site where your rhododendrons will get some shade. Most varieties will burn in full sun and will struggle in hot, dry weather. The west side of a house is one of the worst possible sites for winter injury. A plant in this location can be tricked into thinking it should come out of dormancy; then the sun sets and temperatures plummet. It is also desirable to stay away from excessive wind, which can cause leaves to dehydrate in winter. Another serious problem is standing water. Rhododendrons have no tolerance for wet feet. Be very careful to check the location of your downspouts when making a foundation planting. Even in ground with good drainage, downspouts can cause water to stand long enough to do damage.

HOW TO PLANT

The addition of organic matter to the soil is very beneficial. Do not add lime; these plants prefer an acid soil. Use an organic mulch to keep the soil cool and moist and to reduce weed pressure. Rhododendron's roots are very near the surface. Cultivation can damage delicate roots, so it is best not to cultivate if possible.

CARE AND MAINTENANCE

Water thoroughly when necessary. This may include a thorough watering in the fall (it is not wise to send a rhododendron into winter under water stress). Prune as necessary after rhododendron blooms. This will also remove the spent flowers. You will not want plant energy to be wasted on seed production, so snap off the spent blooms even if you are not pruning. Rhododendrons face two major problems in New Jersey: borers and black vine weevils. Control borers by spraying at 10-day intervals in May. Black vine weevils are evidenced by notches in the leaves, and the larvae feed on plant roots. You can try to control the adults, but they are difficult to eliminate and you may need professional help.

ADDITIONAL INFORMATION

There is a Rhododendron Garden at the Rutgers Gardens in New Brunswick, an old collection that is being updated. It is a lovely walk in the woods, and warrants more than one visit as different varieties come into bloom at different times. There are three chapters of the American Rhododendron Society in New Jersey. They may be difficult to locate since the president changes regularly; the name of the current president of the Princeton chapter is always on file at the Princeton Public Library.

ADDITIONAL SPECIES, CULTIVARS, OR VARIETIES

There are thousands of rhododendrons. The American Rhododendron Society gives high rankings to the following: 'Lem's Stormcloud' grows to 5 ft., is hardy to minus 15 degrees Fahrenheit, and has bright-red flowers; 'Lodestar' is hardy to minus 20 degrees Fahrenheit, grows to 5 ft., and has white or very pale lilac flowers; 'Scintillation' is hardy to minus 15 degrees Fahrenheit, reaches 5 ft., and has pink flowers.

Saint Johnswort

Hypericum prolificum

Other Names: Shrubby Saint Johnswort,
Broombrush
Height: Up to 4 ft.
Spread: Up to 5 ft.
Flowers: Bright yellow buttercuplike flowers,
1 in. diameter
Bloom Period: June, July, and August
Zones: 3, 4, ,5, **6, 7,** 8

Light Requirement:

*A*ny woody ornamental that blooms in summer deserves a
second look, and this one you can't miss. The first burst of
Saint Johnswort's summer flowers is usually quite spectacular, and the
rest of the summer display is wonderful as well. It produces not just a
single flower here or there but a significant number of sunny yellow
blooms at any given time. A Saint Johnswort bloom has been compared to a single rose, although it is not nearly as fussy as the queen
of flowers. Saint Johnswort produces its abundance of blooms on new
growth; this means it can, and sometimes should, be pruned severely
in the spring. Saint Johnswort originated right here in the Garden State
as well as south to Georgia and west to Iowa, and offers the advantages of native plant material. It has no serious pests and is adaptable
to a wide range of soil types; it is a good choice for poorer soils and
will tolerate dry conditions.

WHEN TO PLANT

Early spring is the best planting time, in late March or early April.

WHERE TO PLANT

Saint Johnswort likes sun but will do well in light shade. It is a
good choice for dry rocky conditions. Saint Johnswort can be effectively used for mass planting or as part of a mixed border. With its
mounded shape, Saint Johnswort doesn't have enough character to
be used a specimen plant. Nor is it a great choice for a foundation
plant since it is not very attractive in the winter, but since it stays on
the small side and can be pruned, you can try it as a foundation
plant if soil conditions limit other options.

How to Plant

Several sources suggest using only container grown plants, but Saint Johnswort suckers readily, and divisions made in early spring are almost always successful. It is very tolerant of dry, rocky soil, but don't push your luck; it is still a good idea to prepare soil properly. Break up a hardpan with a pickaxe if necessary and add some organic matter. A layer of mulch will help retain whatever moisture the soil is able to hold.

Care and Maintenance

This plant has no significant pests of any kind, which makes care easy. Prune hard in the spring. This will encourage a fuller plant that flowers with enthusiasm. If you want to divide Saint Johnswort, that should also be done in the early spring.

Additional Information

There has been tremendous publicity recently regarding the use of a species of Saint Johnswort as a medicinal herb. That species is *H. perforatum*, a herbaceous perennial that creeps along the ground, sending out roots as it runs along the soil surface. One of its key active ingredients is "hypericin," which is not found in significant quantities in the ornamental varieties. *H. perforatum* was introduced into the United States from Europe and is now considered a serious weed.

Additional Species, Cultivars, or Varieties

There are many species, but not many selected cultivars or varieties. 'Hidcote' is a variety of *H. patulum* and the most commonly grown. It is small and low growing, with 2 in. flowers that appear in significant numbers all summer. Unfortunately, it is often killed to the ground in winter and so should be treated like a herbaceous perennial. It is an excellent choice for rock gardens; even after a severe winter it will come back from the roots. *H. frondosum* is the shrubby hypericum that has lots of yellow flowers and is hardy to Zone 5. Each blossom has brushlike stamens which add character. *H. kalmianum* is one of the most hardy and does well up to Zone 4. Many of the others may only be hardy to Zone 6 or 7.

Sand Cherry

Prunus × cistena

Other Names: Purple Leaf Sand Cherry,
Dwarf Red Leaf Plum
Height: 7 to 10 ft.; up to 15 ft.
Spread: Almost as wide as tall
Flowers: Many fragrant, pale pink single blossoms
that open with the leaves
Bloom Period: Late April to early May
Zones: 2, 3, 4, **5, 6, 7,** 8

Light Requirement:

---

*T*his is a wonderful shrub that can be trained as a small tree.
It is a cross between *P. pumila*, the sand cherry, and *P. cerasifera*
'Atropurpurea', the purple leafed plum. It has been around since
1909 when it was released by Dr. N. E. Hanson of South Dakota State
University. (That explains why it is so hardy, but not why it took so
long to be available in the trade.) The leaves are more dark red than
purple, and the pale-pink flowers are spectacular against the emerging
foliage. The overall shape of the plant tends to be roundish, and the
branches are upright to spreading but not drooping. Its greatest claim
to fame is the rich leaf color which it maintains to perfection throughout the season. It may get small blackish fruits. The fruits are not
obvious, but the birds will enjoy them. Sand cherry is often recommended for container culture. A more important use for this little gem
is in exposed locations in the colder part of the state. The combination
of later flowers and extreme cold hardiness make this a dependable
bloomer even after tough winters.

WHEN TO PLANT
Plant in early spring; late March or early April is best.

WHERE TO PLANT
Plant in a sunny location. Sand cherry is a nice choice for a specimen
plant in a very small yard and is small enough to do well in containers on patios and decks. It is extremely cold hardy and is good for
more exposed locations where many spring flowering shrubs suffer
winter damage or flower bud injury from late spring frosts. It is not
pollution tolerant.

HOW TO PLANT

Sand cherries are not particularly fussy about soil type or pH. They do require good drainage, so be sure to add organic matter to heavy clay soils. If you prefer a tree form, it may be necessary to select the main trunk at the time of planting. Prune accordingly.

CARE AND MAINTENANCE

This sand cherry is considered a dwarf. It stays on the small side and maintains an attractive round shape. The little pruning it requires should be done after flowering, although this will remove developing fruits. Be sure to take any suckers from the base if you are trying to maintain a small tree. Although it is a close relative of the purple leaf plum, it does not appear quite as susceptible to the many pests that plague that species.

ADDITIONAL INFORMATION

Up until about 5 years ago, the sand cherry was almost unknown by local plant professionals. It can now be found easily, even if it is not yet available everywhere. The name "cistena" comes from the Sioux and means "baby." It is surprising that this "baby" has taken almost 100 years to become popular. It is so lovely. (We have a patch of sand cherries at Blooming Acres. They are magnificent while in bloom. One summer one was accidentally mowed, and it was mowed repeatedly the rest of the summer. That fall I rescued the pitiful thing and moved it into a bed by the house. It survived, grew the following year, and bloomed the next spring. This is a great little plant.)

ADDITIONAL SPECIES, CULTIVARS, OR VARIETIES

There is only one named variety mentioned in the literature: 'Big Cis' reaches 14 ft. It has a very round habit and lots of pale pink flowers which are very fragrant.

Vanhoutte Spirea

Spiraea × vanhouttei

Other Name: Vanhoutte Bridalwreath
Height: 6 to 8 ft.; up to 10 ft.
Spread: 12 ft.
Flowers: Cascades of white flowers carried
  in clusters
Bloom Period: May
Zones: 4, 5, 6, 7, 8

Light Requirement:

A border planting of Vanhoutte spirea in full bloom is spectacular. The graceful way the branches arch up, over, and down until they sweep the ground is simply royal. The number of snow-white flowers is astronomical. The leaves are a subtle bluish green. Don't look for dramatic fall color, but the foliage may turn slightly purple. Vanhoutte spirea has been around since the mid-1800s. Its parents are *S. triloba* and *S. cantoniensis*. It has gone up and down in popularity and may not be receiving as much favor now as it did in the past. For a dependable, easy-care, low-maintenance shrub, it is still a good choice. It grows relatively quickly and can make a good privacy hedge or mass planting. Spirea can be mistreated with electric hedge shears just as forsythia are often brutalized. If you shear and squeeze it into a formal hedge, it will survive like that for years, but it will be very ugly. There are other plants and even other spireas that will stay compact and work well in tight places. This one needs room to spread its wings. Plant it and let it be, or plant something else.

WHEN TO PLANT
Plant in early spring or early fall.

WHERE TO PLANT
Give this plant a sunny spot with room to stretch out. It can be part of a group or used as a border or privacy planting, or even as a specimen. Moist, well-drained soil is preferred, but it is very flexible regarding soil type and pH.

How to Plant

Vanhoutte spirea has no special planting requirements. Improve your soil before planting, as needed. The addition of organic matter is always helpful.

Care and Maintenance

This shrub has no significant pest problems and is virtually trouble-free. Every 2 or 3 years it is a good idea to *selectively* prune out the oldest wood at the base right after it finishes blooming. Take a pair of long-handled loppers and cut out the oldest shoots right at or near the ground. When you do that, you will be thinning out the top at the same time. Use hand pruners to shape and thin the rest. Do not shear this plant; shearing cuts off all the grace and leaves only what is ugly.

Additional Information

Try planting Vanhoutte spirea, forsythia, and weigela together in a border planting or informal hedge. The three have similar growth habits and bloom sequentially.

Additional Species, Cultivars, or Varieties

S. triloba is much smaller than its offspring, the Vanhoutte, reaching only about 5 ft. It also has a more compact habit. The variety 'Swan Lake' is particularly floriferous and may make a better choice than Vanhoutte for an informal hedge in tight spaces. 'Fairy Queen' is another option. There are many other species and many named varieties within each of the species. Be sure you understand the potential height, width, and bloom period of the variety you choose. There are tremendous differences among them, so pick the one that best suits your needs.

Virginia Sweetspire

Itea virginica

Height: 3 to 5 ft.; up to 10 ft.
Spread: 2 to 4 ft.; up to 12 ft.
Flowers: Tiny, fragrant white flowers in
    spikes up to 6 in. tall
Bloom Period: June and July
Zones: 5, 6, 7, 8, 9

Light Requirement:

This is a lovely summer blooming native shrub that requires little fussing and provides dependable flowers. It is still blooming when most woody ornamentals have finished, and it is well suited for the wet spots in your yard where most plants don't stand a chance. It is a good choice for planting along the edges of ponds or stream banks. Sweetspire can be found in the New Jersey Pine Barrens and south all the way to Florida. It spreads by suckers, so in some places it will form large patches. It is not too aggressive, so don't worry that it will take over. Each leaf is about 4 in. long and dark green during the summer, but it turns purple-red or even brilliant red in fall. The leaves are tenacious and provide fall color for an extended period. This native is another testimony to the idea of using indigenous plants for an environmentally sound landscape. It is a rugged small plant with dependable flowers and no serious pest problems, and it requires little special attention when properly sited.

WHEN TO PLANT

Plant in early spring. Container material is not too particular about planting time, but if you are dividing suckers to propagate your planting, that should be done in late March or early April.

WHERE TO PLANT

Choose a moist to moderately wet site in full sun or partial shade. A good spot is at the water's edge, or try low spots in your yard or drainage swales. These plants are small enough to be useful in foundation plantings, especially near downspouts where they will tolerate the extra moisture. Their summer flowers and attractive, long-lasting fall foliage give them interest for much of the year, an important consideration when you have a plant by the front door. Sweetspire will also tolerate container culture.

How to Plant

These plants can be massed together, or plant a few and let them fill in on their own. Be sure to add copious amounts of organic matter to sandy soil to hold on to the needed soil moisture. An organic mulch will help cut down on evaporation.

Care and Maintenance

Sweetspire does not require an excessive amount of maintenance. It has no significant pests. In the spring, a little shaping and a little pruning of dead wood may be required. That is also the time to remove any suckers if you want them contained, or to transplant the suckers if you want them to spread. Hot, dry summers will warrant occasional deep watering. Keep the plants mulched to retain soil moisture. This sounds like a little work, but if the plants are in moist soil with some room to grow, you can ignore them most of the time.

Additional Information

Until recently, you would find sweetspire only in the wild. It was almost unheard of in cultivation. The movement towards planting native plants has contributed to its slow rise in availability. It truly is a nice addition to the landscape, especially for wet spots where options are so limited.

Additional Species, Cultivars, or Varieties

'Henry's Garnet' is readily available in the trade; it has larger flower clusters and garnet red fall foliage that is supposed to be spectacular. 'Saturnalia' is more compact with yellow, orange, and red fall color. (I once saw a pink-flowered variety at a nursery in Sussex, New Jersey. I am very sorry I didn't pick it up then, because I have never seen another one.)

Winged Euonymus

Euonymus alatus

Other Names: Burning Bush, Corkbush,
Spindle Tree
Height: 8 to 10 ft.; up to 20 ft.
Spread: 10 ft.; up to 20 ft.
Flowers: Insignificant
Zones: 3, 4, **5, 6, 7,** 8

Light Requirement:

The winged euonymus gets its name from the corky ridges that develop along the length of its branches. Since most of these species are grown from seed, there can be significant variation in the degree of corkiness from plant to plant. This feature is completely hidden while the plant is in leaf, but it becomes an attraction after the leaves drop. These curious branches can make an artistic contribution to creating a dramatic look in both fresh and dried floral arrangements. One of the other common names, "Burning Bush," is another appropriate name, since the fall foliage is such a brilliant red it looks like a blaze of color. The rest of the year, winged euonymus is an attractive easy care plant, but without any features that capture the eye. The shape is gracefully spreading without ever getting the "tangled" look that some shrubs get. Its growth rate is slow, so it doesn't need a major pruning every time you turn around. It is an excellent choice for a hedge or border planting, especially as a backdrop for more-colorful summer plantings. Burning bush also works well in front of an evergreen border where its fall color stands out like a neon sign. As a specimen plant, it might work better if pruned to maintain the form of a small tree. Winged euonymus is never a problem in the landscape. It is virtually trouble free. The euonymus scale that affects many of its relatives has little interest in this winged version. Winged euonymus is a landscape workhorse that has major "zing" in fall.

WHEN TO PLANT
Plant in early spring or early fall.

WHERE TO PLANT
Winged euonymus will thrive in full sun, partial sun, or shade, but its fall color may not be quite as vivid in shade. Since it does well as

a specimen, massed with others, as an informal border, or as a formal hedge, you can put it almost anywhere. It is flexible regarding soil types and pH. Avoid waterlogged soils.

How to Plant

This very easy, adaptable plant requires no particular fuss. Young plants, probably from seed, can appear beneath the spreading branches. Transplant these in early spring for best results.

Care and Maintenance

Winged euonymus is a trouble free plant. Since it is slow growing, it rarely needs pruning more than every other year. Do this in spring before new growth emerges. While it can be sheared, you may lose its graceful vase shape and end up with an unnatural-looking box. Selective pruning with long handled loppers and hand pruners will produce a more attractive result.

Additional Information

The wood was once used for specialty items such as spindles (hence the other common name), bows for violins, and until the 19th century, for piano and organ keys. The name "Euonymus" is often mispronounced. The correct pronunciation is "yew-ON-im-us." In the 1922 edition of *Bailey's Cyclopedia of Horticulture*, the species is listed under "Evonymus," and it is still occasionally written this old fashioned way.

Additional Species, Cultivars, or Varieties

'Compacta' is slightly smaller and lacks the corky wings, but it can still reach 10 ft. 'Rudy Haag' is more compact, reaching only 5 ft. 'Monstrosa' has extra large corky ridges. In the world of euonymus, there are over 170 species; these are mostly native to Asia. Some are evergreen, some are groundcovers, and others are deciduous shrubs. They are readily available and extensively used. Most have serious infestation problems with the evil euonymus scale. As a result, they require constant monitoring and quick action when scale is discovered. One species is *E. americanus*. It is native to the eastern United States, and it is interesting if for no other reason than its common name, "hearts-a-burstin." This whimsical appellation comes from the warty seed capsules that open in September or October to display the scarlet seeds within. It also has red fall foliage, but it is only borderline hardy in Zone 5.

Winterberry Holly

Ilex verticillata

Other Names: Black Alder, Coralberry, Michigan Holly **Height:** 6 to 10 ft.; up to 20 ft. **Spread:** 6 to 10 ft.; up to 20 ft. **Flowers:** Male and female flowers on separate plants; ornamental berries on female specimens **Bloom Period:** Berries August to January **Zones:** 3, 4, **5, 6, 7,** 8, 9	**Light Requirement:**

There is nothing prettier than a mass planting of winterberry holly with its red berries sparkling against newfallen snow. This plant is native to the eastern United States where it can be found in boggy places. That means it is a good choice for those difficult wet sites. Acid soil is best, and most New Jersey soils are acid. Winterberry holly is not a fast grower, but it may need occasional pruning to keep it from getting leggy. It will eventually sucker itself into a patch if you let it. You will need a least one male plant to produce the copious quantities of berries that are this plant's claim to fame. If space is really limited, it is possible to graft a male branch onto a female tree, but finding room for these small plants should not be too difficult. The berries appear in large numbers and will sometimes last until January if the birds don't eat them—a flock of lovely cedar waxwings stopping for a meal on the fly can make quite a dent in the display.

WHEN TO PLANT

Plant in early spring or early fall.

WHERE TO PLANT

Winterberry holly is a great choice for a soggy spot in the yard or at the water's edge. It will do well in a sunny location or in a little shade. The red berries are dramatic in front of a planting of evergreens. When planted en masse in a grassy field, they look lovely with their berries against the background of green, and spectacular when the field is covered in snow.

HOW TO PLANT

These plants are not particularly fussy and will adapt to drier soils than those of their native habitat. Since they prefer boggy soils rich in organic matter, give them a good start by adding the organic matter they favor to the soil. Leaf compost is an excellent source.

CARE AND MAINTENANCE

Water thoroughly during hot weather when the ground gets dry. Prune in late winter by removing the oldest shoots to keep fruit production at its best. The leaves will show signs of chlorosis if the pH gets too high. This is not likely to be a problem in most New Jersey soils, but foundation walls sometimes leach lime, which raises the pH in the surrounding beds. Avoid the use of marble chips as a mulch; marble is compressed lime and will cause the pH to skyrocket.

ADDITIONAL INFORMATION

If you have hopes of using the heavily berried branches during holiday festivities, be sure to cut them in early November. They can be stored outside in a bucket of water in a spot where they will be a little protected from the wind. If you wait until the holidays are upon you to gather your branches, you may find the birds have beat you to it or that they at least have thinned the fruits so the sprays aren't as pretty.

ADDITIONAL SPECIES, CULTIVARS, OR VARIETIES

'Nana' has exceptionally large red fruits on a compact plant that stays 3 to 4 ft. tall. 'Afterglow' stays under 6 ft. and has orange-red berries. 'Chrysocarpa' has yellow berries. Many outstanding varieties have been developed by crossing *I. verticillata* with *I. serrata*. 'Sparkleberry' receives great praise in the literature for its abundant and persistent fruit as well as for its multistemmed growth habit. It has a male counterpart, 'Apollo', that has a similar size and shape. These two were introduced by the National Arboretum. Our own Dr. Elwin Orton at Rutgers University released two hybrids of the same parentage: 'Autumn Glo' has orange yellow fall foliage in addition to its red fruit; 'Harvest Red' has red purple fall color. The male 'Raritan Chief', also released by Dr. Orton, is an excellent pollinator for most female varieties since it has an extended season of bloom.

Witch Hazel

Hamamelis virginiana

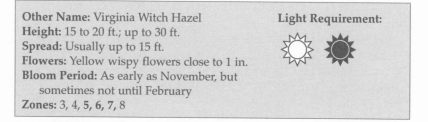

Other Name: Virginia Witch Hazel **Height:** 15 to 20 ft.; up to 30 ft. **Spread:** Usually up to 15 ft. **Flowers:** Yellow wispy flowers close to 1 in. **Bloom Period:** As early as November, but sometimes not until February **Zones:** 3, 4, **5, 6, 7,** 8	**Light Requirement:**

The witch hazel is native from Canada to Georgia. It can be found in the deeper part of a woods growing in the shade of its taller neighbors. It is easily recognized, even without leaves, by its beige fuzzy buds shaped like a butter knife. The flowers often appear in the fall, making it one of the last shrubs to bloom. The bright-yellow color of the fall foliage can mask the flowers when they appear together, but that does not always happen. Sometimes the flowers will not open until the leaves have fallen, and occasionally they wait until early February. Then they adorn the first shrub to flower in the new season. Because it is so shade dependent, this is a very useful shrub or small tree. The time of flowering is an important characteristic, since it is usually the only woody ornamental blooming when it decides to grace us with its flowers. Its habit is open and a little wild, so occasional pruning is necessary to keep it in line. It will also sucker and spread; if this is a problem, you will have to remove the suckers whenever they get annoying. In the right spot, this habit may be advantageous.

WHEN TO PLANT
Plant in early spring or early fall.

WHERE TO PLANT
Witch hazel is hard to beat for those difficult shady places. It thrives in the shade but maintains an open habit. If you choose to grow it in full sun, it will be a much fuller plant, but you will have to pay more careful attention to its water needs in hot weather. The leaves may burn up when under drought stress. Although a woodland

native, witch hazel shows a significant tolerance for urban settings. It will tolerate poor soil, but try to avoid dry conditions.

How to Plant

Woodland soil is almost always high in organic matter from the leaves falling year after year. By adding leaf compost, you can approximate witch hazel's native forest soil. An organic mulch will help as well. Don't let the soil get overly dry.

Care and Maintenance

Occasional pruning in early spring after witch hazel blooms will keep it from getting gangly. Prune out suckers to keep this plant from becoming a thicket (unless you want a thicket, which can be very nice for creating a woodsy atmosphere). Witch hazel doesn't have any serious insect or disease problems.

Additional Information

Witch hazel has some interesting uses. It is the wood of choice for making "divining rods," those Y-shaped branches used to locate underground sources of water. The bark from the plant is distilled to make the extract "witch hazel" that is used medicinally. If you break off a twig and crush it, you can get a whiff. The name "Hamamelis" is derived from two words: "hama," which means "together with," and "melis," which means "the apple." In her book *Garden Shrubs and their Histories*, Alice M. Coats theorizes that this name was applied to the witch hazel because its small fruits, which take 12 months to ripen, appear on the plant the same time as the next season's flowers.

Additional Species, Cultivars, or Varieties

H. vernalis is the vernal witch hazel. This one has fragrant flowers that always open in February or March. *H. mollis* is the Chinese witch hazel. It is the largest species, reaching 30 ft., and has the largest flowers. It suffers occasional flower bud kill in Zone 5. *H. × intermedia* is a cross between *H. japonica* and *H. mollis*. These hybrids can have yellow, orange, red, or dark-red flowers in spring. Fall foliage is yellow to red and very showy. 'Diana' is considered one of the best red flowering selections. 'Jelena' glows like copper when seen from a distance. Its scented flowers are golden yellow with a claret red base.

Yew

Taxus cuspidata, T. × media

Other names: Japanese Yew, Intermediate Yew   **Light Requirement:**
Height: Variable; up to 40 ft.
Spread: Variable, but often with an equal
    or greater spread
Zones: 4, 5, 6, 7

Yews are adaptable evergreens with soft 1-in. needles that are a rich dark green on the upper surface and pale green below. The new growth is yellow-green and feather soft, giving them an advantage over the ubiquitous sharply pointed junipers. There are a zillion varieties and tremendous variation among them. The narrowest is probably 'Flushing', developed by Pete Vermeulen, a plantsman located in Neshanic Station, New Jersey. When 'Flushing' reaches 8 ft., it is only 18 in. wide. When 'Wardii' is 6 ft. tall, it will be 19 ft. wide. Other yews may fall anywhere in between these extremes. The red berries on female plants are an added attraction. Seeds will sometimes sprout beneath a shrub, but these seedlings will probably differ significantly from the parent. The biggest problem to avoid is wet ground; yews do not like to sit in water. They are adamant about having good drainage. Even if plants in waterlogged soil do not die outright, they will never thrive. Once yews start to yellow, it is hard for them to recover. That means site selection and soil preparation are even more important for yews than for some other evergreens. Once established, they are hardy easy-care plants that maintain their color throughout the winter. Keep in mind that deer like to eat yews. If deer are a problem in your area, put up a deer fence or plant something else. The only other significant problem originates with the gardener. It is that electric hedge shears addiction that turns normal, reasonable gardeners into buzzing, glassy-eyed maniacs. Yews are not meant to look like hockey pucks, meatballs, or snowcones. A yew pruned this way develops short, twiggy growth with no needles on the inside. A little hand-pruning with loppers and hand-pruners will keep a yew in line and maintain a healthy natural habit. If the one you have is constantly outgrowing its allotted space, move it or toss it and plant another variety that will fit the spot. There are plenty from which to choose.

WHEN TO PLANT
Plant in early spring or early fall.

WHERE TO PLANT
Plant in sun or shade. Avoid extremely windy locations and avoid wet sites. Yews are flexible regarding soil type, as long as they are well drained. They have more than an average amount of tolerance for urban conditions.

HOW TO PLANT
Dig an extra-large hole and break up any hardpan that may prevent drainage. Be sure to avoid the "bucket" effect in heavy clay, where you amend the soil to backfill the hole (water will flow into the hole as it follows the path of least resistance and just sit there). If drainage is poor, prepare the entire bed with a 2:1 mixture of organic matter and sand, or plant the ball a little high if you have no other choice. Raised beds are another option.

CARE AND MAINTENANCE
To keep the plant full, prune in the early spring before growth starts. Unlike many other evergreens, it can take severe pruning and will resprout on dormant wood, but a little selective pruning now and then is really all you should need.

ADDITIONAL INFORMATION
If you must have a formal sheared hedge, yews are an excellent choice. They are also suitable for topiary since they tolerate heavy pruning. There is a big difference, however, between the art of topiary and meatball madness. In old England, yews were used to make bows, perhaps even those of Robin Hood and his merry men.

ADDITIONAL SPECIES, CULTIVARS, OR VARIETIES
T. baccata is the English yew. It has been cultivated in England for centuries, but it is less hardy than *T. cuspidata* or *T. × media*. The intermediate yew is actually a cross between the English and the Japanese yews, but it retains the hardiness of the Japanese. *T. canadensis* is very hardy but will not grow in Zone 7. It is sometimes used as a groundcover. Japanese yews to look for include 'Capitata', which is pyramidal and can reach 50 ft., and 'Intermedia', a dwarf, round, slow growing form. Intermediate yews include 'Hicksii', a wide columnar form, and 'Sentinalis', which is almost as narrow as 'Flushing'.

CHAPTER FIVE

Plants for Winter Interest

ONCE THE LEAVES ARE SHED IN AUTUMN, THERE IS A DEFINITE LULL IN THE EXCITEMENT OF MOST GARDENS. Winter tends towards a medium shade of gray with only an occasional snowstorm to break the monotony. There can be, however, a hidden beauty to the winter landscape. It takes careful planning and an appreciative eye to find it.

Certainly evergreens are an important component of the winter scene. The massive green-needled trees move from background to center stage. When they become the focal point, their subtle differences become more obvious. You may suddenly notice that "ever green" comes in an infinite variety of shades, and that two blue spruces are not the same blue at all. The thick needles of the bluish white fir look nothing like the long, graceful needles of the Himalayan pine, which differ from the scalelike leaves of the arborvitae. Mixing species and adding an occasional young evergreen tree will provide differences in height and texture.

Once you establish your landscape's character with a variety of elegant evergreens, you can get more daring. Add a weeping Norway spruce or a 'Zebrina' Himalayan pine, whose needles are variegated in green and yellow. A weeping blue atlas cedar is hardy only to Zone 6, but it might be worth a try in Zone 5 in a protected nook. It is magnificent—you might almost look forward to leaf drop just to eliminate any distractions from its dignified grace. A contorted white pine is another fascinating plant. It is a slow-growing pyramidal tree whose branches and needles are both slightly twisted.

Think beyond evergreens to perk things up in winter. Deciduous trees are sometimes more intriguing without their leaves. Harry Lauder's walking stick is a prime example. All summer it looks like a green mound. Once it drops its leaves, it looks as if it has a curly perm. The dangling catkins are an added bonus. The contorted

Chapter Five

mulberry sends twisted branches in all directions and the corkscrew willow sends spiraling branches almost straight up. The Japanese fan-tail willow is more like a shrub. It has branches which grow flat and spreading, like a fan, but also twist and curl. You won't even notice the curling while it still has leaves. The redosier dogwood comes in several varieties. One variety has bright red stems on current year's growth which are stunning against a backdrop of snow, and the red is an eye-catcher all winter long. There is even a bright yellow variety, 'Flaviramea'.

Vines that twist and turn add character. An old wisteria can ramble in impossible directions. The velvety seedpods dangle down and last well into winter; then they twist open to release the seeds. A thick tangle of silver fleece vine breaks up straight lines all year long.

Fruits and berries add another level of interest. The brilliant red berries of the winterberry holly are spectacular against the snow or a field of green. The paper lantern pods of the goldenraintree are so beautiful they are used as dried flowers. They persist into early winter. Pyracantha can be covered in berries. These berries last most of the winter since the birds do not seem to favor them.

Beyond trees and shrubs is a world of interesting perennials that can add a surprising twist to the winter landscape. The Christmas rose, *Helleborus niger*, gets 3 in. flowers in December and can hold on to them until spring. The sensitive fern has tightly curled sporulating fronds that last all winter. These fronds are so engaging they are sometimes dipped in gold to be made into jewelry. The rising tide of interest in ornamental grasses offers many varieties that maintain decorative plumes for most of the winter. They are excellent for decorative indoor use.

If you just let your winter landscape happen, you might be surprised by something wonderful, but some things are best not left to chance. Gardeners sometimes struggle with cabin fever during a long cold winter. Plan your winter garden with as much care as your summer flowers. It will give you something to look forward to besides the winter blahs.

Contorted Mulberry and Weeping Mulberry

Morus 'Contorta' and *Morus alba* 'Pendula'

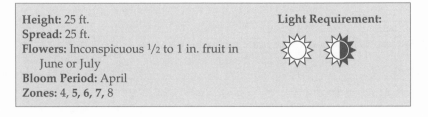

Height: 25 ft.
Spread: 25 ft.
Flowers: Inconspicuous $1/2$ to 1 in. fruit in June or July
Bloom Period: April
Zones: 4, 5, 6, 7, 8

Light Requirement:

The white mulberry, *M. alba*, is native to China and is the primary food of silkworms. It has been cultivated for centuries as part of the silk industry and was introduced to North America at Jamestown in an attempt to establish a silk industry here in the United States. Those efforts failed, but the tree has naturalized throughout the east and south. The white mulberry was brought under cultivation along the Mediterranean coast in the 12th century. It is unclear when the weeping variety was developed. The weeping mulberry is a small tree with multitudinous slender branches that drape down to the ground. These trees were popular with Italian immigrants to the U.S. earlier in the century and could be commonly found in Newark's Italian communities. You can still find an occasional gnarled old tree in the most surprising of places. This variety generally stays under 12 ft. Its long branches form a curtain of strong vertical lines, creating a dramatic winter look. People either love the fruit or hate it. It looks much like a blackberry, but is infinitely sweeter. The fruit is formed only on female trees, so choose a male or "fruitless" variety if you have no interest in the berries. The contorted mulberry is sold under many botanical names; this can make finding one difficult. There is really only one variety of this fast-growing tree. It has an open spreading habit with branches that twist and turn fantastically. It makes a wonderful winter feature in your yard. The branches are prized for flower arrangements.

WHEN TO PLANT

Plant in early spring or early fall.

WHERE TO PLANT

Plant in full sun or partial shade. Weeping mulberries are an excellent choice for small urban yards. They take up little space and are tolerant of city growing conditions. The contorted mulberry needs a little more room: its branches grow in all directions and it does not blend in very well with other trees. Mulberries have some tolerance for seaside conditions. They are flexible regarding both soil type and pH.

HOW TO PLANT

Both varieties transplant readily and will survive with minimal soil preparation. Water during the first season when needed. Once they are established the trees will withstand drought.

CARE AND MAINTENANCE

Mulberries are susceptible to some leaf spot diseases and an occasional infestation of mites or scale. These problems are usually not serious. Prune in early spring. The contorted variety can tolerate significant pruning if you want to cut branches for indoor use.

ADDITIONAL INFORMATION

When I was a child, we had a weeping mulberry to one side of our enormous, old Victorian home. I used to hide beneath the branches and eat the fruit from the behind the curtain of leaves. The little stems on the fruit always gave me a hard time. Sometimes I tried to pick them off. Sometimes I just ate them. I was certain no one knew I was there; it was my secret place. Many years later, I wrote about my childhood memories of the old mulberry and sent copies to my seven siblings. My oldest brother asked if I had copied the story from his book. He had written about an identical childhood experience twenty years earlier.

ADDITIONAL SPECIES, CULTIVARS, OR VARIETIES

The contorted mulberry may be available as *M. nigra* 'Contorta', *M. australis* 'Unryu', or *M. bombycis* 'Unryu'. It is believed that these are all the same, though it is by no means certain. If you cannot find specimens locally, they are available through two Oregon nurseries, Northwoods Nursery and Forest Farm. The weeping mulberry 'Pendula' is also sold as 'Teas'. This is a fruit-bearing female clone. 'Urbana' and 'Chaparral' are non-fruit-bearing male varieties. Weeping mulberries, usually female trees, are extremely popular in Canada. They are hardy to minus 20 degrees Fahrenheit and are suitable for the small yards of many new homes.

Dragon's Eye Pine

Pinus densiflora 'Oculus-draconis'

Height: Up to 35 ft. **Spread:** Up to 35 ft. **Zones:** 4, 5, 6, 7	**Light Requirement:**

*D*ragon's Eye Pine is a novelty evergreen that is a compact, variegated version of the Japanese red pine. The species can sometimes reach 100 ft., but this variety stays much smaller. The needles are quite distinctive—each one is marked with two irregular yellow bands. When you view the branch from its end, you can see alternating circular bands of yellow and green. This is (supposedly) absolutely identical to the pattern in a dragon's eye. The cones start out with a bluish tinge, turn brown as they age, and stay on the tree for several years. Dragon's eye pine produces cones at quite a young age. The habit of young trees is open and somewhat irregular in shape. The literature is completely inconsistent regarding the rate of growth. The catalog from Weston Nurseries in Massachusetts says these trees are fast growing. Michael Dirr rates them as slow growers. The Burpee catalog says they grow very slowly. (The 'Oculus-draconis' planted in my front yard is not shooting up like a weed, but it makes noticeable growth each year. A slow to medium growth rate for this specimen is probably accurate. My tree may be a *P. thunbergiana* 'Oculus-draconis'. It is hard to tell the difference—even the nursery did not know.)

WHEN TO PLANT
Plant in early spring or early fall.

WHERE TO PLANT
Choose a sunny, well-drained location. As a general rule, variegated plants are a little more finicky than their all green relatives. Pick the best location possible. Because its foliage is so unusual, dragon's eye pine makes a good specimen plant. While many plant professionals consider it an oddball, there is no reason it can't be mainstreamed if

you like it. Mix it in with other evergreens as part of a border or mass planting to break up the monotony of green.

How to Plant

There is nothing particularly difficult about establishing this plant. It would be wise to stake the tree, at least until it gets established. An evergreen's bulk causes it to capture wind and snow. A little support will keep it upright until the roots can take over the job.

Care and Maintenance

Little pruning should be necessary. To make this naturally open plant a little fuller, you can pinch the candles back halfway when they elongate in the spring. Dragon's eye pine has no serious insect or disease problems.

Additional Information

According to Michael Dirr, there is some indication that the needles turn muddy brown over the winter. The specimen at Blooming Acres holds its green and yellow color year long.

Additional Species, Cultivars, or Varieties

There are two other species of pine that have varieties called 'Oculus-draconis'. One is the Himalayan pine, *P. wallichiana*. It is believed to be the same as the variety 'Zebrina' and is more commonly available under that name. The other species, *P. thunbergiana*, is the Japanese black pine. It is not attributed with muddy needles in the winter. The Himalayan pine's needles are bunched together in fives, making it easily distinguishable from the Japanese black and red pines, both of which have needles in groups of two. There is a mature 'Zebrina' at the National Arboretum in Washington that is spectacular. The Japanese black pine was not available in any of the catalogs or local nurseries I checked. Some local sources, however, had trees labeled only *Pinus* 'Oculus-draconis'. These could have been specimens of either species. You would have to compare the buds side by side to be sure. Though there may be a bit of confusion regarding the variety and species, if you see a dragon's eye pine you will never forget it.

Harry Lauder's Walking Stick

Corylus avellana 'Contorta'

Other Name: Contorted Filbert
Height: 8 to 10 ft.
Spread: 10 ft. or more
Flowers: Attractive male catkins
Bloom Period: Catkins dangle all winter,
  then open in April
Zones: 4, 5, 6, 7, 8, 9

Light Requirement:

*H*arry Lauder was an entertainer who carried a twisted and gnarled walking stick as part of his act. The branches on this wildly contorted small tree are reminiscent of the famous staff, hence the common name. The plant itself was discovered growing in a hedgerow in England in the mid-1800s. It is a variety of the European filbert, a tree grown for the commercial production of its nuts. Harry Lauder's walking stick is a fabulous choice for winter interest. When covered in leaves, it is impossible to see the twisting and spiraling of the branches without putting your nose right into the plant. In full leaf, it makes an excellent backdrop for spring bulbs, perennials, and summer flowers. Once the season winds down and the wind blows away the wavy leaves, you are faced with the most outrageous of plants. It commands the attention of all who pass. The branches are absolute treasures for floral design but crafters will desire them as well. The small catkins look like built-in Christmas ornaments and are most beautiful when they elongate in early spring. They can reach up to 6 in. in length when they are in bloom. They blow in the wind like delicate threads of gold.

WHEN TO PLANT
Plant in early spring or early fall.

WHERE TO PLANT
Harry does well in full sun but is also tolerant of shade. Its rate of growth is slow and it stays small. This makes it a good choice for

planting in a rock garden or mixing with small evergreens. When choosing a location for this tree, take into consideration that it is at its peak in winter. Planting it near a path to the front door might be better than putting it out back by the pool.

HOW TO PLANT

There is nothing tricky about getting Harry established. Choose well-drained loamy soil if you have a choice. It is fairly adaptable to different pH and soil types.

CARE AND MAINTENANCE

Most Harrys are grafted, so it is critical that you remove any suckers emerging at the base. These will not be contorted and will have a much faster growth rate. If they are not removed, straight shoots will dominate the plant in short order. It is possible to layer 1 to 2 year old shoots to get plants to grow on their own roots. You also need to watch out for Japanese beetles. These hungry critters will make quite a meal of the leaves. Spray at the first sign of damage. Michael Dirr reports a leaf and twig blight that is not common.

ADDITIONAL INFORMATION

Harry Lauder's walking stick has been a featured plant in gardens designed for the pleasure of gardeners who have visual difficulties. These gardens consist of plants that you can touch and smell. Harry's curling branches and dangling catkins are unmistakable. (At Blooming Acres we have holiday reindeer made from white birch logs—one even has a red nose. Branches from the Harry make the *best* antlers.)

ADDITIONAL SPECIES, CULTIVARS, OR VARIETIES

Harry Lauder's walking stick is a one-of-a-kind tree.

Japanese Fantail Willow

Salix sachalinensis 'Sekka'

Other Names: *S. udensis* 'Sekka', also 'Sekko'
Height: Usually under 10 ft., but up to 30 ft.
Spread: Wide spreading
Zones: 4, 5, 6, 7

Light Requirement:

---

*P*lants do not get much stranger than this one. Japanese fantail willow is definitely a novelty plant. You would probably not want more than one in your landscape, though it is absolutely remarkable in the garden as well as in cut arrangements. It produces catkins in the spring that are similar to those of the pussy willow, but smaller. They look particularly strange on the twisted, curled, fan shaped branches that are characteristic of this variety. Like other willows, Japanese fantail willow is an excellent choice for wet sites where many other plants "melt" in short order. It will do well in any moist soil. Willows are generally weak wooded and fast growing, and this plant is no exception. Cut it back hard in the early spring to keep it compact and vigorous. To use the cut branches dry, do not put them in water. They can last for years. If you use them as part of fresh flower arrangements, they may produce roots. Willows are one of the easiest plants to propagate in moist sand or even a glass of water. When grown from cuttings, plants exhibit the variety's typical contortion within one or two years.

WHEN TO PLANT

Planting in early spring or early fall is best, but in most cases any time from spring to fall will be successful.

WHERE TO PLANT

Choose a sunny location with moist soil conditions. Japanese fantail willow is an excellent choice for wet sites or low spots in the yard. It can get a little wild looking, so you may not want to plant it in a featured spot, but be sure to plant this tree where you can enjoy it in the winter when the contorted growth shows at its best.

HOW TO PLANT

Take cuttings almost any time to root in moist sand or a glass of water. In sandy soil you will need to add organic matter to help retain soil moisture. If bunnies are a problem, be sure to cage this plant when it is young or it will be nibbled to the ground over the winter. Once established, it grows so quickly that what the bunnies eat can be sacrificed.

CARE AND MAINTENANCE

Prune Japanese fantail willow hard, in part to keep it from getting wild but also to use the amazing branches indoors. It can be pruned almost any time of year, but prune in early spring to reap the benefit of the fuzzy catkins. In dry hot summers a thorough watering now and then will be appreciated, especially in sandy soils.

ADDITIONAL INFORMATION

The bizarre growth that distinguishes this variety from others is probably caused by a bacteria, *Corynebacterium fascians*. The phenomenon is called *fasciation* or *cresting*. The plant loses its ability to grow upright and appears to grow as though many stems had fused together. The cause of fasciation is not entirely understood. In her authoritative tome *Plant Disease Handbook*, Cynthia Wescott recommends controlling the disease by using sterilized soil and seed. This implies that it can be spread in the soil. Dr. Spencer Davis, an extremely knowledgeable retired plant pathologist from Rutgers University, says that if this disease were actually transmissible through the soil, more plants would exhibit the symptoms, though he knows of no other factor that could cause this type of growth. At Blooming Acres we have pruned off the occasional fasciated apple branch, have found fasciation on squash plants, and it recently appeared on true lilies that had been in the ground for several years. They were truly bizarre.

ADDITIONAL SPECIES, CULTIVARS, OR VARIETIES

There are no other fasciated willows, but all pussy willows offer winter interest in the form of swollen buds that appear in late winter. These include *S. caprea*; *S. gracilistyla*, rosegold pussy willow; and *S. melanostachys*, the black pussy willow. There are few plants that exhibit fasciation as part of the variety. One may be the annual flower cockscomb, *Celosia cristata*.

PLANTS FOR WINTER INTEREST

Lacebark Pine

Pinus bungeana

Height: Usually to 50 ft., but up to 75 ft. **Spread:** Usually to 25 ft., sometimes more **Zones:** 4, 5, 6, 7, 8	**Light Requirement:**

*T*here are many pine trees that are hardy in New Jersey. Most have desirable attributes that make them useful. A few are classic, almost indispensable, landscape plants. Some are valued for their foliage, others for their tolerance of environmental conditions. Some are used for Christmas trees, and even others are planted to take advantage of their rate of growth. Lacebark pine is special because of its bark—the bark sheds and peels like the bark of a sycamore. Young branches are green with bits of white and brown. As the bark matures, it turns chalky white, as if covered in a lace veil. It is beautiful all year long, but its subtle charm is better appreciated in the gray of winter. In many cases this tree is grown with a multistemmed trunk. This creates more trunk to see at eye level where it can be enjoyed. On occasion, the lower branches are removed to make the bark more visible. Lacebark pine is very slow growing. It can be pyramidal, though the branches spread with age and with the tree's number of trunks. The 4 in. long needles are produced in bunches of three and persist for up to 5 years. They are sharp, stiff, and dark green. Because it grows so slowly, lacebark pine would be a poor choice for border plantings, but it makes an excellent specimen where it can be viewed up close.

WHEN TO PLANT
Plant in early spring or early fall.

WHERE TO PLANT
Lacebark pine prefers a sunny location and well-drained soils. Michael Dirr suggests that it be used at the corners of large buildings. It would be lovely in that type of location, but watch out for any snow that may slide off the roof. The wood is weak and brittle, and winter ice and snow can cause damage. To use this tree to its best advantage, plant it in a location where you can see the bark.

How to Plant

Balled and burlapped trees should be root pruned prior to digging. Many commercially produced specimens are now container grown, which eliminates the need for root pruning. Add organic matter and sand to heavy clay soils.

Care and Maintenance

Pines are subject to a variety of insects and diseases but there is no specific pest or disease that affects the lacebark pine. You can prune by trimming the candles in the spring, but this tree is such a slow grower that it may not be necessary. Proper pruning of any winter damage is wise. Because lacebark pine is susceptible to damage from winter ice and snow, it may pay to shake off accumulations of snow, if possible, before the damage is done.

Additional Information

Lacebark pine is grown by many wholesale nurseries and should not be difficult to locate. If you would like to see one to get a better idea of these trees' appeal, you can visit the 15 ft. specimen in the evergreen collection at Rutgers Gardens in New Brunswick. Several mature lacebark pines can be found at the Willowwood Arboretum in Chester Township. It is surprising that this pine is not more commonly used.

Additional Species, Cultivars, or Varieties

With their evergreen needles and various shapes and sizes, all pines offer some kind of winter interest. Lacebark pine, however, is the only pine noted for spectacular bark.

Paperbark Maple

Acer griseum

Height: 25 ft. **Spread:** Up to 25 ft. **Flowers:** Inconspicuous red flowers that develop into showy winged seeds **Bloom Period:** Spring **Zones:** 4, 5, 6, 7, 8	**Light Requirement:**

*T*he paperbark maple is interesting all year long, but its bark is a special addition to the winter scene. This tree is smaller than many of the popular maples, which makes it useful in tight places where most shade trees would take over the limited space. Its overall shape is oval to round but rather open. The winter silhouette is striking, especially of a mature tree. The leaves are a bit unusual for a maple. They are compound, with 3 leaflets each. Even so, the overview of the leaf is similar to more traditional maple leaves. It is not difficult to see the relationship. Leaves arrive late in the spring and turn orange and red in the fall, providing an early frost does not do them in before their time. The bark is a rich cinnamon brown. It peels in long strips, much like the bark of paperbark birch. The exfoliation on the trunk and branches begins at a very early age, usually when the tree is only two years old. Eventually the trunk stops exfoliating, but mature trees retain their lovely shades of red and brown. Paperbark maple grows slowly. Cuttings are not very cooperative about rooting. This tree produces few viable seeds. These factors make propagation difficult, and this maple tends to be more costly than other trees. Its price is perhaps comparable to that of a Japanese maple. While it is probably not available everywhere, paperbark maple is not difficult to locate.

WHEN TO PLANT

Maples generally do best when planted in spring. Late March or early April is the best time to plant.

WHERE TO PLANT

Choose a place where you can enjoy this lovely small tree. Outside a favorite window where you can see it during the winter might be best. Paperbark maple needs sun and moist, well-drained soils, though it tolerates clay soil better than some.

HOW TO PLANT

Since it prefers well-drained soils but tolerates clay, this tree is a good choice for the heavy clay soils found in central Jersey. It is wise to add organic matter to clay soil in order to improve drainage. Heavy clay soils sometimes have a hardpan several feet down. If you can, break up the soil with a pick. If you have heavy clay soil and improve the soil going back into the hole, watch out for the bucket effect: water follows the path of least resistance and flows into the soil around the roots, where it stays, waterlogging the plant. Make sure the water around your tree has a place to go.

CARE AND MAINTENANCE

Paperbark maple has no serious insect or disease problems. Its slow rate of growth means it requires little pruning. Once established, this is a low maintenance tree.

ADDITIONAL INFORMATION

Michael Dirr says the oldest living paperbark maple in the United States (as of 1983) can be found at the Arnold Arboretum in Massachusetts. (I checked, and the specimen is still there.)

ADDITIONAL SPECIES, CULTIVARS, OR VARIETIES

A. davidii, the David maple, reaches 45 ft. and has bark with white stripes. So does *A. grosseri*, which grows to 30 ft. Together they make up the "snake bark" maples. They provide wonderful winter interest but are difficult to locate. The literature varies greatly regarding hardiness, but these trees are probably hardy to Zone 5, possibly to Zone 4. Forest Farm in Oregon carries both types, but ranks both as hardy only to Zone 6.

Redosier Dogwood

Cornus sericea

Other Names: *C. stolonifera*, Redtwig Dogwood
Height: Up to 10 ft.
Spread: Up to 10 ft.
Flowers: $1^1/2$ to $2^1/2$ in. clusters of small,
    white flowers
Bloom Period: Late May and a few blooms
    all summer
Zones: 2, 3, 4, **5, 6, 7,** 8

Light Requirement:

*W*inter is far more colorful than you would expect if it includes a bank of redtwig dogwood. The new growth is red—really red. Keeping it red requires frequent significant pruning to force the growth of lots of shoots from the roots. If left to grow unattended, the older wood will dominate and you will lose the powerful color impact. While winter color is the prize, this little shrub has other qualities that make it worthwhile. It spreads from the roots and rapidly becomes a thicket. Combine this fact with its tolerance for wet locations and the redosier dogwood may be the plant of choice for stabilizing banks along streams and the water's edge. Spring flowers are attractive, if not spectacular. Redosier dogwood also occasionally blooms in summer. The white fruits appear in late summer and are very pretty up close, though they are often lost in the foliage. Fruits are followed by fall color, which varies from plant to plant but can sometimes be a very attractive red-purple. Choose your location carefully. Since this shrub does spread, it can be overpowering in a confined space. On the other hand, it could work well as a border planting or privacy screen.

WHEN TO PLANT

All dogwoods generally do best with spring planting. Of the group, the redosier dogwood may be the most accepting of planting in the fall. If you try it, be sure to plant in early September.

WHERE TO PLANT

Its native habitat is swampy ground, so it makes sense to plant redosier dogwood in a similar environment for the best performance. It is, however, a very adaptable shrub. It may not thrive in extremely dry locations, but almost anywhere else is acceptable. Sun, light shade, and deep shade will all be tolerated. Plant en masse in open spaces for the best winter effect. Border plantings may be terrific, but remember that the roots will spread in all directions. They can be pruned to keep them under control but consider your neighbor's reaction if the plants should start to spread over the border.

How to Plant
Space plants 5 to 6 ft. apart for a mass planting. Balled-and-burlapped or even bare-root specimens transplant easily. Since they prefer moist soil, be sure to add organic matter to dry, sandy soils to help maintain soil moisture.

Care and Maintenance
Pruning on a regular basis is critical to maintaining this shrub's red color. Specimens can be cut to the ground every spring for maximum color, but that may not work well if you are using them for a privacy screen. Selective pruning of 2 and 3 year old growth in the spring will keep a plant from becoming woody and brown. To control the plant's spread, prune the roots with a spade and prune branches that run along the ground. Redosier dogwood is subject to a twig canker, scale, and the voracious bagworm. (See the Arborvitae entry in the Shrubs section for details on bagworms.) This shrub is native to eastern North America from Newfoundland down to Virginia and Kentucky. Though this native plant does have pest problems, it is very adaptable to a wide range of planting conditions.

Additional Information
Using redosier dogwood along highways is very attractive as well as functional. You can see large plantings of this shrub along the ramps of Route 18 in the New Brunswick area.

Additional Species, Cultivars, or Varieties
'Flaviramea', the yellowtwig dogwood, has all the same characteristics as redosier dogwood, but its twigs are bright yellow. 'Nitida' is the greentwig dogwood. 'Isanti' is a compact redtwig that reaches 5 ft. 'Kelseyi' grows to only 18 to 30 in. *C. sanguinea* is the bloodtwig dogwood; despite its name, it is less red than the redosier. *C. alba* is the tartarian dogwood. Whether the variety 'Siberica' is redder than the redosier is debatable. In the trade these two are sometimes confused. The primary difference is that *C. alba* does not spread from the roots very quickly, while the redosier does.

Weeping Norway Spruce

Picea abies 'Pendula'

Other Name: *P. excelsa* **Height:** Variable **Spread:** Variable **Zones:** 2, 3, 4, **5, 6, 7**	**Light Requirement:**

*T*he species *Picea abies* has slightly pendulous branches and can reach 150 ft. It is overplanted and does not maintain a great shape as it ages, and it is severely prone to canker. The weeping form of Norway spruce is an attractive alternative. Weeping trees generally grow at a slower rate than that of uprights. In *Dwarf and Unusual Conifers Coming of Age*, Sandra McLean Cutle estimates that a 10 year old weeping Norway spruce will generally reach 5 ft. tall and 4 to 5 ft. wide. A species specimen will be 6 to 8 ft. tall at the same age. Still, it is difficult to compare growth rates since weepers grow up a little, then arch over and down, or out and along the ground. The training they receive as young trees in order to establish a trunk and primary branches will affect their growth pattern and ultimate shape. 'Inversa' weeps at both the primary and secondary branches. It is so weepy that if it is not trained it will ramble along the ground. The cones of Norway spruce are up to 6 in. long and persist through most of the winter. The bright green new growth of spring seems to glow against the dark green of older needles. The needles stay on the plant for several years. Because traits can vary by specimen, it is necessary to choose the individual plant with as much care as you have given to choosing the species.

WHEN TO PLANT
Plant in early spring or early fall.

WHERE TO PLANT
Plant in full sun. Weeping Norway spruce is fairly flexible regarding soil type, though it does prefer well-drained sandy soil that is moist rather than dry. Since weeping forms are usually specimen trees, be sure to give your tree a prominent place in the landscape. Weeping Norway spruce is always interesting, but it moves out of the spot-

light while summer color dominates. A site in plain view as you sit inside by the fire might be nice, or you can plant the tree by the mailbox, where you will be able to see it at least once a day.

HOW TO PLANT

Weeping Norway spruce transplants readily. Even larger trees do well since they have shallow, spreading root systems rather than a tap root. Weeping trees grow so slowly that starting with a larger plant will give you an idea of the habit of the particular tree you choose.

CARE AND MAINTENANCE

Prune weeping Norway spruce in early spring if necessary. Weepers occasionally throw off an upright or vigorous shoot that must be removed to maintain the form. It is important to keep Norway spruce well watered, especially in hot, dry weather, for the first few years. Watch out for mites. Control them if necessary in May and September.

ADDITIONAL INFORMATION

At Blooming Acres we have two weeping Norway spruce. One is S-shaped and grows up, down, and up again. The second almost hugs the ground but is slightly mounded. Visitors pass both on their way to the front door and are often intrigued by the appearance of these odd trees, but never more so than when the new growth is out. The contrast of the soft bright green against the stiff dark green seems artificial. You have to touch them—another good reason to place them in a place where you can get up close.

ADDITIONAL SPECIES, CULTIVARS, OR VARIETIES

'Acrocona' is pendulous but irregular. It has extra-large cones that are reddish-purple for a short time in spring. 'Reflexa', 'Pendula', and 'Recurvata' may all be the same variety. You may also find 'Pendula Major' and 'Pendula Monstrosa', two other named cultivars.

Plants for Down the Shore

*T*HOSE OF US WHO GREW UP WITH THE JERSEY SHORE
know it is one of the greatest places in the world, from the wide
beaches of Wildwood to the rocky outcroppings of Sandy Hook
back to the well preserved Island Beach State Park and the Victorian
wonders of Cape May. There are mansions and tiny bungalows,
quiet nooks, and the outrageous boardwalk at Seaside Heights. On
Friday evenings in the summer a large percentage of the state mobi-
lizes and heads "down the shore" to indulge in the sun, sand, and
surf. There is no other place quite like it.

It wasn't long ago when much of the shore area was fairly
deserted outside the summer months, but that is no longer the
case. Year round populations have grown, and new developments
continue to spring up all along the coast. Landscaping these properties is a challenge; the strong winds and salt air make life difficult
for green growing things. Some plants mentioned elsewhere in
this book are very tolerant of these conditions. American holly is
one of the best, and the rugosa rose is a hardy flowering beauty.
Hydrangeas do well, and so does the purple-leaf sand cherry. Not
mentioned (only because of limited space) are the wonderful butterfly bushes, *Buddleia davidii*, which draw butterflies in droves.

Maintenance of the grounds is an important consideration. If you
have a summer home, you probably do not want to spend your time
pruning and spraying the shrubbery while you are there. You can
tell how common this feeling is by the predominance of "pebble
lawns" at summer homes instead of grass. While a little weed control is usually necessary, pebbles eliminate the need for mowing.
Zoysiagrass is another alternative. It tolerates drought and prefers
the sandy soils usually encountered at the beach. Zoysiagrass turns
brown at the first sign of cold weather, but if you only see it in the
summer, it doesn't really matter. Seasonal use also affects your

Chapter Six

choice of flowering shrubs. Early spring bloom doesn't count for much if the home owners don't arrive until the middle of June.

Having a more traditional landscape to meet the needs of the established (and growing) year-round population requires some special consideration. Adding organic matter to the soil will help the soil hold on to moisture. This is important under most growing conditions, but the need for organic matter in sand is even more crucial. It's like telling someone to dress warmly—it has a more-intense meaning at the North Pole.

As you move inland, the salt becomes less of a problem, but sandy soils persist in many areas. Inland plants may still have to be tolerant of dry conditions, or you may spend a lot of time supplying water.

There are a few tips for getting plants established. Starting with young trees in pockets of improved soil may be easier than trying to establish larger trees that have been grown under more advantageous circumstances. This is particularly useful on rocky ridges where there is not enough space to set a larger rootball. If the roots are allowed to find their own way, they may establish themselves in spite of the limitations. While deep planting can be a disaster under normal soil conditions and sure death in wet soils, it may protect the roots from rapid drying in sand.

It is often necessary to stake or support newly planted ornamentals that are planted in sandy soil. The loose soil may not hold them up in the wind. Very deep stakes are required to do the job effectively, or you can use buried logs with guy wires attached.

It is a good idea to do a major pruning at the time of planting. This will help take the pressure off the newly installed root system that is trying to settle in without the benefit of much moisture. It is also helpful for cutting wind pressure and so reducing damage to plants not yet ready to handle heavy off-the-water wind. The closer to the water and the sandier the soil, the more these extra precautions are necessary.

Bayberry

Myrica pensylvanica

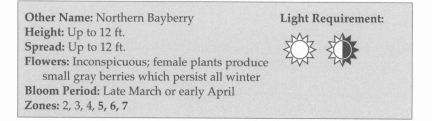

Other Name: Northern Bayberry **Height:** Up to 12 ft. **Spread:** Up to 12 ft. **Flowers:** Inconspicuous; female plants produce small gray berries which persist all winter **Bloom Period:** Late March or early April **Zones:** 2, 3, 4, **5, 6, 7**	**Light Requirement:**

This seaside favorite is native from Newfoundland to Maryland, mostly along the coast. It can be found growing right in the path of direct salt spray and is extremely tolerant of sandy soil conditions. This combination of qualities makes it irreplaceable in the shore landscape. Bayberry usually stays between 5 and 10 ft. but is sometimes taller. The wind at the waterfront tends to sculpt the shape and keep it low to the ground. Inland plants are likely to be taller. Bayberry spreads by root suckers and can grow into a thicket. The sprawling roots help keep it upright in the sand and help to stabilize the sandy soil at the same time. The thick, dark-green, almost leathery leaves are considered semievergreen. They may turn a little purple before they drop (if they drop), but fall color is not a major asset. The berries, which are an important attribute, can form in large numbers on female plants. They have a waxy quality and are the source of the scent in bayberry candles. As an added bonus, bayberry fixes nitrogen in the soil.

WHEN TO PLANT

Plant in early spring. Late March or early April is best. Transplanting bayberries from the wild (or seedlings from around the yard) is not easy. You are more likely to be successful with an early-fall planting if you use container grown plants.

WHERE TO PLANT

Bayberry grows in sun or partial shade. It is extremely tolerant of salt spray and sandy soil conditions. Its spreading root system anchors it in windy conditions, though it may be stunted or "sculpted" in heavy wind. Bayberry can be mass planted or used as a border planting. It has been very successfully employed on highways where winter salt spray overwhelms most plants. Acidic soil conditions are a must, but that is rarely a problem in New Jersey.

How to Plant

If moving a wilding or volunteer plant, take along a large hunk of the original soil to give the plant a better chance for survival. You may be better off purchasing a container-grown plant whose roots have been confined. Bayberry will tolerate very sandy soil, but be sure to mix an abundance of organic matter into the soil prior to planting. Roots will take a while to get established. Organic matter helps the soil retain moisture while roots are settling in.

Care and Maintenance

Bayberry has no serious insect or disease problems. It can be trained as a standard (an upright plant with a single stalk). New shoots grow quickly but older wood has a slower growth rate. Prune away new shoots if you want to keep the plant confined.

Additional Information

It takes $1^1/2$ qts. of berries to make one 8 in. bayberry candle. Gather berries in October or early November. Boil in water for about 5 minutes and skim off the wax or let the wax harden when cooled. It can be used by itself or mixed with tallow. Pure bayberry does not burn as brightly as regular candles, but it does give off a lovely scent. The wax may also be substituted for animal fat in the making of soap. Store bayberry products in plastic bags or sealed containers to preserve the scent.

Additional Species, Cultivars, or Varieties

There are both male and female plants. Female plants produce the berries. To ensure that you get a female plant, look for shrubs that have been propagated by division or from cuttings. There are three other species of *Myrica*. The southern wax myrtle, *M. cerifera*, can reach 35 ft.; it is hardy only to Zone 6. *M. californica* also reaches 35 ft. and has purple berries; it is hardy only to Zone 7. *M. gale* is a small plant—usually under 4 ft.; it is hardy to Zone 1. There is little information about it. It may not grow this far south and is difficult if not impossible to locate.

Beach Plum

Prunus maritima

Other Names: Shore Plum, Black Plum
Height: Usually 6 ft., but up to 12 ft.
Spread: Variable; around 6 ft.
Flowers: Showy white ¹/₂ in. flowers in
    groups of 2 or 3
Bloom Period: May
Zones: 4, 5, 6, 7, 8, 9

Light Requirement:

It is difficult to say whether the little beach plum is prized more for its lovely white flowers in the spring, its tasty fruits for jams and jellies in the fall; or its ability to tolerate sand, salt, and wind. It is native from Maine to Virginia and can be found only along the coast. The plant spreads from suckers but also reproduces from seed; there is, therefore, tremendous variation in the size and habit of the plant and in the size and color of the fruit. The plums range in color from red to purple to yellow and in size from a small crab apple (which is mostly pit) up to 2 in. in diameter. The fruit is almost always round. Its taste is tart, but the jelly produced from this plant is served as a side dressing for meats and is treasured by its devotees. The fruit is harvested in August when it reaches its full color. Beach plum is extremely abundant in Cape Cod and is a local favorite. It can be spotted frequently along the coast in New Jersey at both Island Beach State Park and Sandy Hook. The plants grow in the dunes that flank the trails and paths leading from the parking lots to the beaches. Dunes are very fragile and it is best not to walk on them unnecessarily, so be sure to admire the beach plums from the designated pathways.

WHEN TO PLANT

Plant in early spring. Late March or early April is best.

WHERE TO PLANT

This native plant does best on sandy, acidic soils similar to its native habitat. Beach plums appear in the areas called "secondary dunes" where the salt spray is not as intense and the variation of vegetation is greater. It can be found growing with bayberry, shadbush, and highbush blueberry. It will also thrive in inland locations with heavier soils, but there are so many other choices for those circumstances that it has not become very popular as a mainstream ornamental.

How to Plant

You can propagate beach plums from seed by sowing in place, but if you are seeking particular characteristics of habit or fruit quality, you are better off purchasing a container-grown plant. Add organic matter to help the soil retain moisture. Since this plant suckers, you may be able to propagate an existing plant by division. Do this in the early spring.

Care and Maintenance

The plant stays small but suckers from the base. If this is a problem, prune out the branches in early spring. No particular insects or diseases are noted in the literature for beach plum, but all *Prunus* are prone to scale and some leaf spots.

Additional Information

To make beach plum jelly, take $2^1/2$ lbs. of fully ripe plums and 1 lb. of slightly green plums. Crush in the bottom of an enameled kettle (leaving in the pits and the skin) and cook in $1^1/2$ cups of water. Bring to a boil and simmer for 20 minutes while stirring. Strain in a jelly bag to get 4 cups of juice. Put the juice back into the kettle with 3 cups of sugar. Boil until the mixture reaches 220 degrees Fahrenheit or until jelly sheets from the spoon. Remove from heat, skim, and pour into sterilized $1/2$-pint jars. Leave $1/8$ in. of room at the top of each jar. Cap with two-piece screwband lids. (from *Putting Food By* by Hertzberg, Vaughan and Greene, 1984)

Additional Species, Cultivars, or Varieties

'Flava' produces yellow fruit and is native to Cape Cod. Several other varieties exist as a result of significant research and selection. 'Eastham', 'Hancock', 'Premier', and 'Autumn' are credited with having fruit that is superior in quality to that of the species.

Common Sea Buckthorn

Hippophae rhamnoides

Other Name: Swallow Thorn
Height: Usually 10 ft., but up to 40 ft.
Spread: Usually 10 ft., but up to 40 ft.
Flowers: Small, yellow, inconspicuous
Bloom Period: March or April
Zones: 4, 5, 6, 7

Light Requirement:

*I*ts bright orange berries are one of the common sea buckthorn's primary attractions. The limitations of salt and sand make the colorful fruits more precious than they might be in other areas where plant selection is more diverse. Fruit arrives on female shrubs; fruit production requires a male plant in close proximity. The berries are hard but edible. One reference suggests leaving them for the birds. Another says the fruits persist all winter. This must mean that even the birds don't like them. Sea buckthorn fixes nitrogen. Its foliage is grayish green, 3 in. long, and narrow, similar in appearance to a willow leaf. Leaves do not supply much in the way of fall color, but the berries ripen by September and are striking against the attractive foliage. Fruits are abundant and can last until April. Like many sand-tolerant species, common sea buckthorn can form its own thicket if left unpruned. (This must have something to do with roots evolving to spread in search of water.) Branches can have small thorns and the plant eventually suckers from the base. In a landscape, this tendency can be helpful along a border or in a mass, but in restricted space it can be annoying.

WHEN TO PLANT

This plant is a little uncooperative about getting established. Plant in late March or early April for the best results.

WHERE TO PLANT

Plant in a sunny location in infertile, sandy soil. (Sounds like the beach to me!) Sea buckthorn will tolerate salt spray. It establishes more rapidly in poor soils than it does in fertile soils, and it prefers a damp subsoil. Plant size is usually around 10 ft., so you can use it as a foundation plant if the suckers are removed. Planting sea buckthorn en masse or as a border may be more appropriate. Due to its salt tolerance and stabilizing capability, this plant may be a good choice along highways where salt is a winter problem.

HOW TO PLANT

You can plant up to 6 female plants for every male plant and still have sufficient pollination for fruit set. The plants are pollinated by wind so the male should be in close proximity. Container grown material will probably be the easiest to get established, though you may be able to transplant plants from suckers if you are particularly careful. You can also layer the branches or even grow sea buckthorn from seed if you are willing to be patient. Rooting cuttings is extremely difficult.

CARE AND MAINTENANCE

Prune suckers if desired. Sea buckthorn also benefits from occasional pruning to shape. It has no serious insects or diseases.

ADDITIONAL INFORMATION

Sea buckthorn is native to Europe as well as western and northern China. It is used extensively in Europe along roads and highways. One reference mentions that the fruits, which are very acidic, can be used for making jams or sauce. It is supposed to be very high in vitamin C. Sea buckthorn's wood can be used for turning. This plant may be difficult to locate, but nurseries in the shore area are more likely to carry it than nurseries elsewhere. It is also available from Forest Farm in Oregon.

ADDITIONAL SPECIES, CULTIVARS, OR VARIETIES

There is one other species, *H. salicifolia*. It is larger, has yellow fruit, and is equally salt and sand tolerant. Unfortunately, it is hardy only to Zone 8. The only variety of *H. rhamnoides* mentioned in the literature is 'Procera', which has has yellow to dark red fruit and grows to 60 ft. tall

Japanese Black Pine

Pinus thunbergiana

Other Name: *P. thunbergii*
Height: Usually 20 to 40 ft., but up to 90 ft.
Spread: Usually 20 to 40 ft., but varies
Zones: 5, 6, 7

Light Requirement:

The irregular shape of Japanese black pine is not well suited for a formal setting, but most seaside plantings are far from formal. The tree's habit is open and spreading but somewhat pyramidal. Even young seedlings tend to look like impressionistic pyramids. Whether Japanese black pine is actually hardy to Zone 5 is debated in the literature. The needles may burn if temperatures go below minus 15 degrees Fahrenheit. The shore areas, where this plant is so desirable, are all in Zones 6 or 7 in New Jersey, so this uncertainty should not affect the tree's usefulness as a salt-tolerant seaside plant. Japanese black pine's ability to grow in salty environments is due to its proficiency in blocking the uptake of sodium and chloride. This makes it invaluable as a landscape ornamental for residential settings at the shore, as well as extremely functional in dune stabilization and land reclamation. As the tree ages, the trunk can take on a very crooked appearance. The bark becomes fissured in irregular plates. Cones are up to 3 in. long. The dark-green needles are in bundles of two and last up to 5 years. The seeds produced germinate readily as soon as they are ripe and require no stratification. This is evident by the large number of seedlings that can be found beneath a mature tree. These can be dug and transplanted without much difficulty. If left to grow where they fall, the plants will all grow together, making an irregular tree look even messier. Japanese black pine does not do well in rich soils and so does not generally thrive inland. There are many other pines that are more suitable for those better conditions.

WHEN TO PLANT
Plant in early spring or early fall.

WHERE TO PLANT
Japanese black pine is so salt tolerant that it can be found within a few feet of the high water mark. Find it a sunny location on moist

but well-drained soil. As a border plant, it is irregular and some-what unpredictable in habit. It will sprout from seed and fill in, but its shape is irregular at best. Since it pops up from seed, it can become quite thick. This tree is not a traditional choice for a specimen plant, but the crooked habit may be interesting in the right spot.

How to Plant

Japanese black pine is not difficult to get established. Move seedlings in the early spring. If soil is particularly dry, add organic matter to help it retain moisture. New plants growing in windy situations should be staked.

Care and Maintenance

Snipping of the candles (new growth) in early spring will help keep this unconventional pine more compact and full. Japanese black pine tolerates shearing better than most pines. A type of oyster-shell scale known as *lepidosaphes pini* has recently been found to infest the needles down in the center of the needle clusters. Because this pest is spread by wind, it is more a problem along the shore than any-where else in our state. Applying dormant oil in April will be helpful, though it is difficult to penetrate the clusters. To control *lepidosaphes pini* in the young crawling stage, spray in mid-June and again in August with 1 percent horticultural oil, or check with your County Agricultural Agent for insecticide recommendations.

Additional Information

Japanese black pine is native to Japan. It is considered a good choice for bonsai and an absolute must in Japanese-style gardens.

Additional Species, Cultivars, or Varieties

'Oculis-draconis' has needles with two yellow bands. The Japanese red pine and the Himalayan pine also have varieties of the same description with the same name. The Himalayan's long graceful needles make it easy to distinguish from the others. Japanese red pine looks very similar and is more readily available in the trade. There is some indication in the literature that the black may hold its color better in the winter. 'Thundercloud' has silver-white candles and a compact, mounded growth habit. It grows only 3 to 6 in. per year. 'Yatsubusa' is a low, spreading specimen that grows 3 in. per year.

Summersweet

Clethra alnifolia

Other Names: Sweet Pepperbush, Sweet Alder
Height: 4 to 10 ft.
Spread: Up to 12 ft.
Flowers: Fragrant 4 to 6 in. slim spikes of white or pink
Bloom Period: July and August
Zones: 3, 4, **5, 6, 7,** 8, 9

Light Requirement:

Its fragrant summer blooms are appreciated wherever summersweet puts down roots, but its tolerance of seaside conditions makes it especially attractive in the shore area. Like many of the other plants in this chapter, this shrub will spread by suckers. In most situations this is really not a problem. It can be pruned hard in the spring, if necessary; its lovely blossoms are produced on new growth. Summersweet leafs out rather late. The 2 to 4 in. long leaves are bright green all summer, turn yellow in October, then fade to brown before dropping. Because the flowers arrive on new growth, they grow at the uppermost tips of the branches, which makes them very obvious and easy to appreciate with your eyes or your nose. The flowers are deliciously fragrant but not overpowering. Bees love them. Planting summersweet near your vegetable garden may help with the pollination of summer crops. Summersweet is not an aggressive grower and pruning is not usually necessary. It tends to stay in the small end of its height range unless planted in moist soil under shady conditions.

WHEN TO PLANT

Planting in early spring is preferred. There are hints in the literature that this plant is tricky to get established.

WHERE TO PLANT

You can plant summersweet almost anywhere. The ideal site would be one with a little shade and moist, acidic soil that is high in organic matter, but summersweet will take full sun to heavy shade and gravel soil to wet spots. It is a very adaptable little bush. There are dwarf forms that make good foundation plants, but the species is useful as a border plant, for mass planting, and even as a specimen in small yards. It is tolerant of seaside conditions and is native from Maine to Florida.

How to Plant

Summersweet is generally available in containers, but you may come across a balled specimen on occasion. Suckers can be divided in early spring. Add plenty of organic matter such as leaf compost when you are planting in sandy soil. This helps conserve and maintain soil moisture, giving the plant its best shot at getting established. An organic mulch will help replenish the organic matter in the soil as it dissipates; it will also help keep the soil moist in hot weather.

Care and Maintenance

Little maintenance is required unless you want to keep summersweet from spreading. If this is the case, prune in early spring. Summersweet has no insect or disease problems. Snip off the flower skeletons to keep the bush tidy if desired. Keeping the mulch thick will reduce moisture evaporation from the soil. This native plant is well adapted to the New Jersey climate.

Additional Information

We have a summersweet planted by the path to the front door. It established easily and produces pink flowers for much of the summer. The sweet fragrance and delicate flowers make me smile every time I walk by. It is surprising that summersweet is not more commonly used.

Additional Species, Cultivars, or Varieties

There are quite a few varieties available and more are being introduced all the time. 'Pink Spires' are a soft pink. 'Rosea' has dark-pink buds that open to a very pale pink. 'Hummingbird' is a compact form. 'Ruby Spice' has dark-pink flowers; 'Fern Valley Pink' has bright-pink flowers that are larger than most. *C. barbinervis* is not common, though it is gaining popularity in the trade. It is hardy in Zones 5 to 8 and reaches up to 18 ft. It can be grown as a small tree. Its beautiful bark sometimes exfoliates.

Tamarix

Tamarix ramosissima

Other Names: Tamarisk, Salt Cedar,
  T. pentandra, Five-Stamen Tamarisk
Height: 10 to 15 ft.
Spread: Generally not as wide as it is tall
Flowers: Masses of feathery pink flowers on the
  ends of long, sometimes arching branches
Bloom Period: June and July
Zones: 2, 3, 4, **5, 6, 7**

Light Requirement:

*T*amarix is different. Some may want to plant it for that reason alone, but its tolerance of salty conditions makes it even more desirable. The leaves resemble scales, so even when the plant is in full leaf it maintains a unique appearance. The overall image is "fluffy." This is even more true when tamarix is covered in its delicate pink blossoms. The flowers appear in midsummer and can last for up to 6 weeks. The plant blooms on new growth, so the flowers blossom at the branch tips where they are most conspicuous. Each long flowering branch can be up to 3 ft. long. The dramatic lines created by these branches give the plant a touch of elegance. When the flowers and leaves are gone, tamarix takes on a rather loose, weedy appearance. Michael Dirr suggests it be kept hidden at that time of year. Severe spring pruning will rejuvenate scraggly plants and help keep the minuscule foliage as lush as possible. Since it blooms on new growth, this treatment will not impair the plant's ability to bloom.

WHEN TO PLANT

Early spring (late March or early April) is the best time to plant.

WHERE TO PLANT

Tamarix is extremely salt tolerant and makes a great choice for the shore area. It does not do well in highly fertile soils but will adapt to most other conditions. The ideal location would be in full sun in acidic, well-drained soil. It is best to avoid locating tamarix near water and sewer pipes.

How to Plant

The root systems of this plant are somewhat "minimalistic,' so extra care needs to be given to protect what roots there are. You will be most successful with a container-grown plant. Disturb the roots as little as possible. This plant thrives in sandy soil and does not require extensive soil preparation to get established.

Care and Maintenance

The biggest challenge with tamarix is keeping it from getting leggy. Its unruly habit makes spring pruning very desirable. In some places it is even treated as a herbaceous perennial. If cut down to the ground every year, it sends up a flush of green growth in spring. This is not necessary, but it may make the plant's appearance more acceptable. The fuller, more compact growth which results may allow the home owner to take better advantage of tamarix's salt tolerance and summer flowers. It grows very quickly and will fill in by summer. Tamarix is said by some to be susceptible to several diseases as well as scale. It is listed in *Ortho's Home Gardener's Problem Solver*, however, as being relatively free of insects and diseases. You should have no serious pest or disease difficulties, but as with all plants, keep your eyes open for problems before they become severe.

Additional Information

There is often confusion about the difference between tamarack *Larix decidua* and the tamarisk discussed here. Tamarack looks much like a needled evergreen, but is in fact a very large deciduous tree that reaches up to 100 ft. in height. If its other common name, "larch," were used exclusively instead of 'tamarack,' the confusion would be eliminated. Tamarack and tamarisk do not have the same site preferences, so be sure to ask for and purchase the right one.

Additional Species, Cultivars, or Varieties

'Rubra' has deep pink flowers and is very likely the same as 'Summerglow'. 'Rosea' blooms a little later than the species. 'Pink Cascade' has blue green foliage and an extended bloom. *T. parviflora* is the small flowered tamarix, which blooms in May on old wood. Any necessary pruning should be done right after it finishes blooming.

$\mathscr{V}$INES ADD A NEW DIMENSION TO YOUR GARDEN. They can be manipulated in ways that woody ornamentals cannot. Vines are flexible in the most literal sense as well as in their usefulness. They can be trained over archways, up cinderblock walls, to screen an ugly view, or to draw attention to something beautiful.

A plant is defined as a vine more by how it grows than by the type of plant it is. Vines can be woody, perennial, or annual. The key characteristic is that they need some sort of support to grow upright or they will ramble along the ground.

Most vines continue to grow from the end in a long, continuous shoot. Some root along the way if left on the ground; this tendency can be useful for bank stabilization or erosion control. Sometimes these small, sticky roots can even attach to walls. Some vines have tendrils with cuplike suction ends that are amazingly strong and hold the plant firmly. Others have curly tendrils that latch onto any support the vine touches. There are also twisting vines whose growing shoot spirals around whatever is holding it up. Finally, some vines have no way of attaching themselves and must be tied.

Choosing the right vine requires a careful evaluation of your goal as well as the plant characteristics. For example, vines that cling by roots or suction may not be the best to climb up a wooden house; they might damage the surface and get under the siding. The same vines may do fine growing up a wooden fence or covering a ramshackle shed. Vines with curling tendrils will cling easily to a chain-link fence, but they will have nothing to hold on to if you want them to cover a cinderblock wall.

If you are attempting to block a view, you may need an evergreen vine to keep the ugliness out of sight all year long. While waiting for a woody or perennial vine to get big enough to do the job, you can plant a functional, attractive annual.

Chapter Seven

Vines also have an important application in a small yard. They allow the use of vertical space to build diversity and character. The creative use of vines can turn tight quarters into an intimate nook.

Vines can produce flowers or fruits. If you are looking for summer shade, you can plant pole beans or scarlet runner beans and get a harvest at the same time. Annual flowers that vine include morning glory and its close relative, moonflower. The cheerful black-eyed Susan, *Thunbergia alata*, grows thick and tall in a single season. It can be covered in dark-yellow flowers that have black throats.

Grape vines do triple duty. They provide thick cover for summer shade; the grapes can be luscious if properly tended; and stuffed grape leaves are a Greek or Lebanese delicacy. Be wary of heavy wood vines. They twist and turn and get very interesting, but they can also pull down the trellis or wooden porch that holds them up.

Trellises present another set of variables. Be sure to use treated lumber so the trellises will hold up for a while. Some trellises are now available in plastic, and under some circumstances, metal will work. Wisteria will eventually "crush" a wooden support as it grows. It is a good example of a vine that would benefit from a metal trellis. Metal pipes can be screwed together to make a very durable but unattractive support. If the vines are dense enough, they will eventually cover the support and its ugliness will not matter.

After all the practical aspects of growing vines have been appropriately weighed and measured, there is another very real benefit to consider: vines are magical. As they wind up old wrought-iron gates and fences, they create an instant romantic aura. Is there anything more lovely than walking under an arch of climbing roses? In Frances Hodgson Burnett's *The Secret Garden*, it is vines that hang down and cover the long hidden door to the forbidden garden. And "ivy-covered halls" add character to any institution of higher learning.

Choose, plant, and care for vines with all the careful discrimination you would use in planting anything else in your garden. Then treasure them for their expressive personality and the enchantment that is theirs alone.

Clematis

Clematis hybrids

Height: To 18 ft. but requires support
Flowers: Up to 8 in. in diameter, in a
    wide variety of colors
Bloom Period: Varies
Zones: 5, 6, 7, 8 (some are hardier)

Light Requirement:

*C*lematis is grown primarily for its spectacular flowers. The thin vines are brittle and somewhat delicate, but once established, they just keep growing. To make sense of the hundreds of cultivars and hybrids would fill a large book. Some varieties bloom on old wood in the spring. These varieties occasionally put out a bloom or two throughout the summer (but don't count on it). Some flower only on new growth in the summer and may bloom from July until frost. Others flower on both old and new growth. To make matters more complicated, some varieties sometimes produce double flowers on old growth and single flowers on new. The only way to be sure of the proper treatment of the clematis you have selected for your garden is to know the variety name and follow the directions that come with it. If you prune varieties that bloom on old wood in the early spring, the flowers will be gone for the year. Clematis fanciers sometimes make faces at the idea of growing clematis up a mailbox post or a lamppost. When you work with these plants every day, that treatment may indeed seem monotonous. In your own yard, where clematis are not clinging to every vertical surface, a vine adorning the lamppost can be lovely. But remember that there is room to expand one's horizons when it comes to this plant. It can grow up trellises and pergolas, gazebos and dead maples. Its slender vines can soften the corner of your house or cover a chain-link fence. When used in a foundation planting, clematis can provide vertical interest without taking up a lot of space. These plants can actually thrive in that environment, because the other shrubbery will shade the roots and keep them cool, just the way they like it. With the right collection of clematis, it is possible to have flowers all season, from spring until frost. The decorative seed-pods of some varieties will provide interest into the winter.

WHEN TO PLANT

Plant in early spring. Late March or early April is best.

WHERE TO PLANT

Clematis prefers sun on the leaves, but keep the roots in the shade
to help them stay cool. This is not as difficult as it may sound. Since
clematis grows upright on a support, it is possible to have other
shrubs planted very close by to provide shade. Avoid very hot and
very wet areas. Be sure to provide support—clematis does better
with thin supports rather than thick ones. A 2 x 2 in. piece of wood
is too big for the vines to hold.

HOW TO PLANT

Clematis likes moist, well-drained soil that stays cool. Other shrubs
planted nearby can help shade the roots. At the very least, use a
thick layer of organic mulch to protect the roots. Plants are available
in containers or bare root; container plants generally get established
more easily. Soil preparation should include the addition of organic
matter and lime. These plants are not overly particular about pH,
but they prefer a pH of 6 to 7.5. Since most New Jersey soils tend to
be on the acidic side, a little lime may be beneficial; perform a soil
test to be more precise about the soil's needs.

CARE AND MAINTENANCE

Pruning can be tricky, and proper technique is dependent on variety.
Keep clematis well watered, especially in hot, dry weather. Stem rot
can be a problem. Control it by removing infected shoots below the
soil line and treating the plant with an appropriate fungicide. It is
also subject to a variety of insect pests. Keep an eye out for white fly,
mites, scale, and borer.

ADDITIONAL INFORMATION

One thing gardeners need to recognize is that dormant wood on
clematis looks very dead. Even healthy stems are so brittle they tend
to snap. Look for healthy buds. You may want to wait to prune until
you can see what is growing and what is not. If you do not know
the type of clematis you have, observe it carefully for a year. You
should be able to figure out if it is blooming on new growth or old.

ADDITIONAL SPECIES, CULTIVARS, OR VARIETIES

There are hundreds—possibly thousands—of varieties. Pick the ones
that have the characteristics you like best. (My favorite is 'Henryi',
with its enormous white flowers. It blooms on old wood in June and
repeats in late summer on new wood.)

Climbing Hydrangea

Hydrangea anomala subsp. *petiolaris*

Other Name: *H. petiolaris*
Height: Up to 75 ft.
Spread: Variable
Flowers: Flat clusters of white flowers up
    to 8 in. across
Bloom Period: Late June to early July
Zones: 4, 5, 6, 7

Light Requirement:

The climbing hydrangea is a magnificent plant. It is one of the vines that cling with small aerial roots and attach themselves to any rough surface. It has the ability to grow quite large, up to 75 ft., which means it can turn an ugly cinder-block wall into a vertical jungle of flowering vine. The climbing hydrangea has a three-dimensional growth habit. Its side branches can protrude from the wall up to 3 ft., giving depth, shadows, and mountains of character to an otherwise flat surface. The flower clusters are flattish and up to 8 in. across; they appear in late June and last about two weeks. The blossoms are white and have a light, pleasant scent. The branches extend from a wall in such a way that the plant will have a layered look; this look is particularly effective while the plant is in bloom. The leaves are usually heart-shaped, but they are quite wide, which gives the impression of being round. The leaves are dark green and extremely shiny. They appear very close together on the vine, giving a rich, lush appearance to the plant, and they stay green well into fall. There is a discrepancy in the literature about this plant. Some credit it with golden fall foliage; others say the leaves drop off green. The flower cluster size of seedlings can vary, so there may be leaf variation in seed grown plants as well. (I have several at Blooming Acres and have never seen any noticeable fall color.) As a bonus, the cinnamon red bark exfoliates on mature plants.

WHEN TO PLANT

Plant in early spring or early fall. Late March or early April and early September is best.

WHERE TO PLANT

Climbing hydrangea has flexible light requirements; it will do well in full sun to shade. It will need support, but can cling to any rough surface with its aerial roots. Choose a spot where the plant can grow in rich, fertile soil that has an acidic to neutral pH.

HOW TO PLANT

Be sure to add lots of organic matter, such as leaf compost, to the soil prior to planting. Container-grown plants will grow better if you avoid excessive trauma to their roots. It can take several years before newly transplanted climbing hydrangeas show much growth. This slow growth may be discouraging, but once the plants settle in, they will grow steadily, and they are definitely worth waiting for. It is possible to propagate this vine by laying a side branch on the surface of potted soil. Secure it in place with a wire pin. After it roots, the branch can be cut. Give it some TLC in its container before transplanting and you will have as many new plants as you could possibly desire.

CARE AND MAINTENANCE

Once established, climbing hydrangea is a maintenance-free plant. It requires little pruning and has few, if any, insect or disease problems.

ADDITIONAL INFORMATION

There has been some confusion between this species and *Schizophragma hydrangeoides*. They have a similar appearance, but the petals of the flowers on *Schizophragma* are less showy, and its leaves are not as shiny. The hydrangea is considered the superior of the two.

ADDITIONAL SPECIES, CULTIVARS, OR VARIETIES

The species, *H. anomala*, is similar in flower and habit but has pointy leaves and floppier blooms. It may not be quite as hardy as *H. petiolaris*, but its appearance can be as magnificent.

Fiveleaf Akebia

Akebia quinata

Height: Up to 40 ft.	**Light Requirement:**
Spread: Variable	
Flowers: Small purple dangling flowers; scent of vanilla	
Bloom Period: May	
Zones: 4, 5, 6, 7, 8	

*T*his deciduous vine has a number of unique characteristics that are very appealing. The almost blue green compound leaves are made of five leaflets arranged "palmately" or like an umbrella, 2 to 3 in. across. Each leaflet is rounded and has a notched tip. The result is an attractively delicate appearance. Although they have no noticeable fall color, the leaves persist late into fall. Each May, the vine produces small rosy-purple male flowers and 1 in. eggplant colored female flowers on the same flower spikes. The female flowers sometimes develop into purple, edible fruits up to 4 in. long. The vine may require a little hand pollination to help it along if you want it to bear fruit. Fruits ripen in September or October. Fiveleaf akebia is a twining vine that needs support. It grows quickly with very dense leaves, and in warmer climates it can become invasive to the point of choking out whatever it grows on. If cut down to the ground in late winter, it will stay under control. This very fine foliage vine is useful for covering fences, walls, or trellises. Akebia is adaptable to a wide range of growing conditions and requires little care once it is established.

WHEN TO PLANT
Early spring is best. Try planting in late March or early April.

WHERE TO PLANT
Give this plant room to climb. It does well in sun or shade but prefers rich, fertile soil. It is most useful for covering up a fence or ugly wall, and it can be magnificent growing up a dead tree. Avoid locating it near small plants that can be easily smothered.

How to Plant

This plant can be divided or grown from seed or cuttings, although container grown stock is recommended. Pinch repeatedly to encourage many stems for fullness. Provide support to give the vine something to twine around.

Care and Maintenance

Your biggest maintenance chore with fiveleaf akebia is to prune it regularly to keep it from getting aggressive. It can be thinned to keep it from becoming overwhelming, or you can simply cut it to the ground. It has no serious pest problems acknowledged in the literature. Watch out for suckers that can pop up where you don't want them.

Additional Information

This is a truly pretty vine and very useful, but choose your location carefully. In the South it is evergreen and is sometimes considered a weed; it grows far more slowly in cold-winter areas. New Jersey winters should be sufficient to contain this enthusiastic plant, but keep an eye on it and don't be afraid to prune it hard.

Additional Species, Cultivars, or Varieties

'Alba' has white flowers. 'Rosea' has lavender-pink flowers. *Akebia trifoliata* has three leaflets instead of five. *A.* × *pentaphylla* is a cross between the two; it has some five leaflet and some three leaflet leaves.

Japanese Wisteria

Wisteria floribunda

Other Name: *W. multijuga* (formerly)
Height: 30 ft. to much higher, depending
　　on support
Spread: Variable
Flowers: Shades of violet to white panicles;
　　usually 9 to 20 in.; very fragrant
Bloom Period: Late April to early May
Zones: 4, 5, 6, 7, 8, 9

Light Requirement:

Wisteria may be the queen of flowering vines. There is nothing that can top the splendor of a mature vine, all twisted and gnarled, covered in trailing panicles of violet blooms that fill the surrounding air with an intoxicating scent. Nothing. There comes a point when beauty touches a place that is not quite real, and wisterias can sometimes reach that place. Few species have the ability and even fewer specimens actually get there, but when they do, there is magic in the air. The twining wisteria vines are very powerful. If left to climb an enormous shade tree, they will eventually strangle it. (The tree's ghost, dripping in flowers, is magnificent.) One of the biggest wisteria problems can be failure to bloom. Be sure to start with named cultivars rather than seedlings, and provide plenty of sun. Avoid nitrogen fertilizer, which pushes foliar growth. Root pruning can jump-start blooming. Prune vigorous shoots back to three or four buds and follow with an application of superphosphate. With luck, you will get flowers. With the right variety and growing conditions (and perhaps a handful of fairy dust) you may get panicles 48 in. long. According to Donald Wyman, one flower panicle measured at the Arnold Arboretum reached 36 in.; in Japan, they can get over 5 ft.!

WHEN TO PLANT
Plant in early spring or early fall.

WHERE TO PLANT
Wisteria will tolerate partial shade, but if you want flowers, drench the vines in sunlight. Provide strong support. If you intend to grow them along a porch rail, remember that they can be destructive over time. Plants in poor soil may bloom earlier than plants in deep,

moist, well-drained loam, but the best soil conditions will mean the best specimens in the long run.

How to Plant

Start with a named variety plant, preferably one that is container grown. Do a thorough preparation of the soil, including the addition of large quantities of organic matter. An application of lime will be beneficial. If you are planting in heavy clay, add a mixture of 2 parts organic matter and 1 part sand to the soil. If the plant is not located in front of a structure or dead tree, you will have to provide support. Metal pipe may be the best material for the support, since wisteria can crush wood over time. In lieu of support, you can use severe pruning to develop a free-standing small tree. Support of some type will be necessary to train the trunk of this tree, but it won't be needed for long. An organic mulch will help retain soil moisture.

Care and Maintenance

Failure to bloom is this plant's most frustrating problem (see above). It is a good idea to keep an eye on the vines as they grow; careful planning and guidance of the twining shoots can prevent these plants from wreaking havoc on your home. Wisteria is susceptible to a variety of insects and diseases. Notches in the leaves may indicate that black vine weevil adults are feeding at night; this means the larvae are feeding on the roots as well. Scale can also be a problem.

Additional Information

Twining is Japanese wisteria's method of attachment. If you look closely, you will see it always twists in a clockwise direction—this is an identifying characteristic.

Additional Species, Cultivars, or Varieties

There are many varieties that have been selected for color, scent, and panicle size. 'Longissima alba' has particularly long, white flower panicles. 'Rosea' is fragrant with pale-rose blooms, each tipped in purple. 'Royal Purple' is the darkest purple. There are also double-flowered varieties, but the flowers are often inferior. The Chinese wisteria, *W. sinensis*, is readily available; it is not quite as hardy as the Japanese nor is it as fragrant. Its lovely panicles open all at once. This makes for a display that is even bigger than that of panicles that open sequentially, but the display is shorter lived. The flowers of the Chinese wisteria are considered an edible delicacy in China, where they are collected in full bloom. Although very similar in appearance, the Chinese wisteria can easily be distinguished from the Japanese by its counter-clockwise twining.

Kolomikta Vine

Actinidia kolomikta

Height: 20 ft.	**Light Requirement:**
Spread: Variable	
Flowers: Small, white; inconspicuous but fragrant	
Bloom Period: May and June	
Zones: 3, 4, 5, 6, 7	

*T*his plant needs a common name that is easier to pronounce! "Ornamental Kiwi" might be a good choice. It is related to both the fuzzy kiwi (a popular fruit produced mostly in New Zealand) and the hardy kiwi (a vigorous vine grown both as an ornamental and for the small, smooth fruits similar to those of its fuzzy cousin). The foliage is about 5 in. long, emerges with a hint of purple, and matures mostly dark green. The ornamental value of this vine is found primarily in the male plant's leaves, whose tips are variegated in pink. It looks as if each one was dipped into white paint and then pink. On some leaves just the very tip has color, while others are more than half pink. The color is a gradation of pink, with the deepest color along the edge of the leaf. It is very beautiful. Female plants show some variegation, but it is not as pronounced. Kolomikta vine also produces fruits that resemble the hardy kiwi but are even smaller, about 1 in. You should grow at least one male for every three to four females to ensure fruit set. The fruit will ripen in September and October. To get the best of both worlds, consider alternating males and females. These twining vines will cover a chain-link fence, stay beautiful most of the year, and produce an almost pest-free edible crop in the fall.

WHEN TO PLANT
Early spring is best.

WHERE TO PLANT
This plant will grow in full sun or light shade, although there is some confusion in the literature regarding light. After an exhaustive search, it appears this very cold hardy plant (hardy to -40 degrees Fahrenheit) does not like heat. In hotter climates, it requires shade to

produce its color; in colder climates, it does best in full sun. It will produce the best color in soils high in lime. Miller Nurseries in New York supplies both male and females; give them as much sun as possible. Kolomikta vine is flexible about soil type, but avoid wet ground. Since it is a twining vine, it needs something to hold. It might be the perfect plant to cover a chain-link fence.

How to Plant

Since it does well in soils heavy in lime, you should add lime during the soil preparation process. If you are using the plant to hide an ugly wall or block a view, you need to provide support. Kolomikta will grow from seed planted in the spring, but you will not be certain of the male-to-female ratio for some time. Cuttings taken in June are only moderately successful at rooting. Your best bet is to purchase container-grown material with the sex clearly identified.

Care and Maintenance

Don't be too quick to fertilize this vine; excessive feeding will reduce variegation. Once the plant is big enough, you may be able to propagate it by layering. It is not as vigorous as its relatives, and it reaches maximum height at 20 ft. If pruning is necessary, it can be done at almost any time unless you are growing the plants for fruit production. *A. kolomikta* blooms and fruits on old wood, so prune sparingly in early spring if you want small kiwis in the fall.

Additional Information

According to the Oregon Extension Service, the fruit of *A. kolomikta* has 700 to 1000 mg. of Vitamin C per 100 grams of fruit. This is ten times higher than the amount of C in the fuzzy kiwi, and twenty times higher than the C in citrus.

Additional Species, Cultivars, or Varieties

To be used as an ornamental, Kolomikta vine is often available as 'Arctic Beauty'. This can be male or female, so check the tag on the individual plant to determine its sex. Miller's Nursery offers the species as ornamental beauty kiwi, and you can specify male or female. Female varieties include 'Krupnopladnaya', 'Sentyabraskaya', and 'Pautske'. Two close relatives are *A. arguta* (the small fruited hardy kiwi) and *A. deliciosa*, also called *A. chinensis* (the larger fuzzy kiwi which is hardy only to Zone 7).

Silver Lace Vine

Polygonum aubertii

Other Names: Silver Fleece Vine, Silvervine
Fleeceflower, China Fleece Vine,
Mile-a-Minute Vine
Height: Up to 35 ft.
Spread: Variable
Flowers: Soft, billowy masses of tiny white
to off-white flowers
Bloom Period: July to frost
Zones: 4, 5, 6, 7, 8

Light Requirement:

*S*ilver lace vine is a rapidly-growing plant that produces copious numbers of flowers when not many woody ornamentals are
in bloom. It can grow 25 to 30 ft. its first year. Its climbing habit is to
twine, but not very tightly, so it is rarely harmful to its support. In fact,
it may need a little "help" every now and then to hang on. The leaves
emerge reddish-bronze but mature to a bright green. The leaves are
almost heart-shaped and are evergreen in the southern part of the
plant's range. They have no noticeable fall color. Since it blooms on
new wood, this plant can be pruned severely in early spring to control
its high speed growth. It can even be cut to the ground, although such
a practice will delay bloom significantly. The flowers are truly lacelike.
They cascade down the entire length of vinelike lace curtains blowing
in a breeze, and they have a slight fragrance that is pleasing. This
plant does seem to be pollinated by flies, so you may not want to
plant it by an outside dining table. Silver lace vine is accepting of city
conditions and is also recommended for the shore area. It will tolerate
drought once it is established.

WHEN TO PLANT
Plant in early spring or early fall.

WHERE TO PLANT
Choose a place that receives sun or a little shade. This attractive vine
needs something to twine around, and it's useful for covering an old
fence. Since it clings loosely to its support, it is less likely than other

vines to damage a porch or deck. It is a good choice for dry soils, but is very adaptable to soil conditions.

How to Plant

Silver lace vine transplants easily. It can be propagated by dividing rhizomes in early spring. Cuttings root easily, and plants are generally available in containers. There is nothing tricky about this one. If planted in spring, it will flower its first year.

Care and Maintenance

Severe pruning in the spring will keep it under control. The flies it attracts for pollination can be annoying, but they do no damage to the plant and are not worth controlling. It is better to locate the plant a little distance away so you can enjoy its airy beauty without having to deal with the flies. Japanese beetles can be a problem, and they warrant control when you see them.

Additional Information

We have a silver fleece vine at Blooming Acres. Its vines twine up the pergola to provide shade. It tolerates the abuse young children give it and blooms for an extended period with very little attention. The flies are annoying, but they do not overshadow this vine's beauty and function.

Additional Species, Cultivars, or Varieties

Pink-flowered *P. baldschuanicum*, bokhara fleece vine, is quite similar to *P. aubertii*. There are several other species of *Polygonum* that have a mounded habit, and some that are rather obnoxious weeds. (Don't judge a plant by its relatives!) There do not appear to be any named varieties of silver fleece vine in the trade at this time. That may change in the near future, as there is a great amount of interest in this plant.

Lawns

CCORDING TO THE LAWN INSTITUTE, LOCATED IN TENNESSEE, there are five grass plants in every square inch of lawn, over 850 in every square foot, and somewhere around 8 million in every 10,000 square feet (one-quarter acre) of lawn. That's a lot of grass.

There is a tremendous range in attitudes toward lawns. Some people don't really care what is growing as long as it is mostly green and not poisonous. Others want a rich, uniform, dark-green, perfectly manicured work of art. Most people fall somewhere in between.

There is no doubt that having some green grass where one can wiggle one's toes is one of Nature's great gifts. The work of mowing, fertilizing, liming, seeding, and controlling pests is not, however, a joy. The degree of commitment home owners have to their turf is very individual. If having a picture-perfect lawn is your idea of heaven, then go for it. If not, try to find the balance between effort and pleasure that best fits you and your family's needs.

It is impossible to cover lawn care in great detail in the context of this book. There have been volumes written on this subject alone. The following points are presented in a way to help you evaluate the different aspects of lawn care so that you, the home owner, can make an informed decision about the kind of lawn you want.

SOD

Sod is nothing more than transplanted grass. It is not an excuse for poor soil preparation, and it does not mean that once you put down sod you will have a perfect lawn forever.

What it does mean is that you can have an instant lawn of thick, virtually weed-free grass. It means you will have a thick protective

Chapter Eight

cover that will prevent many weed seeds from having an opportunity to get started. It means you will be able to wiggle your toes in cool green grass in a matter of days.

The use of sod gives you tremendous flexibility in lawn establishment. As long as the ground can be prepared properly, you can install sod. There is no waiting for the right weather to ensure seed germination.

Sod needs to have a high percentage of Kentucky bluegrass to hold it together. Bluegrass spreads by rhizomes and effectively holds the sod together by its network of roots. It is a sun-loving grass, and it will not last long in a shady area. Sod containing fescue, a more shade-tolerant grass, does exist, but it has to be mixed with bluegrass to keep the cut sod from falling apart. Understand your needs and make sure you purchase sod that is "New Jersey certified."

If you decide to use a primarily bluegrass sod in a shady area, you can overseed with fescue in the spring, or even better, in early fall. The fescue will fill in as the bluegrass thins out.

Prepare your yard for sod installation exactly the same as you would for seed. Strip the old grass and weeds. Apply organic matter, lime, and fertilizer as determined by a soil test. Till it all in to a depth of six to eight inches. Level, smooth, then lay your sod. In the long run, you will pay for any skimping in preparation.

COLOR

Grass is green. Even bluegrass is green. The question is: "How green does it need to be?" A rich, dark green lawn that comes up in the spring is a beauty, no doubt about it. Different species and even different varieties vary in color slightly, but to push grass to be as dark as possible can cause difficulties.

Nitrogen is the substance that greens up a lawn. It develops that deep emerald color that glistens in the sun. A dark-green lawn also grows faster and so has to be mowed more often; then you will have to deal with more clippings. It is also very tender and extremely susceptible to many insects and diseases that thrive on the tender growth. Know the consequences of a dark-green lawn, and be prepared to deal with insects and diseases in a timely manner or the dark green can become dead brown in no time.

You can also develop an appreciation for medium green. Medium green can be a very good thing. It is sturdier and slower growing. Moderation in all things—including green.

FERTILIZER

For grass, fertilizer is food. The sun provides part of the food, but fertilizer provides the rest. The numbers on the bag refer to nitrogen (N), phosphorus (P), and potassium (K), always in that order. "Organic" fertilizer needs some explanation since this term has more than one meaning. A very common lawn fertilizer is 10-6-4, 50 percent organic. In this fertilizer, half the nitrogen is in a chemical form that is released quickly and available to the grass plants immediately, like a quick shot in the arm. The other 50 percent is the "organic" component, which is in a chemical form that is released slowly over time to continually supply the grass with what it needs. It is becoming more common to call this "slow-release" fertilizer.

The other type of organic fertilizer is like cow or chicken manure. Such fertilizers are generally not as high in N-P-K, but they may have more minor elements and they also supply "organic matter," an important component of soil structure. It is, however, very difficult to be sure that what comes out of a cow is consistent. Sometimes the nutrient level is not even included on the package, so you cannot be sure how much of the essential elements you are adding. If you feel more comfortable using natural products, this is a very good approach, but it may be more difficult to achieve a perfect lawn. The grass itself doesn't really care whether the nitrogen came out of a cow or out of a fertilizer manufacturing plant.

FERTILIZER APPLICATION

The best way to know how much fertilizer you need is to have your soil tested. Any other approach is nothing but a guess. If you prefer to guess, 10-6-4 50 percent organic (slow release) applied at a rate of 10 pounds per 1,000 square feet is reasonable. Apply in early fall and again in late fall. Sometimes you can skip a spring application, or at least delay it until late spring. Never fertilize in the heat of summer.

The truth is, even if you never fertilize your lawn, you will still have grass, or at least something green. Frequent mowing puts some pressure on broadleaf weeds to keep them from taking over. The grass types that can tolerate lower fertility will dominate. Crabgrass and some broadleaf weeds will fill in any open spaces.

If you choose to fertilize only when the urge grabs you, it is better done in the fall. That is when you get root development, which is more important to make a sturdy lawn than the delicate green top-growth in the spring.

If you have to decide between fertilizing heavily and never fertilizing, go with never. An excess of fertilizer will kill grass, and most other things, in the blink of an eye. Whatever can't be used by the plants just runs off into the environment, causing more problems than it is worth. Your lawn will never win any awards if you don't fertilize, and you will have to settle for yellowish green color, but don't think you will get out of mowing. If there is a lawn, you have to mow.

LIME

Lime is used to alter the pH of the soil. It also supplies calcium. New Jersey soils tend to be on the acidic side, and the addition of lime brings the pH up to a point where the grass will be happy. The only way to know for sure how much lime you need is to have your soil tested. The amount needed is dependent on the existing pH as well as on your soil type. Once you get your soil pH adjusted properly, a maintenance application is 20 to 25 pounds of pulverized or granular limestone per thousand square feet once a year. Test again every three or four years to be sure your pH level is where it should be.

Chapter Eight

THATCH

There are tremendous misconceptions about thatch. It is not made of grass clippings. The top of the grass, the part that gets cut off when you mow, is so tender and delicate that it breaks down in no time. In fact, clippings release nitrogen back into the soil if left on the lawn after mowing. Three or four days after you mow, you will have a hard time finding the clippings you left behind.

Thatch is dead grass *plants*. As the new grass emerges from the growing tip, the oldest part of the plant dies. As it ages and matures, it gets thicker, tougher and almost woody. It develops a texture like coarse straw. This is thatch. The faster you push your lawn to grow—the more nitrogen you apply to get it to "green up"—the more rapidly you will develop thatch.

Thatch creates a blockade to the roots. Water, pesticides, and fertilizer get trapped in the layer of thatch and never get down to the roots where they are needed. Seed will not germinate if it sits on top of a layer of thatch.

Thatching and dethatching are terms sometimes used interchangeably to mean thatch removal. Whatever you call it, when thatch gets one-half inch thick, it is time to get rid of it. Remove thatch in early fall. Small areas can be done by hand with a special rake designed for thatch removal. This is difficult work, so larger areas may require the use of a mechanized de-thatching machine (they can be rented), or you can hire a professional to do the job for you.

MOWING

The frequency of mowing required is dependent on a number of factors, but grass height is the most important. Never mow shorter than one-and-a-half inch. Two to two-and-a-half inches is better, especially during the summer. As a rule, mow when the grass gets twice as tall as the mowing height. For example, if you want to mow the grass to two inches, mow when it reaches four inches. You can allow the clippings to stay on the lawn as long as they do not form a mat on the surface. If they do, they will smother what is underneath. This sounds ridiculously simple, but keep your mower sharp.

SEEDING

The best time to do a major seeding is early September. The ground will still be warm from summer heat, and that will encourage germination. By the time the grass is up, the air temperature will have cooled off and the tiny grasses will enjoy growing in the absence of heat stress.

The type of seed you choose is dependent on the growing conditions. It is always good to have different types of grass in the mix; this is recommended for insect and disease prevention. In a sunny area, use at least 60 percent Kentucky bluegrass, but make sure you have at least two different kinds of bluegrass to make up that 60 percent. The rest should be evenly divided between fine fescues and fine turf-type perennial rye. In the shade, use 60 percent fine fescues and split the rest between Kentucky bluegrass and perennial rye.

Use only high quality seed. This is very important. Bargain seed mixes are no bargain; in fact, they can be a disaster.

When seeding, the rye grass will germinate first, then the fescue. It can take up to twenty-eight days for the bluegrass to germinate.

WEED CONTROL

A thick, healthy lawn is the best weed control, but sometimes weeds will pop up with even the best lawn care. Never use a chemical weed control the same season you seed. Do not apply weed killers in hot weather. You can apply a single broadleaf weed killer or a commercially prepared mix of weed killers in the spring or early fall. The only way to effectively control crabgrass is to use a pre-emergence material, one that will prevent crabgrass from germinating, in the early spring—but most pre-emergence materials prevent desirable grass from germinating as well.

Weed identification is the key to effective weed control. Tolerance of weeds will cut way back on the need for weed control! Some

Chapter Eight

weeds are really undesirable, but a little clover or a few violets may not be so bad. After all, a weed is in the eye of the beholder.

WATER

This is important: if you cannot water correctly, do not water at all. It is a simple concept, but many people don't get it. You need one inch of water a week, put down all at once, in the early morning.

The truth is, most lawns would rather go dormant in hot weather. Giving a lawn a little water, or a lot in small doses, keeps it going but not thriving. If it gets brown from going dormant, it will recover. If it gets stressed from trying to grow when it should be dormant, you are in much worse trouble. It is definitely better not to water than to do it incorrectly.

DISEASE AND INSECTS

There has been more than one doctoral dissertation written on lawn diseases. Let it suffice to say that it is a rare disease that is worth treating after it has become established. Lawn diseases are extremely weather dependent. By the time you get it identified, chances are the disease will have run its course. Often the grass will recover or you can overseed to fill in any bare spots. It is more important to get the disease identified so you can treat preventively the following year. This is especially beneficial if the same disease shows up repeatedly, year after year.

The most common insect pests are grubs, sod webworms, and chinch bugs. Grubs are the larval stage of beetles, usually but not always Japanese beetles. They feed on roots, causing the grass to pull up like a carpet. The white grubs become C-shaped when disturbed. Sod webworm adults are moths that close up their wings like a cigarette. They fly away as you walk across the lawn. It is the larvae of these moths that actually damage turf, but they are most easily identified and located by the presence of adult moths. Chinch bugs are the smallest, about one-fifth inch long. They are black, but their wings fold over their backs so they look whitish.

Chapter Eight

If you have an insect or disease problem, contact your local County Agricultural Extension Agent to find out the current chemical recommendations for control. They can change frequently.

GRASS SPECIES AND VARIETIES

When it comes to grass varieties, you may have no idea how lucky you are to live in New Jersey. Rutgers University has one of the finest turfgrass-breeding programs in the country, if not the world. Dr. Reed Funk has evaluated, developed, and patented many varieties of grass here in the Garden State. That provides New Jersey home owners with some of the best and most well suited grass varieties that can be found. The lawngrasses presented in this book include the most current recommended varieties. They are taken from the New Jersey breeding program and variety trials done around the country. The list has kindly been provided by Dr. William A. Meyer, Professor of Turfgrass Breeding at Cook College, Rutgers University, and the New Jersey Agricultural Experiment Station.

Bentgrass

Agrostis species

Mown Height: 3/4 in. (mow at 1 1/2 in.) **Color:** Medium green **Texture:** Fine **Zones:** 3, 4, **5, 6, 7,** 8, 9, 10 (variety dependent)	**Light Requirement:**

*B*entgrass is not a great choice for a home lawn. It prefers cool temperatures, sunny conditions, and fertile soils. Don't even think about putting it in shade. It is extremely high maintenance; mowing is frequent, sometimes every other day, and it is subject to a wide variety of insects and disease. Bentgrass is commonly found on golf courses. Colonial bentgrass is sometimes used for home lawns but is more often found on fairways; creeping bentgrass is finer and is used on greens; velvet bentgrass is the finest textured of the three and has the best shade tolerance. When bentgrasses are mixed with other lawngrasses they can become patches that stand out and look more like a weed than a desirable grass. Bentgrass is included here because home owners see it looking great on the golf course and want it in the front yard. No turfgrass professional recommends it for home use. Penn Cross is the old standard variety and is still sold in quantity, but it is not as good as the new releases. If you absolutely must have it, be sure to get the new, better varieties.

Recommended varieties of bentgrass include: South Shore, L93, Pennlinks, and Providence.

Hard Fescue

Festuca longifolia

Mown Height: 2 in. (mow at 4 in.)
Color: Deep green
Texture: Fine
Zones: 4, 5, 6, 7, 8, 9
  (variety dependent)

Light Requirement:

Hard fescues are one of the fine fescues, but they deserve a little attention on their own. Fescues will not tolerate wet sites but are the best grasses for shady locations. Avoid close mowing and excessive fertilization. Hard fescues are non-spreading, so bare spots are not likely to fill in. The hard fescue has a fine texture and is low growing. It may do the best in shade of all the fescues and may have better disease resistance as well.

Recommended varieties of hard fescue include: Discovery, SR3100, Reliant II, Warwick, Ecostar, Brigade, Nordic, Spartan, and Aurora.

Kentucky Bluegrass

Poa pratensis

Mown Height: 2 in. (mow at 4 in.)
Color: Rich, deep green
Texture: Medium
Zones: 3, 4, **5, 6, 7,** 8, 9
   (variety dependent)

Light Requirement:

---

*T*here is no doubt that Kentucky bluegrass is the workhorse of the grass industry. It prefers cool temperatures, adequate soil moisture combined with good drainage, and lots of sunshine. To thrive, bluegrass requires lime and fertilizer. It is not tolerant of even moderate shade and deteriorates with close mowing and poor drainage. Bluegrass can go dormant during hot weather, but it has very good recovery when the weather patterns change in late summer and early fall. There is no single variety that is resistant to all the problems that can plague grass, so it is always a good idea to use a blend of several good quality varieties in your seed mix. There are many good varieties from which to choose.

Recommended varieties of Kentucky bluegrass include: Midnight, America, Princeton 105, Blacksburg, SR2,000, Eclipse, Unique, Shamrock, Washington, Preakness, Suffolk, Ram I, Adelphi, Livingston, Glade, Cheri, Lofts 1757, Julia, Apex, Liberty, Challenger, and Moonlight.

Perennial Ryegrass

Lolium perenne

Mown Height: 2 in. (mow at 4 in.)
Color: Medium green (variety dependent)
Texture: Medium
Zones: Zones: **5, 6, 7,** 8, 9, 10
   (variety dependent)

Light Requirement:

One of the advantages of growing perennial ryegrass is its ability to germinate in 5 to 10 days. This provides quick cover to keep the weeds down while other grasses take their time about coming up. Ryegrasses are more tolerant of shade than bluegrass and will grow in a wide range of soil conditions. Newer varieties are greatly improved with regards to color, persistence, texture, density, and lower-growing habit. The fine turf-type ryegrass will blend well with other grasses, but the mixture will need frequent mowing to stay attractive.

Recommended varieties of perennial ryegrass include: Brightstar II, Palmer III, Premier II, Calypso II, Panther, Monterey, Secretariat, Catalina, Prelude III, Repell III, Divine, Laredo, Citation III, Manhattan III, Prizm, Elf, Accent, Top Hat, and Omega III.

Red Fescue

Festuca rubra

Mown Height: 2 in. (mow at 4 in.) **Color:** Medium green **Texture:** Fine **Zones:** 3, 4, **5, 6, 7,** 8, 9 (variety dependent)	**Light Requirement:**

The red fescues include the chewings and creeping fescues. Chewings fescues are fine leafed and low growing, and they spread very little. Creeping fescue is also fine leafed but will spread a little due to small underground rhizomes. Chewings, creeping, and the hard fescues addressed earlier, make up the fine fescues. They are extremely important, as fine fescues can tolerate moderate shade better than any of the other lawngrasses suited for New Jersey. Fine fescues will also tolerate poor, dry soils. Avoid wet locations, excessive fertilization, and close mowing. They mix well with bluegrass. Even in a sunny area, it is recommended that you have approximately 20 percent fine fescue in the mix. Be aware that Boreal, a variety of creeping fescue, is sold in large quantity and is very inexpensive. It is, however, considered a very poor variety. Avoid it if possible and select an alternative from the following list.

Recommended varieties of chewings fescue include: Shadow II, Magic, Victory II, SR5100, Brittany, Tiffany, Brideport, Treazure, Jamestown II, and Banner II.

Recommended varieties of creeping fescue include: Jasper, Flyer II, Shademaster II, and Salem.

Rough-Stalked Bluegrass

Poa trivialis

Mown Height: 2 in. (mow at 4 in.)
Color: Light green
Texture: Fine
Zones: 3, 4, **5, 6, 7,** 8, 9

Light Requirement:

This is another grass you may come across that is not a good choice for home lawns. You need to know about its characteristics when making important decisions about your lawn. Rough-stalked bluegrass gets its name from the rough sheaths on the individual grass plants. It is very intolerant of hot, dry situations but does well in shade where it is cool and moist. Its light-green color and its tendency to spread along the ground when mowed makes it appear out of place in a well tended lawn. If mixed with other, more desirable grasses in a sunny situation, rough-stalked bluegrass can be considered a weed. Think carefully before including it anywhere, but be sure to use the better varieties if you use it at all. There are not a lot of named varieties from which to choose.

Recommended varieties of rough-stalked bluegrass include: Saber, Laser, and Winter Play.

Tall Fescue

Festuca arundinacea

Mown Height: 2 in. (mow at 4 in.)	Light Requirement:
Color: Medium to dark green	
Texture: Medium to coarse	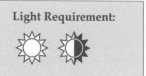
Zones: 5, 6, 7, 8, 9, 10	

*T*all fescue has undergone significant improvements in recent years. It is primarily a bunch-type, cool-season grass, but it spreads ever so slowly from short rhizomes. It also tolerates heat and drought better than the other cool-season grasses and so will hold up in some places where Kentucky bluegrass gives up. Tall fescue is tough and can take foot traffic; it has been used in playgrounds and parks where durability is more important than looks. Definitely more coarse than the fine-leafed bluegrass, it can still be used to mix with bluegrass if mowed regularly. The newer turf-type varieties have been selected for finer texture and better color; objections to their use are dwindling. The new varieties maintain durability but are prettier to look at. The old standby, Kentucky 31, has been around since 1940. It is better than the species, but is still a terrible lawngrass. Stick with the many new and improved varieties.

Recommended varieties of tall fescue include: Crossfire II, Houndog V, Falcon II, Jaguar III, Coyote, Coronado, Southern Choice, Genesis, Pixie, Tomahawk, Barlexas, Lancer, Marksman, Fine Lawn Petite, Virtue, Tulsa, Safari, Rebel Junior, Duster, Cochise, and Apache II.

Zoysiagrass

Zoysia japonica

Mown Height: 1 in. (mow at 2 in.)
Color: Medium to dark green
Texture: Medium
Zones: 5, 6, 7, 8, 9, 10
    (extremely variety dependent)

Light Requirement:

*P*eople either love zoysiagrass or hate it. We receive as many inquiries to learn how to wipe it out as inquiries to learn how to get it established. It is a warm-season grass that will thrive in hot summer weather on dry sandy soils. If you have a shore home that is used primarily in the summer months, it may be a good choice. Once the weather turns cold, zoysiagrass turns brown. It can stay brown for 6 months each year or sometimes even longer. If you aren't there, it doesn't matter, but it is a decided disadvantage for year-round living.

Zoysiagrass is planted from plugs, usually on a grid pattern, and it can take 2 or more years to completely cover an area. Once established, it spreads with enthusiasm and can creep into your neighbor's lawn whether they want it or not. There are not many varieties in the trade and only one recommended for New Jersey.

The recommended variety of zoysiagrass is Meyer.

CHAPTER NINE

Ornamental Grasses

*T*EN YEARS AGO, ORNAMENTAL GRASSES WERE ALMOST UNHEARD OF. The only grass people thought about was that which had to be mowed every Saturday whether they liked it or not. No one ever gave much thought to grasses blooming or being graceful or providing wildlife habitat. Grass formed a lovely green background for everything else.

How things have changed! Ornamental grasses are now front and center. There are grasses for just about every planting need and to suit every environmental possibility. It may come as a big surprise, but many of these grasses are absolutely stunning.

The first time I was impressed with the beauty of grasses was at a large property in Morris County. The landscape was designed by a landscape architect. He wanted to cut down on maintenance and also get the property to blend in with the surrounding rough fields and immature woodland. His suggestion was to simply stop mowing most of the lawn. A half-acre close to the house was still to be tended religiously, but the rest was allowed to do what it wanted. It was mowed once every two years or so and woody material was pulled.

I arrived in late spring. The gently sloping field was a sea of delicate seed stalks proudly waving in the breeze on top of thin green stems. It was so lovely it was breathtaking. What had once been a thick traditional lawn was now something else entirely. The plants were the same, but the effect was dramatically different.

If this can happen with regular lawngrasses, plants selected for their natural beauty have an incredible untapped potential for show-stopping splendor.

Just about every garden center now carries a selection of ornamental grasses, so getting started is not difficult. Unfortunately, grasses in pots can look like a whole lot of nothing. The nature of

Chapter Nine

ornamental grasses is such that many need a mass effect to be seen to their best advantage. Many others can play an important role in the landscape by offering winter interest with their long-lasting plumes. They often will not produce these features in a pot. Don't let scruffy plants in pots discourage you, and don't base your design on what you see at the garden center. Garden catalogs often have pictures that may give a better idea of qualities and attributes than you can get from looking at plants in pots. "Gardening By Mail" by Barbara Barton and published by Mariner Books lists sixty-six mail-order companies that feature ornamental grasses. One of the most complete is from Kurt Bluemel, Inc., located in Baldwin, Maryland. Kurt Bluemel is one of the driving forces behind the explosive ornamental grass industry and has introduced several exceptional new varieties.

The ornamental grasses selected for this book are hardy throughout New Jersey. Great care has been taken to include basic, dependable varieties that are relatively easy-care. The home gardener may enter the world of ornamental grasses with every possible expectation of success. A few less-common varieties have been included to keep things interesting, but none is difficult to grow. All the varieties are available by mail and many can be found at your local garden center.

Ornamental grasses should be an interesting and fun new dimension to your gardening efforts. Don't be afraid to try a plant that is out of the ordinary. These are not oak trees. If you like the results, you will be quite pleased with yourself. If you do not, yank the plants and try something else.

A garden is not something you plant and finish. It is not like laying bricks or pouring concrete. Gardening is an adventure in taming the wilds of nature. It is never really finished, and it is never quite tame. It is the perfect place to try something not quite conventional.

Blue Fescue

Festuca glauca

Other Names: *F. ovina glauca, F. ovina, F. cinerea, F. arvernensis, F. caesia, F. amethystina*, Sheep's Fescue, Blue Sheep's Fescue, Gray Fescue

Light Requirement:

Height: Up to 18 in.
Spread: Up to 12 in.
Flowers: Varies from nonexistent to not showy to very showy
Bloom Period: Summer
Zones: 4, 5, 6, 7, 8

The ornamental fescues are closely related to the lawngrasses but are far more interesting. They are characterized by a blue gray color and a rounded habit. The nomenclature is obviously confused. It is impossible to open a reference book without finding a different grouping of species. The seven botanical names shown above are considered identical to one another in at least one reference, but each is listed as a separate species somewhere else. Your best bet is to stick with named varieties. These are propagated by division and will be consistent regardless of classification. Most of the blue fescues are evergreen clump grasses. Their blue color comes from a glaucous coating on the leaves similar to that on a blue spruce. They are excellent choices for winter interest, for use in a rock garden, or as groundcovers. There are 4 to 6 in. miniature varieties as well as some that may reach 18 in. Most blue fescue are in the 10 to 12 in. range. The close relative *F. gigantea* can reach 2 ft. Some produce very thin, delicate flowers that extend beyond the mounded clump, but blue fescue is cultivated more for its rolled blue gray foliage than for its flowers.

WHEN TO PLANT
Plant in early spring, especially if you are dividing older plants to revitalize them. Early fall is also acceptable.

WHERE TO PLANT
Locate in full sun for the best color. They will survive in light shade, but expect less blue. Choose a well-drained site. They are fun for tucking into rock gardens and for edging paths. The attractive but

neutral color is a good choice for softening bright colors that may clash. In a bed of mixed grasses, blue fescue provide variation in color, height, and habit. The discreet mounds complement the vertical habit of many other popular grasses.

How to Plant

Fescue is drought tolerant, but in really sandy soil you may want to incorporate organic matter into the soil to hold moisture. It establishes easily but may need replanting every 2 to 3 years. You can propagate by seed, but expect variation in height and color. To maintain the characteristics of a named variety, propagate only by division. Set plants 6 to 15 in. apart depending on the variety and the look you desire.

Care and Maintenance

Fescue should be cut back to about 3 in. in the early spring. If the center of the clump has died out, it will be necessary to lift the mound. Remove the outer tufts of healthy fresh growth and replant. Dispose of the older, dead growth from the center. Some varieties will slow down their growth in summer heat. They may even get a little ratty looking. Don't prune while it is hot; the plants do not always recover. In general, they perk up as the weather cools down. If they look really bad, you can prune them in the fall. Because fescues have a mounded shape, they do not provide complete cover of the ground. This means they require frequent weeding. The use of an organic mulch may help reduce the need for hand labor. Insects and diseases are rarely a problem.

Additional Information

Blue fescue is an excellent ornamental grass for use in containers. Its small size and clumping habit allow it to fit without taking over a planter or container. The soft but interesting color allows it to blend with a myriad of colors, and it can tie everything together throughout the season.

Additional Species, Cultivars, or Varieties

There is a long list of varieties; many have names in both German and English. One can only assume that they were developed in Germany and the English translation is provided to make things easier. 'Azurit' (Azure Blue) is 12 to 16 in.; 'Blaufink' (Blue Finch) is a soft blue, fine textured, and 8 to 10 in.; 'Solling' doesn't flower—it reaches 8 in.; 'Daeumling' (Tom Thumb) stays at 4 in. and turns green in summer; 'Elijah Blue' grows to 8 in. It may be the most readily available variety.

Feather Reed Grass

Calamagrostis acutifolia

Other Name: Reed Grass
Height: 5 to 7 ft.
Spread: 24 in.
Flowers: Very slim seedheads that turn
   golden and then golden-brown or silver
Bloom Period: June; seedheads last through
   the following winter
Zones: 5, 6, 7, 8, 9

Light Requirement:

Feather reed grass is a perennial grass that grows in clumps. It can work well mixed with other grasses, but it is showy enough to plant by itself en masse. One of its strong points is its long season of interest. The flowers show up in June with a hint of red; the seedheads mature to a golden tan and last until the following spring. These plumes will tower 3 to 4 ft. over the foliage. They are very useful in dried arrangements or even as filler for fresh flowers. The foliage itself stays at about 2 ft. Grown in full sun, the plumes will be densely packed together and sturdy enough to stay upright through most of the winter. The species will tolerate light shade, but it is not as prolific in flower production as *C. acutifolia*, and its stalks are floppier. This plant's overall look is vertical, but not rigidly so. A single clump can be useful in a small space to create vertical interest year-round without having to use a space-hogging woody ornamental. Although it is not the prominent selling point of this species, the foliage is an attractive arching clump. It will stay evergreen in mild climates, but expect it to be deciduous in most of New Jersey.

WHEN TO PLANT
Spring planting is best in cold climates, but early fall is acceptable in the southern part of the state.

WHERE TO PLANT
A sunny location will encourage the sturdiest plants with the most decorative seedheads. The plant will tolerate light shade if you are just looking for cover. Feather reed grass prefers rich, moist soils, and it will do well in heavy clay. Avoid dry, sandy soils. Planted as

a border plant, it will create a golden band of color for most of the summer and straight through winter. Scattered plants in a mixed border will provide winter interest. Even when used as a single specimen, it can add a dramatic touch. Clumps flanking the front steps can be very interesting, and there is no need to worry that these plants will ever outgrow their allotted space.

How to Plant
Feather reed grass is not difficult to get established. It can be divided in early spring. The addition of organic matter will help it hold on to soil moisture.

Care and Maintenance
Cut feather reed grass back in the spring to see its fresh green growth. Divide in early spring if desired. Water deeply during hot weather. Cut the seed stalks as needed for fresh or dried arrangements. The seeds are generally sterile, so there is little chance that this plant will become invasive. Feather reed grass has no known pest problems.

Additional Information
The botanical name is derived from the Greek word *kalamos*, which means "reed." There are 250 species in the genus, mostly from Europe and Asia. Some species are used as forage grass.

Additional Species, Cultivars, or Varieties
'Karl Foerster' is sometimes listed as *C. arundinacea*. This is a prolific bloomer with sturdy spikes that turn silver-gray. It reaches about 6 ft. and is very popular. 'Stricta' is very similar to 'Karl Foerster', but more golden, with a habit that is slightly more airy. It blooms 2 to 3 weeks later. 'Sierra' turns golden brown. 'Overdam' has foliage variegated in white and green. All of these plants are lovely.

Frost Grass

Spodiopogon sibiricus

Other Names: *Muhlenbergia alpestris,*
Lasiogrostis splendens, Silver Spike,
Graybeard Grass

Height: 2 to 3 ft.; up to 5 ft. when in bloom

Spread: 2 to 3 ft.; spreads with age

Flowers: Upright panicles 3 to 4 in. wide, up
to 12 in. long, held 14 to 18 in. above the
foliage (they emerge with hints of purple
and mature to brown)

Bloom Period: July through August

Zones: 5, 6, 7, 8, 9

Light Requirement:

Frost grass is considered a clump type, but it will spread slowly over time. It has a less typical growth habit since its 6-in. leaves attach to an upright central stalk. The leaves are attractive in their own right. There is a white midrib, and the bright green leaves have a fuzzy quality. In fall they turn brown streaked with shades of deep purple and purple red. The flowers are exceptionally light and airy. Each is covered with fine white hairs. They are held far above the foliage which adds to the feeling of lightness. The spikes appear to be floating above the leaves. At first they have hints of purple, but they mature to a fuzzy brown. The flowers and even the foliage are excellent filler for floral arrangements. The spikes can persist well into winter, but when the foliage begins to deteriorate you may want to cut back the plants. This is a medium sized plant, a good choice for small gardens as well as massing in larger areas. It is not overpowering and provides interesting elements in all seasons but the dead of winter. It gets its common name by being particularly beautiful when its fall color and form are sparkling with an early morning frost.

WHEN TO PLANT
Plant in early spring or early fall.

WHERE TO PLANT
Frost grass prefers full sun but can take a little shade. It is a good choice for use along the edge of woods. Too much shade will cause

the plant to flop over; it will keep growing but will require staking. It is moderately tolerant of shore planting conditions as long as it is not allowed to dry out. Its interesting reedlike leaves and stalks make it suitable for specimen planting or using in clumps. In general, it does better at the northern end of its range, so it should do well just about anywhere in New Jersey.

HOW TO PLANT

It can be planted from seed or divisions in the spring. Container-grown material can be planted in the fall. Since it does not like to dry out, you may have to add significant amounts of organic matter to sandy soils. Cover with a thick layer of organic mulch to help retain soil moisture. It is not difficult to get established.

CARE AND MAINTENANCE

Water thoroughly in hot dry summers. Prune in late fall or early winter if it gets unattractive. It does not appear to have any insect or disease problems.

ADDITIONAL INFORMATION

Frost grass is native to prairies in Siberia. It can also be found in northern China and Korea. Japan introduced it to the rest of the world.

ADDITIONAL SPECIES, CULTIVARS, OR VARIETIES

There are only nine known species in this genus and only the one described here is under cultivation. There are no named varieties mentioned in any of the literature at this time.

Hakonechloa

Hakonechloa macra

Other Names: *Phragmites macra,*
   Hakone Grass
Height: Up to 30 in.
Spread: 24 in. or more
Flowers: Light, open flowers; not very showy
Bloom Period: Late summer
Zones: 4, 5, 6, 7, 8, 9

Light Requirement:

This is one of the better ornamental grasses for growing in shade. It makes an excellent groundcover under tall shade trees (which makes sense because it is native to the forests of Japan). Hakone is an out-of-the-ordinary plant that mixes perfectly with ferns, hostas, and astilbe to add interest to a shady spot. The dark-green color is rich and elegant. Hakonechloa is a slow growing deciduous perennial that spreads from rhizomes but is never invasive. Its habit is almost weeping, but not quite. It will do well on gentle slopes where its graceful arching habit can be best appreciated. Although it does spread, hakone is small enough and sufficiently restrained to be suitable for container culture. It is somewhat exotic, almost like bamboo in appearance, so it makes an excellent choice for Oriental gardens. One of the most wonderful attributes of this plant is its fall color. At first it turns pinkish-red; the winter season ripens it to a rich bronze. It will stay attractive well into winter. To draw attention to its beauty, be sure to plant it among other plants that offer autumn interest.

WHEN TO PLANT
Planting in early spring is best.

WHERE TO PLANT
Hakonechloa needs some shade. Its leaves will burn in full sun, especially during the heat of summer. Plant it under tall shade trees as a groundcover (lawn grass has a hard time growing under these trees). A woodland setting can be lovely, and it will thrive at the edge of woods as well. Since it is suitable for containers and prefers shade, it may be perfect when potted on the front porch or under a pergola. It needs moist soil conditions, good drainage, and high

fertility. It does not want to dry out, nor will it be happy sitting in heavy wet clay. Choosing the right location for hakone grass is essential for success; it will struggle if improperly located.

HOW TO PLANT
It will do best if planted from container stock in the spring. It is also possible to grow it from seed or from divisions made in the spring. If you are starting with heavy clay soil, add a 2:1 mixture of organic matter and sand to lighten the soil and improve drainage. In sandy soils you should add organic matter to hold on to that important soil moisture. Be sure to apply a thick layer of organic mulch to retain soil moisture and keep the soil cool.

CARE AND MAINTENANCE
The most important aspect of care is to keep the plant well watered during hot weather, especially if rainfall has been scant. Replenish the organic mulch as needed. Hakone will do best in a humusy soil, and the mulch will continue to improve the soil as it decomposes. The plant can be cut back in the early spring if necessary. It has no known insect or disease problems.

ADDITIONAL INFORMATION
There are not nearly as many ornamental grasses for shade as there are for sunny areas. The sedges (*Carex species*) are not true grasses, but they are generally grouped with the true grasses because of their similar appearance. They will do well in light shade.

ADDITIONAL SPECIES, CULTIVARS, OR VARIETIES
The variety 'Aureola' is variegated, mostly yellow with streaks of green. It is much easier to find than the species, but it is not as hardy. The literature varies when specifying how far north it will survive; it is hardy to at least Zone 7.

Little Bluestem

Schizachyrium scoparium

Other Names: *Andropogon scoparius*, Prairie
  Beard Grass, Broom Sedge
Height: Generally 2 to 3 ft., may grow up
  to 5 ft.
Spread: 12 to 18 in.
Flowers: Small flower spikes that mature to
  fluffy seedheads
Bloom Period: Spikes emerge July through
  September and last into winter
Zones: 4, 5, 6, 7, 8, 9

Light Requirement:

---

ittle bluestem is not really that little, but it is smaller than its relative 'Big Bluestem', which can reach 6 ft. This species is not even very blue. Its stems are mostly green, and they have a blue cast near the base. The foliage starts out as a light shade of green, and ages to a darker color. Each leaf is up to 1/2 in. wide and 12 to 16 in. long. The leaves are slightly hairy. Little bluestem is native to North America and can be found from Canada south to Florida. It is a prairie grass that grows as far west as Utah, though it is far more common in the east. Little bluestem is a clump grass that can be very effective when planted in a mixed perennial border. Its fall color is its most dramatic attribute. It can turn a golden orange to bronze and is particularly eye-catching after a rain. Its flexible stems endure wind and snow, and the plant holds some color into the winter months. This makes it an excellent choice for mixing with other plants that feature fall and winter interest (such as asters and mums). Little bluestem will thrive in sandy soils and is extremely drought tolerant. It would blend beautifully with the orange berries of sea buckthorn, a medium-sized shrub that is also very tolerant of sandy soil. Little bluestem is adaptable, and will do well in all but soggy ground. When planted in more average soils, little bluestem's lovely fall color can complement the cinnamon colored exfoliating bark of the paper bark maple.

WHEN TO PLANT
Plant early spring or early fall.

WHERE TO PLANT

Little bluestem does best in full sun, but it will tolerate light shade. Its drought tolerance makes it ideal for dry, sandy soils, but it requires a little water during the hottest part of the year. It can be used as part of a mixed border or a mass planting. It is also impressive as a specimen in the right place, perhaps in a small garden. Little bluestem is very effective for erosion control. It is popular in transitional zones between wild areas and those under cultivation. It may reseed and so will probably persist over time.

HOW TO PLANT

Little bluestem can be planted from seed but is more commonly grown from container stock or divisions. You may choose to grow it from seed in a large area; *Taylor's Guide to Ornamental Grasses* suggests the seed be pressed into prepared soil with a lawn roller to help with germination. Little bluestem is flexible regarding soil types and requires no particular attention in order to become established.

CARE AND MAINTENANCE

Cut little bluestem back hard in the early spring. It can be divided at that time if desired. The literature is mixed regarding this plant's ability to reseed. One source credits it with little or no reseeding, while others say it is a potential pest problem. Since it naturally covers a large area, it must have the ability to spread. Just keep an eye on it to make sure it doesn't get out of control. It has no known insects or disease problems, so there is little maintenance required.

ADDITIONAL INFORMATION

The flowers and dried foliage of little bluestem both have ornamental value. The bright fall color is a lovely addition to an arrangement, and the foliage is even suitable for craft projects. The seeds are a natural attraction for small birds.

ADDITIONAL SPECIES, CULTIVARS, OR VARIETIES

There are two varieties currently available. 'Blaze' has pink, orange, red, or purple fall color. 'The Blues' is more blue than the species and has pink stems; it turns rusty red in the fall.

Maiden Grass

Miscanthus sinensis

Other Names: Eulalia Grass, Japanese Silver
Grass, Chinese Silver Grass
Height: 3 to 12 ft.
Spread: 3 ft. and up
Flowers: Silver, tan, reddish, pink, coppery
red, or white; matures to buff or silver
Bloom Period: July to September
Zones: Most varieties **5, 6, 7,** 8, 9

Light Requirement:

---

*M*aiden grass is one of the most popular and versatile of the ornamental grasses. Its many varieties are prized for their graceful foliage that can be variegated green-and-white or green-and-yellow. There are varieties tipped in silver and streaked with red. Fall color can be spectacular. Most are tall and arching, but some are almost rigidly upright. They grow in clumps that get bigger over time, but they do not spread or become invasive. Maiden grass varieties are not particular about soil, and many are commonly planted at the water's edge. Some can even tolerate standing water. Established plants will tolerate drought, although they will look better if watered. They will adapt to an acid or alkaline pH. Although the lovely foliage and cooperative personality do much to recommend these plants, it is the flowers that capture the hearts of grass fanciers. Maiden grass has a long season of bloom and its fluffy seedheads hang on well into winter. The flower spikes emerge in a wide variety of colors, a rare quality in the world of grasses. Almost all the varieties go dormant tan by winter, but the strong lines of the foliage and the skeletons of seedheads continue to add interest until they are cut back in early spring. With the enormous selection of varieties available, many of them modestly priced, there is a *Miscanthus* variety for almost every garden.

WHEN TO PLANT
Miscanthus does best when planted in spring.

WHERE TO PLANT
Certainly planting location will be dependent on the variety. There are dwarf varieties suitable for small gardens, and tall ones that can

make excellent hedges. Mix the varieties with other perennials in a border planting or bed. They are an excellent choice for planting near water, but they are also considered adaptable to shore locations in sandy soil. Sunny locations are best. They will behave acceptably in light shade but may need support.

HOW TO PLANT

They are generally available in containers, although very large clumps can be balled in burlap. They are so adaptable to different types of soil that soil amendments are usually not necessary. It is probably best to avoid seeding since the cultivars will not breed true.

CARE AND MAINTENANCE

Miscanthus should be cut back in early spring. That is when the plants can be divided, if desired, but the impenetrable root system requires an ax or saw to make the divisions. In general, they have no serious insects or diseases, but occasional rust and mealybugs do show up. The plants generally recover on their own from all but the most serious cases. Flopping can be a problem with some varieties, as can dying out in the center of the clump.

ADDITIONAL INFORMATION

Some varieties have been reported to be under cultivation in Asia for centuries. Here in the United States, maiden grass was very popular in Victorian times. Old clumps can still be spotted near old houses.

ADDITIONAL SPECIES, CULTIVARS, OR VARIETIES

The following is just a sampling of what is currently available. 'Gracillimus' is one of the oldest; very fine but very hardy, it can reach 6 ft. 'Morning Light' is newer and smaller (5 ft.). It is similar to 'Gracillimus' but has a white stripe on its foliage; its late flowers emerge pinkish bronze. 'Little Fountain' stays 3 to 4 ft. and blooms for weeks; it is a good choice for a smaller garden or in front of taller varieties. Some credit 'Sirene' with having the best plumes; the abundant flowers rise above the 5 to 6 ft. foliage. 'Strictus' is variegated green-and-yellow with an upright habit; 'Zebrinus' is very similar but has an arching habit. 'Purpurascens' is called flame grass because of its spectacular red orange fall color which matures to purple red; it may be hardy only to Zone 6. 'Hercules' is similar in habit. It is also red in the fall but not quite as brilliant as flame grass; it is, however, hardy to Zone 5.

Moor Grass

Molinia caerulea

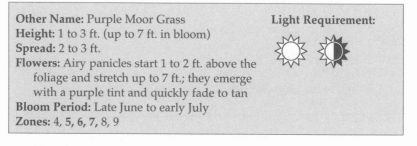

Other Name: Purple Moor Grass
Height: 1 to 3 ft. (up to 7 ft. in bloom)
Spread: 2 to 3 ft.
Flowers: Airy panicles start 1 to 2 ft. above the
    foliage and stretch up to 7 ft.; they emerge
    with a purple tint and quickly fade to tan
Bloom Period: Late June to early July
Zones: 4, 5, 6, 7, 8, 9

Light Requirement:

*M*oor grasses are native to Europe and Asia. They can be found in bogs and in open moors, which accounts for their common name. Moor grass has several distinctive characteristics that can be used to advantage in many garden settings. The plants themselves stay compact. They are unusually slow growing and form tight mounds of slightly arching foliage. Some varieties are variegated. In fall, most turn a bright yellow with an occasional hint of orange. 'Moorflamme' turns orange red. The abundant flowers emerge in early summer and tower over the compact plants. The panicles shoot up on stiff but delicate stems. The spike does not initiate until the stem has risen several ft. above the leaves. Each panicle is long and open; the panicles add the impression of height without blocking the view. Since moor grass grows slowly, it may take two or three years in the garden before you see a bloom. If you start with the biggest clumps possible, you cut down on the wait. But don't let the wait discourage you—moor grass is worth waiting for. The flowers will last well into fall but not through the winter. Moor grass is one of the few ornamental grasses (actually one of the few perennials) that completely sheds its old growth. The leaves and stems break off near ground surface where the plant has bulblike structures. If you want winter interest, this plant is not a good choice. When the grass is planted near gazebos, ponds, swimming pools, and other places less frequently visited in winter, its self-pruning will cut down on maintenance chores, and there will be no loss of summer beauty. Moor grass will eventually self-sow, but the plants take so long to grow to any size that this is rarely a problem.

WHEN TO PLANT
Moor grass does best when planted in spring.

WHERE TO PLANT
Moor grass is happiest in full sun but will accept light shade. Moist, fertile ground is best; definitely avoid dry alkaline soils. It will do well in the shore area, but perhaps not right on the beach. Mix with perennials or other grasses in a bed or border. In the right spot, the tight, slow growing mound can make a lovely specimen plant.

HOW TO PLANT
The addition of organic matter will help keep the soil moist. Do not add lime. Start with divisions or potted plants that are as large as possible. This will cut down on the wait for flowers. To get flowers the first year, plant divisions the size of a softball. You can grow moor grass from seed, but it will be years before the plants mature enough to bloom.

CARE AND MAINTENANCE
Moor grass requires little care since it self-cleans and grows slowly. Water in hot, dry summers will be appreciated. It has no known pest problems. You may want to cut the elegant flowers for both fresh and dried arrangements.

ADDITIONAL INFORMATION
Consider planting moor grass against a dark backdrop. Its open, airy flowers are profuse but transparent; with a contrasting background they will show to perfection.

ADDITIONAL SPECIES, CULTIVARS, OR VARIETIES
Tall moor grass (*M. litorialis, M. c. var. arundinacea, M. arundinacea* or *M. a. var. altissima*) has larger foliage and taller flowers. 'Skyracer' can reach 8 to 9 ft. Varieties of moor grass include the popular 'Variegata', whose leaves are striped in creamy white. 'Heidebraut' ('Heather Bride') has very upright flowers in large numbers. 'Dauerstrahl' ('Faithful Ray') has arching flowers that create a pleasing rounded outline; it blooms in July and August.

ORNAMENTAL GRASSES

Northern Sea Oats

Chasmanthium latifolium

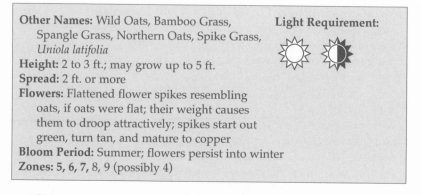

Other Names: Wild Oats, Bamboo Grass,
   Spangle Grass, Northern Oats, Spike Grass,
   Uniola latifolia
Height: 2 to 3 ft.; may grow up to 5 ft.
Spread: 2 ft. or more
Flowers: Flattened flower spikes resembling
   oats, if oats were flat; their weight causes
   them to droop attractively; spikes start out
   green, turn tan, and mature to copper
Bloom Period: Summer; flowers persist into winter
Zones: 5, 6, 7, 8, 9 (possibly 4)

Light Requirement:

The drooping clusters of seeds of northern sea oats are irresistible. This plant has an upright habit, but its heavy seeds weigh down its branches. The highly ornamental seed clusters can be an inch wide and 2 in. long. They arch gracefully over the branches and dangle, bob, and sway in the tiniest whispers of breeze. Spikes emerge green but mature to tan, and are ultimately tinged with copper. Northern sea oats seed spikes can hold up well into winter. They look most dramatic against a snowy setting. The spikes are coveted for use in dried arrangements, as they last for up to a year. The foliage color will be dark green if planted in its preferred site of partial shade. The more sun this plant receives, the lighter green it will be. The leaves are wide for grass, up to 3/4 in., and they are set along a central stalk. This gives the plant the bamboolike appearance which accounts for one of its many common names. The clumps will increase in size, but unlike bamboo, they are (thankfully!) not aggressive from the roots. There may be more of a problem with self-sowing. Northern sea oats will spread from seed, sometimes rapidly. This is a bigger problem in areas of high moisture; dry ground tends to slow it down significantly.

WHEN TO PLANT

Northern sea oats does best when planted in spring.

Where to Plant

This plant can grow in sun or shade, but in dry soil, the tips of the leaves will tend to dry in full sun. Northern sea oats is salt tolerant and recommended for shore plantings. Its dangling seedheads can be particularly lovely for use by ponds and water gardens. It does well when planted in containers or mass planted on slopes and open fields.

How to Plant

Moist, fertile soil is preferred, so the addition of organic matter, such as leaf compost, will be beneficial. Plants are usually available in containers. They can be grown from seed, or established plants can be divided in the early spring. Recommended spacing for mass planting is 2 ft.

Care and Maintenance

Northern sea oats will have to be cut back severely in late winter or early spring. Keep an eye out for seedlings, and prevent them from spreading where you do not want them. Divide if clumps are overgrown and flowering has become disappointing. This plant has no known pest problems, which helps keep it low-maintenance. In full sun, it will appreciate an occasional deep watering during hot, dry weather.

Additional Information

Northern sea oats is native to North America. It can be found wild from Pennsylvania south to Florida and west to Texas. Donald Wyman considers it one of the best native ornamental grasses.

Additional Species, Cultivars, or Varieties

There are five species in the genus, but only *C. latifolium* is cultivated to any significant degree. This one has enough common names to start its own tribe, but they are all the same plant. There are no known cultivars available at this time, but with the rising tide of interest in ornamental grasses, that may change at any time.

Plantain-Leaved Sedge

Carex plantaginea

Height: 1 to 2 ft. **Spread:** 1 to 1½ ft. **Flowers:** Separate male and female flowers on three-sided stalks **Bloom Period:** Early spring **Zones:** 5, 6, 7, 8, 9 (possibly 4)	**Light Requirement:**

*S*edges are not true grasses, but they have grasslike foliage and are generally planted with true grasses for ornamental purposes. *Carex* species have one distinct advantage over true grasses: they are very tolerant of shade. The foliage of many *Carex* species is evergreen, and the clumps they form are generally well behaved. The narrow leaves come in a variety of colors including copper, gold, silver, white stripes, pink new growth, blue green, and yellow borders. The leaves can be straight, curled, whorled, palmlike, or draping. Most sedges tend to be small. The largest reach 3 ft., but many petite varieties stay under a foot (as tiny as 4 inches!). The smaller varieties are suitable for container culture and for tucking into the nooks of rock gardens. A few don't get any taller than 3 ft. but have leaves that trail for 6 ft. Out of this enormous selection, many are hardy only to Zone 7, so be sure to inquire about the ones that pique your interest. There are plenty from which to choose for New Jersey gardens. Plantain-leaved sedge was selected here due to its hardiness and easy care. Its bright-green leaves make an excellent groundcover in shady areas. It looks very much at home planted with ferns, hostas, and trilliums, or mixed into a bed of periwinkle for contrast. The spring flowers are typical of sedges, although slightly showier than most. They are brown, almost black, and held above the newly emerging spring leaves. They are attractive when cut for a vase.

WHEN TO PLANT
Plant in early spring or early fall.

WHERE TO PLANT
Plantain-leaved sedge is a good choice for planting near water, as long as it is receives some shade. It does best in moist, fertile soil,

but since New Jersey is the northern part of its range, it will tolerate drier conditions as long as it is out of the sun. Use it to line paths or fill in around azaleas and rhododendrons. It makes an attractive groundcover that will spread but not be invasive.

How to Plant

This *Carex*, like many others, is not difficult to establish. It is wise to add a generous amount of organic matter to hold soil moisture in dry soils. The use of a thick organic mulch will help recreate the forest floor environment similar to its native habitat. It is generally available as a container grown plant, but it can be started from divisions or seed.

Care and Maintenance

Water in hot, dry weather is essential, especially in sunnier locations. If brown tips develop on the leaves, they can be trimmed with sharp scissors. Keep them thoroughly mulched. They may self-sow when grown under preferred conditions. Plantain-leaved sedge is a low maintenance plant with no known significant problems.

Additional Information

There are over 2,000 species of sedges found all around the world, most in cool, wet climates. In addition, there are many varieties and selections. Some do well in dry or sunny situations, while others will tolerate occasional submersion. Plantain-leaved sedge is native to the Eastern forests of North America. It is an excellent example of a high-quality native plant that can be tamed in the garden.

Additional Species, Cultivars, or Varieties

The following varieties all have hardiness ratings that include Zones 5, 6, and 7 and so are hardy throughout the Garden State. *C. digitata* reaches only 8 in. *C. elata* 'Bowles Golden' is 2 to 3 ft. tall; it has yellow foliage with green edges. *C. glauca* is the blue sedge; it remains at 6 in. *C. nigra*, the black-blooming sedge, grows 6 to 9 in. and is a good choice for rock gardens. *C. pendula* is the drooping sedge grass. The last one is a must for anyone who has a soft spot in their heart for the '60s! It is *C. speciosa* 'The Beatles', the mop-headed sedge grass. It is tiny, reaching only 4 in.

Prairie Dropseed

Sporobolus heterolepsis

Other Name: Northern Dropseed
Height: Up to 3 ft.
Spread: Up to 2 ft.
Flowers: Panicles of delicate, fragrant flowers held 2 to 3 ft. above the leaves; the heavy seeds may weigh down the stems
Bloom Period: August through October
Zones: 4, 5, 6, 7, 8, 9

Light Requirement:

This native American grass once filled the western prairies, and its seed was harvested for food by Native Americans. The common name "dropseed" comes from the plant's tendency to easily drop its seed from mature seedheads. Its natural range has been devastated by excessive grazing and modern agriculture. Of the many ornamental grasses available to home gardeners, this species is considered a good choice for beginners. The graceful mounds blend with other perennials in a border or bed or even as a foundation plant. It can make a smooth transition between wild and cultivated areas. The delicate sweet scent of the flowers lasts through September. This fragrance is not typical of flowers, and it has been compared to buttered popcorn. The autumn foliage color is a uniform, rich orange-gold. As winter progresses, the color matures to creamy brown. It stays very attractive through the winter. Prairie dropseed will tolerate dry, rocky soil, a trait not common among ornamental grasses. It prefers full sun but will tolerate light shade. Sometimes flopping becomes a problem if there is too much shade. It is extremely heat and drought tolerant.

When to Plant

It is best planted in spring, although some sources indicate fall planting is successful.

Where to Plant

Full sun is much preferred. This plant will tolerate dry, rocky soil, and it will do just fine in a wide range of soil conditions. Prairie dropseed does need the soil to be well-drained. It can be planted as a groundcover for large areas, but in most gardens it will be used to its best advantage when mixed with other grasses or perennials.

How to Plant

Prairie dropseed is generally available as a container plant. Try to find 2 year plants, if possible, as it grows slowly and takes 3 years to bloom. Prairie dropseed requires little soil preparation unless drainage is an issue. If mowed in the spring it will drop its seed and may be self-sowing, but it is not invasive. It can also be divided in spring, but make the division a large size to cut down on the time it takes to get established.

Care and Maintenance

This plant should be cut back in the spring. Its slow growth rate eliminates the need for frequent division. It has no pest problems, so it should be very easy to maintain.

Additional Information

The seeds of prairie dropseed are attractive to birds and other wildlife.

Additional Species, Cultivars, or Varieties

There are about 100 species from different parts of the world, but few are under cultivation. *S. airoides* is the alkali dropseed. It is used for mass planting, but is hardy only to Zone 7. There are no varieties of prairie dropseed at this time.

Snowy Wood Rush

Luzula nivea

Other Name: *Juncoides* (old)
Height: 2 ft.
Spread: 8 to 12 in.
Flowers: Almost white flowers in umbels
  1/2 to 3/4 in. across
Bloom Period: Very early spring
Zones: 4, **5, 6, 7,** 8, 9

Light Requirement:

Snowy wood rush is not a true grass, but it has grasslike foliage. There are about 80 species in the wood rush genus, all perennial. Some are native to North America, but those under cultivation are primarily of European origin. *Luzula* is in the same family as *Juncus*, the true rushes, but it differs in that it has tiny hairs along the leaf margins or completely covering the leaf surface. True rushes thrive in boggy, wet sites, while their drier woodland cousins prefer moist, humusy soil in a shady spot. *L. nivea* may be the most ornamental of the wood rushes. It is one of the European species and can be found in the wild from Spain to Poland. The diminutive clumps are pleasing both to the eye and to touch. The tiny hairs on the gray-green leaves give the plant a soft, velvety feel. The species is considered evergreen, but it may not hold up to perfection through the entire winter. The very early spring flowers of snowy wood rush are among the first to bloom. In the shade they love, snowy wood rush can be planted with trilliums, bloodroot, and violets. The flowers are an ivory white and arranged in "umbels" (clusters that resemble an upside-down umbrella). The flowers are taller than the leafy mounds and quite showy. The ivory color mellows to a creamy beige as the flowers dry, continuing to add their appeal above the foliage after other spring blooms are gone. The slender stems are tall enough to make excellent cut flowers, fresh or dry.

WHEN TO PLANT
Snowy wood rush can be planted in early spring or early fall.

WHERE TO PLANT
A woodland setting of rich, moist, humusy soil is ideal, but these are cooperative small plants. They burn in the hottest part of their

range if planted in full sun, but they will likely survive full sun in most of New Jersey. They can be used under trees as a groundcover, mixed in a border with other perennials, or used as a specimen. Snowy wood rush is an excellent choice for shaded rock gardens.

How to Plant
It is always a good idea to try to copy the conditions of a plant's natural environment. Woodland soil is rich in organic matter from the annual dropping of leaves. The addition of significant amounts of leaf compost will make a close approximation. The use of an organic mulch is beneficial as well. Snowy wood rush is usually grown from container stock. The species can be propagated by seed. Divide established plants in early spring.

Care and Maintenance
Prune back flower stalks as needed. Cut back foliage in late winter if it looks less than acceptable. Snowy wood rush has no known pests or other problems.

Additional Information
The delicate leaf hairs of this plant catch and hold moisture. *L. nivea* is particularly lovely when the morning sun shines across its dew-laden leaves. One source credits this sight with the origin of its botanical name. *Luzula* is derived from the Latin "luciola," which means "glowworm." Another source says it comes from the Latin "lux," meaning "light." At least they both seem to be on the same track.

Additional Species, Cultivars, or Varieties
L. nivea has two varieties you may be able to locate. 'Snowbird' has pure-white flowers; 'Schneehaeschen' or 'Snow Hare' has long-haired white flowers. There are some related species, including *L. pilosa*, the hairy wood rush, whose foliage is quite fuzzy. The variety 'Gruenfink' or 'Green finch' is considered an improvement on this species. *L. purpurea* has a purple tint in its foliage later in the season. *L. maxima* (*L. sylvatica*) is the greater wood rush (even though it is really quite small). It stays at 1 ft., is more reliably evergreen, and has yellow-green flowers in March or April. There are several available varieties: 'Hohe Tatra' forms upright clumps, 'Marginata' has gold edges on its leaves, 'Farnfreund' or 'Fern Friend' is a compact variety, and 'Tauern Pass' has a matlike habit.

Switch Grass

Panicum virgatum

Other Name: Panic Grass
Height: 3 to 7 ft.
Spread: 2 to 3 ft.
Flowers: Panicles lightly tinted in pink,
    red, or silver; they grow 1 to 2 ft.
    above the leaves
Bloom Period: Open in July; persist all winter
Zones: 5, 6, 7, 8, 9

Light Requirement:

This native American has long been cultivated in Europe, especially in Germany, but it is only recently gaining popularity as an ornamental in the States. Perhaps it is difficult to appreciate what is in one's own backyard. Switch grass can be found across the entire eastern United States and west to Colorado. The tall-grass prairies were once a sea of switch grass undulating in the breeze. Between the tall, upright plants and the flowers towering above, this must have been a spectacular sight. Add the thought of its vivid fall color and the image can boggle the mind. Today, switch-grass is making great strides in the ornamental industry. New varieties are being regularly released. It is easy to grow and is adaptable to a wide range of soil types and moisture conditions. It even tolerates wind and salt spray for shore plantings. The clump habit may spread slightly, but it does not usually become a problem. Since it holds its winter foliage, it can be used as a border planting. The bold shape and flower skeletons can be particularly interesting when covered in snow. In summer, use switch grass to hide a view, or even better, to carve out a private nook. The flowers shoot straight up like a rocket and then splay open like fireworks. They are beautiful as fresh flowers, or elegant and long lasting once they dry. To all these features add remarkable fall color. Strong shades of yellow dominate, but there are varieties with orange red to rusty red to purple red autumn foliage.

WHEN TO PLANT
Plant in early spring or early fall.

WHERE TO PLANT

Switch grass will do best in a sunny location, but it will tolerate light shade. Too much shade will cause it to flop over. Moist, fertile soil is ideal, but it will grow even under extreme conditions. Use it as an untamed hedge or as part of a mixed planting of grasses and perennials. It works well as a screen, or place a pair of clumps as a focal point. In a natural setting, switch grass will attract wildlife. Its inborn tolerance for seashore conditions makes it indispensable in that setting. That same tough quality gives it distinct advantages for growing along highways and roadsides. It is used for groundcover as erosion control and in land reclamation projects.

HOW TO PLANT

Switch grass can be planted from seed, but take care with mixed prairie seedings, as switch grass can take over a seed mix. It is most commonly planted from container grown stock. Propagation is by division, especially of named varieties, in the spring. It is not difficult to get established and requires no particular preparation of most soils.

CARE AND MAINTENANCE

It can be cut back in the spring, but the new growth will grow up through the old without much fuss if you prefer not to bother. This native is drought tolerant, but it may look better with an occasional watering during a hot, dry summer. Switch grass has no known pest problems.

ADDITIONAL INFORMATION

There are over 600 species of *Panicum* grasses. The genus name is taken from the old Latin name for Italian millet. *P. miliaceum* is the true millet, cultivated for its small round white seeds commonly used in birdseed mixtures.

ADDITIONAL SPECIES, CULTIVARS, OR VARIETIES

'Cloud Nine' grows 4 to 6 ft. tall with blue-gray foliage and reddish flower plumes. It gets rave reviews in all the literature. 'Heavy Metal' is a little smaller, in the 3 to 5 ft. range. It also has metallic blue foliage, but it maintains an almost columnar habit. 'Rotstrahlbusch' or 'Red rays' is considered the reddest of the reds. 'Squaw' has pink flower spikes in August with red fall color, but it stays small—3 to 4 ft. 'Warrior' is similar and has even redder fall color, but it is a little taller.

Gardening
is an adventure
in taming
the wilds of
nature.

The New Jersey Gardener's Guide

Photographic gallery of featured plants

Selective photography courtesy of the author

SHADE TREES

Ginkgo
Ginkgo biloba

Heritage River Birch
Betula nigra 'Heritage'

October Glory Red Maple
Acer rubrum 'October Glory'

Purple Beech
Fagus sylvatica 'Riversii'

Red Oak
Quercus rubra

Tulip Tree
Liriodendron tulipifera

EVERGREEN TREES

American Holly
Ilex opaca

Colorado Blue Spruce
Picea pungens

Cryptomeria
Cryptomeria japonica

Douglas Fir
Pseudotsuga menziesii

Fraser Fir
Abies fraseri

Himalyan Pine
Pinus wallichiana

Serbian Spruce
Picea omorika

Swiss Stone Pine
Pinus cembra

Umbrella Pine
Sciadopitys verticillata

White Fir
Abies concolor

White Pine
Pinus strobus

Flowering Crab Apple
Malus species

Franklinia
Franklinia alatamaha

Fringetree
Chionanthus virginicus

Japanese Snowbell
Styrax japonicus

Kousa Dogwood
Cornus kousa

Kwanzan Cherry
Prunus serrulata 'Kwanzan'

Purple Leaf Plum
Prunus cerasifera
'Atropurpurea'

Stellar Series Hybrid Dogwoods
Cornus kousa × C. florida

Saucer Magnolia
Magnolia × soulangiana

Scholartree
Sophora japonica

Stewartia
Stewartia pseudocamellia

Weeping Japanese Cherry
Prunus subhirtella 'Pendula'

Arborvitae
Thuja occidentalis

Andromeda
Pieris japonica

Azalea
Rhododendron hybrids

Bumald Spirea
Spirea × bumalda

Doublefile Viburnum
Viburnum plicatum var. *tomentosum*

Dwarf Alberta Spruce
Picea glauca 'Conica'

Eastern Redcedar
Juniperus virginiana

Forsythia
Forsythia × intermedia

Junipers
Juniperus species

Lilac
Syringa vulgaris

Oak Leaf Hydrangea
Hydrangea quercifolia

Old Fashioned Weigela
Weigela florida

PeeGee Hydrangea
Hydrangea paniculata 'Grandiflora'

Rhododendron
Rhododendron catawbiense

Saint Johnswort
Hypericum prolificum

Sand Cherry
Prunus × cistena

Vanhoutte Spirea
Spiraea × vanhouttei

Virginia Sweetspire
Itea virginica

Winged Euonymus
Euonymus alatus

PLANTS FOR WINTER INTEREST

PLANTS FOR DOWN THE SHORE

Winterberry Holly
Ilex verticillata

Witch Hazel
Hamamelis virginiana

Yew
Taxus cuspidata

Contorted Mulberry
Morus 'Contorta'

Dragon's Eye Pine
Pinus densiflora 'Oculus-draconis'

Harry Lauder's Walking Stick
Corylus avellana 'Contorta'

Japanese Fantail Willow
Salix saçhalinensis 'Sekka'

Lacebark Pine
Pinus bungeana

Paperbark Maple
Acer griseum

Redosier Dogwood
Cornus sericea

Weeping Norway Spruce
Picea abies 'Pendula'

Bayberry
Myrica pensylvanica

Beach Plum
Prunus maritima

Common Sea Buckthorn
Hippophae rhamnoides

Japanese Black Pine
Pinus thunbergiana

Summersweet
Clethra alnifolia

Tamarix
Tamarix ramosissima

Clematis
Clematis hybrids

Climbing Hydrangea
Hydrangea anomala subsp. *petiolaris*

Fiveleaf Akebia
Akebia quinata

Japanese Wisteria
Wisteria floribunda

Kolomikta Vine
Actinidia kolomikta

Silver Lace Vine
Polygonum aubertii

Blue Fescue
Festuca glauca

Feather Reed Grass
Calamagrostis acutifolia

Frost Grass
Spodiopogon sibiricus

Hakonechloa
Hakonechloa macra

Little Bluestem
Schizachyrium scoparium

Maiden Grass
Miscanthus sinensis

Moor Grass
Molinia caerulea

Northern Sea Oats
Chasmanthium latifolium

Plantain-Leaved Sedge
Carex plantaginea

Prairie Dropseed
Sporobolus heterolepis

Snowy Wood Rush
Luzula nivea

Switch Grass
Panicum virgatum

Bugleweed
Ajuga reptans

Creeping Juniper
Juniperus horizontalis

Dwarf Japanese Juniper
Juniperus procumbens 'Nana'

English Ivy
Hedera helix

Lamb's Ears
Stachys byzantina

Moss Pink
Phlox subulata

Pachysandra
Pachysandra terminalis

Periwinkle
Vinca minor

Sweet Woodruff
Galium odoratum

Wintergreen
Gaultheria procumbens

'Carefree Beauty' Shrub Rose
Rosa

'Fragrant Cloud' Hybrid Tea Rose
Rosa

'Love' Grandiflora Rose
Rosa

'New Dawn' Climbing Rose
Rosa

'Rise 'N' Shine' Miniature Rose
Rosa

Rugosa Rose
Rosa Rugosa

'Trumpeter' Floribunda Rose
Rosa

Asters
Aster species

Astilbe
Astilbe × arendsii

Bee Balm
Monarda didyma

Black-Eyed Susan
Rudbeckia fulgida

Blanketflower
Gaillardia × grandiflora

Bleeding Heart
Dicentra spectabilis

Candytuft
Iberis sempervirens

Christmas Rose
Helleborus niger

Columbine
Aquilegia × hybrida

Daylily
Hemerocallis hybrids

Evening Primrose
Oenothera species

False Dragonhead
Physostegia virginiana

Hosta
Hosta species

Iris
Iris species

Mums
Chrysanthemum species

Oriental Poppy
Papaver orientale

Peonies
Paeonia lactiflora

Purple Coneflower
Echinacea purpurea

Rose Mallow
Hibiscus moscheutos

Shasta Daisy
Chrysanthemum × superbum

Yarrow
Achillea millefolium

Autumn Crocus
Colchicum autumnale

Calla Lily
Zantedeschia species

Canna
Canna × *generalis*

Crocus
Crocus species

Crown Imperial
Fritillaria imperialis

Daffodil
Narcissus species

Dahlia
Dahlia pinnata hybrids

Dogtooth Violet
Erythronium americanum

Fall Blooming Crocus
Crocus species

Flowering Onion
Allium species

Gladiolus
Gladiolus × *hortulanus*

Glory-of-the-Snow
Chionodoxa luciliae

Grape Hyacinth
Muscari armeniacum

Hyacinth
Hyacinthus orientalis

Lily
Lilium species

Magic Lily
Lycoris squamigera

Peruvian Daffodil
Hymenocallis narcissiflora

Reticulated Iris
Iris reticulata

Snowdrop
Galanthus elwesii

Tulip
Tulipa species

Wild Hyacinth
Camassia leichtlinii

Winter Aconite
Eranthis hyemalis

Alyssum
Lobularia maritima

ANNUALS

Annual Vinca
Catharanthus roseus

Bachelor's Buttons
Centaurea cyanus

Begonia
Begonia semperflorens-cultorum

Black-Eyed Susan Vine
Thunbergia alata

Celosia
Celosia cristata

Cosmos
Cosmos bipinnatus

Geranium
Pelargonium × hortorum

Globe Amaranth
Gomphrena globosa

Impatiens
Impatiens wallerana

Lobelia
Lobelia erinus

Marigold
Tagetes species

Ornamental Cabbage
Brassica oleracea

Pansy
Viola wittrockiana

Petunia
Petunia × hybrida

Poppy
Papaver rhoeas

Portulaca
Portulaca grandiflora

Snapdragon
Antirrhinum majus

Spider Flower
Cleome hasslerna

Strawflower
Helichrysum bracteatum

Sunflower
Helianthus annuus

Verbena
Verbena × hybrida

Wishbone Flower
Torenia fournieri

Zinnia
Zinnia elegans

USDA PLANT
HARDINESS MAP

New Jersey

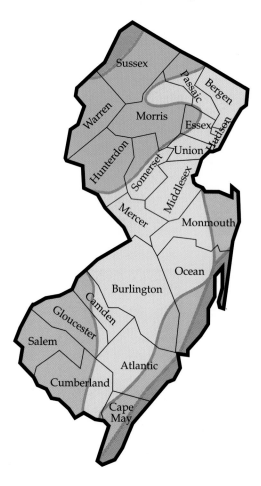

AVERAGE ANNUAL MINIMUM TEMPERATURE

Temperature (C°)				Temperature (F°)		
-23.4	to	-26.1	5B	-10	to	-15
-20.6	to	-23.3	6A	-5	to	-10
-17.8	to	-20.5	6B	-0	to	-5
-15.0	to	-17.7	7A	5	to	0
-12.3	to	-15.0	7B	10	to	5

*It is never
really finished,
and it is never
quite tame.
It is the perfect
place to try
something
not quite
conventional.*

CHAPTER TEN

Groundcovers

*G*ROUNDCOVERS ARE EXTREMELY USEFUL FOR COVER-ING THE GROUND. This may sound like an oversimplification, but it is the practical truth. If you don't cover the ground with something, nature takes over and you begin the natural stages of succession. Wait long enough and you will have a mature forest.

The most popular groundcover is grass. This ubiquitous green carpet holds up under foot traffic, is pleasing to the eye, and creates an environment conducive to family life. Good quality grass is, however, rather high maintenance. Forcing grass to grow where it doesn't feel comfortable can be a constant battle.

There are also places where grass is inappropriate. You wouldn't want grass under the shrubs, and no one wants to mow in a rock garden. Steep slopes can be dangerous, and you may not want to spend your time mowing the grass at a weekend getaway house.

Determine how much grass you need to satisfy the demands of your family's activities. Then decide how much of what is left you can cover with groundcover.

Groundcovers add interest. They have texture and color and sometimes even flowers. Most groundcovers hug the ground and stay under eighteen inches tall. Up to three feet may be acceptable, but the size of the groundcover needs to be in proportion to the scope of the ground you are covering.

The popular switch grass, *Panicum variagata*, reaches seven feet, and it did a fine job of covering the vast grass prairies. It is a good choice for erosion control and taming open fields in a hurry. The tiny leafed, six-inch saxifrage 'London Pride' is perfect in a rock garden outside a new townhouse, but it isn't going to keep three acres of soil in place.

The amount of sunlight available also affects your choice. If a townhouse rock garden is in blazing sun, you may want to try one of the sedums.

A great place to substitute groundcovers for grass is beneath shade trees. The shade, along with the root competition from the trees, can make growing grass almost impossible. Mowing whatever does grow is another problem, since surface roots will interfere, and an occasional nick in the bark is not good for the tree.

Any of the "Big Three" (pachysandra, ivy, and myrtle) will do the job, but try something a little different. Bunchberry is related to our native dogwood; it is a beautiful groundcover that thrives in the shade, but only in the coldest part of the state. Liriope is an evergreen with strappy leaves and late-summer flowers. Pink-flowered lily of the valley is a dusty pink.

Grass doesn't stand a chance in wet ground, but you can try *Houttuynia cordata* 'Chameleon'. It grows vigorously in full sun and gives you a blast of color with leaves showing yellow, green, bronze, and scarlet. It prefers very moist soil and tolerates soil that is constantly wet.

Use groundcovers to connect beds and to provide definition of space. They can be helpful in directing the flow of foot traffic. Once established, they are invaluable in controlling weeds.

Grass is a basic component of your landscape design. Groundcovers help grass be at its best by eliminating places where grass is less than ideal. While groundcovers will never replace your perennials and woody ornamentals for interest, they do offer a bit of zing to the otherwise mundane. If grass were a loaf of sandwich bread, then groundcovers are English muffins and bagels and crusty Italian bread and maybe even corn muffins. Indulge a little!

Bugleweed

Ajuga reptans

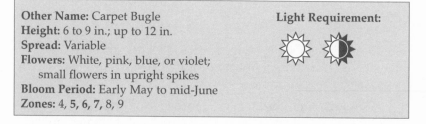

Other Name: Carpet Bugle
Height: 6 to 9 in.; up to 12 in.
Spread: Variable
Flowers: White, pink, blue, or violet;
   small flowers in upright spikes
Bloom Period: Early May to mid-June
Zones: 4, 5, 6, 7, 8, 9

Light Requirement:

Bugleweed forms a solid mat of leaves that are interesting both in texture and color. The species is dark green, but the varieties get outrageous with purple and even multicolored variegation. In partial shade, the leaves reach 4 in. Full sun keeps them slightly smaller, but the colors are more vivid. *Ajuga* is in the mint family and has mint's enthusiasm for spreading. The plants send out runners up to 10 in. long, and they can put down roots along the way. If left to fend for itself, bugleweed will creep its way into the lawn and may become a weed problem. The use of substantial edging such as railroad ties or larger rocks will cut down on its "creepiness." The flowers are held above the foliage in 4- to 5-in. spikes. For such a small plant, it puts on a significant display. It will eventually reseed itself, but the seedlings tend to revert back to the species type. If you have planted a particular variety and you wish to maintain it, weeding out the volunteer seedlings is a must. You can also replant the bed whenever it gets all jumbled together. Mowing the flowers as they fade, but before the seeds mature, will cut back on seed dispersal.

WHEN TO PLANT
Planting in early spring is best.

WHERE TO PLANT
It will do well in both sun and shade, but its colors are brighter in sun. Avoid very hot and dry locations. It is an excellent choice for under trees or along borders. Since it will invade your lawn, use as an edge planting can be risky unless you install something sturdy to contain it.

How to Plant

Bugleweed can be planted from seed, but that usually results in species type plants. Container grown plants are generally available, and you can sometimes purchase them by the flat. In the spring, divide the established plants or transplant some of the rooted runners the plant conveniently provides. Direct the runners to fill in bare spots by pinning them to the soil in the direction you wish them to grow. Once they root, remove the pins. Plant bugleweed 6 to 12 in. apart in moist, well-drained soil. The addition of organic matter is beneficial.

Care and Maintenance

Water during hot weather. A light application of spring fertilizer will give the plants a growth spurt. Take care not to be overly generous, as heavy feeding encourages root diseases, especially in poorly drained soils. Keep a close eye on creepers that may invade the space of other plants, especially your lawn. Pot up the escapees and give them to a friend, or plant them elsewhere in your garden. If you don't want them, *don't* throw them on the compost pile. They will probably root there, too. To control seedling volunteers, remove seedheads before they shatter.

Additional Information

Bugleweed is considered evergreen in most of New Jersey, but it may get a little ratty by spring. A nip and tuck here and there will tidy things up. Its big blast of flowers is in early spring, but it may surprise you by throwing up an occasional spike throughout the summer.

Additional Species, Cultivars, or Varieties

'Alba' has light-green foliage and abundant white flowers. 'Atropurpurea' is sometimes called 'Purpurea'. It has slightly larger leaves that are a dark purple-bronze, and its flowers are blue. 'Rosea' has pink flowers. 'Multicolor Rainbow' is not as sturdy as the species, but it has variegated foliage in a whole whirlwind of colors. *Ajuga pyramidalis* 'Metallica Crispa' has a clumped habit and is a good choice for rock gardens. Its flowers are deep blue, and its crinkly foliage is a brownish red color with a metallic sheen.

Creeping Juniper

Juniperus horizontalis

Other Names: Creeping Savin Juniper, Creeping Cedar
Height: 1 to 2 ft.
Spread: 4 to 8 ft., but variable
Zones: 3, 4, **5, 6, 7,** 8, 9

Light Requirement:

Creeping junipers are workhorses among groundcovers. The number of varieties is endless. They are native to the northeastern United States where they can be found on sea cliffs as well as in swamps. This accounts for their being particularly tolerant of rocky, sandy soil conditions and hot, dry locations. They are very adaptable for use in the landscape (which is not surprising since they can be found in the wild in swamps as well as on sea cliffs). The leaves of all varieties are "glaucous," which means the needles are covered in a grayish, bluish, or whitish waxy coating that can be easily wiped off. These plants can be green, blue green, or metallic blue. Many have a purple tint in fall and winter that can vary from plum to silvery purple or bronze purple. Creeping junipers are useful for rock gardens, on steep slopes, and for mass planting. They even tolerate container culture. To break up the uniformity of a large planting, daffodils can be planted directly beneath the branches; they will come up right through the foliage. Junipers are, in general, among the easiest plants to grow. They are a good choice for urban conditions since they hold up under pollution and city grime. Creeping junipers may need an occasional branch removed if they are spreading beyond their bounds, but they are not overly demanding. They are extremely functional. To be perfectly honest, they tend to be a little boring when planted in large numbers. If you have an expanse to cover, consider mixing in a few interesting rocks with an assortment of creeping junipers. Try different shades of green or blue junipers, a few mat types, and a few that are on the shrubby side. Just to break things up, throw in one with a little leaf variegation.

WHEN TO PLANT

Plant in early spring or early fall. Container grown material can be planted almost any time the ground can be worked.

WHERE TO PLANT

Plant in just about any sunny situation. These plants tend to become open and scraggly in the shade. Dry rocky soil or heavy clay soil is acceptable. Creeping junipers tolerate a higher pH, but they do not demand it. Scattered in a rock garden, where you can see the outline of their branches, they can be very attractive. They are effective in preventing erosion on a slope, and they can take the heat of a south or west facing exposure. They are popular choices for larger planter boxes.

HOW TO PLANT

Creeping junipers are readily established with very little fuss. The addition of organic matter will improve any New Jersey soil, but for junipers this is not a requirement.

CARE AND MAINTENANCE

Occasional pruning of dead or straying branches may be necessary. Wear gloves, as the plants can be irritating. Always prune back to a side shoot or you will lose the branch entirely. Bagworms can completely defoliate a juniper if left unattended. Juniper blight usually affects the twigs, but it can kill an entire plant.

ADDITIONAL INFORMATION

Juniper berries can used to make gin, and four berries can be substituted for a bay leaf in cooking. You can also try putting a few juniper branches on the outside grill. This is supposed to impart a interesting smoky flavor to the meats cooking there.

ADDITIONAL SPECIES, CULTIVARS, OR VARIETIES

'Wiltoni' is also known as 'Blue Rug'. It is 4 to 6 in. high but can reach 8 ft. in diameter. 'Plumosa' is also known as the Andorra juniper, having been released by Andorra Nurseries in 1907. It can grow up to 2 ft. tall and 10 ft. wide, and turns an attractive plum color in the winter. 'Blue Chip' is a very low-spreading form that has excellent blue color. 'Douglasii' is also called 'Waukegan'. It is a fast grower with steel blue foliage, and can grow $1^1/2$ ft. high and up to 9 ft. wide. 'Sun Spot' is similar, but it has spots of yellow throughout. The list seems endless.

Dwarf Japanese Juniper

Juniperus procumbens 'Nana'

Other Names: *Juniperus chinensis procumbens* 'Nana', Japanese Garden Juniper
Height: 1 ft.
Spread: 4 to 5 ft.; up to 12 ft.
Zones: 4, **5, 6, 7,** 8, 9

Light Requirement:

---

*O*f all the groundhugging junipers, this is the most beautiful. That may be because it doesn't look much like a juniper. Its small needles and layered branches are far more exotic than most, and it is the perfect choice for a Japanese garden or even for starting a bonsai. *J. p.* 'Nana' is an absolute must for draping over a wall. A rock wall is best, but any wall will show off the many layers of branches as they cascade over and down. (I once had a tiered garden in an urban setting. 'Nana' was planted in one corner of the uppermost tier. It draped down the four railroad ties and spread out on the lowest tier, two levels below. It was stunning!) Mature needles have a bluish cast, but they emerge a bright green that turns slightly purple in winter. The needles are small, densely packed together—and sharp! The overall effect is more like moss than a juniper. When planted as a groundcover, 'Nana' eventually makes an impenetrable barrier to weeds. It is a slow grower, so be patient. Look for about 6 to 8 in. each year.

WHEN TO PLANT
Plant in early spring or early fall.

WHERE TO PLANT
This plant needs full sun, but it is very flexible regarding soils and moisture content. It needs room to spread. It is also suitable for container culture. The root containment may even help prevent the plant from reverting to the species. It is excellent for climbing over walls and embankments. Try using it on slopes, terraces, or on flat ground as an interesting groundcover. *J. p.* 'Nana' is even tolerant of shore planting conditions.

HOW TO PLANT

As is true of most junipers, there is nothing particular about this one's requirements, although some say it is more difficult to establish than others. (I have planted several over the years, in very different environments, with no difficulty.) It is not the kind of plant that you need in large numbers. Its detail is best viewed up fairly close. It is an excellent choice for a specimen plant in small yards, but have it climb over something to best show off its abundant character.

CARE AND MAINTENANCE

It is very tolerant of the pruning needed to keep it in line, and even of the pruning required if you want to use it as bonsai. Take care to prune back to a side shoot. As with all junipers, if you prune to bare wood the branch is not likely to resprout. The Phomopsis twig blight that affects other junipers affects this one severely, so you may not want to overindulge in this species. A single plant is often enough, even from a design point of view. The disease can be controlled by spraying an appropriate fungicide at budbreak and at 14-day intervals. When pruning an infected plant, always dip the pruners in a solution of household bleach between cuts. This will reduce the spread of the disease.

ADDITIONAL INFORMATION

Don't let the threat of Phomopsis keep you from enjoying this truly beautiful plant. If you have problems, you can always pull it up and plant something else. Most of the time it does just fine. There are some absolutely magnificent old plants in the Dwarf Conifer Garden at the National Arboretum in Washington, D.C. If you are in that area, even a drive through visit is worthwhile.

ADDITIONAL SPECIES, CULTIVARS, OR VARIETIES

Juniperus procumbens 'Variegata' is streaked in creamy white. 'Nana Californica' is bluer, finer textured, and even slower growing than 'Nana'. It will eventually get 8 in. tall and 4 ft. wide. 'Nana Greenmound' is similar but more green.

English Ivy

Hedera helix

Other Name: Evergreen Ivy
Height: 6 to 8 in. as a groundcover; 90 ft.
  up a wall as a vine
Spread: Variable
Flowers: Small greenish white flowers
  in umbels
Bloom Period: October
Zones: 4, **5, 6, 7,** 8, 9 (depending on variety)

Light Requirement:

*W*hat would ivy covered halls be without this dependable old favorite? Just boring brick walls! English ivy is native to many parts of Europe and was one of the earliest plants brought over by settlers. It is amazingly flexible about light, but it will appreciate sending its roots into rich, moist soil that is high in organic matter. English ivy is an excellent evergreen groundcover for use under trees. The same aerial roots it uses to climb buildings and trees help it spread and root as a groundcover. It develops roots so readily that you can root cuttings in water almost any time of year. Because it is a vine, it tends to climb things in its path. Take care not to let it encircle the trunk of a woody ornamental. As the vine grows and the woody ornamental grows, the vine will eventually strangle the branch or trunk. This is true even of mature shade trees. It is easy to keep the vine from surrounding the main trunk, but when it reaches the upper branches, there is nothing to prevent it from encircling major limbs. While healthy trees can endure this situation for some time, it is a good idea not to let ivy get so high it is out of control. English ivy will produce small clusters of flowers called "umbels" in October. The branches with the ability to bloom have a more simple foliage type and are considered the "adult" leaves. The adult branches grow more like a woody plant and less vigorously than the juvenile foliage most people recognize. The flowers develop into black berrylike fruits that are poisonous.

WHEN TO PLANT
Plant in early spring or early fall.

Where to Plant

Since it can grow in sun or shade, you can plant it almost anywhere. It will stay the most attractive, however, out of winter sun and wind. Ivy tolerates a wide range of soil pH. Plant it in beds under shade trees, along slopes that may be difficult to mow, on steep banks for erosion control, or up a wall. Ivy will cover a chain-link fence, but it will have to be woven into the fence since there is not enough substance for the clinging air roots to hold. On the ground you can use it to spread over an old broken black-topped area or concrete patio, or even an ugly old shed. Put the roots in good soil and let the ivy grow. It will adapt to containers and shows some tolerance for shore growing conditions.

How to Plant

Ivy can be purchased by the pot, bare root, or in flats. If you take cuttings from a friend's overgrown patch, try to get pieces that have a few roots already started. Pop cuttings without roots into water and they will usually root. The use of a rooting hormone and sterile potting medium will increase the chances of success. Since English ivy prefers deep, rich, humusy soil, double-dig the soil and add copious amounts of organic matter.

Care and Maintenance

Established patches can grow with an excess of enthusiasm, requiring the occasional significant haircut. Ivy is subject to mites, which can be particularly bad on potted plants indoors in the winter but will show up outdoors as well. Leaf spots can also be difficult. Control mites whenever they appear. Leaf spots require treatment with an appropriate fungicide at budbreak, 10 days later, and then 20 days later.

Additional Information

After planting, be patient. There is an old saying about ivy: "The first year it sleeps. The second year it creeps. The third year it leaps!"

Additional Species, Cultivars, or Varieties

There are many cultivars available, but many are not hardy throughout New Jersey, so make your purchases carefully. The following are considered very hardy: 'Baltica', 'Bulgaria', 'Hebron', 'Rochester', 'Rumania', 'Thorndale', and 'Wilson'.

Lamb's Ears

Stachys byzantina

Other Names: Woolly Betony, Woundwort,
    S. lanata, S. olympica
Height: 6 to 8 in; up to 18 in. in bloom
Spread: 18 to 24 in.
Flowers: "Interrupted spikes" of small purple
    flowers arranged in whorls
Bloom Period: Late June through July;
    sporadic until frost
Zones: 4, 5, 6, 7, 8, 9

Light Requirement:

The common name of this plant is quite appropriate. Its leaves are shaped much like the ear of a lamb and are *incredibly* soft. Each leaf is thickly covered in silver hairs that are addicting to touch—the young leaves just emerging are the best. Because of this seductive attribute, lamb's ears have been featured in gardens for the blind. The silvery foliage makes an attractive groundcover. The color contrasts beautifully with other foliage and forms a wonderful background for colorful blossoms as well. Pale pinks and soft blues may benefit the most from this type of background, but it is hard to argue with brilliant red or deep purple splashed against the silver. The plants form a thick mat relatively quickly. They are almost evergreen, but they look tattered in the spring and will require some cleanup. If the centers of the clumps have died out, the plants can be divided. When the center is only mildly deteriorated, they can often be rejuvenated with a significant pruning. The flowers receive mixed reviews. The very straight spikes produce "interrupted" blooms. This means the flowers at the tip have a few leaves, beneath that is bare stem, then come more flowers sitting on more leaves. This continues for the length of the flowering stem. They can be cut for their flowers, which look lovely with iris that bloom at the same time, or the flowers can be left on the spikes to dry for use later on. Some gardeners remove them immediately to keep the focus on the foliage. If left on the plant too long, they get funky looking—but this is certainly a matter of personal taste.

WHEN TO PLANT
You can plant the species from seed in the spring. Divide established plants or start from potted plants in spring or fall.

WHERE TO PLANT
These plants will do best with sun, although light shade is not devastating. Use lamb's ears as a groundcover by itself, or for contrast mixed with other, darker groundcovers. It works very well in beds of spring bulbs that are followed by summer annuals; it accomplishes the task of groundcover but acts as a connecting link for the two seasons. The velvety texture provides outrageous contrast when tucked into a rock garden. These are tough, fuzzy little plants. Well-drained average soil is adequate for them. They will even endure shore planting conditions.

HOW TO PLANT
If you plant from seed, you will get plants typical of the species. There are not many varieties available, but if they have characteristics that interest you, stick to potted plants or divisions. Space the plants 12 to 18 in. apart for groundcover. Lamb's ears are easy to establish with little fuss.

CARE AND MAINTENANCE
Spring tidying up is the biggest chore. Dead centers require division and replanting of the young shoots. Sometimes they will volunteer from seed, but not aggressively. Yank the unwanted seedlings, especially if you are striving for uniformity of a particular variety—or move them or give them to a friend. Cut flower stalks before they get too ugly. These plants can have some fungus problems in hot humid weather, but it is not usually a problem in well-drained soils in full sun.

ADDITIONAL INFORMATION
Known as betony in the herb world, this plant has a long, interesting history. According to *Rodale's Illustrated Encyclopedia of Herbs*, it was used to ward off evil spirits. The English volume *Demonology and Witchcraft* states: "The house where *Herba Betonica* is sown is free from all mischief." Well, it can't hurt.

ADDITIONAL SPECIES, CULTIVARS, OR VARIETIES
'Silver Carpet' is supposedly free of flowers but has exceptional foliage. The occasional flower spike it does throw is ugly. 'Helene von Stein' has pink flowers. Lime-green and variegated varieties supposedly exist, but they must be a well-kept secret.

Moss Pink

Phlox subulata

Other Names: Ground Pink, Mountain Pink, Moss Phlox
Height: 6 in.
Spread: 1 to 3 ft.
Flowers: A solid mat of 3/4 in. flowers; white, pink, lilac, magenta, purple, and variegated varieties
Bloom Period: March through May
Zones: 4, **5, 6, 7,** 8, 9

Light Requirement:

*M*oss pinks produce an *amazing* number of flowers for an extended season of bloom. They create a sea of brilliant color that looks best in a rock garden or draped over a wall. At the peak of flowering, it is difficult to see the foliage through the flowers. After bloom, the 1/2 in. leaves form a dense mat. They are dark green, needlelike, and packed together like sardines. The flowers fade to a green carpet in time to form a perfect background for summer flowers. The leaves are almost evergreen, but don't expect this plant to get through the winter looking picture perfect. To keep the plants as dense as possible for groundcover, shear them back halfway after they finish blooming. If you have a significant area, you can use the lawn mower set high. A single plant can cover a large expanse. It will creep along on stems that are almost woody. Eventually the center will die out and the plant will have to be divided. This is best done in the fall. Moss pinks are native to the northeast. They can be found from New York to North Carolina.

WHEN TO PLANT
Install potted plants in early spring or early fall. Divide established plants in the fall.

WHERE TO PLANT
Moss pinks do best in full sun with loose, well-drained soil. Rock gardens show this plant off to perfection, but mixed borders and

any sunny open area will be suitable. When mass planted, the drive-by impact is spectacular. Moss pinks are tolerant of shore planting conditions.

How to Plant
In heavy soil conditions, add a 2:1 mixture of organic matter and sand to loosen up the soil. You may try planting in raised beds or on a slope. Moss pinks are not difficult to get established. Plant 12 in. apart for quick cover.

Care and Maintenance
Moss pinks will have to be divided every few years to keep them full and blooming with enthusiasm. Division is best done in the fall. Shearing or mowing in the spring when they finish blooming will promote new growth and keep them thick enough to control most weeds. Spider mites can be a problem, but moss pinks are not nearly as susceptible to powdery mildew as their upright cousins, garden phlox.

Additional Information
When I was a young child, my family had no garden. Someone came to mow the grass and that was about it. Then one day my father asked the landscaper to put in a few "pinks" where the yard sloped down to the driveway. They were so beautiful I could hardly believe my eyes. Years later, when my passion for horticulture was just taking hold, I saw *Phlox subulata* blooming at a nursery and instantly recognized it as my childhood favorite. It is amazing how much impact something as simple as a bank of flowers can have. After all the flowers I have grown, I can still picture those "pinks" as clearly as if they were planted yesterday.

Additional Species, Cultivars, or Varieties
If you have a spot that has partial shade, consider using *P. stolonifera*, creeping phlox, instead of moss pinks. It may not be quite as floriferous, but it prefers the lower light conditions under which moss pinks struggle. Varieties of moss pinks include 'Candy Stripe', with pink-and-white-striped flowers; 'Millstream Daphne', with clear-pink flowers that have a dark eye; and 'Scarlet Flame', one of the best reds. 'White Delight' has large white blooms; 'Blue Hills' and 'Emerald Blue' are blue; 'Emerald Pink' has bright-pink flowers; and 'Laurel Beth' has variegated green-and-white foliage with rosy-pink flowers.

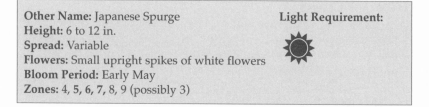

Pachysandra

Pachysandra terminalis

Other Name: Japanese Spurge
Height: 6 to 12 in.
Spread: Variable
Flowers: Small upright spikes of white flowers
Bloom Period: Early May
Zones: 4, 5, 6, 7, 8, 9 (possibly 3)

Light Requirement:

It would not be possible to write about groundcovers and exclude pachysandra. It is one of the "big three" (the other two being ivy and myrtle). The dark green leaves are up to 4 in. long and 1½ in. wide. They are *dentate*, which means they have indentations along their edges. They are arranged alternately along the stem but form a rosette at the shoot tip. Pachysandra thrives in deep shade where many other plants melt into nothingness. It is dependable, glossy green, evergreen, and non-invasive, and it competes effectively with tree roots. (If only it weren't so *boring*!) Pachysandra spreads by "stolons" or stems that run along the ground sending out new roots and shoots. It grows at a moderate rate which is not problematic. Shoots with roots transplant easily to fill in bare spots or to start a new bed. The flowers are not dramatic, but they add a little interest in early spring. The flowers are followed by white berries in the fall. Donald Wyman observed that the plants are more likely to produce fruit if the bed comes from more than one clone. If several clones are present and there are bees to do the work, fruits develop annually.

WHEN TO PLANT
Plant in early spring or early fall.

WHERE TO PLANT
Plant in shade and acid soil conditions. Pachysandra will yellow in full sun, even in the winter. It is an excellent choice for use under shade trees, mature evergreens, smaller trees, shrubs, and in any other shady nook. In semi-urban settings where houses are so close together they are separated by alleyways, pachysandra can be an

effective groundcover provided there is adequate soil preparation. Avoid exposed locations in sun and wind or the foliage will suffer.

How to Plant

Pachysandra needs an abundance of organic matter in moist but well-drained soil. Pile on the leaf compost and till it in. Transplant cuttings with roots already started. Plants are often sold by the flat or possibly bare root. Water thoroughly after planting, but don't keep the soil waterlogged. Plant 6 in. apart for quick cover. Use an organic mulch; it will help control weeds until the pachysandra fill in, and it will add organic matter to the soil as it decomposes.

Care and Maintenance

Trim back at the edges if it starts to creep beyond its bounds. Water in times of drought. Once established, it is an effective weed barrier. Pachysandra canker can be a major problem. If you see circular areas where the plants are brown and flopped over from the base, there is a good chance it is this rampant disease. If not controlled, it can take out the entire planting. The use of an appropriate fungicide three times at 10 to 14 day intervals should solve the problem. Add a "spreader sticker" to the solution. This will help the fungicide stick to the shiny, slippery leaves.

Additional Information

In *The Complete Shade Gardener* by George Schenk, the author observes that in his 3-month study of gardens in Japan, he never found a planting of this native plant, even though the Japanese use groundcovers extensively in many situations. It is unfortunate the Japanese do not appreciate this little plant that is native to their islands. It is also a shame that it is used to the point of monoculture in far too many places in our northeast. Save it for truly deep shade where not much else will grow. In other sites, try something with a little more spunk in its personality.

Additional Species, Cultivars, or Varieties

'Green Carpet' is lower growing and darker green than the species. 'Variegata' is also called 'Silver Edge'; its leaves are edged in white, but it is not quite as vigorous as the species. *Pachysandra procumbens* is native to eastern Kentucky and West Virginia. It is not as shiny as its Japanese cousin, but it has a blue-green cast. It offers an alternative for deep shade, but it may be hard to find.

Periwinkle

Vinca minor

Other Names: Vinca, Myrtle, Dwarf Periwinkle, Common Periwinkle, Lesser Periwinkle
Height: 3 to 6 in.
Spread: Can spread indefinitely
Flowers: Lilac blue, 5 petals, 3/4 in. across; look like tiny pinwheels
Bloom Period: Late April
Zones: 3, 4, **5, 6, 7,** 8, 9

Light Requirement:

This is the last member of the "big three" (myrtle, ivy, pachysandra) and my personal favorite. Not only is it an excellent groundcover for shade, but it gets *flowers*! The plant stays low and compact. The dark-green leaves are in pairs, 2 in. long and richly glossy. (The elves come out at night and polish each one with a soft cloth.) It spreads by putting down roots as its stems run along the ground. Periwinkle is evergreen and often holds its color through the winter. In winter sun, the foliage may turn purple bronze. This is not a plant that can be appreciated as a broad expanse. Get up close and personal to enjoy its leaves and delicate flowers. The new growth emerges a bright green at about the same time as the flowers. There can be many blooms, and they last for several weeks. The more sun, the more flowers. If you are lucky, you may even get a few flowers sporadically during the summer. The flowers are never dramatic, but they are delightful. When faced with ivy and pachysandra as alternatives, they are irresistible. Unfortunately, periwinkle may not flower in very deep shade. Periwinkle is native to Europe and western Asia but has naturalized in some areas of the eastern United States. Once established, beds are very long lived, requiring no particular care.

WHEN TO PLANT
Plant in early spring or early fall.

WHERE TO PLANT
Light shade is best. It will grow in full sun but may have winter leaf discoloration; it will grow in deep shade but may not bloom. It is a

great choice for planting under shade trees where it successfully competes with surface roots. Periwinkle is useful on banks and slopes. It has tenacious roots that can prevent erosion. It can even be a substitute for the traditional lawn, although it will not withstand heavy foot traffic.

How to Plant

This plant does best in moist soil that is high in organic matter. It will endure poor soils but will grow and fill in much more slowly. It can be planted from divisions and roots easily from cuttings. It can also be propagated by layering. Plant rooted cuttings 6 in. apart for cover the first year. If you have the time (or want to cut back on expenses), rooted cuttings can be planted 12 in. apart. It is particularly important to keep the bed moist the first year.

Care and Maintenance

Established plantings can endure drought, but newly planted beds need extra attention to soil moisture. You can shear or prune long runners to force branching. An annual shearing is suggested to keep the plant vigorous, but is not always necessary. Michael Dirr lists a host of diseases that can be encountered by myrtle, but it usually thrives without incident.

Additional Information

There is some confusion about a flower known as annual vinca and incorrectly referred to as *Vinca rosea* or *V. major*. The flower is similar to that of periwinkle, but it is white or pink. While related to true vincas, this plant falls into a different genus. The correct name is *Catharanthus roseus*. *V. major* is a perennial groundcover, but it is hardy onlyto Zone 7. The variegated form is commonly used as an annual vine for container gardens. Within its hardiness zones, *V. major* is a common groundcover. It produces larger flowers than its smaller cousin and grows more aggressively. *V. major* rarely blooms in containers but may, on occasion, overwinter in Zone 6 in a protected spot. Make sure you get the one you really want!

Additional Species, Cultivars, or Varieties

There are many varieties of *V. minor*. For large plantings, consider mixing them together. Use different-colored flowers and even variegated leaves to add interest and diversity. 'Alba', 'Emily Joy', and 'Gertrude Jekyll' have white flowers. 'Bowles' is a dwarf with blue flowers. 'Purpurea' has bright burgundy blooms. 'Variegata' has leaves with cream colored edges and deep blue flowers. 'Sterling Silver' is variegated with lavender flowers.

Sweet Woodruff

Galium odoratum

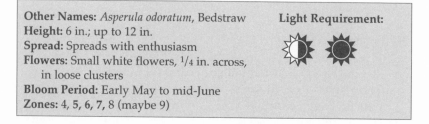

Other Names: *Asperula odoratum*, Bedstraw
Height: 6 in.; up to 12 in.
Spread: Spreads with enthusiasm
Flowers: Small white flowers, 1/4 in. across, in loose clusters
Bloom Period: Early May to mid-June
Zones: 4, 5, 6, 7, 8 (maybe 9)

Light Requirement:

*S*weet woodruff has many fine qualities, not the least of which is its ability to grow in deep shade. From an aesthetic perspective, it has unusual leaves, delicate spring flowers, and a lovely aroma used in perfumes as well as to flavor wine. It is listed throughout the literature as evergreen or semi-evergreen, but that is a stretch in New Jersey. It may last into winter, but by spring it emerges almost entirely from the roots. Perhaps it holds up longer in milder parts of its hardiness zones. The leaves are *wonderful*! They are arranged in whorls of 6 to 8 slender, inch-long leaves around a thin square stem. The whorls repeat every inch. It is the leaves more than the flowers that have the delicious scent. The fragrance becomes more noticeable as the leaves dry. It has been compared to fresh-cut hay, which may account for its common name "bedstraw." Other noses offer such descriptions as vanilla scented or honey-and-horehound. It is a common addition to May wines as part of a tradition marking the passage of winter. It is also said to improve the flavor of otherwise harsh tasting wine. The white flowers are 4 petaled and 1/4 in. across. They are not showy but are very sweet. The small "cymes" (branched clusters that bloom from the center) are held above the leaves and continue to blossom for 4 to 6 weeks.

WHEN TO PLANT
Plant in early spring or early fall.

WHERE TO PLANT
Plant in partial to deep shade. It can be used under shade trees or lower growing shade shrubs such as rhododendron and mountain laurel. It would be lovely under a stretching dogwood. It will spread

rapidly in deep humusy soil. Sweet woodruff will volunteer from seed, so choose a place where you can let it naturalize instead of locating it in a formal setting. The flowers and leaves are best appreciated by viewing up close.

How to Plant

Spring plantings of small divisions spaced 7 in. apart will fill in by autumn if grown in ideal soil conditions. Sweet woodruff has a deep woodsy aura. It looks perfectly at home with trilliums poking up through its foliage or a few interesting ferns scattered through its domain. Soil amended with abundant organic matter will make this sweet thing content. It needs generous moisture, and organic matter will help retain the water that is there. An organic mulch will be beneficial as well, at least until the plants fill in. Sweet woodruff prefers an acid soil, so do not add lime. Seed is available, or you can collect it from an established bed. Spring planting of seed is possible, but it can take 200 days to germinate. Potted plants are generally available locally.

Care and Maintenance

The biggest problem is keeping this plant from creeping beyond its bounds. It can spread from its roots as well as seeds. The beds may need a little tidying up in the spring when the previous year's foliage dies down. Water in hot, dry weather. There are no diseases or insects mentioned in any of the literature. Overall, sweet woodruff is an easy-care groundcover with many virtues.

Additional Information

The folklore and herbal history of sweet woodruff is extensive. During the Victorian era the leaves and flowers were mixed with other herbs in sachets as a protection against moths. It has been used in wreath making to provide aroma, and even to stuff mattresses. During medieval times it was used to decorate churches for religious holidays. A tan dye can be made from the leaves and a red dye from the roots.

Additional Species, Cultivars, or Varieties

It appears that no varieties of sweet woodruff exist. *Hortus III* lists about 12 species, but they do not seem available in the trade. *Asperula azurea* or *A. orientalis* (woodruff) is the only available species that comes even close to sweet woodruff. It is considered a hardy annual. Woodruff is also fragrant, and its lavender blue flowers are recommended for cutting. Seed is sometimes available from Thompson and Morgan.

Wintergreen

Gaultheria procumbens

Other Names: Checkerberry, Teaberry,
    Mountain Tea
Height: 3 to 6 in.
Spread: Variable
Flowers: Pinkish white, nodding flowers
    1/4 in. long (they become bright-red
    berries 2/5 in. long)
Bloom Period: May to July
Zones: 3, 4, **5, 6, 7**

Light Requirement:

Wintergreen is native to the woods of the northeast. The shiny, inch long dark green leaves and bright red berries are easy to recognize on an autumn walk through the woods. The scent of a crushed leaf is unmistakable any time of year. The plant is evergreen and woody, but its leaves turn a rich burgundy in the fall. The stems creep along the ground half buried. Wintergreen is very slow growing. The flowers appear in spring but continue to open until July. They are white with a hint of pink and resemble a lily-of-the-valley flower. The flowers develop into bright red berrylike fruits. These first appear in July, continue ripening through the fall, and persist until the following spring. Sometimes delicate fresh flowers open in the presence of the previous year's fruit! The berries are edible and have an unusual refreshing taste. Wintergreen was the original source of oil of wintergreen. It was once harvested in large quantities and shipped to distilleries. (It is now almost exclusively laboratory synthesized.) Native Americans made tea from the leaves and so did early colonists—especially while they were having tea problems with the mother country.

WHEN TO PLANT

Plant in early spring or early fall.

WHERE TO PLANT

Plant in shade or partial shade in acid soil. This is not a good choice for a large expanse since it grows so slowly. It is best put to use in a naturalized woodland setting where the rich humusy soil is deep and moist. It is excellent for shaded rock gardens and can be wonderful around azaleas and rhododendrons or along a woodland path.

How to Plant
Transplanting from the wild is difficult, so it is best to use potted plants. Do *not* add lime, but add lots of organic matter, especially leaf compost. It is possible to divide established plants, but it is probably not worth the effort since they grow so slowly. Wintergreen prefers moist soils, so do not let the ground dry out, especially the first year. Pine needles make a good mulch, but any organic mulch will be beneficial. Plant 12 in. apart.

Care and Maintenance
Wintergreen grows slowly and is not invasive. It rarely, if ever, needs to be pruned. Insects and diseases are not mentioned in the literature so are probably not serious. You may have to weed around the plants since they will not fill in quickly; mulch will help with that. Water in hot, dry weather. It sounds easy and it is.

Additional Information
Do you remember the "Teaberry Shuffle"? Teaberry chewing gum has been around forever and you were supposed to do the Teaberry Shuffle when you chewed. The flavor originated in this little wintergreen groundcover. Oil of wintergreen is in many products that are used to treat sore, aching muscles. You can soak a cloth in it, but too long of a direct application may irritate the skin. If you would enjoy a cup of wintergreen tea, use a teaspoon of chopped leaves in a cup of water. Steep to taste.

Additional Species, Cultivars, or Varieties
'Macrocarpa' is a compact variety that is particularly fruitful. It may be difficult to locate. Donald Wyman lists six other species, but they are not readily available. *G. miqueliana* is the miquel wintergreen. *G. ovatifolia* is the Oregon wintergreen. Both reach 1 ft. *G. shallon* reaches 1¹/₂ ft. All three are hardy to Zone 5. Shallon and miquel are carried by Forest Farm in Oregon. *G. hispidula*, creeping pearlberry, reaches 2 ft. and is hardy to Zone 3. Native to North America, it may be available through the Native Plant Society.

CHAPTER ELEVEN

Roses

*I*T HAS BEEN OVER 2,000 YEARS SINCE THE GREEK POET SAPPHO FIRST CALLED THE ROSE "THE QUEEN OF FLOWERS." There are other flowers that may try to seize the title, but roses have reigned for too long to easily give up the throne.

To plant roses in your garden requires serious deliberation. You'll have to find the right location. A sunny, well-drained bed is essential. Trying to grow roses in less than full sun or in wet ground is futile. You will need to do some research to discover the type of rose you want to grow. A climbing rose is not a shrub rose, and neither is likely to produce the flowers of a hybrid tea. The type of rose you choose will also affect the location you choose, so you are back to square one. A climbing rose needs to climb on something. A hybrid tea is not the best choice for blending into a landscape planting— shrub roses may be better for that application.

Roses are not stick-them-in-the-ground-and-forget-about-them plants. All roses need some attention. If you want your roses to bring you pleasure, you have to tend them. Hybrid teas may require the most care, but then they are the classic image of what a perfect rose should be. As is true of most things in life, if you want the best, you will have to work for it. Some shrub roses, including the rugosa roses, may be less demanding and are truly lovely, but you will never get that perfect long-stemmed beauty from a rugosa rose.

GETTING STARTED

Once you have chosen your planting location and have decided you have the time and willingness to do what it takes to grow roses, you can get started. Some gardeners prefer to keep all their roses together in one spot. In Victorian times this was called a "rosary" and is the origin of the term "rosarian," which means rose gardener.

Chapter Eleven

Such a grouping certainly makes caring for roses easier and draws attention to their magnificent flowers while in bloom. The plants themselves, however, are often not very exciting while not in bloom. And not everyone has room for a special "rosary."

Soil Preparation

Whether your roses will stand alone or be part of your landscape design, you will have to do some serious soil preparation. Drainage is critical. The addition of organic matter to heavy clay soil will help prevent the soil from staying waterlogged. It may be necessary to raise the bed or install a drainage pipe to remove excess water. The addition of organic matter will help sandy soil hold on to soil moisture. It is especially important in hard-packed clay soil to double-dig the soil in order to prepare it deeply for a root system to expand.

Planting

When you are ready to purchase your roses, you may be able to find the varieties you want locally. These will, in most cases, be available in containers. The best time to plant is early spring. Plant them very carefully. Try not to let the soil fall away from the roots as you pull the plant out of the pot or you may tear the delicate feeder roots that are just developing.

Roses shipped to you will arrive bare root, usually at the time of year best suited for the planting of roses in your area. When they arrive, check them right away to see that they are moist. If your new roses cannot be planted immediately, moisten the roots and wrap them in plastic. Store at 35 to 40 degrees Fahrenheit. Check them every two or three days to make sure they don't dry out. Two weeks is about as long as you can keep them like this. If you must wait longer to plant, bury the plants about a foot down with their branches pointing up at a 45 degree angle. If the temperature is expected to drop below freezing, cover them with leaves and plastic. If temperatures go above freezing, be sure to get out there and pull off the protection or the plants will cook.

Soak the roots overnight or up to twenty-four hours before planting. Cover the whole plant with water for the last two or three hours before planting. When you are ready to plant, prune off any broken roots. Prune off any damaged canes while you are busy snipping. Prune all the canes to ten to twelve inches tall.

When digging the hole, make it big; then make it a little bigger. You will want the entire root system to fit inside. Put most of the soil back in the hole, forming a mound in the center. Spread the roots evenly over the mound. The bud union, a fat knot, should be two inches belowground in places where the temperature goes below zero degrees Fahrenheit in winter. Since temperatures in some winters can hit zero throughout the state, that is a good rule. Orient the bush so the bud side of the knot faces north. That is the side on which most of the canes will develop. The canes will reach for the sunnier side, helping to establish a well shaped bush.

Fill the hole and tamp it down firmly with your hands. If you use your foot for tamping, it may get packed too hard. Water thoroughly. Let the water soak in and water again.

PRUNING

If you want long, straight stems and large blooms, it will be necessary to remove the side buds that grow along the canes below the terminal bud you want to keep. If all the buds grow, you will have many shorter branches with many smaller flowers. You can prevent unwanted branching by snapping off the buds with your thumb.

Pruning to remove dead flowers is done by removing the stem back to the first complete leaf; this will encourage branching and future flower production. Rose leaves generally consist of five leaflets, but beneath the flower they may have only three or even just one. Cutting back to the second complete leaf will result in longer stems and larger blooms but fewer flowers.

In the autumn, allow the last flowers to die on the plant. Pruning them late in the season may trigger new growth that will be tender going into winter. When the plant is dormant, prune the branches lightly to prevent injury due to wind, ice, and snow.

Major pruning is done in late March or early April. First remove any dead, diseased, or broken canes. Then remove canes growing towards the center, or these will crisscross and make a mess. If two canes are rubbing, even if they are both arching out nicely, one must be removed. You want to leave three to five healthy canes that are as large as a pencil or larger. The secondary canes that emerge from the canes you keep will never be larger than the original, and they are usually smaller.

Prune to a height of eighteen inches, pruning to an outside bud. The buds develop into branches that grow in the direction the bud points. Inside buds eventually become crisscrossing branches. Make your cut at a 45 degree angle pointing down towards the center of the bush. After making the cut, examine the "pith" or center of the cane. If it is white, the cane is in good shape. If it has a brown center, continue to remove small increments until you reach healthy tissue. After a severe winter, there may not be much left. You may be forced to settle for a little brown in the center to save the cane. Sealing the cut ends with nail polish, white glue, petroleum jelly, or tree wound compound helps prevent borers from getting into the canes.

CLIMBING ROSES

Climbers may bloom once in the spring, or they may repeat-bloom in the summer. Even on those varieties that bloom again, the bulk of the flower display will be in the spring. The spring flowers are all on "old wood," which means wood that grew the previous growing season. Prune away only those canes that suffered winter damage or die-back; anything else will remove the blooms. The dead flowers of repeat bloomers should be removed to the first five leaflet leaf. If they are not eliminated, the dead flowers will make "hips," or seeds, and plant energy will go into seed production instead of into making new flowers.

FERTILIZER

Apply fertilizer to new roses after the first round of blooms. Established roses can be fed once a month beginning six weeks before the first bloom (in New Jersey, the first feeding will be mid- to late April). Finish fertilizing six weeks before the last bloom (early September in New Jersey).

If you are not religious about your fertilizer schedule, at least remember to feed on three holidays: Memorial Day, Fourth of July, and Labor Day.

There are many commercial formulations available for roses. The three numbers on the bag represent the percentage of nitrogen, phosphorus, and potassium, always in that order. How much you should apply depends on the exact formulation of the product you buy. Follow the directions. A soil test will supply the exact requirement for your garden. Contact your County Extension office for having your soil tested through Rutgers University.

CONTROLLING INSECTS AND DISEASE

Unfortunately, roses have many pest problems. Breeders are paying particular attention to these issues as they develop new varieties. Some old varieties, including shrub roses, may have more natural resistance than the more popular hybrid teas.

Starting in late May, a weekly spray schedule of an all-purpose rose spray will keep the problems from getting out of hand. Of the many insects you may encounter, spring caterpillars, Japanese beetles, aphids, and mites are probably the biggest offenders. Black spot and powdery mildew may be the worst of the diseases.

For more details on insect and disease problems of roses, consult one of the are many good references that are dedicated to the cultivation of these finicky beauties.

WINTER CARE

The final pruning is done after the plants are fully dormant, and it is done only to prevent winter damage from snow and wind. It is a good idea at that time to mound soil, or a mixture of soil and mulch, or even mulch alone, to a height of ten to twelve inches around the base of the plant. This is particularly important for white and yellow roses, which have the most difficult time surviving winter.

ROSES FOR NEW JERSEY

In order to create a list of the best roses for New Jersey, it seemed wise to consult with the ultimate in rose specialists. There are thousands of varieties, and unless one dedicates their life to the thorny species, it is difficult to evaluate all the possibilities.

I spoke with Fred Edmund, the recently retired founder of Edmund Roses in Oregon. While delightful and informative, Mr. Edmund felt the best person to answer questions about New Jersey was Frank Benardella, a past president of the American Rose Society and long-time New Jersey resident. Mr. Benardella has grown thousands of roses and has had firsthand experience in our climate. Mr. Edmund was unsure of where Mr. Benardella now lives, but thought it was on a farm either in New Jersey or Pennsylvania. It turns out that Mr. Benardella now lives in my own neighborhood.

My meeting with him and his wife was delightful. He was knowledgeable and full of enthusiasm. One of his suggestions for an outstanding climbing rose was 'New Dawn'. This was introduced in 1932 and was developed in New Jersey. It received the very first plant patent, #0001. In fact, it was recently voted the favorite rose for the past three years by the World Federation of Rose Societies. This international organization represents thirty-three countries and meets every three years. They have an oil painting done of the honored rose which is usually presented to the party responsible for its introduction. In this case, because the rose was introduced so long ago, there was no trace of the originator.

Chapter Eleven

Life works in mysterious ways. It just so happens I know the family that received the very first plant patent, although I had never before heard the variety name. After meeting the Benardellas, I contacted Carl Bosenberg, a retired landscape contractor whose business has long been on Livingston Avenue (a street I lived on for eight years) in North Brunswick. His father, Henry F. Bosenberg, founder of the family business, was the person who actually discovered the rose. It was a "sport" (a naturally occurring branch that differs from the rest of the plant) of 'Dr. W. Van Fleet', a popular rose of the time. The sport appeared on a plant growing in the yard of company headquarters. It was cultivated and released by the Somerset Rose Nursery, another family business.

Mr. Benardella offered many suggestions for roses to be grown in New Jersey and included in this book. He also went to a meeting of the Garden State Rose Club and had the members vote on their favorites. All the final selections are generally available in the trade.

Climbing Roses

Rosa

Height: Many 8 to 10 ft., some up to 20 ft.	**Light Requirement:**
Flowers: White, pink, yellow, red	
Bloom Period: June (some rebloom in summer)	
Zones: 5, 6, 7	

Climbers are roses that can be trained to grow up a trellis, arbor, pergola, or other support. They bloom profusely in spring on previous year's growth. Some climbers can have large blooms, and a few will even rebloom in the summer.

The difference between a climber and a true rambler sometimes gets a little fuzzy. In fact, ramblers are a type of climbing rose. They have very pliable canes for sculpting over archways and around gazebos. Ramblers bloom only in spring on old growth, and they generally have an abundance of small flowers. When left on their own, they can grow in all directions. Some rosarians prune ramblers to the ground after they bloom to start over for the following year.

Climbing rose varieties include: 'Autumn Sunset' (apricot gold), 'Westerland' (apricot blend), 'New Dawn' (light pink), 'Handel' (pink blend), 'Red Fountain' (bright red), 'Dortmund' (red and white single), 'Sally Holmes' (white single, sometimes considered a shrub), 'Climbing Iceberg' (white), and 'Jeanne LaJoie' (pink miniature).

Floribunda

Rosa

Height: 2 to 7 ft., many about 3 ft.
Flowers: Many colors; in clusters
Bloom Period: June (most with
   good rebloom)
Zones: 5, 6, 7

Light Requirement:

Floribundas are modern roses, the result of crossing polyantha roses with hybrid teas. This cross was first successfully accomplished as part of a breeding program in Denmark in the 1920s. Floribundas have an extended season of bloom and are available in a wide range of colors. The flowers are not as large as those of hybrid teas, but they grow in clusters with many flowers per cluster. The flowers are becoming larger as new varieties are developed. They may soon approach the size of those of the large-flowered parent.

Floribundas may not be quite as finicky as hybrid teas, but they are far more demanding than many shrub roses. To keep them blooming, remove the spent blooms and follow a regular maintenance program.

Floribunda varieties include: 'Iceberg' (white), 'Sunsprite' (yellow, fragrant), 'Showbiz' (medium red), 'Scentimental' (red and white stripe), 'Playboy' (orange and scarlet with a yellow center, single), 'Sexy Rexy' (pink), 'Dicky' (pink), 'First Edition' (coral orange), and 'Trumpeter' (orange red).

Grandiflora

Rosa

Height: 3 to 7 ft., many about 3 ft. **Flowers:** White, pink, red, yellow (yellow often not as hardy) **Bloom Period:** Most bloom all season **Zones:** 5, 6, 7	**Light Requirement:**

Grandifloras are even newer than floribundas. They are a result of crossing floribundas with hybrid teas. The first grandiflora was introduced in 1954. It took an act of Parliament to establish formal approval to name the lovely new pink rose 'Queen Elizabeth'. It is still considered the standard by which other grandifloras are judged.

The idea behind the hybridization was to combine the hardiness of the floribundas with the long stems and flowers of the hybrid teas. In England, this classification is not even recognized; what are called grandifloras in the United States are lumped in with floribundas by English gardeners. Even so, many hybridizers continue to work with this group, and new varieties are being introduced all the time.

In general, grandifloras are taller than both parents, more vigorous and slightly hardier than the hybrid tea. Their numerous blooms have the form of the hybrid tea.

Grandiflora varieties include: 'Queen Elizabeth' (pink), 'Love' (red and white), 'Gold Medal' (medium yellow; needs winter protection), 'Tournament of Roses' (pink), 'Pink Parfait' (pink), 'Aquarius' (light pink), and 'Camelot' (coral pink).

Hybrid Tea Roses

Rosa

Height: 2¹/₂ to 9 ft., many 3 to 4 ft.	**Light Requirement:**
Flowers: Many colors; up to 6 in. diameter	
Bloom Period: All season	
Zones: 5, 6, 7	

When the romantic image of a large, beautiful red rose on a long stem comes to mind, that is a hybrid tea rose. They are the result of crossing the hybrid perpetual rose with tea roses introduced from China.

The hybridization was started late in the last century. The targeted traits were the repeat blooming capabilities of the tea roses and the flower type of the hybrid perpetuals. The early experiments resulted in repeat bloomers, but fewer flowers in the first flush. The flowers and hardiness were an improvement over the teas, but they were less hardy and sturdy than the perpetuals.

Over the years, breeders have expanded the palette of colors to an incredible range. These are, hands down, the most popular roses under cultivation in greenhouses and backyards, and have been for over fifty years. Unfortunately, hybrid teas continue to be the most difficult to grow successfully. In recent years, breeders have put more efforts into developing insect and disease resistance as well as hardiness. Some new varieties show marked improvement in these important characteristics. There are also older varieties that are extremely worthwhile. Keep in mind that there are no pure-yellow varieties that are truly hardy in New Jersey.

Hybrid tea varieties include: 'Mr. Lincoln' (dark red), 'Olympiad' (medium red), 'Touch of Class' (coral pink), 'Elina' (creamy white), 'Pristine' (white), 'Peace' (yellow blend), 'Double Delight' (red-and-white blend), 'Signature' (deep pink), 'Fragrant Cloud' (orange red), and 'Sheer Bliss' (white).

Miniature Roses

Rosa

Height: Up to 18 in. **Flowers:** Many colors **Bloom Period:** June (good repeat bloomers) **Zones:** 5, 6, 7	**Light Requirement:**

here is a miniature rose planted outside my office window in plain view. Every year it blooms in profusion until December. When all the other roses are long gone—when everything else is long gone—it still blooms. It brings great joy.

Miniature roses are generally about a foot tall but they can be up to 18 in. A few climbing miniatures can reach 5 ft. They are hardy little things and extremely floriferous. They have been crossed and recrossed with so many traditional roses that the color options are phenomenal.

Miniature roses grow on their own roots, so you can root cuttings and have many miniatures. Minis can be cultivated indoors, but only if you have an abundance of light. At the very least, you need an unblocked southern exposure window, and you may want to supplement that with florescent light in the winter.

Miniature rose varieties include: 'Kristin' (red blend), 'Jean Kenneally' (apricot blend), 'Figurine' (white), 'Starina' (orange red), 'Black Jade' (dark red), 'Snow Bride' (white), 'Rainbow's End' (yellow blend), 'Old Glory' (medium red), 'Rise 'N' Shine' (yellow), and 'Loving Touch' (apricot blend).

Rugosa Roses

Rosa rugosa

Height: 2 to 12 ft. (variety dependent)
Flowers: White, pink, red
Bloom Period: June (many have good
    repeat bloom)
Zones: 5, 6, 7

Light Requirement:

---

ugosa roses are shrublike, with heavily textured foliage. They make an excellent choice for mass planting, and are probably among the most care free plants in the world of roses. Their flowers are usually single, but they are large, fragrant, and produced most of the season. Their hips, commonly used for tea, are among the best— they are bright orange-red and grow the size of cherry tomatoes. All rose hips are very high in vitamin C. The rugosa rose is also one of the best plants for use at the shore. It is especially tolerant of cold, wind, sand, and salt spray.

Rugosa rose varieties include: 'Alba' (white), *Rosa rugosa* (deep pink), 'Linda Campbell' (velvety bright red), 'Blanc Double DeCoubert' (white double), 'Grootendorst Pink' (pink), and 'F.J. Grootendorst' (red).

Shrub Roses

Rosa

Height: 1½ to 12 ft.; many about 6 ft. **Flowers:** White, yellow (often not hardy), pink, red **Bloom Period:** June; some repeat bloom **Zones:** 5, 6, 7	**Light Requirement:**

*S*hrub roses are a broad group that often includes roses that don't quite fit anywhere else. These roses are generally among the varieties that are most suited for landscaping purposes. They are bushlike in habit, but they may be tall and arching or compact and tidy. They have very diverse origins. Shrub roses are usually vigorous, low maintenance, hardy, and pest resistant.

Shrub rose varieties include: 'Carefree Beauty' (pink), 'Bonica' (pale pink), 'Sea Foam' (white), 'Flower Carpet' (pink; very disease resistant), 'Scarlet Meidiland' (bright red), 'White Meidiland' (white), and 'The Fairy' (very pale pink).

Perennials

GARDENING IS AN ART FORM THAT INCLUDES FOUR DIMENSIONS. The fourth dimension is that it changes over time. What may be perfectly balanced today can be out of whack before too much time has passed. Trees grow, light conditions change, groundcovers spread, vines climb. You can measure the passage of time by watching a shade tree stretch and grow over the years.

When you work with perennials, you put that progression over time into high gear. Perennials will develop from year to year, but they also change the look of your garden dramatically from spring through fall. They are simple enough to move from spot to spot if the mood suits you. Virginia bluebells, primrose, columbine, and bleeding heart in spring look nothing like liatris, evening primrose, and monarda in summer, which are completely different from false dragonhead, asters, chrysanthemums, and anemones in the fall. You can have a similar progression with the right assortment of woody ornamentals, but you can have many perennials in the amount of space that would accommodate only a few trees or shrubs.

Annuals need to be replanted every spring. You can mix them up and change the scheme from year to year, but it will look the same for the entire season. Perennials stay in the same place for two or three years at least (some can stay fifty years), but your garden will appear to be many different gardens in the same year. Making room for some of each gives you the best of both worlds.

Determine whether you want the same variety planted in a mass, or whether you want to collect different varieties. An enormous planting of raspberry parfait peonies will stop traffic cold while in bloom, but when it's over, it's over. If you plant twenty varieties of peonies carefully selected for color and time of bloom, you will have a much longer peony season, but to appreciate the sometimes subtle differences you need to be at sniffing distance. In a small yard, up close and personal is all you have, so make it work for you. In large sprawling grounds, a single plant is often lost. You need to plan the right amount of clustering with enough variety to suit the size of your yard and your own personal interests, with an overall pleasing effect.

Don't think you have to get it all right with the first planting. What really tickles your fancy can be divided and spread out. Plants that fall flat can be replaced. Annuals can provide big blasts of color that camouflage the lulls in the progression of the perennials. Fill in with something perennial when you find just the right plant. One of the wonderful things about perennials is that it only takes a shovel to change things around. If you don't like it, move it. If you love it, divide it and you will have more. If you really hate it, toss it on the compost pile and try something new. It is not like digging out an oak tree because you decided you prefer maples.

On occasion, a particular perennial will capture your heart and run away with it. That is when you become a specialist. It is not difficult to become totally devoted to daylilies. Once you see how fabulous they can be and how many colors and varieties there are to choose from, you may find yourself wanting many. The same can be said for iris, or peonies, or chrysanthemums. There are societies or clubs for many popular perennials. The American Hosta Society, The American Iris Society, The American Peony Society, The American Primrose Society, and The National Chrysanthemum Society are a few. These specialty organizations will often offer plant exchanges or opportunities to get unusual, new, or historic varieties that are not readily available in the trade.

It doesn't matter whether you have row upon row of perennials or just a few tucked into a corner. When their time to bloom is approaching, you will peek and check and anticipate their beauty. There are perennials for shade or sun and spring, summer or fall. They can be tall or short and come in every color imaginable. They will bring you joy. You may find that your absolute favorite is the one blooming right now.

Asters

Aster species

Other Name: Michaelmas Daisy
Height: 6 in. to 8 ft., depending on species
Spread: Variable
Flowers: Disc surrounded by ray flowers
Bloom Period: September and October
Zones: Most are hardy in 4, **5, 6, 7,** 8, 9
   (some 3 or 10)

Light Requirement:

*A*sters are fall blooming perennials. They can be found growing as wildflowers in almost every abandoned field but are not used in gardens as often as you might expect. There are over 600 species as well as an enormous number of hybrids and varieties. People sometimes think only of chrysanthemums as fall flowers. It is true that autumn without mums would be disappointing, but asters offer an easy-to-grow alternative. These flowers belong to the composite or daisy family. The flat disc in the center is surrounded by "ray" flowers or petals. Wild asters often produce small flowers—only 1/4 in. across—that grow in large clusters. The New York aster, *A. novi-belgii*, has deep-violet flowers 2 in. across. Hybrids tend to develop powdery mildew while the species rarely have this problem. Hybrid asters make up a significant number of the garden varieties available. They generally grow to between 1 and 3 ft. in height. One hybrid, *A. × frikartii* 'Monch', receives high praise in the literature and in catalog listings. It reaches 3 ft. in height, needs no support, and produces 2 1/2-in. lavender-blue flowers for an extended season. *A. tataricus*, a native of Siberia, produces many small lavender blooms with yellow centers and towers 6 to 8 ft. in the air. *Aster* 'Alert' grows to 1 ft. and has crimson red flowers. To search for and find any particular variety or species may be difficult, but there are many offered at local nurseries and by mail-order. Be sure to get all the available information on the asters you purchase so that you can use them to their best advantage.

WHEN TO PLANT

In New Jersey, it is always better to plant fall-blooming perennials in the spring. This will give them a chance to establish roots before winter. Once they begin to produce flowers, perennials do very little in the way of growing roots. If you plant them in the fall while they are in bloom, you may have to treat them as annuals. If fall planted asters come back in spring, consider it a bonus.

WHERE TO PLANT

Asters need full sun and some room to spread. They can be mixed with other fall-blooming perennials for an autumn display, or can be used to bring color in their turn to a multi-seasonal bed. Asters prefer rich, moderately dry soil.

HOW TO PLANT

Asters are usually available as potted plants, sometimes by the flat. Because asters prefer their soil on the dry side, it is best to amend the soil with a 2:1 mixture of organic matter and sand rather than with organic matter alone.

CARE AND MAINTENANCE

Powdery mildew can be a problem. Use a fungicide at the first sign of white spots. When watering, water thoroughly, making sure to water the ground around the plants and not the plants themselves. Keeping water off the leaves will slow down the spread of the disease. While asters prefer soil on the dry side, overly dry soil makes them more susceptible to powdery mildew. Asters usually spread from their roots. The centers of plantings can become less productive over time and will need to be dug out every 2 or 3 years. Replace old centers with young divisions from the outer edge of the planting. This will prevent excessive spread and keep the patch blooming with enthusiasm. Asters also spread from seed, so keep an eye out for volunteer plants in the garden.

ADDITIONAL INFORMATION

Victorian literature contains many references to Michaelmas and the Michaelmas daisy. As a Brontë and Austin devotee, I often wondered what this meant. I discovered that Michaelmas is a religious day honoring the archangel Michael. It takes place every September 29, which also happens to be right around the time when most asters (or Michaelmas daisies) are in full bloom.

ADDITIONAL SPECIES, CULTIVARS, OR VARIETIES

'Alma Potschke' is a German variety with warm-pink blooms that last for 6 weeks. 'Purple Dome' is a dwarf with of 1 in. purple flowers. 'Marie Ballard' has light blue double blooms. 'Rudelsburg' has salmon flowers and can reach 4 ft. There are many more.

Astilbe

Astilbe × arendsii

Other Names: False Spirea, Meadow Sweet
Height: Usually 2 ft., but can be anywhere
    between 1^1/$_2$ to 4 ft.
Spread: 1^1/$_2$ to 2^1/$_2$ ft.
Flowers: Soft, fluffy panicles with a great
    many tiny flowers in a variety of colors
Bloom Period: June through August
Zones: 4, 5, 6, 7, 8
	Light Requirement:

*T*here are about 14 species of astilbe, two of which are native to North America. The rest originate in eastern Asia. The popular garden varieties are usually hybrids of four or five species. All have a similar general appearance but may vary in particulars. Leaves are compound and look much like fern fronds. They may be shiny or dull, dark green or with hints of bronze or purple. The inflorescence varies from 12 to 18 in. and may grow on stems as tall as 3 ft. Flowers can be white, coral, apricot, various shades of pink, or subtle-to-bright shades of red. Early-, mid-, and late-season varieties bloom respectively in June, July, and August. The astilbe is an easy care perennial and a great boon to the shade gardener. These flowers are very effective in small bursts. They can be scattered about a mixed border in groups of three or five. Plant all of one variety in a group to make a big impact in a small spot. It doesn't take many astilbes to add zing to a bed of leafy hosta or soft green ferns, but a single plant will be lost. Planting just a few of several different varieties will not show any of them to their best advantage. Try different varieties for more color or to extend the blooming season, but always grow at least three of the same kind together. For major impact, a mass planting of a single variety or large patches of complementing colors is stunning. A large mass of astilbes in a woodland clearing grows thick enough to function as a groundcover but is brilliant enough to be magical.

WHEN TO PLANT
Plant astilbe in early spring or early fall.

WHERE TO PLANT

Astilbes are treasured for their enthusiasm in the shade, but they will tolerate full sun as long as the spot is not excessively hot and soil is kept adequately moist. I would not recommend planting in a western exposure up against a dark house, but bright morning sun with good air movement should be fine. Astilbes planted in open spaces in a wooded area can be spectacular. Try growing them along a bank under tall trees or in patches right through myrtle or pachysandra for a little midsummer color. They mix beautifully with ferns, hostas, and lily-of-the-valley. Plant around azaleas and rhododendrons. Astilbes come into their season just as these shade-loving shrubs are finishing up.

HOW TO PLANT

Astilbe demands deep moist soil that is high in organic matter. That means you need to incorporate copious quantities of organic matter into the soil prior to planting. Leaf compost is best, but peat moss can also be used. Dig deeply to ensure good soil drainage. Remember that high soil moisture is not the same as soggy ground.

CARE AND MAINTENANCE

Astilbes have few problems, but they need to be divided every 4 or 5 years to maintain vigor. Remove spent flowers to keep the plants looking attractive and to prevent seed formation. Water during hot, dry summer weather. Apply an organic mulch to retain soil moisture and to moderate fluctuations in temperature.

ADDITIONAL INFORMATION

Astilbes can make very attractive cut flowers if you cut them when they are only partially open. They make beautiful bouquets when combined with roses. The flowers resemble the soft delicate blooms of baby's breath, but in bright colors. Try red astilbe with yellow roses for zing or soft pink astilbe with white roses for a more delicate look.

ADDITIONAL SPECIES, CULTIVARS, OR VARIETIES

A. biternata is native to the mountains of Kentucky and Virginia. The creamy white flowers are meager compared to garden varieties, but the rich dark green foliage is lush. This plant is a good choice for the darkest corner of your shade garden. 'Avalanche', 'Bridal Veil', 'Bergkristall', and 'Brautschleier' are white garden varieties. 'Bonn', 'Anita Pfeifer', and 'Bressingham Beauty' are pink. 'Fanal', 'Granat', and 'Koblenz' are red. 'Cattleya' is orchid pink. If you want purple-blooming astilbe, try *A. chinensis* varieties, especially 'Purpurlanze'.

Bee Balm

Monarda didyma

Other Names: Bergamot, Oswego Tea,
  Horsemint, Monarda
Height: 3 ft.
Spread: Generally 2 ft., but varies
Flowers: Tubular blooms arrayed like a
  sputnik, available in many colors
Bloom Period: June through August
Zones: 4, 5, 6, 7, 8

Light Requirement:

Once you see bee balm in full bloom, you will never forget it. These flowers are otherworldly. They start out resembling a sputnik, then develop a central disc, sometimes sending out more tubes in a tiered effect. They make an unusual-looking addition to cutflower arrangements and can be white, pink, red, or purple. They look like nothing else in the garden. You will appreciate the butterflies, bees, and hummingbirds this plant draws to your neighborhood. Hummingbirds find the red flowered types particularly appealing. Bee balm spreads, sometimes too energetically, so be sure to give it plenty of room. It comes back year after year with no fuss. The bloom period is fairly long, especially if you remove dead flowers. Bee balm tends to get powdery mildew later in the season. You can minimize the plant's susceptibility by keeping the soil moist and planting where there is good air circulation. Powdery mildew can also be controlled with fungicides, or you may choose to just ignore it. The plants return yearly whether you treat or not. If you can tolerate the resulting end-of-season rattiness, it may not be worth the trouble to treat this disease. Bee balm stems are very square, a typical characteristic of plants in the mint family. The leaves resemble mint leaves but are generally larger. They have a fragrance all their own, with just a hint of citrus, and are commonly used for tea. Native to eastern North America from Canada to Tennessee, bee balm was one of the plants used to substitute for the black tea that irate colonists dumped in Boston Harbor.

WHEN TO PLANT

Plant bee balm in spring. Fall plantings do not usually survive the winter. This may be surprising given the plant's vigor, but it is true enough to avoid fall planting.

WHERE TO PLANT

A location in partial shade with deep rich soil is best. Bee balm can take full sun if planted where the soil never dries out. Air movement will also help minimize powdery mildew. If at all possible, choose a location where you can see the plant in bloom from indoors. It is entirely possible you may get to watch a hummer race from flower to flower. Because it spreads with enthusiasm and can become ragged and sad looking from mildew at season's end, you may not want to plant bee balm in a formal garden or right outside the front door.

HOW TO PLANT

Maintain soil moisture by adding plenty of organic matter to the native soil. An organic mulch will help keep soil moist. Bee balm can be an overpowering plant. Do not plant it next to anything small and delicate. Space plants 18 in. apart.

CARE AND MAINTENANCE

A severe pruning after bee balm finishes blooming often triggers a second bloom in the fall. Removal of dead flowers during the season can extend the first round of blooms for over 2 months. Begin spraying for powdery mildew as soon as you see white spots. If you want to dry the leaves for tea, harvest those you want before you start to spray. Cut the plants down to the ground in the fall. Divide in the spring every 2 or 3 years.

ADDITIONAL INFORMATION

Oswego tea is named for the Oswego (or Otsego) Indians who first introduced early settlers to its pleasures. It is primarily a drink imbibed for its pleasant taste, but it is sometimes taken to treat coughs or a sore throat. John Bartram, a famous American botanist in the 1700s, sent seeds of this plant to England. It has been cultivated throughout Europe since that time, where it is known as golden melissa or Indian nettle.

ADDITIONAL SPECIES, CULTIVARS, OR VARIETIES

M. fistula is a little taller and a little more unruly than *M. didyma*, though its lavender flowers are similiar in appearance. It is extremely drought tolerant. Varieties of *M. didyma* include 'Adam', 'Cambridge Scarlet' (an old favorite), 'Gardenview Scarlet' (a new favorite), and 'Squaw'', which all produce red flowers. 'Mahogany' and 'Raspberry Wine' are dark red. 'Marshall's Delight' and 'Croftway' are pink. 'Snow Queen' seems to be the only white available. 'Blue Stocking' and 'Prairienacht' are violet-purple; 'Purpurkrone' is a true purple variety.

Black-Eyed Susan

Rudbeckia fulgida

Other Names: Showy Coneflower,
   Orange Coneflower
Height: Usually 1¹/₂ to 4 ft., but up to 12 ft.
Spread: 24 in.; varies
Flowers: 2 to 4 in. wide, golden orange petals
Bloom Period: July to October
Zones: 4, **5**, **6**, **7**, 8, 9

Light Requirement:

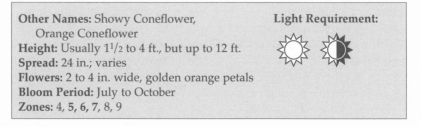

The color of a black-eyed Susan is hard to describe. It is golden orange, but the color has an intensity that is difficult to put into words. A field in bloom is electric. The full, hairy plants can grow up to 12 ft. tall in moist fertile soil, but garden varieties are usually smaller. The flowers have brown-to-black center discs that mature to a raised cone shape surrounded by golden orange petals. The leaves are about 6 in. long. Black-eyed Susans spread by rhizomes, and clumps often get quite large. The plant's stem branches and produces many flowers along its length. The flowers are excellent for cutting and blend beautifully with zinnias and giant marigolds in a brilliant summer bouquet. Regular cutting will extend the bloom period, though black-eyed Susan always enjoys a long season of bloom. The conelike seedpods that follow are useful in dried arrangements. Plants often volunteer from the seed that drops. Named varieties are far more compact and floriferous than the species. You may not be happy with volunteer seedlings; they invariably revert to the species type and lack the productivity and uniformity of the varieties. If you want more plants, keep in mind that they grow at a snappy rate and can be divided in spring. Black-eyed Susan is native from New Jersey to Florida and west to Michigan. It is generally found in open fields.

WHEN TO PLANT

It is best to plant or divide black-eyed Susan in early spring.

WHERE TO PLANT

Black-eyed Susan prefers full sun but will tolerate light shade. It will grow in a wide range of soils with almost any degree of moisture content, though it will not survive in soggy sites. It spreads and shows to its best advantage when planted en masse, so give this plant room to stretch out. It also works well in an informal perennial bed or as the perennial in an annual cutflower garden. Plant in an iris bed, and the summer blooming black-eyed Susan will take over after the irises have finished up.

HOW TO PLANT

Black-eyed Susans are not fussy and establish easily. Potted plants are usually available in spring. If you see them in bloom in containers in the summer, you can just pop them in your garden. They will usually do well. Just be sure to keep newly planted black-eyed Susans well watered during the heat of summer, and mulch heavily in the fall.

CARE AND MAINTENANCE

Leaf miners and powdery mildew can affect the plant, but they are rarely serious problems. Control when you see you have one of these problems. Continual removal of dead flowers will encourage more flower production. Divide every 3 or 4 years.

ADDITIONAL INFORMATION

There is another species, commonly a roadside plant, *R. hirta*, which includes among its named varieties the beautiful gloriosa daisy. These plants make wonderful additions to your garden, either as annuals or biennials grown as annuals. While they may self-sow, they are not perennial. To avoid disappointment, be sure to get the species you want. The flowers of these two species can be very similar and are easily confused.

ADDITIONAL SPECIES, CULTIVARS, OR VARIETIES

The most popular black-eyed Susan is 'Goldsturm'. It has 4-in. flowers on 2 ft. stems. Propagate by cuttings only. Plants from seed are sometimes sold as 'Goldstrum strain', but they will not be uniform. *R. f. deamii* is more floriferous than the species and has broader foliage.

Blanketflower

Gaillardia × grandiflora

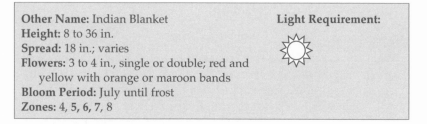

Other Name: Indian Blanket	**Light Requirement:**
Height: 8 to 36 in.	
Spread: 18 in.; varies	
Flowers: 3 to 4 in., single or double; red and yellow with orange or maroon bands	
Bloom Period: July until frost	
Zones: 4, 5, 6, 7, 8	

lanketflower creates a colorful, long-lasting display. Its tolerance of dry growing conditions makes it invaluable. The large showy flowers are very attractive and make excellent cut flowers. Flower petals are almost raggedy tipped. Blanketflower's colors combine beautifully with yellow and orange marigolds in the garden or in a vase. The biggest blast of color comes in early spring, but blanketflower will continue to produce a significant number of blooms for the rest of the summer. If you regularly remove the dead flowers as they fade, flower production will be more generous. Before you prune off every dead flower, keep in mind that the seedheads are also attractive and last a long time. *G. × grandiflora* is a cross between the perennial *G. aristata* (which has yellow flowers), a native of North Dakota, Colorado, and Oregon, and the painted gaillardia *G. pulchella*, native from Virginia to Florida and west to New Mexico. According to *Hortus III*, the hybrid has now naturalized in the west.

WHEN TO PLANT

Strains of blanketflower can be planted from seed in the spring and will bloom the first year. Plant container grown plants in spring or fall.

WHERE TO PLANT

Grow blanketflower in full sun in loose, well-drained soil. It works well in a cutflower garden, as part of a perennial border, in rock gardens, in containers, or even as a groundcover for small areas. Blanketflower tolerates heat better than many other summer flowers.

How to Plant

It is best to plant from divisions. Space plants about 18 in. apart.
Heavy soils, especially those that stay wet over the winter, are
deadly to the blanketflower. Add a 2:1 mixture of organic matter
and sand to loosen soil. *Never* add sand to heavy clay soil without
adding organic matter as well, even if the plants prefer sandy soil.
Sand and clay make concrete, and no plant will grow in it.

Care and Maintenance

The plants are not very long lived. The clumps sometimes die out in
the center and require division every 2 or 3 years. A major pruning
in late summer will encourage a late fall bloom. Removal of spent
blooms keeps fresh flowers coming.

Additional Information

The Department of Parks in New Brunswick planted blanketflower
in the island bed in the middle of Albany Street (a main road in the
downtown area). The plants were planted under very young shade
trees, with black-topped road and busy car traffic on either side of
the site. These blanketflowers tolerated their adverse environment
amazingly well. They bloomed late every spring and sporadically
through the summer for 3 or 4 years with very little attention.

Additional Species, Cultivars, or Varieties

'Baby Cole' is a dwarf that grows from 6 to 8 in. tall. 'Burgundy'
has wine red flowers and can reach 5 ft. 'Goblin' has dark-red
flowers with a yellow border. It grows to only about 1 ft. 'Yellow
Queen' is all yellow and reaches 2 to 5 ft. tall. 'Monarch' is the
same size. Its flowers come in a range of colors from yellow and
orange to dark red.

Bleeding Heart

Dicentra spectabilis

Other Names: Common Bleeding Heart,
Old Fashioned Bleeding Heart
Height: 1 to 3 ft.
Spread: 1 to 3 ft.
Flowers: Deep-rose, 1¹/₂ in. dangling
heart shaped flowers
Bloom Period: May and June
Zones: 4, 5, 6, 7, 8

Light Requirement:

There is no flower as romantic as the bleeding heart. Each heart-shaped blossom is pierced at the point with a white dagger. Each row of pierced blossoms dangles from horizontal stems like a necklace Cupid would wear. They are delicate and graceful, and their shape is the poet's perfect symbol for a broken heart. Do not let the romantic whimsy of the author dissuade you from planting these gentle beauties: bleeding hearts are dependable perennials that return year after year with very little fuss. Though the plant dies back by midsummer, you can plant summer annuals at the base of each bleeding heart and by the time the perennial fades, the annuals will have taken over, lasting until frost. The foliage of the bleeding heart has its own appeal. The leaves are compound and graceful. The stems grow up and arch over. The upper part of the stem has a hint of red that turns yellow in hot weather, but does not become shabby looking. When bleeding hearts fade, cut them back and let your summer annuals fill in the gap.

WHEN TO PLANT

Early spring is the best time to plant.

WHERE TO PLANT

Plant bleeding heart in deep woodland soils in sites with partial to deep shade. This plant is an excellent choice for a shaded rock garden, under shade trees, or in a romantic nook.

HOW TO PLANT

Prepare the soil as for any woodland plant. Double dig, if necessary, in hard compact soils. Add large amounts of organic matter and use an organic mulch. Mix bleeding heart with spring flowers such as trillium, bloodroot, and violet. This plant works well with ferns and hostas, which can fill in easily when the bleeding heart has finished blooming.

CARE AND MAINTENANCE

Keeping the plants well watered in hot weather will prolong the seasonal life of the foliage. Regular attention to an organic mulch will help replenish the organic matter in the soil. Bleeding heart has no serious insect or disease problems. It can live for years with little or no attention. Be sure to mark the location of the plant in order to avoid inadvertently digging it up in the fall. Plants can be divided in early spring.

ADDITIONAL INFORMATION

The plant does not produce enough flowers to allow you to cut them often, but a few mixed in with a spring bouquet of tulips can be stunning. The contrast of flower size and shape, as well as the horizontal carriage of the bleeding heart blooms on their stems, creates a special image. (A few sprigs in a bridal bouquet would be very romantic.)

ADDITIONAL SPECIES, CULTIVARS, OR VARIETIES

The only variety of *D. spectabilis* is 'Alba'. It is pure white but not quite as hardy as the species. Fringed bleeding heart, *D. eximia*, has fernlike foliage and pink dangling hearts that appear throughout the summer. It forms neat clumps which do not spread from the roots, but seedlings can pop up anywhere. They are easily weeded if you don't want them, though they add to a natural woodland setting. There are also hybrids of *D. eximia* and *D. formosa* available. 'Luxuriant' has dark reddish-pink flowers. 'Bountiful' has red blooms.

Candytuft

Iberis sempervirens

Other Name: Evergreen Candytuft
Height: 4 to 12 in.
Spread: Up to 3 ft.
Flowers: 1½ in. white flowers in flat or
   rounded clusters
Bloom Period: Late May through June
Zones: 4, 5, 6, 7, 8 (possibly 3 and 9)

Light Requirement:

The snowdrift effect of candytuft in bloom is a large part of this dainty but durable perennial's appeal. Its flowers completely cover the plant. The narrow, dark green, 1 to 2 in. long leaves stay green year round. They form a thick mat that can be used as a ground-cover in small spaces. Once the long-lasting flowers fade, upright bright green seedpods take their place. These should be removed at some point so that the plant will fill in and stay dense, but they are so interesting you will want to enjoy them for a while. Candytuft looks its absolute best when draped over a coarse gray rock. Walls cloaked in the veil of white are also impressive. Candytuft is ideal for rock gardens, borders, slopes, and terraced gardens, and in front of ever-green shrubs. Mix it with patches of columbine. The contrasting flower types complement each other rather than compete, as the creeping habit of the candytuft complements the arching branches of the colum-bine. In shady sites, blend in bleeding hearts and violets. In gardens that get full sun, late season tulips popping up through a carpet of candytuft is gorgeous. While you're at it, roll out the white carpet under azaleas and rhododendrons. This can create a stunning effect.

WHEN TO PLANT
Plant candytuft in early spring or early fall.

WHERE TO PLANT
Plant in deep, rich, well-drained soil. Candytuft is prized for use in partially shaded environments but will do well in full sun if kept moist. It will even tolerate deep shade, though you can't expect quite the same avalanche of flowers. Candytuft is one of the best

plants for planting in a rock garden and is simply lovely tucked here, there, and everywhere.

HOW TO PLANT

Plants are usually available in pots but can sometimes be purchased by the flat if you have an aggressive planting plan that calls for a large number of specimens. Candytuft is easily divided in early spring. This plant does not do well in soggy soil, especially in winter, so pile on the organic matter and till it in to insure good drainage.

CARE AND MAINTENANCE

As fascinating as the round green seedpods are, you need to remove them before they fully mature. If the seedpods are not removed, the plants become stretched out and bare at the base of the stems. An allover shearing will have them "thick as thieves" in no time. With some varieties, this pruning will trigger a second bloom in the fall. Keep candytuft watered, especially while it is in bloom. Dry soil shortens the blooming season.

ADDITIONAL INFORMATION

Though color in the garden is one of the major thrills of gardening, white candytuft combined with tall spurred white columbine and white tulips creates a place for angels to visit. Bees will come, too. They love candytuft.

ADDITIONAL SPECIES, CULTIVARS, OR VARIETIES

There are a number of related species, but none are readily available in the trade. The related perennial species are not as hardy, but the annuals may prove interesting. Thompson and Morgan carries seed. Varieties of *I. sempervirens* include 'Alexander's White', one of the most floriferous but hardy only in Zones 6, 7, and 8; and 'Snowflake', which stays at 8 in. but has larger flowers. 'Autumnalis', 'Autumn Snow', and 'Autumn Beauty' all rebloom in the fall.

Christmas and Lenten Rose

Helleborus niger and *H. orientalis*

> **Other Names:** Hellebores
> **Height:** 1 to 2 ft.
> **Spread:** 1 to 2 ft.
> **Flowers:** 2 to 4 in. flowers; creamy white, speckled, purple, or greenish
> **Bloom Period:** December and early spring
> **Zones:** 4, 5, 6, 7, 8
>
> **Light Requirement:**

Hellebores bloom with enthusiasm when most of the outdoor world has snuggled down for a long winter's nap. Don't be disappointed by the fact that they are not really roses. In size and shape the blooms do resemble a single rose, and a Christmas rose by any name is wonderful. Christmas rose blooms in December and the flowers last until spring. Lenten rose will open in January in a mild winter, but almost certainly by February. The nodding blooms are slightly camouflaged by the foliage, so those with creamy white or greenish blooms need to be appreciated up close. Purple or speckled blooms are easier to see. It is true that competition with giant zinnias or softball-sized peonies would make hellebores all but invisible, but in the bleakness of winter there is no competition. That is why the gutsy little hellebores are so striking. The flowers are certainly the main event, but the palmately divided leaves are also quite pleasing. They are almost evergreen, but the leaves can become a little ratty over the winter. In recent years, these plants and some of their relatives have skyrocketed in popularity. It wasn't long ago when an interested gardener had to search high and low to find a single offering in a catalog. Now there are new varieties, hybrids, and unusual species everywhere. The only surprise is that it took so long for them to be appreciated.

WHEN TO PLANT

Plant in early spring or early fall. Divide established plants in early fall.

WHERE TO PLANT

Plant in partial shade to deep shade. Hellebores like deep, rich, moist soil that is high in lime. Choose a location where you will be able to appreciate them in the winter. These plants do not like to be disturbed, so be sure to plant them where they can settle in and stay a while.

HOW TO PLANT

Use potted plants in order to disturb the roots as little as possible in the planting process. Dig deeply or double dig in hard-packed soil. Incorporate significant amounts of organic matter and be sure to lime thoroughly. An organic mulch will help retain soil moisture.

CARE AND MAINTENANCE

Hellebores are very long-lived and have no serious pest problems. They do not like to be disturbed, so divide these plants only if you have a compelling need. If you must divide, do so in August or September. It will take a while for the plants to reestablish. Lenten rose will sometimes spread from seed but is never invasive. Pot up unwanted seedlings and give them away. These plants are too wonderful to waste. Always wear gloves when you work with hellebores; plant juices can cause a skin irritation. Hellebores are also poisonous if ingested.

ADDITIONAL INFORMATION

The Christmas rose was an integral part of a Victorian Christmas. The open flowers floated in a bowl of water as a table centerpiece. To be sure they would be available, the flowers were sometimes forced in a greenhouse. English ivy, barberry, or holly may have been used as the greenery. It is quite curious that this flower went out of fashion. We must be glad that they are back. One source says that hellebores will make long-lasting cut flowers if the stems are split. Another source recommends searing the cut ends or dipping them in boiling water.

ADDITIONAL SPECIES, CULTIVARS, OR VARIETIES

Several species that are now available were unheard of a few years ago. *H. foetidus* bears the awful name "stinking hellebore" or "bears-foot hellebore." It blooms in early spring and has very attractive lanceolate leaves. *H. odorous* is hardy only in Zones 6, 7, and 8, so avoid planting it in northwest New Jersey. There are quite a few hybrids (crosses of the different species) available now. 'Atrorubens' is quite popular and has purple flowers.

Columbine

Aquilegia × hybrida

Height: 1¹/₂ to 3 ft.
Spread: 18 in.
Flowers: Equally ornate sepals and petals,
    often in contrasting colors; available
    in many colors
Bloom Period: May and June
Zones: 5, 6, 7, 8, 9
	Light Requirement:

ood elves live among the columbine. No other flower has enough beauty and whimsy to keep the mythical creatures content. Columbine leaves are reminiscent of a maidenhair fern, though they are not quite as finely carved. The exquisite buds shyly nod their heads, pointing their long threadlike spurs into the air. Some open to face the sun, at which time the long spurs point down. Columbines are so fragile that they don't seem real. But they are—a real and special gift to remind us of the wonders of nature. Most columbines have spurs, though the length varies. A species from Texas and Mexico, *A. longissima*, has spurs up to 6 in. long! (There are even some without spurs, but why bother?) Double-flowered types are interesting but don't have the ethereal quality that makes the singles seem so unreal. Columbines are not difficult to grow. They prefer partial shade and tolerate slightly more, but very deep shade may cut down on flower production. These plants can endure full sun, but be sure to avoid hot western exposures, and water adequately to keep them from drying out. Columbines are excellent for rock gardens, where they seem to have sprung up by magic. They are too free-spirited to work in a formal design but can be mixed with ferns or trilliums in a naturalized setting. Early daffodils can be planted under shade trees to take advantage of the sun before the tree leafs out. Columbines follow daffodils in sequence of bloom, and the ferny columbine leaves help camouflage the fading daffodil foliage.

WHEN TO PLANT
Plant columbine in early spring.

WHERE TO PLANT

Plant in partial shade in a naturalized or informal setting. Columbines look wonderful with candytuft, coral bells, later daffodils, violets, ferns, and hostas. Tucking them into the nooks and crannies of a rock garden may show off their whimsical nature to best advantage. The foliage will not last all summer, so mixing columbine with leafy hostas and summer annuals will make for a smooth transition.

HOW TO PLANT

Plants can be grown from seed sown in the garden in early spring, but they will not set flower until their second year. Plants grown from fall-sown seed will bloom the first spring if overwintered in a greenhouse. If you take this approach, be sure to use commercial seed. The plants hybridize with gay abandon, so the seed collected from garden plants is not likely to come true. Plants are available in containers in the early spring. Space about 18 in. apart. Be sure to amend the soil with lots of compost or other organic matter. Columbines are not fussy about soil, but it must be well-drained.

CARE AND MAINTENANCE

Watch out for leaf miners. They disfigure the leaves and cause early deterioration of the plant. Control at the first sign of the characteristic wavy lines on the leaf surface. Hand pick the damaged leaves and destroy them. Spray with an appropriate insecticide according to package directions. Because the plants reseed, flower quality will eventually be inferior to what it was when the plants were first planted. Trying to rejuvenate a patch after a leaf miner infestation is not worth the effort. Start over with fresh plants every 3 or 4 years.

ADDITIONAL INFORMATION

I once planted a patch of multicolored columbine that came up its second year with enormous pure white flowers. Perhaps the original plants reseeded themselves, but they certainly appeared to be the same plants in the exact same spots. They continued to come up in the same spots, with the same enormous white flowers, for years afterward. None of the possible explanations ever seemed to fit quite right. I concluded it must have been the hand of the wood elves.

ADDITIONAL SPECIES, CULTIVARS, OR VARIETIES

The Beidermeier strain comes in many colors with white-tipped petals. 'Crimson Star' and 'Red Star' have long red spurs. The Dragonfly hybrids produce large flowers in many colors. The McKana hybrids are similar but taller. Many more cultivars exist.

Daylily

Hemerocallis hybrids

Other Name: Tiger Lily
Height: 1 to 6 ft.
Spread: 2 to 3 ft.
Flowers: Large trumpet shaped flowers,
  each lasting only a day, in a variety
  of colors
Bloom Period: Summer
Zones: 4, **5, 6, 7,** 8, 9

Light Requirement:

There are 35,000 registered varieties of daylily. Surely there must be one that you like! There are probably many. Once you start with daylilies, you may want more than you can possibly plant. Even if you are not an avid gardener, you are likely familiar with the wild daylilies that can be found growing along the road and at the wood's edge. These are sometimes referred to as "tiger lilies," though in truth that name is reserved for a species of true lily. Ancestors of the daylily were brought over by early colonists. The plants' free spirit and care-free habits allowed them to spread. All the plants you see as you drive along the highway are escapees from the original cultivated specimens. This is amazing when you consider that daylilies are sterile and spread only from the roots. The botanical name *Hemerocallis* comes from the Greek for "beautiful for a day." It refers to the fact that each bloom lasts for only one day. Don't be discouraged! One day is enough. Each plant produces so many flowers during the season that there is never a shortage of color. If you choose varieties whose bloom seasons are staggered, you can have flowers for most of the summer. A few varieties even rebloom in the fall. There are so many colors of daylily from which to choose that you may struggle to decide on the perfect shade of red, yellow, gold, pink, coral, red, maroon, lavender, or purple. Choosing is the hardest part of growing daylilies. If you can't find what you want locally, you can purchase plants from one of the many mail-order companies that either specialize in daylilies or carry a large selection. Catalogs usually contain outstanding color photographs to help with the selection process.

WHEN TO PLANT

Early spring is the best time to plant, but planting any time from spring until mid-October is acceptable.

WHERE TO PLANT

Plant in full sun for the most flowers. Light shade in the late afternoon will prevent color fading in those varieties that tend to be bleached by strong sun. Daylilies can tolerate up to half a day of shade, but don't expect the same number of blooms. They are not particular about soil type, though moist soil conditions (not soggy) will encourage flower production.

HOW TO PLANT

The spacing of daylilies is variety dependent, but 12 to 24 in. apart is the usual range, and 16 in. is the most common. Plants are usually shipped bare root. Plant so that the roots are covered by about $1/2$ in. of soil. Plant potted specimens at the same depth they were growing in their containers. Mulch to help control weeds and retain soil moisture.

CARE AND MAINTENANCE

You can divide clumps any time from spring until about a month before the first hard freeze. Unless you have a compelling reason, try not to divide in summer, as this will disturb the blooming cycle. Keep daylilies well watered in hot weather to prolong bloom. Remove "scapes" (flower stalks) when all the buds have opened. You don't want energy going into making seeds when it can go into making more flowers. Daylilies have no serious pests.

ADDITIONAL INFORMATION

If you want to try something different, you can eat your daylilies. Leaves have the best flavor when they are 3 to 5 in. long. They are often stir-fried in oil or butter. Flower buds can be eaten raw in salads or cooked in a variety of ways. They are supposed to be particularly luscious when steamed with snow peas. You can even eat the day old flowers dipped in batter and deep-fried.

ADDITIONAL SPECIES, CULTIVARS, OR VARIETIES

There are too many varieties to describe. Make your selection based on color, time of bloom, and size. It is difficult to go wrong—they are all beautiful. (My personal favorite is a pink called 'Tani'.)

Evening Primrose

Oenothera species

Other Names: Sundrop, Suncup
Height: Usually 2 to 4 ft.; up to 10 ft.
Spread: Variable
Flowers: Fragrant, 1 to 4 in. wide flowers; usually yellow, sometimes white or pink
Bloom Period: May through July or longer
Zones: 5, 6, 7, 8, 9 (sometimes 4 and 10)

Light Requirement:

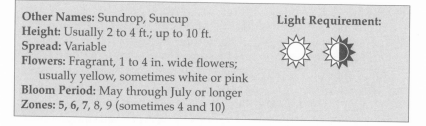

Oenothera is native to North America. There are over 100 species, of which at least one or two can be found in every state, so it is only natural that there is some confusion regarding this plant's common names. In theory, evening primrose opens in late afternoon as the sun sets. The flowers stay open all night, releasing an intoxicating fragrance until they close again at sunrise. Sundrops or suncups are supposed to open with the rising sun and stay open all day. They, too, are fragrant, though not quite as intense. Then there is *O. missouriensis,* equally well known as Ozark sundrop or Missouri primrose, which opens in the afternoon. Nomenclature confusion aside, these large, delicate flowers bring much cheer to the perennial border. Most of the species produce bright yellow flowers, but the blooms of showy primrose, *O. speciosa,* are a lovely shade of pink. All *Oenothera* spread with enthusiasm, so do not try to squeeze them into areas that are too tight. These plants spread so rapidly that they can be used successfully as a groundcover. Sundrops are particularly useful in hot, dry soils where many other perennials can become overwhelmed.

WHEN TO PLANT

Early spring is the best time to plant. Evening primrose can be started from seed in spring.

WHERE TO PLANT

Evening primrose thrives in full sun but can withstand light shade. Be sure to avoid wet sites. This plant does well in hot, dry locations in poorer soil. Though the flowers can be enjoyed all summer long, don't plant them in a confined bed close to the house. They spread, sometimes too aggressively, so you must give them room to stretch out, or prepare yourself for a perpetual battle to keep them confined. If you must have the flowers in a patch close to the house where you can best appreciate their fragrance, plant evening primrose in a container. Keep in mind that it will probably not overwinter if planted above ground.

How to Plant

Plants are easily established from potted specimens. They prefer drier soils and do well in most New Jersey landscapes as long as the area is well-drained. Heavy clay soils that stay wet will have to be double dug. Add organic matter and sand (in a 2:1 ratio) to keep the water from sitting. If you plant evening primrose in a large clay pot, you can sink the pot in the bed to both enjoy the flowers and contain the roots. Evening primrose can, for better or worse, also spread from seed. Space plants 1 to 2 ft. apart, depending on the species and on how quickly you need them to fill in.

Care and Maintenance

Japanese beetles seem to enjoy munching on evening primrose. Spray at the first sign of dining. Prune off the flower stalks as they finish blooming to keep plants from spreading by seed. This may also increase the number of blooms. Your biggest challenge with evening primrose will probably be to keep it in bounds. Choose the right site to eliminate or minimize this chore. If you want to divide an established patch, it is best done in spring.

Additional Information

O. biennis is the common evening primrose. The "skeletons," flower stalks left behind after the seeds have been released, make outstanding additions to dried arrangements. The pods open and curve back to resemble a flower. Soak the stalks in a solution of household bleach to lighten their color, then soak them in a bucket of fabric dye in the color of your choice. The inside surface of the seedpods will be a different shade from the outside surface. The effect is lovely.

Additional Species, Cultivars, or Varieties

O. speciosa produces pink blooms. It is sold as showy primrose or Mexican evening primrose, but it opens during the day. 'Siskiyou' has silvery pink flowers. *O. fruticosa*, the common sundrop that blooms during the day, is often called or confused with *O. tetragona*. Varieties include 'Fireworks', 'Yellow River', and 'Highlight'.

False Dragonhead

Physosegia virginiana

> **Other Names:** Obedient Plant, Lion's Heart, *Dracocephalum* spp.
> **Height:** Usually 3 ft., but can grow up to 5 ft.
> **Spread:** 18 in. and more
> **Flowers:** Tall spikes of pink or white; individual blooms resemble snapdragon flowers
> **Bloom Period:** August through September
> **Zones:** 4, 5, 6, 7, 8
>
> **Light Requirement:**

*P*hysostegia comes into bloom at a time when it is really needed. By August, summer annuals may be showing signs of wear. Powdery mildew is appearing, petunias are all stretched out, and pansies are finished. Then along comes false dragonhead like a seventh inning relief pitcher. The game isn't over, but it is time for a change. Each flowering stalk on this plant can produce many 8 to 10 in. flower spikes. One spike grows at the top, and several (called "axillary" spikes) grow along the sides. Each spike begins opening at the bottom and works its way up. The spikes at the top open sooner than the spikes that grow lower down on the plant. The entire process of blooming can last for 6 weeks, which will bring you all the way to early season chrysanthemums. False dragonhead is a member of the mint family and has the classic square stems to prove it. The leaves are toothed, oblong, and grow up to 5 in. long. Each individual flower resembles a snapdragon flower, hence the common name. The flowers will supposedly remain in place if twisted or jostled, which earns this plant its other common name, "obedient plant." *Physostegia* is native to North America and can be found growing from New England west to Minnesota and south to the Carolinas and Texas. The plants spread rapidly, but not viciously. The spikes make excellent cut flowers. They look very pretty in a vase with large flowered zinnias or a large bouquet of cosmos.

WHEN TO PLANT

Early spring is the best time to plant.

278

WHERE TO PLANT

False dragonhead does best in full sun but can tolerate slight shade. Well-drained soil is important. When growing this perennial in shade, the soil should be kept on the dry side to avoid problems. *Physostegia* is a tall plant, so place it toward the middle or back of borders. It can also work in a rock garden, though not in a tiny one. The roots are tenacious, making this plant a good choice for a mild slope.

HOW TO PLANT

You can plant false dragonhead from seed, but the better selections are best grown from division. They require better-than-average drainage, so be sure to amend soil with a 2:1 mixture of organic matter and sand and/or plant in a raised bed. These plants look very attractive popping up through low growing evergreens for late season color. The sight of pink flowers against the dark green groundcover is particularly pleasing. Make the biggest splash by mixing false dragonhead with perennial hibiscus, lythrum, and purple coneflowers for a major onslaught of passionate pink.

CARE AND MAINTENANCE

Division every 2 to 3 years is recommended. You may also want to keep an eye out for volunteers since this plant can spread from seed. False dragonhead is an easy care plant. (The only problem I have ever had with it was during a particularly soggy summer when the plants came down with a root rot that took out about 3/4 of the planting. The next year was drier and the plants recovered.)

ADDITIONAL INFORMATION

I searched extensively for some interesting tidbit of information about this plant; a medicinal use, Indian folklore, a craft or dye, food for the birds, a romantic story, something, anything. I found nothing, which is unusual when you consider that it is a native American plant. You will have to plant it based on its beauty alone.

ADDITIONAL SPECIES, CULTIVARS, OR VARIETIES

'Alba' and 'Summer Snow' are both white, though 'Alba' has a greater tendency to spread. 'Rosy Spire' produces rosy crimson flowers. 'Vivid' is bright pink or rose. 'Variegata' has green, gray, and cream foliage with lilac blooms.

Hosta

Hosta species

Other Names: Plantain Lily, *Funkia*
Height: 1 to 3 ft., taller when in bloom
Spread: Variable
Flowers: White, lavender, or violet flowers
    on one-sided racemes
Bloom Period: Summer
Zones: 4, **5, 6, 7,** 8, 9

Light Requirement:

*H*ostas are to shade gardeners what flour is to the baker. It is hard to bake without flour, but flour by itself is not much. (Okay, I admit it! I think *Hostas* are boring.) Hostas are absolutely dependable in deep shade where your options are limited. There are over 800 registered varieties. The main event is the rich leafy foliage, but don't forget about the flowers. Most bloom during the summer, some are quite showy, and others have a wonderful sweet fragrance. The flowers appear on spikes that grow straight up with flower buds all on one side. Those that have been selected for bloom may have flowers bold enough to resemble lilies, but make your choices carefully if you want spectacular flowers to accompany your spectacular leaves. Leaves are the distinguishing feature for the large majority of hostas. They come in infinite shades of green, green and white, green and yellow, blue green, blue green and green, and other color combinations. They can be as wide as they are long or long and narrow, heart shaped or almost round. The texture can be paper thin, thick and deeply veined, smooth, crinkled, or wavy edged. The leaves die down completely in the winter. Once established, hostas will last for years. The plants spread like a thick mat and make an excellent groundcover. If left undisturbed, a single clump may eventually reach 5 ft. across. The plants are not invasive, however, and spread slowly. Hostas plod along year after year. You may even forget they are there. For many people this might be the perfect garden plant.

WHEN TO PLANT

Hostas can be planted in early spring or early fall.

WHERE TO PLANT

Hostas prefer partial shade or even deep shade. Some will tolerate sun, but there are so many other choices for sunny sites that you might as well keep hostas in the shade where they will be happiest. The dappled shade under trees is ideal. Well-drained soil is important, especially in the winter, so be sure to avoid wet sites.

HOW TO PLANT

Plant from potted plants or divisions. Hostas need woodsy soil that is deep, fertile, high in organic matter, and well-drained. Be sure to provide better than average soil preparation. Hostas establish slowly and will do best when left where they were originally planted. Add a large quantity of organic matter such as leaf compost and double dig heavy soils. Mix hostas with bleeding hearts, ferns, trilliums, and violets. For summer color, add a mass planting of one color impatiens or begonias. The contrast can be very pleasing.

CARE AND MAINTENANCE

Hostas prefer not to be moved so don't divide them unless necessary. An annual application of fertilizer will help produce an abundance of lush leaves. Remove spent flower stalks to keep the plant's energy going into leaf and root production. Clean up dead leaves in the fall to keep the garden tidy and to avoid harboring pests. And now we come to hostas' major drawback: Slugs *love* hostas. Slugs thrive in the moist shady environment that encourages healthy plants. When slugs eat developing foliage, leaves open to reveal a series of chew marks all across the surface. Control with slug baits or diatomaceous earth. Hostas with thicker, waxy, textured leaves are somewhat less susceptible than the more delicate varieties.

ADDITIONAL INFORMATION

Some people adore hostas. If you happen to be one of them, you might be interested in joining the American Hosta Society. Their headquarters are in Vancouver, Washington. If you are seeking an unusual hosta, contact the catalog companies that specialize or feature these plants. Plant Delights Nursery in Raleigh, North Carolina, has an excellent selection, as does Klehm Nursery in Illinois.

ADDITIONAL SPECIES, CULTIVARS, OR VARIETIES

There are too many varieties to list. One particular variety may be hard to find. My personal favorites are those with very large, deeply textured blue leaves such as 'Elegans', 'Blue Mammoth', 'Krossa Regal', or a new variety called 'Abiqua Drinking Gourd'.

PERENNIALS

Iris

Iris species

Other Names: Flag, Rainbow Flower
Height: Up to 4 ft.
Spread: Variable
Flowers: Six-petaled (3 outer "falls," generally curved back, and 3 inner "standards," more upright); available in a variety of colors
Bloom Period: From early spring to early summer, depending on variety
Zones: 4, **5**, **6**, **7**, 8, or 9, depending on the species

Light Requirement:

There is probably no other grouping of plants more complicated than the iris. The Siberian iris blooms in June and has narrower leaves. It can tolerate some shade. The flowers have no "beards" (fuzzy filaments on the falls that look like a caterpillar), but they are easy to grow and very dependable. Japanese iris are stunningly beautiful. They require acidic soil that is constantly moist. Yellow Flag can grow in shallow standing water and is probably the "Fleur de lis" of the kings of France. Of all the irises (and there are many more than can be addressed here), the most popular garden iris is probably the bearded iris. It is a mishmash of crosses and recrosses resulting in some of the most breathtaking flowers grown in the garden. The standards are regally upright and the falls recurve gracefully with long, fuzzy beards, often in contrasting colors. Newer varieties may not produce quite as many blooms as older favorites, but they can produce flowers as large as softballs. A single flower in a vase can dominate a room.

WHEN TO PLANT
Plant in early spring or early fall.

WHERE TO PLANT
Unless the iris you are planting is clearly marked "shade tolerant," plant iris in full sun. Bearded iris must have soil with excellent drainage. For wet sites use Japanese iris or yellow flag.

How to Plant

Plant iris alone for impact or as part of a mixed border. Bearded iris bloom at a time of year when spring bulbs have finished and summer annuals have not yet gotten up to speed. If you mix them with annuals, the foliage will be interesting during the summer but the flowers will dominate while the annuals get established. Try a large bed of iris with cleome planted all around. Cleome reseeds and blooms all summer but offers no competition while iris is in bloom. When planting rhizomes, arrange them in groups of at least three. The rhizomes should barely show at the surface and the fans of leaves should point out so that the three plants do not grow together.

Care and Maintenance

Keep iris well watered during drought, especially the more moisture loving types. Remove dead foliage as it develops and, in the fall in particular, to minimize the overwintering of insects and disease. When all the buds have finished flowering, cut the flower stalks to keep the plants' energy from going into seed production. Most iris need to be divided every 3 or 4 years. Make divisions right after the plants finish blooming, 6 weeks after they finish blooming to give the rhizomes a chance to make fresh growth, or in early fall. The two biggest problems for iris are the iris borer and a bacterium that causes the leaves and rhizomes to rot. Iris borer larvae can be crushed, but you may need to spray with an appropriate insecticide when the leaves are 4 to 6 in. long, repeating the treatment at 10-day intervals. Good sanitation is important for keeping this pest under control. Borer damage sets the plant up for bacterial rot. You can identify the presence of this disease by the horrible stench deteriorating leaves produce. Eliminate infected portions of the rhizome. Do not mulch. Rhizomes need to be exposed to air. Let them dry for several days before replanting. Controlling the borers and good cultivation practices are your best defense against these problems.

Additional Information

The name Iris comes from a Greek messenger of the gods. She travelled on a rainbow that spanned the gap between heavens and earth. This is why iris is sometimes called "rainbow flower."

Additional Species, Cultivars, or Varieties

There are hundreds of species and thousands of varieties of iris. Of those commonly offered in catalogs, the large majority are hardy in New Jersey. Take care if you develop an interest in the Pacific Coast species, or in the English or Spanish iris—these may not be hardy in our state.

Mums

Chrysanthemum species

> **Other Names:** Chrysanthemum, Daisy
> **Height:** Up to 4 ft.
> **Spread:** Variable
> **Flowers:** Spoon petal, pompons, spiders, buttons, and doubles, wide color range
> **Bloom Period:** Late summer through fall
> **Zones:** Most are hardy in 4, **5, 6, 7**, 8, 9
>
> **Light Requirement:**

The world of chrysanthemums is another complex and convoluted maze. Those who choose to enter will find that most of these plants give spectacular results with minimal effort. Mums are the foundation of any end-of-season display. They come in an extraordinary range of colors that are rich rather than bright. Flowers grow in a variety of sizes and shapes. Giant pompon "football" mums can be almost the size of softballs; little "button" mums are about the size of a dime. "Doubles" have so many petals that you cannot see the center disc. Then there are "fried egg" types, whose large, domed, bright yellow discs are surrounded by white petals, truly resembling an egg. Spoon" mums have tubular petals that open at the tip like long handled spoons. "Spider" mums have long, twisted petals. The American Chrysanthemum Society lists 15 official flower types and over 3,000 different varieties. They come and go in the trade, but there are always plenty of mums from which to choose. Because most have been crossed and recrossed, most garden varieties of this plant have a highly questionable lineage. They are lumped together as *C. × morifolium* and commonly referred to as "Garden Mums." Local "field-grown" mums are generally hardy while florist types may not be. Filling your yard with blooming plants in September is a wonderful way to replace fading annuals and have a festive autumn. Fall planted mums often do not survive the winter. Small mums planted in early spring will grow enough roots to survive their first winter and may last for years.

WHEN TO PLANT

Plant mums in early spring after danger of frost has passed. Early fall is fine for autumn color, but think of these plants as annuals.

WHERE TO PLANT

Plant in full sun with good drainage. Plant en masse, as a specimen, with other perennials, in containers, in rock gardens, in cutflower gardens, in front of foundation plantings, next to the mailbox, by the front walk, or in any nook or sun-filled cranny.

HOW TO PLANT

It is best to plant small plants in early spring. It is difficult to think of mums in the spring, but if you want to grow them as perennials you must force yourself to do so. Once they begin producing flowers, these plants don't make many roots. They will not get established well enough to handle winter weather if you plant pretty plants already in bloom. Prepare the soil with plenty of organic matter to help keep soil moist and to improve drainage. Mums can get fairly large, so give them room. Mulch to help retain soil moisture and to control weeds. Mums are shallow rooted. Be sure not to do much hoeing or digging where they are planted.

CARE AND MAINTENANCE

An annual dose of fertilizer gives mums a healthy push. Pinch out the tiny leaves at the branch tips regularly until early to mid-July. This causes branching. More branches mean shorter, more compact plants with more flowers that will be less likely to flop over when it rains. Prune in late fall, after the plants brown. Take care not to damage the tiny green shoots at the base. These are next year's plants already getting started. If you don't get around to pruning in the fall, then early spring is fine. It makes a nice project for a sunny day in February. Divide in early spring.

ADDITIONAL INFORMATION

Like many flowers, mums have meaning when sent as a gift. Red mum flowers say "I love," yellow flowers mean "slighted love," and white flowers symbolize "truth." Choose your flowers, and your message, carefully.

ADDITIONAL SPECIES, CULTIVARS, OR VARIETIES

Varieties change too rapidly to list. Pick colors and flower types that best suit your fancy. *C. nipponicum* is the Nippon or Montauk daisy. It is different enough to warrant special attention. The leaves are almost succulent and the stems almost woody. This plant tolerates shore planting conditions. It blooms quite late, takes a wee bit of shade, and has large, classic yellow and white daisy flowers.

Oriental Poppy

Papaver orientale

Other Name: *P. bracteatum*
Height: 2 to 4 ft.
Spread: 2 to 3 ft.
Flowers: One 4 to 6 in. goblet shaped flower
    per stem; available in white, pink,
    orange, red
Bloom Period: Late May and June.
Zones: 4, 5, 6, 7 (maybe 3 and 8)

Light Requirement:

---

*P*oppies, irises, and peonies are important links between spring-flowering bulbs and summer annuals. Peonies and iris have soft colors that lean towards pastel. Poppies, on the other hand, are hot. Their colors, especially the reds, seem charged with electricity. The black centers and occasional black blotches at the base of the petals give intensity to even the lighter shades of pink. Flowers are large, with delicate, crepe-paper petals. The coarse, bristly leaves are up to 12 in. long and "pinnately dissected" (very deeply lobed) much like a feather. Each lobe is also toothed. To use the vernacular, the leaves are big, pointy, hairy, almost raggedy things. Actually, they are quite interesting in habit and appearance. By midsummer, poppy plants will have completely died down. This can leave a gap in the garden, but the creative use of annuals can fill in that space. In late summer or early fall, the plants reappear in a tight clump and stay that way until the following spring. Poppies make excellent cut flowers. Combine them with coral bells or cut branches of Van Houtte spirea, which both bloom at about the same time.

When to Plant

Potted poppies can be planted in early spring. Root divisions are made during the summer dormancy, or the clumps can be divided in early fall.

Where to Plant

Plant poppies in a site with plenty of sun and well-drained soil. They will not survive in soil that stays wet in winter. Poppy colors are spectacular when planted en masse, but remember that the plants die down over the summer. If you don't mind mixing colors together in the garden, you can plant poppies with other perennials, but if it's harmony you want, be sure to choose your colors carefully.

How to Plant

Plant root divisions 3 in. deep. If at all possible, start with potted plants; you will be much more likely to have success. Plant potted poppies at the same depth they were growing in their containers. Be sure to lighten heavy soils, as drainage is very important. Add organic matter (such as leaf compost) and sand in a 2:1 ratio to amend the soil prior to planting. Space the plants 2 to 3 ft. apart. They will eventually fill in this space.

Care and Maintenance

Plants will need to be divided every 4 or 5 years. It is best to do this in the early fall after the new rosette of leaves has emerged. Cut flowers for indoor use at night, just before the buds open. You will know they are almost ready when the nodding buds begin to straighten up. Sear the cut end before placing the stem in water. The flowers should open by morning. The seedpods are also very ornamental for use in dried arrangements. Dahlias planted around poppies in the spring will grow large and leafy enough to cover the gaps caused by the summer dormancy (dahlias also thrive in loose, well-drained soil in full sun).

Additional Information

Poppies have held magical qualities for me ever since I saw Dorothy and Toto fall asleep in the poppy field in *The Wizard of Oz*. Some gardeners, however, may find that poppies spread with a little too much enthusiasm. Because of their tendency to spread and their intense flower colors, a few specimens planted in a confined area is probably enough. In a large area, you can let them go. They will be *wonderful*.

Additional Species, Cultivars, or Varieties

'Fatima' and 'White King' produce white flowers. 'Turkenlouis' is bright red with fringed petals. 'Raspberry Queen' is a vivid raspberry pink with black blotches. 'Juliane' is pink without spots.

Peonies

Paeonia lactiflora

Other Names: *P. albiflora, P. chinensis, P. edulis, P. fragrans,* Chinese Peony, Garden Peony
Height: 1½ to 4 ft.
Spread: 3 ft.
Flowers: Four flower types, some up to 6 in. across; available in white, pink, or red with yellow centers
Bloom Period: May and June
Zones: 2,3, 4, **5, 6, 7,** 8

Light Requirement:

---

*I*f peonies had a longer season of bloom, they would be a contender for the most wonderful flower of all time. The blooming period is fairly short, however, and a really good storm can blow apart a beautiful display like feathers in a pillow fight. The beauty of these plants is transient, but they are absolutely magnificent. What peonies lack in duration within a season they make up for in longevity. A single plant can stay in the same spot for 50 years with a minimum of attention. New shoots, often tinted red, emerge in early spring and unfurl lovely compound leaves that add interest throughout the season. Early varieties open in early May while the latest hold off until June. Klehm Nursery in Champaign, Illinois, is one of the largest breeders and suppliers of peonies in the country. They describe four flower types: "Single," which has one or two rows of petals and many bright yellow stamens in the center; "Double," which produces numerous petals and is often fragrant; "Japanese," five or more rows of outer petals with a center full of "staminodium" or abortive anthers; and "Bomb," which has outer petals and a center tuft of very dense petals.

WHEN TO PLANT

Plant any time in the fall when the ground is not frozen. September and October are the best times to plant. Spring planting of potted plants is fine.

WHERE TO PLANT

Peonies need full sun and well-drained soil. A mass planting can be appreciated from a little distance, but specimen plants or a selection of varieties should be located where you can get very friendly. Avoid locating peonies close to large trees, as they will compete for nutrients and moisture.

How to Plant

Prepare the soil at least 1 ft. deep. These plants will be in this spot for a long time, so help them get cozy. Make sure the "eyes," or growing points, are facing up. In the colder portion of the state, set the eyes 2 in. below the surface. They can be planted closer to the surface in the south. Mulch is recommended, especially during the first season.

Care and Maintenance

Peonies are not fussy. Some varieties benefit from the use of a support. The weight of the flowers, especially when they are wet, can bend the stems to the ground. Remove spent flowers to prevent seed formation. Cut back when foliage turns brown in the fall. The only problem peonies may experience is *Botrytis*, or gray mold. Flowers suffering from this disease turn gray and never open. Plants are more likely to be affected in wet seasons. Control with a fungicide, beginning when the flowers are pea-sized. Spray weekly until they finish blooming.

Additional Information

Ants are often found crawling all over the buds and open flowers. They do not damage the plant or the flowers. They simply enjoy the sweet exudate that covers the buds. You may want to shake ants off before bringing in cut flowers, but there is no need to use commercial insecticides.

Additional Species, Cultivars, or Varieties

This is another flower that has thousands of listed varieties. Have fun, but watch out. They can become addicting. Tree peonies, *P. suffruticosa*, are hardy plants with a small treelike habit. They can reach 7 ft. and bloom about one month earlier than the herbaceous peonies. There are several true yellow tree peonies which are not readily available in the herbaceous peonies. Fern-leaf peony, *P. tenuifolia*, is small and slow growing, and usually produces red flowers. This species is not as easy-going as the others.

Purple Coneflower

Echinacea purpurea

Other Names: *Rudbeckia purpurea* (commonly used but incorrect), *Brauneria purpurea* (also incorrect), Hedgehog Coneflower
Height: Usually 3 ft.; up to 6 ft.
Spread: Usually 2 ft.
Flowers: Open with a flat disc and rose-purple ray flowers up to 6 in. across; disc develops into a spiny cone
Bloom Period: Late July to frost
Zones: 4, 5, 6, 7, 8, 9

Light Requirement:

Purple coneflower is a wildflower that can be found throughout the central, east, and southeastern United States. It is a wonderful native perennial that spreads but is not invasive, and it flowers its little heart out for much of the summer and early fall. With its large coarse leaves and an open habit, this is not exactly a delicate looking plant, but the enormous daisylike flowers are cheerful and long lasting. Petals are often flat, like a classic daisy, but they can sometimes be a little droopy in an appealing kind of way. They make outstanding cut flowers that look fabulous with Queen Anne's lace for a wildflower bouquet or mixed with garden annuals like zinnias and cosmos. Purple coneflower can tolerate heat, drought, and wind better than most. It is among the perennials suggested for planting at the shore where it will look lovely planted with the fuzzy silver leaves of lamb's ears. Plants are best placed at the back of a border where their less-than-meticulous growth habit won't be a problem. Bees and butterflies will flock to purple coneflowers wherever they are planted.

WHEN TO PLANT
Plant in spring or early fall.

WHERE TO PLANT
Give purple coneflowers plenty of sun and a little room to stretch. They are not enormous plants but are likely to be among the tallest in the perennial border. They can tolerate moderately dry soils. The seeds are often included in wildflower mixes for meadow planting

or along roadsides. They look lovely naturalizing in a meadow with tall ornamental grasses like *Panicum* 'Heavy Metal', which is a tall, straight grass with metallic-blue foliage.

How to Plant
This plant is not particular about its soil, but good soil preparation is always beneficial. Purple coneflowers are easy to establish and will usually bloom the first year. Potted plants will be the easiest but seed germinates readily.

Care and Maintenance
Take lots of cut flowers and remove the rest as they fade. This will encourage flower production right up until frost. Powdery mildew can be a problem but is not as serious as it is on other plants like phlox or bee balm. Watch out for Japanese beetles. Spray as soon as you see them munching.

Additional Information
Purple coneflower is the *Echinacea* of herbal fame. The entire plant is used in the industry: leaves, stems, flowers, and seeds are usually processed together. The roots are processed separately. Until recently, plants were collected from the wild, but constant increases in demand have introduced the plant to commercial cultivation right here in the Garden State. *Echinacea* is often used to make a tea that is supposed to boost the immune system.

Additional Species, Cultivars, or Varieties
'Alba' and 'White Swan' produce white flowers. 'Magnus' is a very red purple. 'Bravado' has extra large flowers that tend not to droop. 'Robert Bloom' has crimson purple flowers with a particularly long period of bloom. *E. pallida* has larger flowers that are pale purple, have more slender petals, and almost always droop. This plant is rare as an ornamental but is important as an herb.

Rose Mallow

Hibiscus moscheutos

<table>
<tr><td>

Other Names: Mallow Rose, Swamp Rose
Mallow
Height: 3 to 8 ft.
Spread: 3 ft.
Flowers: Five petaled blooms grow up to
12 in. wide; available in white, pink, or red
Bloom Period: August and September
Zones: 5, 6, 7, 8, 9

</td><td>

Light Requirement:

</td></tr>
</table>

*R*ose mallow flowers are so enormous that they don't seem real. The show stopping extravaganza of frisbee-sized flowers is like nothing else in the garden. Even a single plant will make passersby point and exclaim. A mass planting will stop traffic. The size and vivid color of the blooms are certainly the best reasons for growing rose mallow in the garden. Happily, rose mallow provides these pleasures with very little effort on the part of the gardener. Once established, a plant will return for years. The clump always stays about the same size and does not need to be divided. It actually does best when left undisturbed. Under the right conditions, rose mallow will spread from seed, but years of fabulous flowers may not produce a single volunteer seedling. Then one year you may find a patch of seedlings to yank or transplant as the spirit moves you. One aspect of this plant's growth habit is worth noting: it shows no signs of life until very late in the spring. Just as you are ready to give up hope, a tiny green shoot emerges. Then the plant grows so fast you that don't have time to blink. This habit can be frustrating for those who impatiently await the blooms, but use it to your advantage. When planted in a bed of spring flowering bulbs, rose mallow offer no competition for the flowers that rule spring gardens, but its fast growing foliage will help camouflage the bulbs' fading leaves. As the plants fill in, they become a solid mass of large leaves. By late summer you get a second blast of color in the same bed. Rose mallow grows best in wet ground where many other garden favorites cannot survive. They make an excellent choice for planting in the arduous conditions at the shore.

WHEN TO PLANT
Plant in spring.

WHERE TO PLANT

Rose mallow will be happiest in full sun in moist-to-wet soil. It will survive in soils that are average to slightly dry if you water during hot weather. Rose mallow will also tolerate light shade. It makes for great "drive-by" impact on the corner or by the mailbox. In a mass planting the flowers are spectacular. Mix with bulbs and the plants will fill in to hide deteriorating foliage. As part of a perennial border, they bloom later in the season when most other perennials have finished. They never spread out of their space or crowd out smaller plants. Choose a spot where these plants can stay put for a few years.

HOW TO PLANT

Rose mallow's native habitat is North American wetlands, so do your best to plant in soil that will retain moisture. Add copious amounts of organic matter such as leaf compost to the soil prior to planting. Your best chance for success is to plant potted plants in the spring. Seed is readily available and can be sown indoors in March to bloom the following summer. Starting seed outdoors when the ground warms up will produce plants, but they may not flower in the first year. Always use an organic mulch to retain soil moisture. Space plants 3 ft. apart.

CARE AND MAINTENANCE

Don't bother trying to cut the flowers for indoor use. They wilt almost immediately. Keep mulch intact to prevent the soil from drying out. Remove spent flowers to conserve plant energy. Cut back the plants when the stalks yellow in late fall or early spring. Don't divide. This plant prefers to be left alone. Rose mallow has no serious insect or disease problems.

ADDITIONAL INFORMATION

On a local country road is a stretch that goes through a very soggy patch of marshy woods. Early one late summer morning, I drove past this patch as the sun streamed through the raggedy marsh trees. In an open area, in every nook and cranny right up to the tree line, pink rose mallows were opened with their faces tilted to catch the morning sun. The thousands of huge flowers in perfect uniformity were one of the most beautiful sights nature has ever offered me.

ADDITIONAL SPECIES, CULTIVARS, OR VARIETIES

'Southern Belle' is often sold as a mixed-color cultivar. 'Disco Belle' is a dwarf that grows to 2 ft. 'Lady Baltimore' has leaves similar to a large maple leaf and bright pink flowers with large red centers. 'Lord Baltimore' has intense red flowers. 'Blue River II' is pure white.

Shasta Daisy

Chrysanthemum × superbum

Other Names: *C. maximum, Leucanthemum,* Pyrenees Chrysanthemum **Height:** 1 to 4 ft. **Spread:** Up to 2 ft. **Flowers:** White with yellow center; up to 6 in. across **Bloom Period:** June through August **Zones: 5, 6, 7,** 8 (possibly 4)	**Light Requirement:**

*T*he shasta daisy is the classic daisy flower. The blooms are large with single or double white petals and sunny yellow centers. These are the *friendliest* of all flowers. Shastas are cheerful, free flowering, and unpretentious, and they make people smile. This is one of the few mums that bloom early in the year. It was developed by Luther Burbank (1849-1926), which accounts for the confusion of the botanical name. Burbank was an incredible plant breeder and a terrible recordkeeper. *C.* × *superbum* is probably a hybrid of *C. maximum* and *C. lacustre*, but there have been so many crosses and selections that the pedigree is quite fuzzy. Regardless of the exact route of development, the shasta daisy is a wonderful addition to the perennial garden. It produces a big blast of flowers early in the season, and will continue to put out flowers here and there for most of the summer. If you remove dead flowers regularly, you will be rewarded with more prolific flowering. This should not be difficult since shasta daisies make outstanding cut flowers. The leaves are quite shiny, toothed, and almost evergreen but not quite. The foliage forms a thick mat from which the 2 to 4 ft. tall stems shoot up to produce the flowers. Shasta daisies are not fussy, but they are not particularly long-lived. Divide every 2 or 3 years to keep them thriving.

WHEN TO PLANT

Plant shasta daisies in spring.

WHERE TO PLANT

Shasta daisies prefer full sun but will adapt to a little shade. Whether they should be planted in the back or front of the perennial border depends on the variety. Short varieties stay about 1 ft. tall while others can reach 4 ft. Shasta daisies are a good choice for mixing in with bulbs and annuals. They bloom in June after bulbs have finished and before annuals really take off. The flowers are large enough and bright enough to be appreciated from a distance. They will even have "drive-by" impact if you plant a large patch or border.

How to Plant

Like other chrysanthemums, shastas need well-drained soil. Adding organic matter before planting is always a good idea, especially in heavy clay. Mulch to protect the shallow roots. Space most varieties 12 in. apart. Larger types may need a little more room.

Care and Maintenance

Regular removal of the dead flowers will encourage bloom throughout the season. Early pinching of tall varieties will make for more compact plants that produce a larger number of smaller flowers. If you prefer larger flowers, combine pinching with some disbudding (removal of flower buds) for compact plants that have big flowers. Control aphids when you see them. Divide plants every 2 or 3 years.

Additional Information

In the language of flowers, the daisy is said to represent "innocence." A very old-fashioned name is "bairn-wort," which means "children's flower." There may be many daisies other than the shasta, but these are the ideal. Choose this plant when you need to know if "he loves me" or "she loves me not."

Additional Species, Cultivars, or Varieties

'Alaska' is considered more cold tolerant than most and is hardy to Zone 4. 'Dwarf Snow Lady' and 'Little Miss Muffet' are dwarfs that grow to 1 ft. tall. 'Becky' has a particularly long period of bloom. 'Aglaya' is a frilly double. *C. coccineum*, the painted daisy, produces the classic daisy flower in intense pinks and reds as well as white. It is an excellent cut or garden flower. Painted daisy is another *Chrysanthemum* that blooms in spring. Look for its brilliant flowers in June and July. The flowers are not usually as large as the shasta, but they mix well together in the garden or in a vase.

Yarrow

Achillea millefolium

Other Names: Milfoil, Sneezewort
Height: 1 to 3 ft.
Spread: About 2 ft.
Flowers: 2 in. "corymbs" (flat clusters of tiny
 flowers); commonly white but also in
 shades of pink, lilac, and red
Bloom Period: July to September
Zones: 3, 4, **5, 6, 7**, 8, 9

Light Requirement:

*T*his yarrow is native to Europe but has naturalized over much
of North America. The wild type is almost always white, but may
occasionally have hints of pink. Selection and hybridization have
developed a slight tendency to pink into many wonderful pink-to-
red varieties. Yarrow is an outstanding perennial for sunny, hot, dry
places in less-than-ideal soil. If you really want to take advantage of
its cooperative nature, mow it down after it blooms and it will start
all over. Flowers first open in early summer. After the initial bloom, a
significant number of blossoms continue to be produced. Yarrow is
sometimes the last flower left blooming in the fall. This plant may on
occasion spread with too much enthusiasm. The cultivars are less
likely to do this than is the wild type. In most cases, pulling out a few
handfuls when it stretches over the line is sufficient to keep it under
control. Yarrow's creeping and tenacious root system make it perfect
for use as a groundcover, or to secure soil on slopes and banks. It
is also a primary ingredient in wildflower mixes. Yarrow's feathery
foliage is colored the dark, dusty green of the ocean when angry. It
can be used to make an olive green dye. The leaves are covered in
soft hairs and have a very distinctive aroma when crushed. The list of
yarrow's medicinal uses in old European lore and American Indian
lore seems endless. With the rising interest in herbs today, it is among
the plants in highest demand.

When to Plant
Potted plants can be planted any time from spring through fall.
Seed started indoors in late winter will bloom the first year. Make
divisions in spring or fall.

Where to Plant

Plant yarrow in a very sunny location. It adapts to different soil types but will not do well in wet ground. Take advantage of its durability and plant yarrow in skimpy dry soils where most plants languish. Although it spreads, yarrow looks very natural rambling over large rocks in a rock garden. Plant it on a slope or bank as a pretty groundcover, or mix it with perennials and annuals in a cut-flower garden. The delicate foliage and clusters of tiny blooms make an interesting contrast to the large flowered daylilies which bloom at the same time. Choose your colors carefully.

How to Plant

There is nothing tricky about planting yarrow. The plants will do their absolute best in good loamy soil, but average garden soil will suffice as long as it is not soggy. Direct seed in early spring or early fall. If you spring seed, you may have to wait until the second year for flowers. Space plants 12 to 24 in. apart.

Care and Maintenance

Cut back after bloom to keep plants attractive and to encourage repeat bloom. Mow yarrow once a year when it is used as a groundcover. Divide plants every 3 or 4 years. Powdery mildew can make an appearance, but it is not usually serious.

Additional Information

Yarrow makes outstanding dried flowers. Cut at the peak of bloom and hang upside down in a dry, shady place. Even the dried brown clusters of wild yarrow or garden varieties can be used. Cut them after they have dried in the field. They can be soaked upside down in a solution of household bleach and subsequently dyed with fabric dye. Spray paint or floral sprays can also be effective.

Additional Species, Cultivars, or Varieties

The many varieties of yarrow now available include selections and hybrids of *A. millefolium* with *A. × taygetea*. The Galaxy hybrids have a wonderful array of colors such as 'Appleblossom' pink, 'Salmon Beauty', 'Great Expectations' yellow, and 'The Beacon' red. Other varieties include 'Fireland', an intense red, and 'Cerise Queen', cherry red. *A. filipendulina* is the classic yellow yarrow. The standard variety is 'Coronation Gold'. *A. ptarmica* 'The Pearl' is a delicate white yarrow that can be used as a lovely alternative to baby's breath.

Bulbs, Corms, and Tubers

*B*ULBS, CORMS, AND TUBERS ARE SOME OF THE MORE MAGICAL ASPECTS OF THE PLANT WORLD. You take a little brown lumpy thing, stick it in the ground, wave a magic wand, and POOF, you have flowers.

Fall is the time to plant many bulbs for flowers in the spring. It doesn't matter how many you plant, come spring you will always wish you had planted more. The actual planting is almost an act of faith. You know that if you plant these flowers, you truly believe in your heart that spring will come. It is a hex sign against Old Man Winter. No matter how hard winter may try to hang on, these bulbs are going to push out of the ground and burst forth in spring. The thrill of seeing the tiny green tips poking up in spring and the first hint of purple crocus, sometimes right through the snow, is an incredible lift to sagging spirits. Winter doldrums fly out the window. It *proves* that spring is coming: the rebirth of life, a fresh start.

It is hard to pick a favorite spring bulb. Crocus are first and thus very powerful little flowers in the battle against winter. Plant hundreds, even thousands in your lawn. They will bloom a sea of color while the rest of the world barely stirs. By the time you need to mow the grass, they will be long gone. Add snowdrops, winter aconite, and miniature iris as an army to fight back winter.

Daffodils offer the next big push. Daffodils can go under shade trees since they bloom before the leaves come out. They will naturalize and spread; each year you will have more than the year before. Try pink ones, and butterfly flowers, and tiny Rip Van Winkles in the rock garden. Daffodils are easy and make the best cut flowers. Mix them all together or plant a patch of one kind.

The daffodil season overlaps the tulip season. There is nothing like tulips for an explosion of color. You get your biggest impact if you plant a mass of one kind. You get your longest season of bloom if you plant in small patches with carefully selected varieties for early- through late-season bloom. A big bed of one kind with patches scattered about gives you the best of both worlds. Watch out for bunnies, deer, and squirrels. Rabbits and deer will eat the flower buds and maybe the leaves, too. Squirrels dig out the bulbs. When planning your tulip beds you need to know that tulips do not naturalize and need to be replaced every three to five years. If you plant by the hundreds, this is a lot of work.

Follow your tulips with alliums. These are close cousins of the onions we eat but are grown for the fabulous flowers, not the bulbs. Yes, they do smell like onions, but this is a small price to pay for long lived, easy care flowers throughout the month of June.

Mix up your spring display with crown imperials, foxtail lilies, Persian bells, hyacinth, grape hyacinth, scilla, and some other little secrets like glory-of-the-snow and dogtooth violets.

When spring warms to summer, you enter the domain of the lilies. True lilies have bulbs that look like artichokes and flowers that look like the brass section of Glenn Miller's band. Asiatic lilies open in June, Aurelian hybrids in July, and Oriental hybrids finish the season in August. Plant them once and watch them return year after year.

The season ends with fall blooming bulbs such as true fall blooming crocus and the *Colchicum* species called autumn crocus. The pink flowers of the hardy cyclamen are treasures in the October garden and the yellow *Sternbergia* bloom in September and October.

All this, and then there is another universe of summer bulbs to plant in spring and store in winter. The gorgeous calla lily and the giant canna fall into this group. There are no better cut flowers to bring to a dinner party than an armful of gladiolus or a basket full of dinnerplate dahlias. The exotic Peruvian daffodils look like nothing else on this planet or any other, and the enormous leaves of the *Colocasia* elephant ears allow you to take a bit of tropical rainforest and transplant it into your backyard.

Bulbs are like nothing else in gardening. You can get spectacular results in a very short period of time.

Autumn Crocus

Colchicum autumnale

Other Name: Meadow Saffron
Height: 6 to 10 in.
Spread: Up to 12 in.
Flowers: White or pink cup shaped flowers
Bloom Period: September to October
Zones: 5, 6, 7, 8, 9 (possibly 4)

Light Requirement:

olchicum species plants are a wonderful surprise for the autumn garden. They last for years and bloom in patches of bright pink when most of the garden is turning the golden earthy tones of fall. It is amazing to me that many people are unaware of the existence of these little beauties. The common name "autumn crocus" has created some confusion about *Colchicum*, whose flowers look a lot like over-sized crocus flowers, but are not. This distinction is necessary because there are quite a few true crocus that also bloom in the fall. Both the flowers and bulbs of *Crocus* are much smaller than those of *Colchicum*. One of the really fun aspects of autumn crocus (true crocus, too!) is that it can be planted in summer, even as late as early September, and you will still have flowers that same autumn. This kind of almost-instant gratification is a rare thing in the garden. Don't wait too long to plant, however, or plants may be nipped by an early frost. The flowers emerge without leaves and form a thick cluster, like a bouquet, and the blooming becomes more prolific as the bulbs become established. In spring the leaves are far more abundant than you might expect, and they look something like a loose head of lettuce. Foliage dies down in the summer and the bulbs lay dormant until flowers pop out in fall.

WHEN TO PLANT

Plant *Colchicum* during summer dormancy. It is fine to plant any time from when the foliage dies back until early September, but be sure to do so before the plants start to bloom.

WHERE TO PLANT

Plant *Colchicum* in ordinary, well-drained garden soil in a sunny to lightly shaded site. It is best to choose a location where plants can stay put. Autumn crocuses do best when left in their original spot. Plant in rock gardens or where the plants can be appreciated up close. Keep in mind that the spring foliage will take up more space than the flowers do. Autumn crocus works very nicely planted beneath a groundcover of periwinkle.

How to Plant
Colchicum plants are poisonous; be sure to wear gloves. Place the bottom of the bulb 3 to 4 in. deep in well-drained soil. Space bulbs 6 to 9 in. apart. Leave enough space around the bulbs for the substantial spring foliage. These plants are hardy, but a layer of mulch is suggested. Fertilize the following spring. You can also plant seed from the previous year's flowers. Seed-grown plants may sit dormant for the first year or two, blooming after 3 or 4 more years.

Care and Maintenance
The hardest part of maintaining autumn crocus is putting up with the foliage when it starts to get ugly, which usually occurs in June. Plants can be divided during the summer dormant period and will take 2 years to bloom. Fertilize every spring. Slugs can be a problem.

Additional Information
All the plant parts of an autumn crocus are poisonous, so always wear gloves when you are handling one. The chemical "colchicine" is derived from the plant for medicinal purposes, but it is highly toxic even in small doses. It can be absorbed through the skin when handled, so don't forget your gloves. As a novelty, you can place a dormant autumn crocus bulb on a plate or in a cup, where it will produce its lovely blooms without the help of soil or water. Just make sure it is out of reach of pets and children.

Additional Species, Cultivars, or Varieties
C. speciosum is crimson pink and slightly taller than the more common *C. autumnale*. Though both species are available, many of the most popular varieties are hybrids between the two. The following varieties are of uncertain origin and may be selections or hybrids: 'Waterlily' is a double pink; 'Album' is white; 'The Giant' has large pinkish mauve blooms; and 'Autumn Queen' is deep violet.

Calla Lily

Zantedeschia species

Other Names: *Richardia* (old), Lily of the Nile
Height: 1 to 4 ft.
Spread: Up to 3 ft.
Flowers: White, pink, or yellow bract
    surrounding a central "spadix"
    (columnar spike of tiny flowers)
Bloom Period: Summer
Zones: 9, 10, 11

Light Requirement:

In New Jersey, calla lilies must be grown as tender bulbs. Plant in the spring and then dig the rhizomes in the fall for winter storage. Tender bulbs are difficult to dig and store, but calla lilies are so spectacular that they are worth the extra effort. The classic white calla is *Z. aethiopica*. Very few things in this world are so close to perfection that mere mortals cannot see their flaws—this pure white calla is one of these things. A field of callas in bloom is simply wondrous. The classic calla is unfortunately one of the more difficult callas to grow as a tender bulb. Winter storage is very tricky. Starting with one or two fresh rhizomes each spring might be simpler and would still be worthwhile. To have white callas from one year to the next, try *Z. albomaculata*. The foliage is spotted and the lovely white flowers are smaller versions of the classic. Plants grow to 2 ft. high. *Z. elliottiana* has golden-yellow flowers and spotted leaves; the plants are from 1½ to 2 ft. tall. For pink or red flowers, try *Z. rehmannii*. At 1 to 1½ ft., it is the smallest of the callas. The available varieties are hybrids, crosses, and recrosses of the different species. All have similar requirements. Choose the colors that best suit your garden plan. Because the perception of beauty is so subjective, every gardener must decide for him- or herself which calla is the most exquisite.

WHEN TO PLANT

Plant out in spring after danger of frost has passed. Mid-May is generally safe in New Jersey. Dig plants after a light frost has damaged leaves (usually in mid-October).

WHERE TO PLANT

Choose a location where your callas will get partial shade. Plant where you will be able to appreciate the flowers up close. Callas require a soil with good drainage but do best with plenty of water in the summer. One advantage to digging tender bulbs in the fall is that no location has to be permanent. If you try a spot that turns out to be less than ideal, choose somewhere else the following year.

HOW TO PLANT

Dig deeply to ensure adequate drainage, and add plenty of organic matter. Plant roots 3 in. deep and 6 to 12 in. apart. Use a heavy layer of organic mulch over the top. Planting annual lobelia all around callas can make for an outstanding combination. Lobelia's delicate flowers and foliage complement calla's big leaves and flowers, and it will thrive in the partial shade callas prefer.

CARE AND MAINTENANCE

After foliage has been lightly frosted, dig the rhizomes. Gently remove much of the excess soil. Allow the plants to dry in a shady spot for 2 or 3 days. Make sure they are not exposed to frost but receive good air movement. Pack in slightly damp peat moss and store in a dry place at 40 to 50 degrees Fahrenheit.

ADDITIONAL INFORMATION

My parents were married in 1934. Mother's wedding picture hangs in our hallway. In her arms is an absolutely enormous bunch of large white calla lilies. The flowers are said to represent "magnificent beauty." Every time I look at that picture, I understand why.

ADDITIONAL SPECIES, CULTIVARS, OR VARIETIES

'Flame' opens yellow and matures to a dark red. 'Rubylite Rose' is hot pink. 'Crystal Blush' opens white and matures to light pink. 'Black-eyed Beauty' is white with a black eye. 'Dominique' is dark reddish pink.

Canna

Canna × generalis

Other Names: *Canna × hybrida,*
  C. × indica, Indian Shot
Height: Up to 8 ft.
Spread: Variable
Flowers: Showy spikes at the top of the plant
  in yellow, pink, red, or orange
Bloom Period: Summer
Zones: 7, 8, 9, 10, 11

Light Requirement:

*N*ew Jersey gardeners generally treat cannas as summer bulbs. New varieties are listed as hardy through Zone 7, but many references only credit them as far north as Zone 8. The fantastic growth cannas achieve in a single season, up to 8 feet, is so extraordinary that the hassle of digging them up in the fall is bearable. Cannas look "tropical." They resemble banana plants with big tufts of flowers on top. Cannas appear to best advantage when planted in big patches by themselves. Because of their size and mass, there needs to be a lot of them to make visual sense. Two or 3 cannas in the back of a flower bed looks like a totem pole with leaves. A border planting, in front of a wall, across the front of the property or next to a building, will be dramatic, elegant and a little outrageous. New varieties may have very large petals on more compact plants, some reaching only 2 to 3 ft. Grow them in a container for a bit of the tropics "a la terra cotta" on your deck. Smaller cannas also work better with more traditional garden flowers out in the yard. The big banana leaves are usually green but can also be a dark bronze. New varieties include variegated foliage in green and yellow or green and white; sometimes in stripes, sometimes in big blotches. Variegated flowers start one color as a bud which then opens to a completely different color bloom. The petals may be edged in yellow or covered in speckles. Cannas are giant workhorse plants that are quickly evolving into little Shetland ponies.

WHEN TO PLANT
Plant cannas after the danger of frost, usually in early to mid-May.

WHERE TO PLANT
Plant in a very sunny spot where there is plenty of room. The south

side of a building is a great place. Circular plantings in the middle of the yard or driveway can be very effective if the bed is mounded in the center. Plant around the compost pile. The tubers will thrive in that environment and the plants will hide the pile.

HOW TO PLANT

Prepare the soil deeply, adding plenty of organic matter. Cannas require constant moisture but don't do well in soggy soil. Organic matter will hold moisture while keeping the soil loose enough to drain. Each tuber you plant should have one or two "eyes," or growing points. Plant tubers 4 in. deep and 18 in. apart. The plants will seem to have filled in the gaps before you've had time to put your tools away. An organic mulch will help maintain soil moisture and keep weeds under control until plants are thick enough to squeeze out the weedlings themselves.

CARE AND MAINTENANCE

Cannas benefit from a regular application of fertilizer, but in better soils they will do fine with just a spring boost. Water deeply and regularly in hot or dry weather. Remove dead flower stalks as the flowers fade. The nifty little spherical seedpods eventually become rather unattractive, although they are interesting. Take care not to cut the corpses too far back. The next flower spike will emerge just below the one that is finishing up. Watch out for Japanese beetles, who will feed on cannas like a pack of hungry piranhas. After a frost, cut back the stalks and dig out the tubers. In a good year you will have three to six times what you planted. Allow to surface dry and store in slightly damp peat moss at 40 degrees Fahrenheit.

ADDITIONAL INFORMATION

If you want to experiment, dig out all the tubers you will need for next spring, throwing in a few extra to make up for winter loss. Cover the rest with 6 to 8 in. of wood chips. If tubers are close to the house on the sunny south side, you may find that they over-winter just fine. If it works, you have eliminated a big job. If not, plant the ones you stored.

ADDITIONAL SPECIES, CULTIVARS, OR VARIETIES

'The President' is a classic tall red. 'Yellow King Humbert' has yellow flowers with red spots. 'Bengal Tiger' or 'Pretoria' is a new canna with orange flowers and green and yellow foliage. 'Stuttgart' foliage is green and white in large block patterns. 'Tropical Rose' is a very pretty dwarf form with large dark pink flowers.

Crocus

Crocus species

Height: 4 to 12 in. **Spread:** Up to 12 in. **Flowers:** 4-in. cup-shaped flowers in white, yellow, lilac, purple, or stripes **Bloom Period:** Early spring **Zones:** 4, **5, 6, 7,** 8 (maybe 3 and 9)	**Light Requirement:**

*S*pring without crocus would be like a summer without Jersey tomatoes: just not quite right. When we think of spring there are many wonderful plants and flowers that come to mind. The flowering dogwood is called "the harbinger of spring." The forsythia, with its bright yellow flowers everywhere, says it's spring with a trumpet blast; but it is the little crocus that does the real job. While the rest of the plant world still have the covers pulled over their heads, crocus are struggling to push skinny green leaves up through ground that is still frozen, sometimes under the snow. They are the first line of attack to free the world from winter's icy grip. Gardeners are busy building fires and looking for lost mittens while crocus are preparing for the primeval battle. Onward, upward they fight. Strong. Steady. Brave. A few get trampled by the dog. Another succumbs to a pair of snow boots. It doesn't stop them. They keep coming. Then it happens. They burst forth in unison like a cannon shot and winter goes down with a crash. The little soliders wave their victory flags in a sea of color. For just a second our hearts will stop. The crocus are blooming! The crocus are blooming! It doesn't matter what feeble attempts winter will make now. The crocus are blooming! They have taken the ground and the battle is won. Spring is ours! After that, any flower announcing spring is reading yesterday's news.

WHEN TO PLANT
Plant crocus in fall any time from mid-September until Thanksgiving.

WHERE TO PLANT
Plant in sun or partial shade. The earliest flowers will appear in warm, sunny locations. Crocus is not fussy about planting condi-

tions but it does require good drainage. Plant bulbs in the lawn right through the sod, or plant groups of crocus under deciduous trees and shrubs; they will be gone before the leaves come out. If you tried to design a flower for rock gardens, you could not do any better than crocus. You can plant them with peonies and irises or in the rose garden. Crocuses fit in anywhere and everywhere.

How to Plant

Crocuses are easy to grow. Plant them in clumps to get the best effect. While mixed colors are very pretty up close, large patches of one color are far more dramatic from a distance. Good soil preparation is beneficial to all plants, though that may be difficult if you are planting through sod. Make a deep hole and refill it with improved soil. Plant bulbs 3 to 4 in. deep and 3 to 4 in. apart.

Care and Maintenance

You can leave crocus in the ground for years. Each plant will spread into a thick clump. Crocus will be happiest, however, if you divide the clumps every 3 or 4 years. Divide in late spring when leaves are fading but are still attached; replant immediately. You can also divide in early fall, though the bulbs may be difficult to locate. Fertilize with bonemeal in fall.

Additional Information

While crocus are by far the most popular of the early spring bulbs, there are others to add diversity. Miniature iris bloom very early in the season and have large flowers for such little plants. They may even beat the crocus to bloom, though they do not spread and so never have quite the same impact. Winter aconite has cheerful yellow flowers that resemble a cross between a crocus and a buttercup. The foliage is very pretty. Snowdrops are white and look a little like dainty, drooping airplane propellers.

Additional Species, Cultivars, or Varieties

"Snow crocus" is really a group of all the earliest blooming species of crocus. The flowers are smaller than the giant crocus and bloom 3 weeks earlier. This grouping includes *C. sieberi*, *C. tomasinianus*, and *C. chrysanthus*. Many colors are available; some are even variegated. Giant crocus are a little larger and bloom later. *C. vernus* is the most common of this type. *C. flavus* is a deep yellow-orange.

Crown Imperial

Fritillaria imperialis

Other Name: Imperial Fritillary
Height: 3 to 4 ft.
Spread: 1 ft.
Flowers: A ring of red, yellow, or orange blooms dangling upside down at the top of a 3 to 4 ft. stalk
Bloom Period: April
Zones: 5, 6, 7, 8

Light Requirement:

The crown imperial looks like something Mother Nature would wear to reign at the Mayfest. The circle of blooms appears on top of 3 to 4 ft. stems with a tuft of short pointy leaves poking out through the center of the ring. The flowers resemble upside-down tulips and the foliage is often compared to that of lilies. The short, swordlike leaves emerge all around the stem like lily leaves, only wider. They grow from the ground about 2 ft. up the stem, which is bare from that point up to the top, where the flowers form a "crown." If this sounds odd, it is because it is. Crown imperials are native to Persia (now Iran) and were introduced to Europe in the 1500s. They are old fashioned garden favorites that are long lived once they become established. Crown imperials are not as commonplace now as they were at one time. Perhaps they went out of favor because of the way they smell, which is something like skunk cabbage. The odor is supposed to be extremely effective in repelling rodents, moles in particular. The flowers are tall and regal and add vertical interest to the garden. They can be appreciated at enough of a distance that your nose plays no part in the evaluation.

WHEN TO PLANT

Plant bulbs in the fall. Plant as soon as possible after they arrive in the mail or the same day they are purchased locally.

WHERE TO PLANT

Crown imperials are hardy to Zone 5, but to ensure that you have flowers and not just leaves, plant in a spot out of intense wind and cold. A little protection from midday sun is preferred. These plants get tall, so plant bulbs at the back of the spring garden. Keep in mind that crown imperials do not do well if relocated, and pick a spot where they can take up permanent residence.

How to Plant

Plant as soon as possible once you have the bulbs in your possession. They usually come packaged one bulb to a box, which is a tribute to their delicate nature. Prepare the soil down at least 12 in. and backfill the hole with a bed of pebbles and loose soil. Good drainage is critical. Plant the bulb 6 in. deep. Be very careful not to injure any roots that may have begun to grow during shipping. The top of the bulb has a natural depression. Plant a few crown imperials together for both appearance and the well-being of the bulbs. They seem to do better in groups.

Care and Maintenance

Mulch heavily for winter protection. Fertilize every fall. Remove the flower stalks as they yellow. Crown imperials are generally long lived but are subject to botrytis, which can cause the plants to shrivel up in spring. Be careful to ensure good drainage at the time of planting to help avoid this problem.

Additional Information

To camouflage the fading plants, plant specimens that get tall quickly around your crown imperials. Monardas (bee balm) will grow bushy enough to hide the foliage and does quite well with midday shade. You can also try hiding the foliage with Asiatic lilies. Their foliage is similar enough to blend with the leaves of crown imperial and they bloom in June, just in time to draw attention away from the crown imperials as they decline.

Additional Species, Cultivars, or Varieties

'Lutea' has yellow flowers. 'The Premier' is bright orange, and 'Aurora' is orange with a hint of salmon. 'Rubra' is red. Crown imperials look best if all the plants in a clump are of the same variety.

Daffodil

Narcissus species

Other Names: Jonquil, Narcissus
Height: 4 to 20 in.
Spread: Variable
Flowers: A center cup or "corona" surrounded by petals; white, yellow, white and yellow, orange, or pink
Bloom Period: Early to mid-spring
Zones: Most 4, **5, 6, 7,** 8, 9 (Variety dependent)

Light Requirement:

affodils are joyful flowers. They have a simple elegance that is irresistible. The flowers appear early, but not so early that you can't enjoy a walk in the garden to appreciate them. Daffodils are the first spring blooming garden flowers that can be cut for an arrangement. A bunch in a vase, leaning this way and that, radiate cheerfulness all around. The flowers are long lived in a vase, even longer lived in the garden, and the plants seem to last forever. Daffodils naturalize, or spread, and eventually seem to have been planted by Mother Nature herself. Since the flowers bloom before foliage emerges on the trees, bulbs can even be planted under shade trees. They will bloom right through a groundcover of myrtle, creating a pretty display while the myrtle is in bloom. The selection of daffodils is extraordinary. One could get really wrapped up in a discussion of which name is correct for which flower: narcissus vs. daffodil vs. jonquil. This discussion would include talk of the number of blooms per stem, the size relationship of cup to petals, and the angle of the petals themselves. Even if you tried to get the names down to an exact science, there is so much overlap and individual interpretation that it is hardly worth the effort. Unless you happen to be a purist or a breeder, let's call them all daffodils and stick with Narcissus as the genus name. It may not be up to botanical standards, but it works. Pay closer attention to variety names, which will be consistent in characteristics for that variety. The most important factors to consider are whether a variety is hardy in your zone and whether it appeals to your personal taste.

WHEN TO PLANT
Plant from mid-September until Thanksgiving.

WHERE TO PLANT

Plant daffodils in well-drained soil. They do best in sun but can take some shade, especially light shade from trees whose leaves have not yet emerged. Daffodils (the miniature varieties in particular) are terrific for rock gardens. They work well in borders, mixed with shrubs as part of a foundation planting, scattered in a meadow, at the edge of woods, or in any nook that needs a splash of spring color.

HOW TO PLANT

Daffodils do best when they are left in one place; provide extra soil preparation before planting to get them off to a good start. Add organic matter and bonemeal at the time of planting. Don't break up bulbs that have multiple stems. Each "nose" will produce another flower. Plant them the way they arrived and they will continue to multiply in your garden. Daffodils look best planted in bunches. Plant 6 to 8 in. down from the base of the bulb and 6 to 8 in. apart.

CARE AND MAINTENANCE

Remove dead flowers as soon as they get ugly. You don't want to waste plant energy on producing seed that will never be planted. Be sure to allow the foliage to mature before you cut it off. This year's leaves feed the bulb for next year's flowers. Daffodils and daylilies make an excellent combination; daylilies will conceal the daffodils' aging leaves. Divide bulbs when they become crowded and begin to bloom less prolifically. Lift the bulbs as the last of the foliage fades. Divide and replant immediately. You can divide in the fall, but locating the bulbs when there are no leaves is very tricky.

ADDITIONAL INFORMATION

Neither deer nor rabbits will eat these plants. This makes daffodils invaluable in those parts of the state where deer can be a major problem. They must taste really horrid, since deer will eat almost anything if they are hungry enough.

ADDITIONAL SPECIES, CULTIVARS, OR VARIETIES

There are many to choose from. The following are some personal favorites. 'Jack Snipe' is an adorable miniature with bright-yellow cups and pure white petals. Pink cupped varieties hint at being truly pink. 'Romance', 'Replete', and 'Palmares' are all worth trying. 'Kissproof' has cream-colored petals with a deep-orange cup. It is my all-time favorite full-sized, single daffodil.

Dahlia

Dahlia pinnata hybrids

Height: 15 in. to 6 ft., occasionally taller **Spread:** Variable **Flowers:** 1 to 11 in. across in many colors and types **Bloom Period:** Summer until frost **Zones:** 4, **5, 6, 7,** 8, 9, 10 (hardy in 9, 10 only)	**Light Requirement:**

ahlias are not a single kind of flower. They include many different flower types, from small single blossoms that are suitable for containers to enormous "dinner plate" flowers that reach 11 in. across. Some are produced on plants that must be staked to hold the weight of the fully double blooms. There are pompon types, formal and informal doubles, and spiderlike cactus flowered dahlias. The simpler types include single, anemone, and "collarette." This latter type produces a single row of petals with another collection of short fluffy petals around the center disc. Dahlias that produce smaller flowers generally produce lots of them. The largest flowers may produce only 15 blooms in a season. A single huge bloom is very dramatic all by itself. Dahlias are grown from tubers that resemble bunches of skinny potatoes. They are not tolerant of cold weather and must be dug and stored after the first frost. The flowers are so intense that once you grow them, you will do whatever it takes to include these beauties in your garden.

WHEN TO PLANT

Plant dahlias in mid-spring. Planting by April 30 will give you early blooms without much risk of a setback from the cold. Don't plant later than mid-June or you will miss a large part of these plants' blooming potential.

WHERE TO PLANT

Plant in full sun with excellent drainage. The largest flower types are difficult to blend with other garden flowers but look truly sensational in a bed by themselves. They can be effective in the back of a border; a few plants will have major impact. The smaller varieties are much more flexible. Use them in borders or in shrubbery beds, plant them in containers, or mix with annuals or perennials.

HOW TO PLANT

Prepare the soil by adding a significant amount of organic matter. Dahlias demand good drainage. They also benefit from a dose of fertilizer at planting time. Take care not to be too generous. Excess food makes for lush foliage and fewer blooms. The depth and spacing of dahlias depends on the variety. This information is generally given on the package. Larger varieties will require staking. Install a stake at the time of planting to avoid damaging the growing roots later.

CARE AND MAINTENANCE

Keep plants well watered during the season. Mulch for weed control. Cultivation and even hand weeding can damage surface feeder roots. Remove faded blooms when they get ugly. Cut almost fully open blossoms in the early morning for indoor use. Place the stems in warm to hot tap water, then allow the water to cool. Dig tubers after the first frost. Remove any excess soil and allow the tubers to dry for several days in a place where they will not be subject to frost. Store over the winter in a cool, dry location. Divide tubers in spring at the time of planting.

ADDITIONAL INFORMATION

While all dahlias are lovely, the dinner plate varieties are like nothing else. If you saw a dinner plate dahlia made of silk, you would never believe it was a copy of an actual flower. A single flower is spectacular, and a bouquet is unbelievable. Six plants in a bed will make you catch your breath every time you walk by.

ADDITIONAL SPECIES, CULTIVARS, OR VARIETIES

There are many dahlias to choose from. Make your selections based on size and flower type. 'Kelvin Floodlight' is an enormous yellow. 'Lilac Time' is just as large. 'Park Princess' is a very floriferous pink cactus flowered type. 'Young Love' is an unusual-looking cactus type that has white flowers tipped in magenta.

Dogtooth Violet

Erythronium americanum

Other Names: Fawn Lily, Yellow Adder's Tongue, Trout Lily **Height:** 1 ft. **Spread:** 6 to 12 in. **Flowers:** 1 to 1¹/₂ in. yellow flowers **Bloom Period:** April and May **Zones:** 4, 5, 6, 7, 8	**Light Requirement:**

The dogtooth violet is a gentle woodland flower that thrives in moist, rich, humusy well-drained soil. When planted in the right spot, it will reward its keeper year after year with dainty, care-free, long-lasting yellow flowers. This is not a plant for big show. It is very well suited to the shaded rock garden or to a naturalized woodland setting. It is delicate and small but quite noble, holding its shy, nodding flowers up on straight slender stems. As diminutive as the dogtooth violet is, it can still produce 5 to 10 flowers per stem and is quite hardy. There are few bulbs that will be as rewarding in shady nooks where color is hard to find. The foliage is mottled or speckled in patterns that are supposed to resemble the scales of a trout. The flowers look far more like tiny tiger lilies with oversized anthers than they do violets. Perhaps trout lily is the more appropriate name for this plant.

WHEN TO PLANT

Plant as soon as the corms are received in the fall. They have a tendency to dry out quickly.

WHERE TO PLANT

Plant in part shade to deep shade in well-drained humusy soil that holds moisture but is never soggy. Plant at the edge of ponds or streams, along woodland paths, in shaded rock gardens, around azaleas and rhododendrons, or under needled evergreens. Tuck dogtooth violets into any shadowy nook that will benefit from a splash of color. They will blend beautifully with ferns, Jack-in-the-pulpits, trilliums, violets, and bloodroot.

How to Plant

Soil preparation is very important. Dogtooth violets required excellent drainage with constant moisture. Add plenty of organic matter. Plant corms 3 in. deep and 4 to 5 in. apart. Take care not to let the corms dehydrate while handling them for planting. Use an organic mulch to keep the soil from drying out. Dogtooth violets can also be planted from seed, but plants will take 5 years to bloom.

Care and Maintenance

Corms can be left in the ground for years. They prefer not to be divided and have no serious pest problems. This means little maintenance is required. Remove spent flowers to direct energy toward the plant rather than into the production of seed. Keep plants well watered during the summer, especially if it is hot and dry. If you must divide dogtooth violets, do it in late summer and replant immediately. Take care not to let the plants dry in the process.

Additional Information

Years ago, someone brought me a sample of a pretty little woodland plant for identification. I was sure it was a dogtooth violet. My coworker was absolutely sure it was a trout lily. He had 30 years more experience than I, so I didn't want to argue. This was the first in a career long state of confusion caused by the inconsistency of common names. It gets really complicated when botanical names are just as bad.

Additional Species, Cultivars, or Varieties

E. dens-canis is native to Europe. The species has pink flowers but is otherwise similar to *E. americanum*. There are quite a few varieties, including 'Rose Queen', 'Purple King', and 'Snowflake'. *E. revolutum* is a pink flowered American native. 'White Beauty' has white flowers splashed in pink.

BULBS, CORMS AND TUBERS

Fall Blooming Crocus

Crocus species

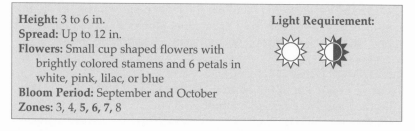

Height: 3 to 6 in. **Spread:** Up to 12 in. **Flowers:** Small cup shaped flowers with brightly colored stamens and 6 petals in white, pink, lilac, or blue **Bloom Period:** September and October **Zones:** 3, 4, **5, 6, 7,** 8	**Light Requirement:**

*I*t is truly surprising that more gardens are not filled with these autumn beauties. They are just as care free as their spring blooming cousins and bring cheerful splashes of color to the garden as most plants are slipping into restful sleep. These happy little flowers are particularly convenient to plant. They are available locally and in catalogs in late summer. Plant as late as the middle of September and you will have flowers in a matter of weeks. This rapid return on the investment of time and labor is very satisfying. Autumnal crocus also naturalize, rewarding you for your efforts for many years to come. It is important that these true crocus not be confused with "autumn crocus," the common name for *Colchicum* species. *Colchicum* is not really a crocus at all. Flowers of the single varieties are similar in appearance but larger than true fall blooming crocus. There are over 20 species of fall blooming crocus, but not all are hardy in New Jersey. In general, however, those commonly available will do just fine here in the Garden State. Among the species that do well in Zones 6 and 7 is *C. sativus*, the saffron crocus. The lovely lilac flowers have darker purple veins with contrasting orange stamens (male parts) and stigmas (female parts). The stigmas are collected to make the spice "saffron." Each stigma is removed by hand for this process. It takes tens of thousands of stigmas to make one pound of the spice.

WHEN TO PLANT

Plant fall blooming crocus in late summer or early fall. Plant as soon as possible after receiving the corms. It is best to plant by mid-September if you want to enjoy blooms the same season.

WHERE TO PLANT

Plant in full sun or light shade. Choose a location where you can see the flowers up close. A swathe across a bed will be visible from a distance, but if you are planting just a few to stretch out summer, they need to be up close and personal to be appreciated. Rock gardens are an ideal location. Although fall blooming crocus naturalize and spread, they are not as suitable as their spring cousins are for lawn planting. They bloom while the lawn is actively growing, which can make mowing a problem.

HOW TO PLANT

As with all bulbs, good drainage is critical. Add organic matter to loosen heavy soil. Clusters of the same variety will have more impact than a mixture of colors. Plant 3 in. deep and 4 in. apart.

CARE AND MAINTENANCE

Crocuses should be divided every 3 or 4 years to keep them vigorous. They make new corms on top of the old ones and will eventually push their way up to the surface. It is very important that you allow the foliage to mature before cutting it back.

ADDITIONAL INFORMATION

If you are interested in harvesting your own saffron, take care to plant the bulbs where they will be easily distinguished from other fall crocus. Check the patch daily while it is blooming. The stigma is located in the center of the flower and is bulbous at the top. There is usually only one. Pluck it out of the flowers while they are fresh. Allow the stigma to dry on a paper towel and then store it in a glass container in a cool, dry place. It takes many thousands of flowers to make a pound of the spice, but since saffron is generally used in tiny amounts, a well-established patch will likely provide enough for home use.

ADDITIONAL SPECIES, CULTIVARS, OR VARIETIES

C. kotschyanus was previously called *C. zonatus*. The species has pinkish lavender flowers; 'Albus' is a white variety. *C. medius* is lilac purple. *C. speciosus* is blue with bright orange stigmas. The variety 'Oxonian' is pastel violet blue.

Flowering Onion

Allium species

Height: 1 to 4 ft. **Spread:** 12 in. **Flowers:** Clusters, often spherical, of tiny flowers in white, pink, blue, magenta, or yellow **Bloom Period:** May or June **Zones: 5, 6, 7,** 8 (many 4 and 9)	**Light Requirement:**

Flowering onions offer an world of spring bulbs that many gardeners don't know exists. They are the best way to extend the spring bulb season, picking up right where tulips leave off and carrying spring right into summer. Alliums include some of the best OOH and AAH generators in the garden. The 10 in. spheres of 'Globemaster' are so flamboyant that they seem like something out of a Dr. Seuss book. A patch of *A. giganteum* will produce 6 in. spheres on top of 4 ft. tall very straight, very naked stems. *Allium* flowers last a long time. If you choose to leave them long enough, they will dry to a light brown and can be saved for dried arrangements. When cut fresh and dried upside down, they often retain their color very well. Even edible onions flower. The chives in your herb garden produce lovely blue spheres that can go into the salad along with the leaves. Leeks produce enormous white spheres in spring if you forget to harvest them in the fall. Garlic chives are prolific bloomers in mid- to late summer. The ornamental varieties are even more beautiful. Not all Alliums are large. The 1 in. *A. caeruleum* is a lovely shade of dusty blue on stems that reach up to 18 in. There is a group of small flowered alliums that produce flat clusters rather than spheres in white, pink, or yellow. These plants reach about 12 in. in height. Alliums will naturalize or can be divided. They make excellent cut flowers, but many do smell like onions. Unless you really like the smell of onions, don't put them in a confined space.

WHEN TO PLANT
Plant alliums in fall.

WHERE TO PLANT

All alliums need full sun to do their best. Their first choice is deep, sandy loam soils but they are not overly particular. Alliums tolerate dry soils better than many other bulbs do. The smaller varieties snuggle well into rock gardens, but the colossal types need a spot all to themselves.

HOW TO PLANT

As a general rule, plant a bulb 2 to 3 times as deep as the height of the bulb itself. For specific instructions, check the packaging of the bulbs you have purchased. Loosen heavy soils by adding a 2:1 mixture of organic matter and sand. Avoid soggy soils.

CARE AND MAINTENANCE

Allium will die to the ground after blooming is over, but don't remove the foliage until it fades. The flowers can be cut for indoor use as fresh flowers, they can be cut fresh and then dried, or they can be dried on the plant and then cut. The bulbs can stay in place for years, but divide them in the fall if they become over-crowded. Fertilize in the spring. Water only if the ground becomes excessively dry.

ADDITIONAL INFORMATION

For years I had a patch of *A. giganteum* planted in front of my New Brunswick home. Every spring I waited impatiently to see the large magenta spheres appear, but every spring, without fail, just as the flowers were about to open they would disappear. I never saw those plants in full bloom. One day when I was moving, a police car stopped in front of the house. The officer informed me that it had been a little old lady who had been stealing my flowers, to take to church. He thought I would want to know. That's where my tulips had gone as well, but she always left me some of those.

ADDITIONAL SPECIES, CULTIVARS, OR VARIETIES

A. christophii is the 'Star of Persia'. It has about eighty 1-in. flowers that form a 10-in. sphere. *A. schubertii* has female flowers on 1 in. stems and male flowers on 8 in. stems. The result is a spidery looking sphere that has over 200 individual pink blooms all together. *A. bulgaricum* (also called *Nectaroscordum siculum*) can reach 30 in. in height and has clusters of burgundy and white drooping flowers. These are slightly different from the others of this species. They are an interesting, more refined novelty in the garden.

Gladiolus

Gladiolus × *hortulanus*

Other Names: Garden Gladiolus, Corn Flag,
    Sword Lily
Height: 2 to 5 ft.
Spread: Up to 1 ft.
Flowers: A tall, narrow spike of large flowers,
    each up to 2 in. across, in a wide range colors
Bloom Period: 65 to 100 days after planting
Zones: Tender in New Jersey (hardy in 8, 9, 10, 11)

Light Requirement:

he common garden gladiolus is far from common in an aesthetic sense. Glads make outstanding cut flowers and are embarrassingly easy to grow. Their colors are anywhere from subtle to vibrant. Three stems in a vase make a statement. A dozen is powerful. The flowers begin opening at the base and work their way up. It is possible to have as many as fourteen flowers open on one stalk at a time. Pluck off the old flowers as they fade. Because of the successive bloom, each stem makes a very long lasting cut flower. Today's glads are the result of crossing and recrossing so many varieties for so many years that the origin is completely obscured. There are now hundreds of named varieties available. The newer tall varieties are sturdy enough to not require staking, even though they reach 4 ft. This is a big improvement. Smaller varieties are available that reach only 2 to 3 ft. These are very easy to grow as garden plants or for cut flowers.

WHEN TO PLANT

Start planting in late April to early May. Plant every 2 weeks until mid-July.

WHERE TO PLANT

Plant in a sunny location that has good drainage. Try to rotate your gladiolus beds from year to year to minimize disease problems. Glads, especially the tall ones, are difficult to blend with other garden flowers. Plant in rows for cut flowers or in clusters of the same color in the back of a mixed flower garden. Five to 10 of the same color make an attractive grouping.

How to Plant

When taking corms out of storage, you may see the shriveled old corm at the base of a fresh, new corm. Twist off the old one and toss it onto the compost pile. Small "cormlets" may be found around the corm. These will produce flowers in 2 to 3 years. The plants grow tall, but they don't take up a lot of space. Plant corms of larger varieties 4 to 5 in. down and 3 in. apart. Add organic matter and fertilizer to the soil at the time of planting. Do not toss fertilizer into the planting holes. It will burn the corms.

Care and Maintenance

A side-dressing of fertilizer is recommended when the plants are showing five leaves. Water deeply once a week if the ground is dry. Keep weeds under control. Organic mulch will help significantly. Cut flowers when the first bud is fully open. Be sure to leave at least four leaves on the plant to nourish the corms. If the flowers are not cut for indoor use, remove them from the plant when they fade. The corms can be dug when the leaves have yellowed. This is usually about 6 weeks after flowering. It is not necessary to wait until frost to dig. Cut the leaves back to 2 in. Dig the corms, shake off the soil, and allow them to dry for a few days, out of the sun and where they will not freeze. You can remove the old corm at this time or wait until the following spring. Store at 40 degrees Fahrenheit in a dry location.

Additional Information

Gladiolus is one of the few flowers that require nothing else with it in a vase to look spectacular. The easiest way to arrange the flowers is to use a large, preferably round or wide, vase with a fairly narrow opening. This will allow the stems to crisscross in the vase. The flowering stems will then fan out to show off the blooms to best advantage. A wide opening gives no support and they will flop. A straight vase crams the flowering parts together so you can't really appreciate each one. Try it. You will look like a pro.

Additional Species, Cultivars, or Varieties

"Butterfly glads" are so named because of the markings on the flower petals, which are supposed to resemble a butterfly's markings. That is a matter of opinion, but they are very attractive nonetheless. Several catalogs offer winter hardy glads, some under the name *G. nanus*. These early blooming glads are supposed to survive the winter up to Zone 5. *Hortus III* says *G. nanus* is really *Babiana nana,* a different species entirely. Still, they may be worth a try.

Glory-of-the-Snow

Chionodoxa luciliae

Other Name: Snow Glories
Height: 3 to 6 in.
Spread: 2 to 4 in.; variable
Flowers: Small blue flower with a white
center; 5 to a cluster
Bloom Period: March
Zones: 3, 4, **5, 6, 7,** 8

Light Requirement:

This is a tiny plant that is treasured for its very early blooms. It will poke through frozen ground with gutsy determination, sometimes even through snow, which accounts for its common name. It makes a good partner for early crocus as it battles back Old Man Winter. Glory-of-the-snow is a great choice for rock gardens, but be sure to pick a place where you can plant it and leave it alone for a few years. It doesn't bloom well its first year, so be patient and be sure not to move it too soon. Once it gets established, glory-of-the-snow will naturalize and settle in for the long haul. It is extremely hardy and produces very blue flowers, about 5 to a cluster. The sweet blue color is a scarcity at any time of the year and very much appreciated against a backdrop of snow. If undisturbed, these plants will spread from seed and roots, eventually providing a solid mat of blue. It is best not to disturb them when they get all thick and wonderful. They look particularly lovely when mixed with white snowdrops, which bloom about the same time. Since glory-of-the-snow tolerates a bit of shade, it can be planted under deciduous shrubs such as forsythia or spirea for early season color. It also does well as a mat beneath the upright foliage of early daffodils. Glory-of-the-snow is an excellent choice for an open woodland type setting where it can naturalize undisturbed.

WHEN TO PLANT

Plant in September or October. Plant as soon as you have the bulbs in your possession.

Where to Plant

Plant in sun or partial shade. Rock gardens are ideal, but any place where the plants will not be disturbed is fine. Plant around shrubbery or in beds with later season perennials.

How to Plant

Glory-of-the-snow needs moist soil with good drainage. Plant bulbs 3 in. deep and 2 to 3 in. apart. These small plants do best in clusters of at least 12, preferably all of the same variety.

Care and Maintenance

These little beauties have few needs and prefer to be left undisturbed. Your biggest problem will be waiting for them to come into their own. The results are worth the wait.

Additional Information

Glory-of-the-snow was discovered in 1842 in a mountain meadow in Turkey. The name *Chionodoxa* is Greek for "glory-of-the-snow." The plant was not introduced to England until 1877, making it a relatively new introduction to cultivation.

Additional Species, Cultivars, or Varieties

'Pink Giant' is a pink variety. 'Alba' is white. *C. gigantea* can reach 10 in. The blooms of *C. sardensis* are darker blue and purple without the white center. The flowers are slightly smaller but there are more per stem.

Grape Hyacinth

Muscari armeniacum

Other Name: Bluebells
Height: 6 to 12 in.
Spread: Bulbs can spread over large areas
Flowers: Spikes of tiny blue bell-shaped flowers
Bloom Period: April and May
Zones: 4, 5, 6, 7, 8

Light Requirement:

Grape hyacinths are free spirited little flowers. They require almost no attention once established and will come back year after year with good cheer. They make a fabulous combination with daffodils. Their true blue color with the daffs' pristine white-and-bright yellow looks like something Van Gogh would have painted. A large batch of them naturalized together in a field is simply delightful. Grape hyacinths are also well suited for rock gardens. In a way that no trowel ever could, their spreading nature allows them to fill in crevices and gaps. They do equally well in full sun or light shade. Be sure to allow the slender foliage to live life to the fullest if you want the plants to naturalize. Avoid the temptation to cut back the leafy patches when they get a little wild looking after blooming is finished. The flower stalks get unattractive as they fade. They can usually be plucked off easily, but if you tug too early, the bulb may come up, too. While the classic grape hyacinth is treasured for its rare true blue color, there are several other species and varieties worth pursuing. Allow solid patches of several different species to spread and overlap one another for a pleasant spring display. There are few flowers that offer as much simple pleasure with so little work.

WHEN TO PLANT

Plant bulbs in the fall as soon as you get them. Seed can be started as soon as it ripens. Sow in flats outside. It can take up to 60 days to germinate. Transplant to the garden in the fall.

WHERE TO PLANT

Plant in a sunny spot or a shady niche. Grape hyacinths are not fussy, but sandy loam soil is best. Avoid soggy sites. Plant in rock gardens, borders, nooks, or crannies. These plants are perfect for a cheery patch outside the back door, planting in open fields for naturalizing, or mixed with spring bulbs.

How to Plant

Prepare the soil as you do for any bulb. Loosen heavy clays to improve drainage and allow roots to stretch out. Add organic matter and sand if needed. Grape hyacinths are very small so plant them in groups. Space 2 to 3 in. apart and plant 3 in. deep.

Care and Maintenance

Allow foliage to mature if you want to keep the plants spreading. They can be divided in autumn, though it is rarely needed. Replant immediately after dividing. Pluck or snip dead flower stems.

Additional Information

In Highland Park, there is a big old mansion that was converted to a YM-YWHA years ago. At the back corner of the grounds you could one find the remnants of a concrete tennis court, with the court lines delineated right in the concrete pad. There were steps down to the dilapidated court and a wrought iron gate at the top of the steps. An ancient twisted wisteria draped the gate in blooms every spring. It was a wonderful spot to be peaceful for a few minutes as my dog ran around sniffing old smells. One day in spring we went for a walk by the old tennis court. From under the gnarled old trees surrounding the court, out to the open grass for almost an acre of ground, grape hyacinths were blooming *everywhere*. There were thousands, if not tens of thousands. They must have spread from the long ago days when the site was a carefully tended garden. Each blue blossom glistened in the sun. It was breathtaking. The next day I returned with a flower-loving friend to share the beauty. The grass had been mowed.

Additional Species, Cultivars, or Varieties

'Blue Spike' produces very fat spikes of double flowers that look more like the true hyacinth than grape hyacinth. 'Fantasy Creation' is another double with long lasting flowers. *M. botryoides* is very similar to *M. armeniacum* but is planted more for the white variety 'Album' than the species. Pink varieties supposedly exist, but if so, they are hard to find. *M. comosum* is the tassel grape hyacinth or feather hyacinth. It looks like a large grape hyacinth with a curly perm. The variety 'Monstrosum' is blue. 'Plumosum' is purple violet. *M. latifolium* is blue at the top of the spike and purple at the bottom. *M. macrocarpum* is yellow, but hardy only to Zone 6.

Hyacinth

Hyacinthus orientalis

Other Names: Dutch Hyacinth, Common
Hyacinth, Garden Hyacinth
Height: Up to 18 in.
Spread: 6 to 12 in.
Flowers: Columnar spike of fragrant, tubular
flowers with petals that open to a star at
the tips; a variety of colors
Bloom Period: March to April
Zones: 5, 6, 7, 8 (possibly 4)

Light Requirement:

Hyacinth flowers look a lot like cotton candy. The prolific blooms surround the stiff stem so that the inflorescence is perfectly uniform on all sides. This is a useful trait when you are arranging cut flowers or planting in an open area where flowers will be viewed from all angles. Hyacinths differ from many other bulbs in that they are not the best choice for mass planting. Their uniformity and stiffness would be extremely formal to the point of being rigid. Use them instead in group plantings to add definition to a more informal or naturalized area. Hyacinths provide splashes of intense color to groups of swaying and unpretentious daffodils. If planting them in a border, be sure to plant in a staggered row, perhaps even leaving skips here and there, or the uniformity will become monotonous. Hyacinths can be used to advantage in a rock garden where the uneven terrain prevents the marching soldier look. Hyacinth flowers are cherished for their sweet, powerful scent. A single patch by the front door will captivate all who enter. The bulbs are often forced for indoor bloom, in part for the beauty of the flowers, but at least as much for the breath of spring that will float through your home. Forcing hyacinths in pots or in vases designed especially for hyacinth bulbs is a pleasant winter project that brings very satisfactory results. It is only fair to warn you, however, that some people find the scent overpowering.

WHEN TO PLANT

Plant in September or October. If you fall behind in your planting, you may be able to plant as late as Thanksgiving. Hyacinths are slightly less hardy than tulips and daffodils, however, so it's best not to take a chance.

WHERE TO PLANT

Choose a bright, sunny location with good drainage. Avoid western exposures where afternoon sun will encourage freezing and thawing of the ground in winter. Avoid planting large expanses of hyacinth alone. Clusters around shrubbery will provide early spring color. Patches mixed in with early tulips or daffodils can be exceptionally pretty. Take advantage of the symmetry and plant by entranceways, mailboxes, or lampposts where you will see them from all angles but add something taller or shorter to keep it interesting.

HOW TO PLANT

Like all bulbs, hyacinths require well-drained soil. They also need a heavy layer of mulch to minimize the freezing and thawing that naturally occurs in winter and that will cause an eventual decrease in flowering. Plant hyacinth bulbs 5 to 6 in. deep and 5 to 6 in. apart. Work the soil deeply (at least 1 ft. deep). Mix in fertilizer with manures and/or bonemeal, but be sure not to allow fertilizer to come in direct contact with the bulb.

CARE AND MAINTENANCE

Remove the flower stalks as the blooms finish up. Keep the plants mulched, especially during the winter. Fertilize after they finish blooming in the spring and again in the fall. Allow leaves to age naturally before removal. They generally need to be replaced every 3 to 4 years.

ADDITIONAL INFORMATION

Hyacinths were described as common as far back as 1596. At that time, they were not cultivated on a large scale because the flowers were not very pretty, even though they displayed nice color and scent. It took about 100 years for hyacinths to come into their own, and by 1734 they had become one of the six most popular garden flowers. The Dutch government was extremely concerned that their popularity would result in a duplication of the tulip mania that occurred 100 years earlier, and so published a history of the economic depression which resulted. Hyacinth mania avoided.

ADDITIONAL SPECIES, CULTIVARS, OR VARIETIES

There are many varieties, all hybrids of the original *H. orientalis*. Simply choose the colors you like best.

Lily

Lilium species

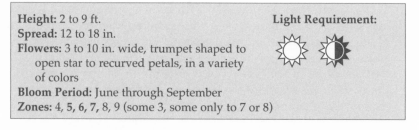

Height: 2 to 9 ft.	**Light Requirement:**
Spread: 12 to 18 in.	
Flowers: 3 to 10 in. wide, trumpet shaped to open star to recurved petals, in a variety of colors	
Bloom Period: June through September	
Zones: 4, **5, 6, 7,** 8, 9 (some 3, some only to 7 or 8)	

ilies are gorgeous. They are regaining popularity, but it is amazing that they haven't always been at the top of the hit parade. The flowers are regal, colorful, and very showy. The plants are care free, spread into robust patches without becoming invasive, and are the tallest herbaceous plants you are likely to have in your garden. A single stem in a vase makes an arrangement by itself. To get the biggest flowers, plant the Oriental hybrids, which grow up to 48 in. tall and have 10 in. wide starlike flowers that bloom in August. Mix these in a vase with some 11 in. wide dinner plate dahlias for an impressive display. Asiatic hybrids are the earliest lilies to bloom (in June) and produce small star shaped flowers. Each plant produces many blooms in intense colors, including rich reds and hot pinks. Trumpet lilies, also known as Aurelian hybrids, bloom in July. Some varieties can reach a towering 8 ft. once established. Smaller, speckled tiger lilies have the longest period of bloom and are among the best species for naturalizing. Martagon lilies have drooping flowers with petals that curve so far back that the anthers seem to be exploding out of the center.

WHEN TO PLANT

The best time to plant is early fall. Some varieties will be available in the spring, but spring planted bulbs may not give their best show until the second summer. Always plant as soon as possible after you get them.

WHERE TO PLANT

A sunny spot is fine, but flower color may fade in strong sun. Partial shade or protection from midday sun is ideal. Avoid wet ground at all costs. If the bulbs get waterlogged, they rot quickly. You can plant lilies in a bed by themselves for cut flowers, but use their vertical habit to advantage wherever possible. The roots do best in shade. Try tucking bulbs between low, spreading shrubs. Mix lilies in the back of a perennial border. Mums in the same bed will draw attention from the fading lily stems.

How to Plant

Prepare the ground deeply and add plenty of organic matter. Lilies prefer acidic soil so do not add lime. Depth and spacing is variety dependent, but as a rule, plant a bulb 3 times as deep as it is tall. Plant immediately after purchase. Never let the bulbs dry out, and take care not to damage either stem or bulb roots. Use an organic mulch. A groundcover will also help shade the roots if you plant your lilies in full sun.

Care and Maintenance

Varieties that exceed 3 ft. may need staking. Cut off the flowering portion of the stalk when the flowers fade. Divide when they become overcrowded and less vigorous. Mulch heavily in the fall. Cut stalks when they yellow. Do not pull the stalks or you may also remove the developing bulbs at their bases. Bulbs can be propagated by planting the bulblets that grow at the base of the stems, by lifting the bulbs and planting individual bulb scales, or by planting "bulbils," small bulblike growths that appear at the leaf axils of some varieties.

Additional Information

Many people are not aware that the popular Easter lily is a hardy bulb. It can be planted out after all danger of frost has passed. Foliage will die back. On occasion these lilies will produce a second bloom in the fall. In the future you can expect to see flowers in July or August, the Easter lily's natural season. Greenhouse professionals must go through complicated manipulations to get lilies to bloom for the holiday. This is an especially complex process since Easter occurs at a different time each year. In the garden, Easter lilies bloom as the spirit moves them.

Additional Species, Cultivars, or Varieties

There are many different types. 'Casa Blanca' is a stunning pure white Oriental. 'Lolypop' is a new white Asiatic whose petals are dipped in deep rose. 'Black Dragon' is a trumpet lily. It grows from 6 to 8 ft. tall and has dark-red buds that open to white.

Magic Lily

Lycoris squamigera

> **Other Names:** Hardy Amaryllis, Resurrection Lily, *Amaryllis hallii*
> **Height:** Up to 3 ft.
> **Spread:** Up to 2 ft.
> **Flowers:** A cluster of deep pink lilylike flowers
> **Bloom Period:** Late August
> **Zones:** 5, 6, 7, 8, 9,10
>
> **Light Requirement:**

The magic lily has every right to its common name. Once the flower stalk emerges, it seems to shoot up an inch or two every time you turn your back. Then *poof*, the flowers are open. No leaves—just an eruption of flowers on top of a very straight, very naked stem. But plants cannot live on flowers along. The leaves emerge in spring, grow long and straplike, then disappear in midsummer. There is no trace of the plant until the sudden appearance of the flower stalk, which seems to bloom before you have time to blink. The leaves can be used to separate colors in the garden or in combination with peonies or sweet William. Plant low growing annuals such as petunias or dwarf marigolds in late May and they will fill in the gaps as magic lily's foliage fades. The flower stalks will shoot up over the annuals when the time comes. They appear so suddenly that it is always a surprise. You'll think Jack traded his mother's cow for bulbs instead of beans.

WHEN TO PLANT

Plant when the bulbs are available. This may be in the spring before the foliage comes out, in the summer before they bloom, or in the fall after they finish.

WHERE TO PLANT

Plant in a sunny spot or in light shade. Be sure to provide a little protection from the worst of winter weather, especially in the northwestern part of the state. It might be best to plant magic lily against a south wall of the house, especially if there are shrubs there to protect the area from northern winds.

How to Plant
Plant 4 to 6 in. deep and 8 in. apart. In northwestern New Jersey, plant bulbs 6 in. deep. Prepare the soil deeply to ensure good drainage. Mulch heavily. Plant with alyssum, annual baby's breath, petunias, or spring bulbs. You don't want to hide magic lily with the foliage or flowers of other plants. If they are too crowded you won't be able to appreciate their magical appearance in late summer.

Care and Maintenance
Bulbs should be left in place for many years. You may want to mark the areas where the bulbs are planted to avoid damaging them during their several dormant periods. Fertilize while the leaves are growing in the spring. Water during dry periods. Let the leaves mature fully before cutting them back. Cut the flower stalks when they finish blooming. Mulch heavily during the winter.

Additional Information
Years ago I planted a patch of magic lilies in deep shade under an enormous old ailanthus tree. Every spring they sent up leaves. The leaves eventually got buried in the daylilies that came up later. No magic lily flower ever appeared. Three or four years went by, and I completely forgot about the magic lilies. Early one spring, I had major professional pruning done to the ailanthus tree. Late that summer, something strange poked up in the shadiest part of the garden. I had no idea what it was. It shot up like a rocket. Not a single leaf; just this soldier straight stem with a bulbous tip. Then it bloomed. A single magic lily erupted into a full cluster of pink flowers. It was the closest thing to a magic plant that ever appeared in my garden.

Additional Species, Cultivars, or Varieties
The literature mentions a purple magic lily, var. 'Purpurea', but the only one that is readily available in catalogs is the species pink. Perhaps these references are really to *L. sprengeri*, which has a smaller but similar purple flower. It is listed as equally hardy. Other species of *Lycoris* are hardy only to Zone 7 and must be dug and stored for the winter. *L. radiata*, the spider lily, has red flowers and long spidery filaments. 'Alba' is a white variety. *L. africana* or *L. aurea* is the golden spider lily. *L. sanquinea* is bright red orange. There is little information about this species, but there are hints that it may be more hardy than some of the others.

Peruvian Daffodil

Hymenocallis narcissiflora

Other Names: Spider Lily, Basketflower,
Ismene calathina, H. calathina
Height: 2 ft.
Spread: 12 to 18 in.
Flowers: Fragrant; white or pale yellow
Bloom Period: Summer
Zones: 8, 9, 10 (treat as a tender bulb
in New Jersey)

Light Requirement:

These totally outrageous flowers resemble nothing else in the garden. They have petals and a central cup like the traditional daffodil, but the petals are long, almost threadlike, and they curl back. These wispy petals are what has generated the common name "spider lily," which it shares with some of the *Lycoris* species. The center cup is larger than any daffodil and so resembles a small white lily. Since the plant is native to Peru, there is a reasonable explanation for its more universal common name, "Peruvian daffodil." Whatever its appellation, a patch in bloom looks like something right out of Munchkinland. The bulbs are quite large, and closely resemble an Amaryllis bulb, which is a relative. If you happen to be lucky enough to travel to the Caribbean for a winter vacation, you will see Peruvian daffodils blooming everywhere as lush landscape plants. Back in the Garden State, they can be grown in pots or potted up and transplanted out after danger of frost.

WHEN TO PLANT
Direct plant in spring after danger of frost has passed (usually around May 15). You can start the bulbs in pots earlier.

WHERE TO PLANT
Plant in a sunny, well-drained spot. You will want visitors to gasp when they see this one in bloom, so make sure it will be plainly visible. If you plant in a bed with low growing annuals such as ageratum, petunias, or verbena, the flowers will take center stage while in bloom. Mixed with something taller, such as red zinnias, they will blend nicely but not be so quick to upstage everything else.

HOW TO PLANT

Plant 6 in. deep and 12 to 18 in. apart. Be sure to prepare the soil deeply. The bulbs need plenty of water until they bloom, but be sure to keep the area well drained. The addition of organic matter at planting time is recommended. Plant at least 6 bulbs together to appreciate the truly singular blooms.

CARE AND MAINTENANCE

Water deeply from the time the bulbs are planted until they bloom. Fertilize regularly; every 2 to 3 weeks is suggested, but it really depends on the fertilizer you use. If you have enough to cut, Peruvian daffodils make excellent cut flowers. Their fragrance is lovely. Be sure to remove the spent flower stalk if you haven't cut it previously. Dig the bulbs after the plants have been lightly frosted. Take extra care not to rip the roots from the bulb while extricating it from the soil—do not cut or damage the roots in any way. Store bulbs where they will be cool and dry, but warmer than most bulbs. 50 to 59 degrees Fahrenheit is ideal.

ADDITIONAL INFORMATION

Several years ago an elderly gentleman gardener approached me with a twinkle in his eye. He asked if I could identify the flower he held. I immediately recognized it as a Peruvian daffodil. He was trying to stump me, and was impressed that I recognized the unusual flower. The bulbs from which the flower grew had been handed down from his grandmother and he really did not expect me to know what they were. As a reward for the correct response, he was kind enough to send me a shoebox full of the bulbs the following spring. The large healthy bulbs bloomed with enthusiasm. I heard shortly after that gardening season, that the gentleman had passed away. He left me with a treasure for which I will be forever grateful.

ADDITIONAL SPECIES, CULTIVARS, OR VARIETIES

There are not many varieties, but you may come across a few if you are diligent. 'Daphne' has larger flowers than the species. *H. × festalis* is sometimes listed as a variety and sometimes as a hybrid between *H. narcissiflora* and *H. longipetala*. It has extra-long wispy petals. 'Sulphur Queen' is pale yellow.

Reticulated Iris

Iris reticulata

Other Names: Dwarf Iris, Netted Iris
Height: 4 to 6 in.
Spread: Up to 12 in. across
Flowers: Fragrant, beardless blooms;
   classic iris appearance
Bloom Period: February to April
Zones: 4, **5, 6, 7,** 8, 9

Light Requirement:

The world of iris is extremely complicated. The large German bearded iris is by far the most commonly cultivated. These little bulb irises are early spring treasures that don't compare in impact to their giant cousins, but have the tough job of blooming while winter is still gleefully blowing a cold wind. Each flower is short lived, but an established patch will produce so many blooms that you will have color for several weeks. *Iris reticulata* spreads, though at a sleepy snail's pace. It will never naturalize over large areas, but it does create compact patches full of delightful little flowers. In a sunny, protected nook, plants may bloom as early as January. Plant this bulb iris by the front door or the path to the car, under the mailbox, or in some other place you visit often. You will want to be able to soak up its cheer when you need a winter boost. If you plant reticulated iris in the back forty, the flowers will be up and gone before you ever see them. If you can get close enough to the blooms, poke your nose in for a pleasant surprise. They are sweetly fragrant, a little like grapes. On a cold day the scent may be hidden, so if your nose is dissatisfied, try again when winter sun is warming the earth.

WHEN TO PLANT
Plant from mid-September to mid-November.

WHERE TO PLANT
Planting in a sunny warm spot will result in the earliest blooms, but *I. reticulata* can put up with a little shade. Tuck the bulbs into rock gardens or any nook where the early spring flowers will be appreciated. As with all bulbs, avoid soggy ground.

How to Plant

Dig deeply. These plants like sandy soil, so add a 2:1 mixture of organic matter and sand to loosen things up. Plant 3 to 4 in. deep and space 3 to 4 in. apart. If planting *I. reticulata* in containers, place bulbs 1 in. deep and 2 in. apart. Store in a cold basement or garage. Bring indoors in late winter to enjoy early flowers.

Care and Maintenance

Make sure the plants stay moist in the fall and again in the spring until they finish blooming. Keep the area well mulched in winter. Fertilize in the spring. Allow the foliage to mature fully before cutting it back. Because they spread so slowly, reticulated iris rarely need division. Potted bulbs can be planted out after the weather warms up.

Additional Information

Years ago I visited a greenhouse that specialized in containerized bulbs. They had a large pile of *Iris reticulata* potted plants ready for the trash heap. The plants had bloomed and faded without being sold. The leaves were mostly yellow. I rescued a bagful of the unwanted plants and put them in my garden. They bloomed the following spring and for many years after that. They are sweet little flowers, but tough little plants.

Additional Species, Cultivars, or Varieties

'Harmony' is a very dark blue with a splotch of yellow. 'Cantab' is light blue. 'Danfordiae' is neon yellow. 'Joyce' is sky blue with a blotch of orange. 'J. S. Dyt' has purplish red flowers. 'Natascha' is ivory with green veins.

Snowdrop

Galanthus elwesii

Other Names: Giant Snowdrop, Milk Flower
Height: 8 to 10 in.
Spread: 3 to 4 in.
Flowers: White, nodding small flowers with 3 larger petals and tiny inner petals
Bloom Period: February to March
Zones: 3, 4, 5, 6, 7, 8

Light Requirement:

A patch of dainty white snowdrops poking up in late winter creates gentle ripples of excitement like a small pebble in the pond. The pristine white flowers nod their heads shyly as their three petals droop gracefully toward the ground. The flowers of the giant snowdrop are 1¼ in. long and reach up to 10 in. in height. Their close cousin, the common snowdrop, *G. nivalis*, has flowers that may reach 1 in. wide but grow only 6 in. tall. Both prefer a bit of shade (remember, these are shy creatures). Plants closest to the house will bloom first and may be the very first flowers of spring. It is difficult to choose between the two species. The larger species makes a bigger splash and actually looks coarse next to its diminutive relative. The common snowdrop spreads more enthusiastically, so it may have the greatest impact over time. Neither species likes to be disturbed.

WHEN TO PLANT

Plant in early fall as soon as you get the bulbs.

WHERE TO PLANT

Snowdrops are a woodland plant and prefer partial shade or full shade to full sun. They are cooperative, however, and will grow in full sun if they must. If you locate them close to the house they will bloom earlier. Naturalize snowdrops under evergreen trees, along a wooded path, or in a rock garden.

HOW TO PLANT

Plant in large patches or these little flowers will be lost. They make a stunning purple and white combination with dwarf iris. Plant quickly when you receive the bulbs so that they don't have a chance to dry out. Because snowdrops are a woodland plant, they prefer a moist, humusy soil. Add plenty of organic matter to the native soil. Plant 3 in. deep and 3 in. apart.

CARE AND MAINTENANCE
Do not disturb these plants if at all possible. They do not like to be moved. Allow the foliage to fully mature before cutting it back. Snowdrops are one of the earliest flowers to bloom, and they finish up early in the season. If you plant them in a shady part of the lawn, they will usually have finished before it is time to mow the grass. A little winter mulch is beneficial for snowdrops planted in beds.

ADDITIONAL INFORMATION
The name *Galanthus* is Greek for "milk flower." This is a fairly well established fact. Not so well known is the origin of the name "snowdrop." According to the Farmer's Almanac's "Flower Gardening Secrets," it comes from a German word "schneetropfen." "Schnee" means snow, but the word actually refers to a popular-style earring from the 1600s. Personally, I think they look more like droopy airplane propellers than earrings.

ADDITIONAL SPECIES, CULTIVARS, OR VARIETIES
According to *Bailey's Standard Cyclopedia of Horticulture* from 1922, there are yellow snowdrops and even fall blooming snowdrops. I could find no other mention of these in any resource, not even in *Hortus III*, the bible of American horticulture. What a shame that they have been lost. One other variety that is commonly available is *G. nivalis* 'Flore pleno'. The inner petals are double white with streaks of green.

Tulip

Tulipa species

Height: 2 to 36 in.
Spread: 12 in.
Flowers: Cup shaped with 6 petals in a
variety of colors
Bloom Period: March through May
Zones: 3, 4, **5, 6, 7** (most 8, some 9)

Light Requirement:

Tulips are lovely flowers, but their claim to fame is color: intense, vivid, rich blasts of color. There are late season parrot tulips with ripply edged petals, fringed tulips with petals that appear to be rimmed with soft bristles, and even lily flowered tulips with pointed petals. On a hot day, they open wide like a stargazer lily. The yellow 'Maja' fringed tulip has captured the afternoon sunshine in its petals, and 'Top Parrot' is the color of a red silk petticoat. Somehow even the pastels are passionate. It is this captivating quality that has given rise to an incredible and somewhat mysterious history. Tulips appeared in Turkey in about 1554 where they were under cultivation in the Sultan's garden. For how long they had been cultivated prior to that time is unknown; there are no wild types that can be clearly traced. Less than 100 years later, one of the biggest economic collapses in the history of the modern world took place. Tulips had become such a craze that they were being sold on speculation. Bulbs were sold and resold, sometimes before they had ever bloomed. Prices for a single bulb were phenomenal. One bulb was traded for 12 acres of land. When this artificial economic structure collapsed in 1637, many people suffered tremendous financial loss. This catastrophe has been equated with the stock market crash of 1929. Although tulips lost favor as a result, breeding and selection continued, particularly in Holland, but throughout Europe and America as well. The tulip went through another crisis during the German occupation of Holland during World War II. Tulip bulbs were ground and mixed with flour for food. The Dutch were able to spare the best varieties so that after the war the tulip industry resumed its growth. Today we enjoy the tulip for its spring cheer, ease of cultivation, and tremendous variety.

When to Plant

Plant tulips in the fall, from mid-September until Thanksgiving.

Where to Plant

Plant in a well-drained sunny spot. Tuck clumps in among shrubs, add to a perennial border for early color, plant along the road for drive-by impact, or grow in a rock garden for splashes of zing.

How to Plant

Prepare the soil deeply and thoroughly. Dig down at least 12 in. Add a 2:1 mixture of organic matter and sand as well as some bonemeal. Be sure to provide plenty of moisture and excellent drainage. The general recommendations are to plant 4 to 8 in. deep and 4 to 8 in. apart. Larger bulbs go deeper and require more space. To encourage tulips to perennialize, or to last for more than 2 or 3 years, plant them 8 to 10 in. deep.

Care and Maintenance

Remove dead flowers immediately. It is estimated that seed production can take up to 30 percent of the bulb's energy. Allow the foliage to completely yellow before removing it. Hide ripening foliage with colorful annuals. If you intend to add bulbs to the bed, take care to mark either the areas where it is safe to dig or those areas where you have bulbs that should not be disturbed. It is easy to damage bulbs when you can't see the leaves. Fertilize in the fall or spring when new leaves emerge. Tulips need plenty of water in the spring. If they don't get 1 in. of rain a week while they are growing, they will require supplemental watering. Replace when the flowers' quality begins to decline. Bulbs usually last 3 to 5 years.

Additional Information

Tulips make splendid cut flowers, but they they continue to grow after they are cut. A bunch in a vase with some greenery and baby's breath is no problem. When used in a centerpiece, however, the stems may elongate several more inches, ruining whatever balance you were striving to create. As long as you are aware of this, you can plan accordingly.

Additional Species, Cultivars, or Varieties

Species tulips are small tulips that work well in rock gardens and for naturalizing. *T. clusiana* is the candy stick tulip. It has red and white stripes on the outside but opens white with a red eye. *T. wilsoniana* is 4 to 6 in. tall and a dark vermillion red. When choosing garden tulips, choose the colors, season, and flower type you like best.

Wild Hyacinth

Camassia leichtlinii

Other Names: Camass, Indian Hyacinth, Zuamach, Quamash, *Quamasia*
Height: Up to 4 ft.
Spread: 10 in.
Flowers: Starlike blossoms in blue or white carried in tall, loose spikes
Bloom Period: May
Zones: 4, **5**, **6**, **7**, 8 (possibly 3)

Light Requirement:

These soft blue flower spikes resemble wood hyacinth, a species of *Scilla*, far more than they do the true garden hyacinth. The flowers spikes are tall and airy. Their stature and timing command attention. The blooms arrive when the big spring flush of color is fading. The late May flowers will take you right up to *Alliums* and all the rest of the garden display that explodes in June. All wild hyacinths are native Americans. This is one of the few garden bulbs that can make that claim. Wild hyacinth prefers a touch of shade and heavy, moist soils, another unusual characteristic for bulb flowers. These wild beauties are only semi-tamed; they will naturalize if left undisturbed. The loose spikes of blossoms have an unrefined elegance like handspun yarn. They were valued as food in many Indian cultures where they were roasted, cooked in soups, or pounded and made into loaves. The flavor is supposed to be quite sweet and, according to the 1852 *Farmer's Encyclopedia*, tastes like licorice. In her wonderful book *Who Named the Daisy*, Mary Durant quotes Mary Elizabeth Parsons: "Grizzly bears, when more plentiful in the early days, were particularly fond of the bulbs. Indians today (1900), value them very highly as an article of diet . . . Indeed, the Nez Perce Indian war in Idaho (1877) was caused by encroachments upon territory which was especially rich in these bulbs." And you thought it was just a pretty flower.

WHEN TO PLANT

Plant in fall after the weather cools to prevent sprouting. Mid-October should be fine.

Where to Plant

A site with partial shade is preferred, but these adaptable plants will endure full sun. Choose a site with heavy, moist soils but no standing water. Wild hyacinth does not like to be disturbed, so plant the bulbs where they can stay a while. It will naturalize if given room to spread and can be used in mixed beds, as borders, or at the water's edge.

How to Plant

Add organic matter to sandy soils to help retain soil moisture. Plant bulbs 3 to 4 in. deep and 6 in. apart. Use a mulch to prevent the soil from drying in hot weather. Plants can also be grown from seed but it will be 4 to 5 years before they bloom. Sow seed as soon as it is ripe. Germination will take anywhere from 30 to 180 days.

Care and Maintenance

Keep *Camassia* well watered during the growing season. Use an organic mulch to prevent soil from drying out. Allow foliage to fully mature before removal. For the best display, do not disturb the plants. Divide in September only after clumps become over-crowded. Replant bulbs immediately. Wild hyacinth makes excellent cut flowers.

Additional Information

There is another plant, "death camass," that has white flowers and looks very similar to the wild hyacinth. It can be found growing wild in the same regions, primarily the Northwest and California. The species is *Zigadenus elegans*. The true camass has blue flowers, but the bulbs themselves are easily confused. It is suggested that you not eat any of these wild plants.

Additional Species, Cultivars, or Varieties

C. leichtlinii 'Alba' is a variety with white flowers. 'Semiplena' is creamy white with semidouble flowers. 'Blue Danube' has very large spikes of dark blue flowers. The flowers of *C. cusickii* are pale blue and the foliage is bluish green. *C. quamash* is shorter, growing to about 2 ft. The flowers are dark bluish purple.

Winter Aconite

Eranthis hyemalis

Height: 3 to 4 in.
Spread: 2 to 3 in.
Flowers: 1¹/₂-in. fragrant, bright-yellow, buttercuplike flowers
Bloom Period: February to March
Zones: 5, 6, 7, 8 (possibly 4)

Light Requirement:

---

*T*his plant needs a new common name, one that expresses its intense good cheer. "Sunspots" isn't bad, or maybe "yellow zingers." "Winter aconite" doesn't even give a hint of its charms. The glowing yellow flowers appear in late winter. While the world is still cold and barren, these tiny flowers burst forth as if the sun were melting and drops of sunshine landed here and there in your yard. Winter aconite does not spread rapidly, but with a slow determination they can fill large swathes of ground as if the golden drips flow into a meandering stream. Winter aconite is part of the army that fights back winter while gardeners fuss over houseplants and mark catalog pages with sticky notes. It is a quiet battle that crocus, dwarf iris, snowdrops and winter aconite wage, but it cries out in a silent world it is time to awaken; that the circle of life is about to begin anew. Each honey scented blossom has 5 to 9 petal like sepals and a pincushion center full of anthers and filaments. In a cool spring, the flowers will last for weeks, maybe even months. The flowers are surrounded by a ruffle of green leaves like an Elizabethan collar. The leaves emerge after the flowers. They are slightly rounded but finely divided and form attractive little clumps that will spread if left undisturbed. The seed capsules look like tiny bean pods. The plant will self sow, but it can take years before the volunteers bloom. The leaves die down and the plant sleeps quietly over the summer.

WHEN TO PLANT

Plant in late summer or early fall. Late August is best. Potted plants are sometimes available for sale after they have finished blooming in later winter. Plant these immediately.

Where to Plant

Winter aconite prefers sun while in flower but shade later on. That makes it ideal for planting under shade trees. If you can be patient, plant many corms at a slight distance from your favorite window where they will eventually spread into a golden sea. A patch outside the front door will bring cheer until the tide comes in on the sea of gold.

How to Plant

Plant as soon as possible after obtaining the corms. They should be soaked for 24 hours prior to planting. Winter aconite prefers moist, well-drained soil. It is adaptable to different soils but prefers soil with an alkaline pH. A application of lime would be helpful since most New Jersey soils are somewhat acidic. Plant large patches of this tiny flower. Space the corms 3 in. apart and plant 3 in. deep.

Care and Maintenance

The most important thing you can do for winter aconite is leave it alone. There is a twist, however. More than one reference suggests that for best results you should transplant the plants while in bloom. If you try this, get as large a clump as possible to avoid damaging the tubers. Allow the foliage to fully mature before you cut it back. Mice and chipmunks can be a problem.

Additional Information

Winter aconite is native to Europe and has been under cultivation since at least the 1500s. In 1948's *Bulbs for Home Gardens*, John Wister quotes John Gerard's circa 1500s description of the power of winter aconite to protect against scorpions: "It is of such force, that if the scorpion passe by where it groweth and touche the same, presently he becometh dull, heavy and senseless."

Additional Species, Cultivars, or Varieties

'Glory' has lemon yellow flowers. *E. cilicica* has larger flowers and bronze leaves. *E. × tubergenii* gets taller, up to 8 in., and has larger, deep yellow blooms.

*A*NNUAL FLOWERS IN THE LANDSCAPE ARE LIKE ACCESSORIES TO A PERFECT OUTFIT. You can try a single strand of short pearls, or try a floor-length feather boa with sparkles everywhere. You can do monochromatic elegance this year and all-colors-go-together-in-the-garden next year.

In all likelihood, however, you will find that you are a fairly consistent creature. If you wear bright colors and decorate your home in bright colors, you will probably do something similar in the yard. Your garden is an extension of your personality and you can express that in a windowbox or on ten acres.

I once heard a distinguished landscape architect from Rutgers University give a seminar on landscaping principles. He stressed the importance of making the front yard, or "public space," very conservative and subdued. He said to save the big flower gardens and colorful displays for the more private back yard. I guess I was a bit of a gardening radical, because my very first thought was: "Why do all that work for only my family to see?" Years later, I will add to that: "Why do all that work for the kids to trample?"

Your own version of annual flower planting principles must be to plant what and where makes you happy. Your garden is for your personal pleasure. That includes both the act of gardening itself and the results of your efforts. Make your garden work for your lifestyle.

First decide what you want your annual flowers to accomplish. If you are primarily concerned with cut flowers, you may want a separate bed allotted to the task. If your concern is summer color with as little work as possible, you need to choose plants that will shed their dead flowers and pack in close enough to keep weeds under control. There are a few species that come back from seed each year. These can be gorgeous and easy, but they come up where the mood suits

Chapter Fourteen

them and usually have a free-spirited air about them. If you want something dignified, try something else.

Color is a tricky thing. Up close, most colors do go together in a garden, especially for a cutflower bouquet. From a distance, however, all colors together look like those bottles with layers of colored sand that someone shook too hard. If you plant colors in repeated stretches, or use one as the foundation color with complementing splashes, it may be more effective. Even consider using all one color for each species, and soften it with another flower altogether. Dark-purple petunias and red salvia make an intense color combination with interesting variations in height and texture. Try white alyssum and pink periwinkle for something more delicate.

Always keep in mind that gardening is an art form with four dimensions. It will change continually over time. Annual flowers will be the most consistent part of your summer garden in any one season, but the rest of the garden will be changing around them. Use your annuals to fill in gaps as spring bulbs fade, but remember that a misplaced giant marigold will conceal your spectacular Oriental lilies in August. Your perennial chrysanthemum plants can get bush-sized before they bloom. Annuals packed in too close will just get in the way.

The very best part of annuals is their transient nature. You can try *anything*. If there is a secret part of you that would love to go with the feather boa but you always wear pearls, the garden is a safe place to go a little wild. Circle the house with giant sunflowers! Mix purple and red and hot pink together! Grow morning glories up the porch rail! Plant enormous trumpet-shaped white moonflowers! Substitute ornamental peppers for petunias! Throw cosmos seed all along the edge of the property and let them go crazy!

You can have perfectly trimmed hedges, the obligatory dogwood, and a manicured lawn; but somewhere, somehow, sometime, let your annual flowers be at least a little outrageous.

Alyssum

Lobularia maritima

Other Names: Sweet Alyssum, Snowdrift,
Alyssum maritimum
Height: Up to 12 in.
Spread: Up to 18 in.
Flowers: Tiny, fragrant, prolific flowers in
rounded clusters of white, lilac, or pink
Bloom Period: Summer

Light Requirement:

Alyssum is soft, sweet, and "fluffy." It is an excellent choice for edging around shrubs or other flowers. It can be grown from seeds started indoors or out. You can also purchase transplants. Alyssum spreads and forms a dense mass of white flowers like a skyful of cumulus clouds landed in your garden. The flowers mature to small round pods, each holding a single seed. The long slender leaves are dark green. The plants are perennial in Zones 9 and 10 and can get slightly woody. In New Jersey they will not survive winter but can tolerate a light frost, and they will generally bloom into early winter. Alyssum self sows, so it may surprise you with a return visit even if the original plants don't survive winter weather. Most varieties stay quite small; some grow to only 6 in. Others, such as 'Tetra Snowdrift', are tall enough to be used as cut flowers. Alyssum does well in containers. It spills gracefully over the edge like a lace shawl. Keep alyssum watered during hot weather and it will bloom until frost. If the heat does take its toll, a midsummer shearing will rejuvenate the plant and encourage a burst of fall flowers. Just before frost, shear your potted alyssum once again and bring the plant indoors. In a sunny window it will make an agreeable houseplant. You can even pot up a few garden plants if you want its cheery company indoors.

WHEN TO PLANT

Start seed indoors in early April. Direct seed in the garden in early May. Transplant potted alyssum in late May. Because it self sows, you can also direct seed alyssum in the fall. A second seeding in June will ensure a showy late season display.

WHERE TO PLANT

Alyssum will grow in full sun, though shade in the hottest part of the day is ideal. This plant is not happy in extreme heat, so choose your location accordingly. A western exposure might be overwhelming. Alyssum is ideal for edging, as filler, in front of shrubs (especially small flowering shrubs like azaleas and potentilla), and in containers. It is gorgeous tumbling about the rock garden. The contrast of soft fluff and hard rock is very satisfying.

How to Plant

Alyssum prefers a moist, loamy soil but will tolerate a wide range of soil conditions. The addition of organic matter will be beneficial. When sowing seed, place it on the soil surface. Germination takes 5 to 14 days and flowers are produced in as soon as 6 weeks. A second seeding in June will give the best fall display. Plant alyssum in a staggered row for edging. It can be very effective concealing the fading foliage of spring bulbs. Space small varieties 6 to 8 in. apart. Place larger ones 8 to 12 in. apart.

Care and Maintenance

Keep plants well watered in hot weather. Shear if they get ratty in midsummer. A June seeding will encourage fall bloom. The taller varieties can be cut for indoor use—this is the best way to appreciate their honeylike scent. Enjoy potted alyssum as a houseplant for as long as it gives you pleasure. If winter growing conditions weaken the plant, just toss it. There will be plenty more come next spring.

Additional Information

Alyssum is native to Mediterranean Europe. American gardeners first became acquainted with its charms in the late 1700s. By the Victorian era it had come to be a garden favorite. The use of flowers to communicate feelings and messages was refined to perfection during that time. This Victorian language of flowers uses the popular sweet alyssum to convey "worth beyond beauty." It is one of the species worthy to be considered an "heirloom" garden flower, a popular concept in today's gardening world.

Additional Species, Cultivars, or Varieties

'Rosie O'Day' is a pink dwarf first introduced in 1961. Its scent is particularly pleasant. 'Oriental Night' is rich purple. 'Easter Bonnet' is a relatively new introduction with 8 colors selected for consistent timing and habit. 'Snow Crystals', 'Sweet White', and 'Carpet of Snow' are among the many whites.

Annual Vinca

Catharanthus roseus

Other Names: Madagascar Periwinkle, *Vinca rosea* **Height:** 2 ft. **Spread:** 1 ft. **Flowers:** 5 petals up to 2 in. across in pink or white **Bloom Period:** Summer **Zones:** 9, 10 (treat as an annual)	**Light Requirement:**

nnual vinca is a very pleasant garden flower. Its habit is bushy and attractive and its shiny dark green leaves are 1 to 3 in. long. The pinwheel flowers sit against the rich foliage in a way that is subtle but very elegant. The bright, congenial blooms are produced for a long season, sometimes as late as Thanksgiving in a mild autumn. The flowers resemble those of the popular periwinkle groundcover, but they are much showier. The unusual flower buds are about 1 in. long and lance shaped. Each bud unfurls into a flat bloom, often with a contrasting eye. The simple flowers are excellent for indoor arrangements. Left in the garden, the dead flowers drop away on their own. This means that the onerous task of "deadheading" (removal of spent blooms) is eliminated, a real gift to overextended gardeners. Annual vinca is recommended for container culture. If pinched when young, it stays more compact and will branch extensively. It is very effective in a hanging basket surrounded by alyssum and a few dangling branches of *Vinca major*. Annual vinca is native to Madagascar, an island in the Indian Ocean. It has naturalized in most tropical parts of the world and can even be found growing wild in southern parts of the United States.

When to Plant

Sow seed indoors in early March. Seeds require darkness for germination, which takes 15 to 20 days. Transplant potted plants into the garden after danger of frost has passed—usually in late May. Direct-seeding is not recommended in New Jersey.

WHERE TO PLANT

Annual vinca prefers full sun but will tolerate light shade. This can be confusing because the popular vinca that is used as a ground-cover requires shade. Vinca is so dependable and low maintenance that it is an excellent choice for mass planting. Use it in a mixed border, around shrubbery, or in containers. The white varieties do well in almost any setting. The pinks have very strong color and may not look their best with oranges or corals but are spectacular with whites, purples, and other true pinks.

HOW TO PLANT

Plant seed $1/4$ in. down and keep flats or pots in the dark at 70 to 80 degrees Fahrenheit. Pinch when seedlings reach 3 to 4 in. tall to promote branching. Prepare the soil to ensure good drainage. Add organic matter in heavy soils. Space plants 1 ft. apart in a staggered row or in clusters. Annual vinca is a neat plant that will look overly formal if planted in straight rows.

CARE AND MAINTENANCE

Annual vinca thrives in heat and humidity and will tolerate dry soils. It is pest free and generally low maintenance. Repeated early pinching will keep the plants low to the ground—do this if you want to use annual vinca as a groundcover. There are also varieties selected for this purpose. Cuttings taken in early fall can be rooted and kept over with great success.

ADDITIONAL INFORMATION

For centuries, annual vinca has been used as an herbal medication in tropical countries. In the 1950s, it was learned that diabetes was being treated in Jamaica with a tea made from annual vinca. Since that time, a tremendous amount of research has been invested in the study of this plant. Among many important discoveries in this plant are anticancer alkaloids, one of which is particularly useful in the treatment of childhood leukemia. Other alkaloids that reduce blood sugar levels have been found in annual vinca.

ADDITIONAL SPECIES, CULTIVARS, OR VARIETIES

'Tropicana' has four bright-pink colors in a mix. 'Apricot Delight' mixes ivory, apricot, and raspberry. 'Peppermint Cooler' is white with a red eye. 'Parasol' comes very close to true red.

Bachelor's Buttons

Centaurea cyanus

Other Names: Cornflower, Bluebottle,
   Hurtsickle, Ragged Sailor, Blue Bonnet,
   French Pink
Height: 1 to 3 ft.
Spread: 6 to 12 in.
Flowers: Up to 2 in. across; usually blue,
   but available in purple, pink, or white
Bloom Period: Late spring through summer

Light Requirement:

---

*T*his hardy, cheerful plant goes about its business without a care in the world. It self seeds and can pop up just about anywhere. The pretty blue flowers are some of the earliest blooming annual flowers for use in cutflower arrangements. Bachelor's buttons make excellent long lasting cut flowers that look fabulous in a spring bouquet with Shasta daisies (which bloom at the same time). During the Victorian era, this flower was popular for use as a boutonniere, as it stayed fresh for such a long time. This tradition gave it the name "bachelor's button." The plants are native to the Mediterranean but have been cultivated for centuries. They naturalized long ago in fields all over England. The plant was called "cornflower" because it grew wild in corn fields, and "hurtsickle" because its strong stem damaged sickles during harvest. Bachelor's button can also be found naturalized in many places in North America. The flowers appear along straight, downy stems. The foliage is silvery blue. If you cut the flowers as they are opening and store them upside down in a dry, dark place, they will retain the blue and make excellent dried flowers.

WHEN TO PLANT

Start seeds indoors in early April. Direct seed in early May. Plant potted plants out in late May, after all danger of frost has passed.

WHERE TO PLANT

Plant in a sunny location where you don't expect everything to stay in tidy straight rows. Plant bachelor's buttons around your tulips; they will bloom in June after the tulips have finished, just in time to hide the fading leaves. Bachelor's buttons are happiest in cooler weather. Pick a spot with good air movement away from afternoon heat buildup. Bachelor's buttons are ideal for a wildflower meadow and are often included in wildflower seed mixes. Try planting them in an open field.

How to Plant

Space plants 6 to 12 in. apart in well-drained acidic soil. Since most New Jersey soils are slightly to very acidic, this should be no problem.

Care and Maintenance

Remove dead flowers continuously if you want the plants to bloom all summer. You can also do successive seeding throughout the summer to keep the flowers coming. They will bloom 8 weeks from the time of seeding. Water regularly. Fertilize in the spring. Yank unwanted volunteers in the early spring.

Additional Information

There are several versions of how the genus received its name. All relate to the centaurs of Greek mythology. According to one tale, the name represents a centaur who was honored as the father of medicine. In another, the centaur Chiron used the flower "centaury" to cure a wound on the heal of his foot. The last story is the best: The centaur Chiron was wounded by Hercules' poisoned arrows. He covered his wounds with cornflowers and was healed.

Additional Species, Cultivars, or Varieties

'Jubilee Gem' is compact with deep blue flowers. 'Black Ball' is the color of milk chocolate. 'Polka Dot Mixed' mixes all the colors together. 'Blue Diadem' has $2^1/2$-in. double flowers.

Begonia

Begonia semperflorens-cultorum

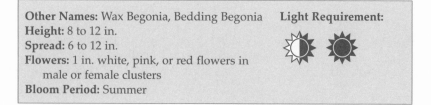

Other Names: Wax Begonia, Bedding Begonia
Height: 8 to 12 in.
Spread: 6 to 12 in.
Flowers: 1 in. white, pink, or red flowers in
    male or female clusters
Bloom Period: Summer

Light Requirement:

right color in the shade garden is hard to find. If it were not
for the dependable begonia, shade gardeners would despair.
Plant begonias in late May and they will bloom their little hearts out
all summer. Wax begonia foliage does have a waxlike quality to it.
The almost round leaves are light to dark green or reddish to deep
bronze. In partial shade the plants get bushy and full. Foliage is
packed tightly together on thriving plants, but the stems are quite
brittle. Handle them gently. You will never have to worry about picking off dead flowers—they must blow away in the wind.

WHEN TO PLANT
Seed needs to be started indoors in January or February. Plant potted plants outside after the middle of May.

WHERE TO PLANT
A partially shaded location is the ideal place to plant. That is where
you will get the most attractive plant and most abundant flowers.
Deep shade is acceptable, but the plants will stretch. Avoid soggy
ground at all costs. Full sun can be tolerated, but choose darker
leaved varieties and never let the soil get excessively dry. Even the
more sun tolerant plants should not have to endure a hot western
exposure. Plant begonias along the edges of paths or tucked in here
and there around your azaleas and rhododendrons. They look wonderful mixed with ferns and can brighten up the dependable but
subdued hostas. Mass planting will work if it is not too sunny, but
be sure to avoid planting in very straight rows; these tidy plants can
get that rigid marching soldier look. Begonias also do well in containers. Bring the pots indoors in the fall. You will enjoy the perky
flowers well into winter while the rest of the garden slips into sleep.

How to Plant

Growing plants from seed is tricky, in part because of the long lead time required for garden-ready plants. The seeds are tiny. Mix them with sand to help evenly disperse the seeds on the soil surface. Keep the temperature at 70 degrees Fahrenheit and wait 15 to 60 days for germination. It may be more practical to purchase plants at a nursery. Plant outdoors in well-drained soil. The addition of organic matter at the time of planting will be beneficial. Provide shade from hot afternoon sun. Place plants 6 to 8 in. apart. When planted in containers, begonias tolerate being packed in fairly tightly. Be sure to provide adequate drainage.

Care and Maintenance

Water when dry. Avoid getting water on the leaves. This can make them more susceptible to mildew, especially if the plant is in deep shade. Fertilize regularly and take care not to let containerized begonias become overly dry. In late fall, bring potted begonias indoors for a little winter cheer. When they get scraggly, take cuttings and root them for spring planting. The mother plant will resprout and eventually fill in. Keep it around if you don't mind looking at it ugly until spring.

Additional Information

There are over 900 species of begonia from all over the world. Most are tropical. The genus is named after Michel Begon, a plant lover and one-time Governor of Canada. Tuberous begonias have the showiest flowers. Others, grown primarily as houseplants in the United States, have outrageous foliage but only occasional flowers. The original wax begonia, *B. semperflorens*, is native to Brazil. It has been crossed and recrossed so often that the current botanical name has become a catch-all for the untraceable hybrids. They may not have an exact pedigree, but they are among the most popular garden flowers. In the Victorian language of flowers, they send an interesting message. A begonia means "dark thoughts."

Additional Species, Cultivars, or Varieties

There are many and they constantly change. Pick the ones you like best.

Black-Eyed Susan Vine

Thunbergia alata

Other Name: Clockvine
Height: 3 to 8 ft.
Spread: Variable
Flowers: Profuse 1¹/₂ in. trumpets in cream
  to deep orange with a dark purple throat
Bloom Period: Summer

Light Requirement:

This wonderful twining vine is an extremely satisfying addition to your garden. It will cover an ugly fence or spill over a bare wall, and it is spectacular in a hanging basket where it will climb up the basket as well as spill over its sides. At first glance, the flowers appear to have 5 petals and a dark central disc. Upon closer inspection you will see that the center is actually a long, dark purple funnel. The vine produces arrowhead leaves with an abundance of flowers along the leaf axils. Black-eyed Susan is an excellent alternative to morning glories, which are lovely but can self-sow to the point of invasiveness. There are new varieties that lack the dark eyes. Though it is a matter of personal taste, I think that varieties without the contrasting center seem less distinctive. Black-eyed Susans are winsome plants that spread with enthusiasm but are not really aggressive. Even so, they like to twine around whatever happens to be handy and can smother smaller plants. They are sometimes suggested as a groundcover, but will become vertical with the first shrub they encounter. In the right spot, black-eyed Susans are simply delightful. Choose your location carefully so you can enjoy them to the fullest.

WHEN TO PLANT

Plant in early April for seed indoors. Transplant potted plants outdoors in May.

WHERE TO PLANT

Black-eyed Susans do well in full sun or partial shade. They are best suited for an isolated planting situation or around other plants that are large enough to resist their twining. If you give sunflowers a head start, black-eyed Susans growing up the stalks can be very pretty. They are perfectly charming flowing over a split-rail fence or up a trellis by the porch. Let them grow over the dog kennel to create summer shade as well as beauty. Hanging baskets bring the hanging gardens of Babylon to your backyard. Potted plants can be brought indoors to a sunroom or closed-in porch for some color into early winter.

How to Plant

When sowing seeds, barely cover them with soil. Use peat pots to make planting easier. Keep seeds at about 70 degrees Fahrenheit. Seeds take 10 to 21 days to germinate. In the garden, add plenty of organic matter to hold soil moisture. Plants need an abundance of moisture to support their rapid growth, but they don't do well with wet feet. Mix fertilizer into the soil at planting time and sidedress at least once during the season. Space plants 12 to 18 in. apart.

Care and Maintenance

Water regularly to keep plants lush and full of flowers. Keep an eye on the vines to prevent them from overwhelming neighboring plants. If you can get the plants to overwinter in a sunny location indoors, you will have an even grander display the following year.

Additional Information

Black-eyed Susan vine is native to tropical Africa. The common name is often confused with the many species of North American *Rudbeckia*. These large daisylike wildflowers are also lovely orange-gold flowers with a dark eye, but they are completely different in habit and are not interchangeable in the garden. The confusion of common names (and sometimes botanical names) is a continual problem in the gardening world.

Additional Species, Cultivars, or Varieties

'Angel Wings' has white flowers and is slightly fragrant. 'Susie Mixed' has different colors in the group, some without dark throats. 'Bakeri' is pure white and 'Alba' is white with dark centers. 'Aurantiaca' has rich orange yellow color.

Celosia

Celosia cristata

Other Names: Cockscomb, Woolflower,
  C. argentea var. 'Cristata'
Height: 1 to 4 ft.
Spread: 1 to 2 ft.
Flowers: Plumelike and feathery or fan shaped
  and crested; various colors
Bloom Period: Summer

Light Requirement:

*C*elosia is a plant that people find either fascinating or ridiculous. When you scan the literature, you will find that some authors describe celosia in terms such as "badly dyed," an "acquired taste" or that it "looks like an alien brain from outer space." Others find it "particularly brilliant" and "unusually effective." There is no doubt that the colors are bright even in the dark. If you are looking for elegance or subtlety, look somewhere else. If you want to have a little fun and be different, give celosia a try. There are two primary flower types. The first type of flower grows as a soft feathery plume, something like the flower spike on ornamental grasses but in intensely bright colors. The second type of flower is a crested form that comes in the same shocking colors but more resembles a 'brain from outer space.' Both types are available in dwarf and tall varieties. All are long-lived in the garden and can be dried to make outstanding winter bouquets. Some varieties have variegated foliage. Celosia's biggest drawback is that it resents transplanting. If the plants go into shock, they simply wither away. Direct seeding or extremely gentle handling are necessary for success.

WHEN TO PLANT
Start seed in late March or early April. Plant outdoors in late May.

WHERE TO PLANT
Celosia will do well in full sun or partial shade. Since the colors are so brilliant, they can be planted at some distance and still be appreciated. (I am certain some people will say they are *better* appreciated at some distance.) Plant in beds of spring perennials such as iris or peonies. Celosia will bloom for a second season of color after the

perennials have finished. Dwarf varieties can be used as edging. In the cutflower garden, plant tall varieties in rows for easy access.

How to Plant

If starting seed indoors, use peat pots to minimize transplant shock. Barely cover the seed with soil. Keep pots at 70 to 75 degrees Fahrenheit. Seeds will take 6 to 14 days to germinate. You may need to put the peat pot in a larger pot before planting out. You can direct seed in the garden after danger of frost, but it will be 90 days before you see flowers. Bloom will be delayed until the middle of August. Plant out transplants in late May. Prepare the soil with organic matter and lime. Celosia prefers a neutral pH. Space 12 to 18 in. apart depending on the variety. Plant en masse for the biggest effect. Use different flower types, colors, and sizes to create an explosion of color.

Care and Maintenance

If the plants establish after transplanting, they are very low maintenance. Water during dry weather. Sidedress once during the growing season. Cut in full bloom for drying. Remove all unnecessary parts and hang plants singly upside down in a dry, warm, dark room. If you want to shape the drying flowers, wire and bend them while they are still fresh.

Additional Information

Every year the gardener of a home on a main street in the town of North Brunswick has a definite theme for the small yard. It always has outstanding drive-by impact. One year the entire yard was shades of purple. Included among the flowers was a circular bed of enormous, deep purple crested celosia. The monochromatic use of color brought the height, habit, and texture of the different flowers into center stage. Though they are usually difficult to blend with more traditional flowers, the addition of celosia to this garden took it from interesting to outstanding.

Additional Species, Cultivars, or Varieties

Seeds sold in mixed colors make real color impact more difficult to attain. Individual varieties give more satisfactory results. 'Flamingo Feather' is soft pink. 'Century Rose' is deep pink. 'Apricot Brandy' was an All-America winner a few years ago. 'Red Velvet' is a crested type and 'Wine Sparkler' is plumed.

Cosmos

Cosmos bipinnatus

Other Name: Mexican Aster **Height:** 6 to 10 ft. **Spread:** 2 to 3 ft. **Flowers:** 3 to 4 in. single blooms in white and many shades of pink to red **Bloom Period:** Summer to fall	**Light Requirement:**

*C*osmos is one of the most rewarding garden flowers for the not overly fastidious gardener. Plant transplants or sow seed once and enjoy their exuberant return year after year. This free-spirited attitude may not fit in with tidy rows of ageratum and geranium, but this flower's airy lightheartedness brings joy wherever it sprouts up. The foliage is fernlike and open. The plants can get quite tall, and many sources recommend staking. To me, that sounds too much like work. Don't fertilize, and cut big bouquets for indoor use when the plants start to get too tall. The flowers work well in an arrangement with almost anything, but a favorite is a large bunch of cosmos with a few pink roses. If the plants volunteer their charms in places you think are off limits, yank them out or transplant them somewhere more acceptable. Big patches at the back of the property allow you to enjoy them from a distance without having to fuss with keeping them too tidy. They also work in beds of spring bulbs where their self-seeding works to your advantage. You won't have to worry about injuring the bulbs while planting annuals for summer color.

WHEN TO PLANT

Sow seed indoors in late April. Direct seed in mid- to late May. Plant transplants in late May.

WHERE TO PLANT

Cosmos requires full sun to do its best. Sun loving plants stretch in lower light. This particular plant doesn't need to get any leggier than it is on its own. Plant cosmos in a sunny place where untamed plants will not seem unsightly. Try planting them in the back of borders, in a meadow, or even scattered in foundation plantings if it suits your taste. Just don't try to force these plants into nice straight rows.

How to Plant

Plant seeds $1/8$ in. deep. Keep at 70 to 75 degrees Fahrenheit and you will see seedlings pop up in 3 to 10 days. Space plants in the garden 18 in. apart. Don't fuss with the soil too much. Plants will flower more abundantly in poorer soils. Do not lime. Cosmos prefers an acidic pH.

Care and Maintenance

Thin seedlings if they come up thick. Pinch young plants so that they branch. This will make them shorter and less likely to blow over. Water during dry spells. Continual removal of dead flowers will extend the bloom into fall. For cut flowers, take the blooms in the early morning and place in water immediately. Carry a bucket of water with you into the garden. Leave the larger buds on the stems you cut. They will open indoors. Cut the plants back after frost.

Additional Information

Cosmos is Greek for "beauty," but the plant is actually from Mexico. This untamed species was found flitting around the Mexican countryside in 1799. The wild type was made available to catalog customers in the mid-1800s as "Late Cosmos." This is the unruly plant that gives rise to all the talk about staking. At 10 ft. tall, it will blow over in a puff of wind. A few varieties were selected over the years, but it wasn't until 1930 that 'Sensation' became available. It is shorter, sturdier, and blooms earlier than the species. It was the breakthrough needed to take this plant from being a stubborn wild creature to being a sweet thing that still has a mind of its own. (This sounds like something from Shakespeare's *Taming of the Shrew*.)

Additional Species, Cultivars, or Varieties

'Sensation' is still available and very popular. 'Versailles' series is a little more compact with a range of colors that may include a redder red. 'Daydream' has smaller white blooms with rosy pink at the base of the petals. It is self cleaning, so deadheading is not required. 'Sea Shells' has lovely tubular petals in a variety of colors. 'Pied Piper Red' is dark red with similar tubular petals. The species *C. sulphureus* has yellow flowers. There are several varieties.

Geranium

Pelargonium × hortorum

Other Names: Fish Geranium, Zonal
   Geranium, House Geranium,
   Bedding Geranium,
   Horseshoe Geranium
Height: 1 to 2 ft.
Spread: 1 to 2 ft.
Flowers: Large umbels of many flowers
   in bright colors
Bloom Period: Late spring to fall

Light Requirement:

Garden geraniums are a very popular garden flower. Red geraniums are classic, but some of the intense pinks and beautiful salmon varieties available in recent years are spectacular. Geranium plants are usually available already in bloom. It may seem painful, but if you remove existing flower buds at the time of planting, the plant will produce more flowers throughout the summer. Bud removal gives it a chance to make a few roots before it heads full steam back into making flowers. Each individual blossom is about 1 in. across. It has five petals and is not much different in appearance from an annual vinca flower or even an impatiens. Unlike either of these two, however, geranium flowers develop in "umbels," or flat-topped clusters. The stems are stiff and hold the umbels erect, usually above the flowers. The leaves are almost round with a slight ripple to the edges. The entire plant is covered in a very soft, fine fuzz. Geraniums are dependable bloomers in the garden or in containers. A few plants clustered together will cheer up a spot outside the back door. A mass planting is very colorful. They are commonly planted with low growing annuals such as alyssum or petunia. Unfortunately, geraniums are overused to the point of being boring. If you must have them, try mixing geraniums with hare's tail grass, asparagus fern, or gazania for a less-traditional look.

WHEN TO PLANT

Start seed indoors in late March. Root cuttings in March or April. Plant out in late May after danger of frost has passed.

WHERE TO PLANT

Plant geraniums in a sunny, well-drained location. They do well in containers, as edging plants, mixed into foundation plantings, or in a cluster outside the front door.

HOW TO PLANT

Prepare the soil to ensure good drainage. Add organic matter and lime. Geraniums prefer a neutral pH. A single geranium will get lost so group at least 3 plants together. Plant in a staggered row for edging. Plant in groups in mixed beds. Vary group sizes to keep the display from looking rigid. Geraniums are formal in appearance and need to be handled in a way that avoids stiffness.

CARE AND MAINTENANCE

Remove the umbels as the flowers age. Fertilize monthly and water if the ground becomes dry. Geraniums can tolerate a very light frost, but if you want to save the plants, bring them indoors at the first sign of frost damage on other plants. Then give them as much sunlight as possible. Water regularly, but keep the plants a little drier than they were outside. They will stretch over the winter but may continue to flower. By the time springs comes, geraniums will need pruning. Root the cuttings in a sterile medium with a light touch of rooting hormone. Plant both the mother plant and the cuttings in late May.

ADDITIONAL INFORMATION

Garden geraniums are not the same as true geraniums. The genus *Geranium* is known as "cranesbill." The developing seed looks very much like a crane's bill. Cranesbill is a lovely garden perennial that is not as showy as *Pelargonium*. Scented geraniums are also *Pelargonium*. They were very popular in the 1800s when breeding scented geraniums was a craze. It is amazing how well geraniums mimicked other scents. Lemon geranium smells very much like lemons. There are rose, peppermint, nutmeg, and even coconut geraniums. During the scented geranium boom there were hundreds of named varieties, but many were lost when they went out of fashion. Today, however, they are again gaining in popularity. There is even a citronella geranium used to keep away mosquitoes.

ADDITIONAL SPECIES, CULTIVARS, OR VARIETIES

There are many varieties of garden geranium, but those available change from year to year. Pick the colors you like best. If you like them enough, take cuttings to keep them through the winter.

Globe Amaranth

Gomphrena globosa

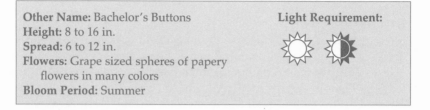

Other Name: Bachelor's Buttons
Height: 8 to 16 in.
Spread: 6 to 12 in.
Flowers: Grape sized spheres of papery
    flowers in many colors
Bloom Period: Summer

Light Requirement:

*G*lobe amaranths are *wonderful* flowers. The plants are very easy to grow. *Gomphrena* comes in a range of colors from sweet pastels to bright, intense shades. The flowers last forever. In the garden they stay lovely right up until frost. When cut and dried they hold their color for years. The round flower heads don't have petals. They look much like a clover flower. Some varieties are quite round and some elongate into a shape more like a Thompson seedless grape. Flowers appear at the tips of the branches as well as in the leaf axils. The blossoms are held very erect and look proud even on such a petite plant. Leaves are about 4 in. long and opposite. The entire plant can be easily dried. Globe amaranth can be started from seed indoors or out. The plants transplant easily and do well in containers. They can be used as edging, for cut flowers fresh or dry, in mass plantings, or in small clusters. Taller varieties mix well in a cutflower garden. Globe amaranth grows thick enough to form a dense mass that minimizes the need for weeding. The plants tolerate heat, humidity, and dry soil. The flowers live so long that you rarely have to deadhead. *Gomphrena* should be a welcome addition to any garden, large or small. It has much to offer and nothing contrary in its personality.

WHEN TO PLANT

Plant seeds indoors in late March or early April. Plant potted plants or direct seed in late May.

WHERE TO PLANT

Full sun is preferred, but these plants will endure light shade. *Gomphrena* is not fussy about soil types but does not do well in soil that is overly rich. It will tolerate dry soil. The flowers are very small and are best seen up close; or you can plant them en masse to enjoy from a distance. A few mixed with other plants might get lost. Shorter varieties of *Gomphrena* are engaging as edging plants and can be very effective in front of foundation plantings. Globe amaranths are a great choice for containers on balconies or decks and can be brought indoors at season's end.

How to Plant

Soak seed for 24 hours and then just barely cover with soil. Keep at 60 to 70 degrees Fahrenheit. Germination takes place in 6 to 15 days. You will probably need to add lime to garden soil, since globe amaranth requires a pH of 6 to 7. Additional amendments are not required in average soils. Space plants 8 to 12 in. apart.

Care and Maintenance

Pinch young plants to make them branch and stay compact. Fertilize when they first start to bloom. Cut flowers for drying just before they reach their peak. Hang up to 10 stems together, upside down in a dry, dark place to dry.

Additional Information

Globe amaranth is one of those plants that doesn't look like much in a six-pack at the nursery. It doesn't really take off until the weather warms up. In mid-May when home owners are busy sprucing up their yards, they go to the nursery and walk past the sluggish *Gomphrena* to the showy petunias and other plants that bloom their hearts out in tiny cell packs. *Gomphrena* gets off to a slow start in cool weather, but once planted in warm summer soil it will provide carefree flowers until frost and plenty of dried flowers for winter bouquets.

Additional Species, Cultivars, or Varieties

Seed is often available in mixed lots. As with many flowers, these mixed lots are fine for cutting but lose garden impact from a distance. Varieties to look for include 'Strawberry Fields', a bright red; 'Professor Plum'; 'Amber Glow'; and 'Innocence', a white variety. The 'Buddy' series are compact varieties in many colors that produce abundant flowers.

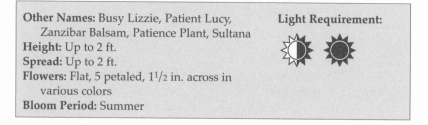

Impatiens

Impatiens wallerana

Other Names: Busy Lizzie, Patient Lucy, Zanzibar Balsam, Patience Plant, Sultana
Height: Up to 2 ft.
Spread: Up to 2 ft.
Flowers: Flat, 5 petaled, 1¹/₂ in. across in various colors
Bloom Period: Summer

Light Requirement:

Impatiens and begonias play tag in the shade garden. Between them they are responsible for most of the summer color in the shadowy nooks of your yard. Impatiens have a broader range of colors but are probably slightly more fragile. The flowers are abundant and self-cleaning, a good combination for a garden plant. Blooms resemble those of the annual vinca. The five petals open flat in front of a single "spur," or wispy, petal like sepal. Of all the plants whose flowers look similar, this wisp is unique to busy Lizzie. It is easier to see when the plant is in bud. Once the flower has unfolded, its stretching petals hide the dainty thread. Impatiens stay low to the ground and form a dense mat that is effective for use as a ground-cover. In a woodland setting, where impatiens wind their way through ferns and around hostas, under a spreading dogwood and up to the azaleas, a single color of impatiens acts like a meandering stream. It brings light and joy wherever it goes, even into the darkest corners of your garden.

WHEN TO PLANT

Plant seed indoors in March. You can direct seed outdoors in late May, but flowers will not bloom till midsummer. Plant potted impatiens in late May.

WHERE TO PLANT

Impatiens need some protection from sun to do their best. If you force them in full sun, plant in a circle. Those in the center will grow taller because they receive the most shade. This creates an attractive mounded appearance. Pay particular attention to watering impatiens in full sun. If they dry out, they rapidly become toast. Plant impatiens in woods, under trees, along shadowy paths, as edging, and en masse in the shade. These plants do well in containers and can be brought indoors for the winter.

How to Plant

Impatiens prefer woodsy soil that is high in humus and has excellent drainage. Prepare the soil by adding organic matter and lime. Impatiens prefer a pH of 6 to 7. Because the flowers are so small, mixed plantings lose color impact quickly. Multiple colors can be very effective, but only if each color is concentrated enough to stand on its own.

Care and Maintenance

Pinch young plants to encourage bushiness. Keep impatiens well watered during hot weather. Light applications of fertilizer once or twice during the season will make happy plants. Before the first frost, take cuttings of impatiens or pot up some of the garden plants or bring in any potted plants. Give them the sunniest spot you have in the house. If they stay lovely, enjoy them. Toss them if they get leggy, or take cuttings and start over.

Additional Information

At my first house in New Brunswick, in a narrow alleyway hidden between the houses, the sun shone overhead for only 20 minutes each day and not even weeds grew. It took a pickaxe to break up the soil. We replaced an enormous amount of crumbly shale with leaf compost from the city's compost program. Several years passed before carefully chosen plants took hold. There were many ferns, azaleas, a witch hazel, and even an evergreen skimmia. Among all these we planted impatiens in a different color every year. The bright flowers lit the alleyway like neon lights. Visitors were always shocked to come upon this out-of-the-way garden. The alley went from barren to bountiful—and the impatiens were the ones who infused it with energy. It was Mary Lennox's Secret Garden in the city and a very special place.

Additional Species, Cultivars, or Varieties

Available varieties change from year to year. Pick the ones you like best. Two interesting relatives are *I. balsamina*, the old fashioned garden balsam, whose double flowers look like roses but are somewhat hidden by the foliage. *I. capensis* is an orange flowered native American known as "jewelweed" which is used as an antidote to poison ivy. Its seeds explode when you touch the ripe pods.

Lobelia

Lobelia erinus

Other Name: Edging Lobelia
Height: 4 to 8 in.
Spread: Up to 12 in.
Flowers: Blue, tubular, with 3 larger lower
    petals and 2 smaller upper petals
Bloom Period: Summer

Light Requirement:

---

*L*obelia is a very common plant for edging beds or paths. The foliage is delicate and airy and billows gracefully, softening the straight lines of sidewalks, bricks, or railroad ties. There are upright and trailing varieties, both of which are suitable for containers, though the trailers are particularly lovely in a hanging basket or tumbling over a wall. Both forms do well meandering through a rock garden. Lobelia is a shade tolerant plant that can take full sun where the summers are cool. In New Jersey it will probably do best with shade during at least the hottest part of the day. Although it is a pleasant alternative for the shade garden, lobelia's small flowers and limited range of colors will never replace impatiens or begonia. Still, it blooms on slender stalks with enthusiasm, has a very long season, and requires little or no attention. The blue color can be very blue which is special since it is so uncommon. The many flowers disappear on their own. A light shearing in midsummer is about the only attention these plants may require.

WHEN TO PLANT
Start seeds indoors in early March. Plant potted plants in late May.

WHERE TO PLANT
Plant in very light to moderate shade. Lobelia is an outstanding plant for lining paths, ringing a flower bed, or snuggling into the crevices of a rock garden. Trailing varieties draped over walls and spilling out of containers are very effective.

HOW TO PLANT
Place seed on the soil surface since lobelia requires light to germinate. Use a sterile soilless mix and water from the bottom. Maintain

temperatures at 65 to 75 degrees Fahrenheit. Seedlings should appear in 15 to 21 days. Expect flowers about 100 days after sowing. Lobelia prefers a rich moist soil with a pH of 6 to 7.5. This means you should add both lime and organic matter at the time of planting. Pinch transplants to encourage bushiness. Space 6 in. apart. Apply an organic mulch to retain soil moisture.

CARE AND MAINTENANCE

Keep lobelia well watered in hot weather. A light pruning in mid-summer will encourage a strong rebloom into fall. Lobelia has no insect pests but will dry out if the soil becomes excessively dry and will rot quickly in soggy soil.

ADDITIONAL INFORMATION

The genus is named after Matthias L'Obel, a Flemish botanist who served King James I of England around 1600. Over 200 years later, while the Victorian language of flowers was evolving, the flower came to mean "malevolence." This seems inappropriate for such a sweet little flower. The plant makes up in quantity what it lacks in size. I once photographed a lobelia blossom up close using slide film. When I saw the image projected onto the screen, I could not identify the gorgeous flower. The intricate detail is incredibly lovely, but impossible to fully appreciate on the Lilliputian scale Nature has given us.

ADDITIONAL SPECIES, CULTIVARS, OR VARIETIES

'Cambridge Blue', 'Emperor William', and 'Mrs. Clibran Improved' are all shades of blue. 'Crystal Palace' is also blue and has bronze foliage. 'Rosamund' is deep cherry red with a white eye. You will find many varieties available in catalogs. *L. cardinalis* is the red cardinal flower. It is a perennial with a tall spike of red flowers in mid- to late summer. It tolerates shade and moisture.

Marigold

Tagetes species

Height: 6 to 36 in.
Spread: Variable
Flowers: 1 to 4 in. single or double flowers in
yellow or orange, sometimes with burgundy
stripes or splashes
Bloom Period: Summer until frost

Light Requirement:

Marigolds are dependable garden plants with an interesting history. The African marigold, *T. erecta*, reaches 3 ft. The French marigold, *T. patula*, can reach 1½ ft. tall, though modern varieties are often smaller. All marigolds are native to Mexico and have been tended for over 400 years. They were introduced to Europe by Spanish explorers in the 1500s and were cultivated in monastery gardens where much of the "state-of-the-art" horticulture occurred. From there they went to Africa and France. From Africa seeds went to India and from India were introduced to England by Huguenot refugees. By the time marigolds made it back to America they had become African and French marigolds. Exactly when they returned is questionable, though we know that Thomas Jefferson had them in his garden. Where and how you use marigolds should depend on the varieties you choose. Because they get so tall, the taller African types do best in the back of a bed. These make outstanding long lasting cut flowers. French marigolds and many modern hybrids are small enough to use as edging plants. Even most of the smaller ones can be cut for indoor use. All marigolds bloom profusely once they get started, continuing to bloom until frost. They look wonderful mixed with zinnias in the garden, but hold up much longer in the fall.

WHEN TO PLANT

Plant seed indoors in early April. Direct seed in the garden in early May. Transfer potted plants to the garden in late May.

WHERE TO PLANT

Marigolds prefer full sun. Small varieties will tolerate some shade, though they will not produce as many flowers. Small marigolds do well in containers, edging areas, rock gardens, or mixed beds, or in front of foundation plantings. Taller varieties can be planted in rows for cut flowers, in informal gardens, in the back of borders, or en masse for impact.

HOW TO PLANT

Sow seed in a sterile potting medium to reduce the risk of rotting. Barely cover the seeds and maintain temperatures at 70 to 75 degrees Fahrenheit. Seeds will germinate in 4 to 14 days. Marigolds will endure dry soil but are less forgiving of soggy ground. Add lime at the time of planting to get the pH up to 6 or 7. The plants will reward you with more flowers if you add organic matter to the soil when you plant. Space small varieties 6 in. apart, medium varieties 12 to 15 in. apart, and giant varieties up to 24 in. apart.

CARE AND MAINTENANCE

Remove dead flowers to keep plants attractive and productive. Water when the ground gets overly dry. Pinch plants when they are young to encourage bushiness. Fertilize once or twice during the season. For cut flowers, take the flowers in early morning the day after a soaking rain or a deep watering. Strip all the foliage—it rots quickly and will clog up the water for the other flowers. Slugs may munch on seedlings but don't usually bother with larger plants.

ADDITIONAL INFORMATION

The marigold's great advances into the modern garden treasure that is must be credited to the W. Atlee Burpee company. David Burpee took over the company in 1915 and began developing the marigold to compensate for waning interest in the sweet pea. The company introduced many varieties, including the first hybrid offered for commercial sale in 1939, and more recently, a white marigold. Over the years I have met W. Atlee Burpee many times—the grandson or perhaps great-grandson of the founder. He works for another seed company now. The family business was sold to another company some years ago.

ADDITIONAL SPECIES, CULTIVARS, OR VARIETIES

Burpee's still offers about 20 different marigolds. The Climax series are all giants that reach 3 ft. There are two whites available: 'French Vanilla' grows to 3 ft. and 'Snowdrift' to 22 in. Thompson and Morgan lists about 40 varieties, including 'Naughty Marietta', a 1947 Burpee introduction. It has single flowers of bright golden yellow with maroon blotches.

Ornamental Cabbage

Brassica oleracea

Other Names: Flowering Cabbage,
Flowering Kale
Height: 12 in.
Spread: 18 in.
Flowers: A terminal spike of yellow or
white 4 petaled flowers.
Bloom Period: (A foliage plant)

Light Requirement:

Ornamental cabbages are not grown for their blooms but the entire plant looks like a giant flower. The relatively recent availability of these upscale cabbages is a gift to gardeners in cooler climates. We can appreciate them here in New Jersey. The cabbages are a confusing group of plants: broccoli, cauliflower, cabbage, kale, brussels sprouts, and kohlrabi all belong to the same genus and species. Each of these veggies has been grown for a different part of its plant—flowers, stem, leaves, or buds. Ornamental cabbages take that natural diversity one step further. They have been selected for the beauty of their leaves. These cabbages are tough and not very flavorful, but they are edible. The plants produce low growing flat rosettes of leaves. Flowering cabbage has an open growth habit and a contrasting center in pink, white, or purple. Flowering kale has frilly leaves in tighter heads. Its center is also pink, white, or purple. Because these plants are of the same species, the differences are sometimes as minute as the differences between brands of cola. The joy of these plants is the color they bring while the rest of the plant world is fading into shades of brown. Cabbages are ready for planting with fall mums but the sprightly plants laugh at the cold. They will often stay perky right up till Christmas and sometimes resprout after a mild winter.

WHEN TO PLANT
Start seed in late June or early July. Plant out in September through October.

WHERE TO PLANT

Start seed in a seedbed for transplanting later. Seeds germinate readily. Transplant to a sunny spot where you will be able to feast your eyes on the cheery plants when there isn't much else to see. Key spots may be around the mailbox, outside the front door, or in a patch you have planted in clear view of the kitchen window. Cabbages make excellent container plants, but if planted above ground they may not be able to fight off the cold as well.

HOW TO PLANT

Plant seeds in a seedbed or flats outdoors. Thin to 2 in. apart. Transplant plants to their winter spot as early as September, but bear in mind that color does not develop until after frost. Use a "collar" (try a cat food can with both ends removed) around the stems or wrap the stems in a strip of newspaper to protect the young plants against cutworms. Transplants are now commonly available at nurseries and ready for planting in the fall. They are not fussy about soils, though fertile, deep, well-drained soils are preferred. The pH is best at 6.5, which means that most New Jersey soils need supplemental lime to provide optimum growing conditions. Mix cabbages with pansies for color and durability.

CARE AND MAINTENANCE

You must thin the seedlings or they will become stretched out and worthless. Keep an eye out for cabbage moth caterpillars. B.T. (*Bacillus thuringiensis*) will provide adequate control. These pests usually slow down when the weather gets really cold.

ADDITIONAL INFORMATION

Ornamental cabbages are definitely better suited for fall planting. They are tall and palmtreelike if spring planted, and their summer color is mostly green. One year we planted cabbages along the steps up to the front door. It was a mild winter and the plants grew into January before they gave up. In early spring, the long stems lay along the soil surface and seemed to be dead. With the first wisp of spring air, the ugly stems sprouted all along their length. They came up thick and colorful like a mat of pink and white roses. Their return was a very welcome surprise. They lasted into spring—early summer weather was their final undoing.

ADDITIONAL SPECIES, CULTIVARS, OR VARIETIES

'Red and White Peacock' kale has highly dissected leaves. 'Cherry Sundae Mixed' cabbage comes in carmine and cream. 'Northern Lights' cabbage comes in white, pink, or rose. There are many others.

Pansy

Viola wittrockiana

Other Names: Ladies Delight, Heartsease, Stepmother's Flower
Height: 6 to 12 in.
Spread: Up to 12 in.
Flowers: Up to 4 in. across with 3 larger petals on the bottom and 2 smaller petals on top in a variety of colors and color combinations
Bloom Period: Autumn into spring and early summer
Zones: Annual or biennial

Light Requirement:

*P*ansies are one of the most underappreciated of all garden flowers. They are popular enough, but they are not recognized for being one of the most cold hardy flowers you can have in the garden. Pansies are *tough*. Plant them in October and enjoy flowers until Christmas or even longer. Then they bloom again in spring right up through the snow. Pansies keep company with such stalwart fellows as crocus, dwarf iris, and snowdrop. They never succumb to winter weather. They *always* come back in the spring. When you plant pansies in the fall, they make lots of roots and get very well established. Then they erupt into color early in the spring. The patches get thick with foliage and are covered in flowers all spring long. The blooms last well into summer. Fall planted pansies are much more heat tolerant because they have deeper roots. The seemingly delicate little flowers look up at you with smiling faces of innocent cheer. Their slender stems bely the threads of steel that run through their veins. Plant them everywhere: in rock gardens, around roses, in containers, under shade trees, and between daffodils. Those with variegated petals are the ones that resemble faces. The solid color flowers have more impact. Try pink or white or even black.

WHEN TO PLANT

To start seed for fall planting, sow in early July. Plant transplants in late September through October. To start seed for spring planting, sow seed indoors in January. Plant well hardened transplants in mid-April.

WHERE TO PLANT

You can plant pansies in every nook and cranny in your garden. Plant under shade trees, where they will bloom in early spring sunlight but benefit from the summer shade. Plant in containers for balcony and deck. Pansies do well in rock gardens.

HOW TO PLANT

Sow seed $1/4$ in. deep. Keep seeds in the dark at 65 to 70 degrees Fahrenheit. Pansies are not the easiest flowers to grow from seed. Most gardeners are happier purchasing transplants. Plant in patches or staggered rows to best display these little beauties. Prepare the soil deeply. Add plenty of organic matter. Lime is probably not necessary since pansies prefer a pH of 5.5 to 6.5. An organic mulch will help plants survive both winter's worst and the heat of summer. Space plants 6 in. apart.

CARE AND MAINTENANCE

Continual plucking of the dead flowers will extend the bloom season. Water deeply, especially during hot weather. If the plants get leggy, give them a pruning and a light sidedressing of fertilizer. If they get really ugly, just yank them out and start over the following fall. With proper planning your summer annuals will be full enough to hide any gaps.

ADDITIONAL INFORMATION

Pansies are an excellent flower for pressing. Simple, inexpensive plant presses are available in many garden centers. You can also make a simple press with newspapers and a few heavy books. Pick the flowers at their prime. Make sure they are completely dry on the surface before you press them. They will dry in a few weeks.

ADDITIONAL SPECIES, CULTIVARS, OR VARIETIES

There are many varieties available. The selection varies from season to season. 'Jolly Joker' is bright orange and purple. 'Imperial Pink' is a mix of all shades of pink. There are several black varieties, including Thompson & Morgan's 'T&M's Black Pansy' and 'King of the Blacks'. They are *really* black.

Petunia

Petunia × hybrida

Other Name: Common Garden Petunia
Height: 6 in. to 3 ft.
Spread: 1 to 4 ft.
Flowers: 2 to 4 in. funnel shaped single or
   double flowers in many colors
Bloom Period: Summer

Light Requirement:

Petunias are versatile, non-stop blooming machines. They are relatively new to cultivation. Most modern petunias are a criss-cross of varieties, but the two species of primary importance in their development are of South American origin. *P. violacea* was found in Argentina in 1830 and *P. axillaris* was discovered in Brazil in 1923. The flowers are large and richly colored. They can be edged in white or have bars of contrasting colors. Eyes can be dark or light. Flowers are single or double, ruffled, fringed, or plain. Some of the old-fashioned "balcony" petunias are supposed to cascade nicely but are not easy to find. There is more flower than leaf to a petunia. The leaves are narrow and small, covered in a fine fuzz, and slightly sticky to touch. The plants get leggy during the season, and a pruning in midsummer keeps them blooming until fall. If you save seeds from hybrid petunias, they will not produce plants close to the production or size of the parents. On the other hand, some of the early varieties had the interesting ability to produce different shades of patterned flowers on the same plant. In *The Heirloom Garden*, JoAnn Gardner suggests trying to recreate the charm of the easy care, small flowered varieties of yesteryear. They may show up in the offspring of a modern hybrid.

WHEN TO PLANT

Start seed indoors in March. Saved seed can be started outdoors in late May, but expensive hybrid seed should be started indoors to avoid loss. Plant potted plants out in late May.

WHERE TO PLANT

Location should be variety dependent. Lower growing plants are excellent for edging. Taller varieties can go in a mixed border. Most petunias spread to varying degrees. This makes them pretty in a rock garden or scrambling over railroad ties. The cascading types are used for windowboxes and hanging baskets. All petunias will give you the best results if you let them bask in sunshine.

How to Plant

Plant seed on the soil surface. Petunias need light to germinate and temperatures of 70 to 80 degrees Fahrenheit. Seeds should pop up in 7 to 21 days. Plant outside in moist, well-drained soil. Incorporate plenty of organic matter. Almost all soils in New Jersey will need lime. Petunias prefer a pH of 6.0 to 7.5. Space most varieties 7 to 10 in. apart. Plant in a staggered row for edging, or group several plants together to get the best color impact. Don't mix too many varieties or the colors will run together like a madras shirt.

Care and Maintenance

Pinch young plants to keep them bushy. Remove dead flowers regularly. Fertilize once or twice during the growing season. Prune in midsummer to revitalize the planting. Watch out for tobacco budworm. These critters feed on the flower petals, leaving them tattered and messy. B.T. (*Bacillus thuringiensis*) may give some control, but if it doesn't help you may have to resort to something stronger.

Additional Information

There was a time when petunias were planted for their fragrance as well as their beauty. The single white types were supposed to be the sweetest. In the many catalog listings I checked, only one mentioned scent as a trait. The variety was 'The Pearl', a mix of old fashioned multiflora petunias with 2 in. flowers. In Shepard's Seed Catalog, it is described as having "a soft sweet fragrance."

Additional Species, Cultivars, or Varieties

If you can find an old fashioned variety, it may be worth trying, especially since the plants will be open pollinated and not as expensive as the modern hybrids. Of the many petunia varieties available, the new "Wave" petunias are something special. 'Purple Wave' stays at 4 in. tall and will spread like a groundcover up to 4 ft. wide. 'Pink Wave' grows up to 8 in. tall and spreads 2 ft. wide.

Poppy

Papaver rhoeas

Other Names: Shirley Poppy, Corn Poppy,
Flanders Poppy
Height: Up to 3 ft.
Spread: 12 to 18 in.
Flowers: 2 to 3 in. wide with 4 petals of
crepe-paper texture; most commonly red,
but available in white, pink, salmon,
and purple
Bloom Period: Summer

Light Requirement:

---

*P*oppies will forever be associated with Dorothy and Toto from
The Wizard of Oz. That field of red as far as the eye could see
was a beautiful sight, even if it was the work of the wicked witch. This
particular poppy is a self seeding annual that is now often incorpo-
rated into wildflower seed mixes. It is not a native of North America
but gets one of its common names from growing wild in the cornfields
of Europe. It is, in fact, the poppy of Flanders Field. The corn poppy
is a wonderful flower to grow around spring flowering bulbs. Poppies
bloom from seed in 60 days. If you mix them with cosmos, the poppies will hide the bulbs' fading foliage, the cosmos will take over as
the poppies finish. Poppy flowers appear on tall, straight, leafless
stems. The buds nod shyly and tilt upward just as they are about to
open. Some flowers open with dramatic dark blotches at their centers.
Foliage is hairy and finely divided. The flowers make beautiful, if not
long-lived, cut flowers. A recommended trick for prolonging the life
of the cut poppy is to sear the cut end immediately after cutting. Or
you can cut them in early morning just as the buds are about to open.
Double corn poppies are gorgeous and last longer, but they don't have
the simple magic of the old fashioned poppies of the field.

WHEN TO PLANT

Plant corn poppies in the early spring. These plants do not transplant happily, so you should direct seed in mid- to late April. You
can also seed in the fall. Seeding again in late spring and early summer will keep poppy flowers blooming until the season's end.

WHERE TO PLANT

Plant in a sunny open area where future self sowing will be an advantage rather than a nuisance. Corn poppies are not suitable for formal gardens or straight rows. Plant in open meadows, wildflower gardens, or along fences—any place they can be free spirited.

HOW TO PLANT

Direct seed while the weather is still cool. In prepared soil, spread the seed with some randomness and then rake it in lightly for a natural look. Just barely cover the seed with soil. Thin the seedlings to about 12 in apart. Poppies require well-drained but moist soil. They do not need heavy applications of fertilizer. Since these poppies prefer a pH of 6 to 7, be sure to add lime to the soil.

CARE AND MAINTENANCE

Deadhead frequently, especially if you want to avoid self-sowing. Save seed if you would like to replant elsewhere or share the seeds with a friend. Yank the plants when they start to fade in hot weather. Avoid the use of pre-emergence weed control in the spring if you want the poppies to return. If you prefer, let the seedpods dry and cut them for use in dried arrangements.

ADDITIONAL INFORMATION

The Shirley poppy is a selection of corn poppy. It was developed in the late 1800s by a Reverend Wilkes, who found a single flower with a white edge and collected its seeds. He replanted year after year, gathering seed only from those flowers that exhibited the variegation. The lovely Shirley poppy is named after the town where Wilkes lived and worked.

ADDITIONAL SPECIES, CULTIVARS, OR VARIETIES

There are not many available cultivars or varieties. 'Mother of Pearl' is a pastel mix in shades of gray, soft blue, dusty pink, and speckled bicolors. 'Angels Choir Mixed' is a colorful mix of double flowered poppies available from Thompson & Morgan. They are especially beautiful.

Portulaca

Portulaca grandiflora

Other Names: Rose Moss, Moss Rose,
    Sun Moss, Wax Pink
Height: Up to 1 ft.
Spread: 1 ft.
Flowers: 1 to 2 in. single or double flowers
    in bright colors
Bloom Period: Summer

Light Requirement:

*P*ortulaca is a delightful low growing annual that blooms profusely under brutal conditions. It spreads out cheerfully in hot, dry locations where most annual flowers cannot survive. Portulaca is also an outstanding container plant that holds up on those inevitable occasions when everyone thought someone else did the watering. A real advantage to planting this plant in containers is that you are more likely to see it at close range. The small flowers are *stunningly* beautiful. The double flowers look like miniature roses in rich, vivid colors. In the parched soils where portulaca thrives, the plants look like someone threw a handful of jewels in the sand. The portulaca plant is succulent, holding a reserve supply of moisture in its stems and needlelike leaves. The foliage is light green and the stems sometimes have a blush of red. The plants form a thick mat that is covered with flowers while the sun is out. The blooms close at the end of the day. On cloudy days you may not see a single flower. Newer varieties have had some of this trait bred out of them. Portulaca blooms throughout the summer and declines as the weather cools. Faded blooms drop agreeably. Portulaca self sows and may return for many years. Volunteers bloom later than transplants do, so choose between earlier flowers and less work.

WHEN TO PLANT

Start seed indoors in late March. Direct seed or plant out transplants in late May.

WHERE TO PLANT

Plant in hot, dry places with sandy soil and lots of sunshine. Portulaca does well as edging along driveways and concrete sidewalks that hold the heat. A dense planting in an open area will do double duty as a groundcover. Portulaca seems to have been created for rock gardens. Weaving between the rocks or spilling over a rock wall shows the brilliant flowers to perfection. Plant in any container that has drainage. Portulaca will not be happy in soggy soil. Try planting it in a strawberry jar. Plants tucked into the small pouches on the side of the jar won't mind its inherent tendency to dry out.

How to Plant

There are differing opinions on the best way to seed portulaca. One approach is to direct seed in the garden. This eliminates transplant-ing—which portulaca does with hesitation—but the flowers will be later and the tiny seed may wash away. Starting seed indoors gives you a head start on summer flowers, but the brittle plants resent excessive handling. Either way, sow seed on the soil surface. It will germinate in 7 to 21 days. Buying transplants eliminates this issue. Space them 12 to 15 in. apart in unimproved sandy soil. Do not fertilize or lime. Portulaca tolerates a pH of 5.5 to 7.5.

Care and Maintenance

Spent portulaca flowers drop on their own. They rarely need water and prefer no fertilizer. If the plants get leggy in late summer, yank them. They will not recover once the weather cools.

Additional Information

P. oleracea is the common garden weed, purslane. It has stems and habit similar to those of portulaca, but its leaves are flat and spatu-late. Purslane can be troublesome, although there are now several ornamental varieties. You may be happy to know that this native of India is quite edible. It is used fresh in salads or can be cooked in a variety of ways. It is supposed to taste like mushrooms when stir-fried. (Though the taste is interesting, I personally don't think it tastes like mushrooms.) If you can't beat it, eat it!

Additional Species, Cultivars, or Varieties

'Cloudbeater Mixed' is a double that does not close during the day. 'Sundial Peppermint' is a pink and red bicolor. 'Sundial Hybrid Mix' comes in a great range of colors.

Snapdragon

Antirrhinum majus

Other Names: Common Snapdragon,
    Toad's Mouth
Height: 6 to 36 in.
Spread: 8 to 18 in.
Flowers: 5 petals (2 upper and 3 lower) forming
    "dragon's jaws" in a variety of colors
Bloom Period: Spring through fall

Light Requirement:

Snapdragons are a welcome addition to any part of the garden, and they add character to a bouquet of cut flowers. Snaps come in a variety of sizes. The tallest ones will need staking, at least until they bush out. The tiniest varieties may be a little floppy. Those in the intermediate 2 foot range usually stay upright on their own and provide long stems for impressive cut flowers. All snapdragon flowers open from the bottom of the spike and work their way up. This results in an extended bloom in the garden or a vase. Snapdragons provide a big blast of flowers in late spring or early summer and continue to bloom all summer. With a little extra attention in the summertime, the plants will give another push of flowers when weather cools off in the fall.

WHEN TO PLANT

Start seeds indoors in early March. Plant outside in late May.

WHERE TO PLANT

Snaps do best in full sun but will endure a bit of shade. The location varies according to the variety you plant. Taller plants go in the back of a border, or you can plant a cluster as a focal point in your foundation plantings. The terminal and secondary spikes look so lush that even when planted in straight rows in the cutflower beds they are extremely inviting. Intermediate varieties may be the most flexible when it comes to choice of location. They do well in mixed borders, in larger containers, along a fence, or in a cutflower garden. The smallest snaps are used in edgings, containers, and rock gardens.

How to Plant

If you are determined to plant from seed, you must take care to purchase rust resistant varieties. Sow seed indoors in a sterile medium such as vermiculite to avoid damping off (a disease that causes seedlings to flop over). Sow on the surface and water from the bottom. Provide seeds with light and keep temperatures at 55 degrees Fahrenheit. You will see signs of life in 10 to 21 days. Pinch seedlings when they have 4 or 5 leaves to encourage bushiness. In heavy clay soils you will need to add a 2:1 mixture of organic matter and sand. Snaps prefer a neutral pH of about 7, so it will probably be necessary to add lime to the soil. Spacing is 6 in. for smallest varieties and up to 12 in. for the intermediate and larger ones.

Care and Maintenance

Plants must be fairly large at the time of planting to ensure that they bloom in early summer. When night temperatures get above 50 degrees Fahrenheit, flower buds may not set. Enjoy the flush of spring flowers. Prune off the dead stems. If plants stop blooming altogether, prune hard, fertilize, and water deeply. They will return for round two at a later date. Watch out for brown spots on the leaves; this is a symptom of rust. To prevent the disease from becoming serious, move your snaps around each year or plant them every other year. Although they are treated as annuals, snapdragons can overwinter in a protected spot or with a thick mulch. Though it is delightful to see them return, this may not be the best way to prevent disease.

Additional Information

New varieties include bell shaped flowers in both single and double forms. But the classic flower shape is part of the whimsical fun of growing snapdragons. The upper and lower petals form the "jaws" of the mythical dragon. If you pinch the sides of the flowers the dragon's mouth will open and close. Snaps are a delight to children (and to the child within). If breeders come up with jawless snapdragons, they really should call them something else.

Additional Species, Cultivars, or Varieties

'Double Madame Butterfly' is an award winning variety that reaches 24 to 30 in. and has double azalealike flowers. 'Giant Forerunner Mixed' is a tall hybrid. Intermediate varieties are more readily available for individual purchase. 'Purple King', 'White Wonder', and 'Yellow Monarch' are just a few. For dwarf varieties, try 'Peaches and Cream' or 'Lavender Bicolor'.

Spider Flower

Cleome hasslerna

Other Name: Spider Plant
Height: Up to 6 ft.
Spread: 4 to 5 ft.
Flowers: 5 to 8 in. spheres of pink, white, or lavender on top of tall stems
Bloom Period: Summer

Light Requirement:

Spider flowers are absolutely charming. They begin blooming in early to midsummer and keep going until frost without any fuss. You never have to remove dead flowers; they evolve into slender seedpods that grow perpendicular to the main stem. New flowers continue to appear at the top, making the plant taller, more bizarre looking, and more wonderful with each passing day. The flowers consist of 4 curved petals with several 2 to 3 in. long stamens. There are many blooms at any one time, making up the large sphere that continually sends up new blooms from the center. The wispy stamen and especially the stretched out seedpods are the foundation of its common name, "spider flower." The foliage is quite interesting. The bright medium-green leaves are palmately lobed, which means they resemble rounded fingers. This plant blooms enthusiastically from summer to fall. It often reseeds and comes back by itself. Spider flower does well planted in an iris bed, where it offers not a speck of competition for the late-spring beauties. By the time the irises have taken their last bow, the foliage of the spider flowers will be lush, with flowers not far behind.

WHEN TO PLANT

Sow seed indoors in late March or early April. Direct seed in late May. Plant out potted plants in early June.

WHERE TO PLANT

Plant in a sunny location, but give *Cleome* plenty of room. The back of a border will be fine. If you scatter plants about the peony or iris beds, they will take over when the perennials finish. They have tremendous drive-by impact and are excellent for planting along the road. You can also plant a large bed at the back of the property and let them go crazy.

How to Plant

For best results, refrigerate seeds in a plastic bag with slightly damp peat moss for 2 weeks before sowing. Sow seeds on the soil surface and keep them at 70 to 75 degrees Fahrenheit. Germination will take place in 10 to 14 days. Outside, spider flowers do fine in average soils and will tolerate dry soils. They prefer a pH of 6 to 7, so you will probably have to add lime. Space 1 to 2 ft. apart.

Care and Maintenance

Spider flowers are drought tolerant and rarely require watering. Fertilizer may result in excessive leafy growth. If you do not want the plants to self-sow, remove the wispy seedpods before they release any seed. If you have selected a planting location where you can take advantage of spider flower's self-sowing, don't do anything. You can use spider flowers as cut flowers; they are sure to impress. If so, side shoots will develop further back, so you will have more, but smaller, blooms. Sometimes you will get secondary blooms as the plants get taller with the primary cluster intact.

Additional Information

If you want the plants to self-sow you have to remember to let the seedlings come up. A pre-emergent material used in the spring to prevent weeds will effectively prevent *Cleome* from germinating as well. *Cleome* seedlings may come up with such enthusiasm that you will think they are weeds. Look for the unusual palmate leaves to sort the wheat from the chaff. Thin seedlings to 1 ft. apart. As a bonus, hummingbirds like spider flowers.

Additional Species, Cultivars, or Varieties

'Rose Queen', 'Violet Queen', 'Cherry Queen', and 'White Queen' are commonly available. 'Helen Campbell' is another white. A related species, *C. lutea*, is native to California. It is smaller, reaching only 3^1/$_2$ ft. with yellow flowers. Yellow cleome is not readily available, but it may be worth trying to find it.

Strawflower

Helichrysum bracteatum

Other Names: Everlasting, Immortelle
Height: 2 to 3 ft., sometimes taller
Spread: 12 to 18 in.
Flowers: 1 to 2½ in., daisylike, with a papery
   texture in a variety of colors
Bloom Period: Summer

Light Requirement:

Strawflower is an old fashioned flower that fits right in with today's world. It is pretty in the garden and is one of the best flowers for preserving in dried arrangements. There is little fuss to growing strawflower, and even less to drying it. Even fresh flowers have a dry, papery quality. Cut the flowers just before they are fully open. Remove the leaves, bundle five or six together with an elastic band, and hang upside down in a warm, dry, dark place. Strawflowers come in many colors, though all hint at the colors of fall. There are many shades of yellow, gold, orange, bronze, and red, as well as a few shades of white and pink. The flowers hold their color remarkably well when dried and will last for years. Each flower has a central disc that is sometimes hidden by the petals. The medium green leaves are 2 to 5 in. long and straplike. The plants branch but maintain a very stiff upright habit. A mixed planting of strawflowers, celosia, and globe amaranth will provide an abundance of material for drying with a minimum of effort. Statice with strawflowers may not be quite as easy, but the combination is fun and worth trying.

WHEN TO PLANT

Start seed indoors in early April. Direct seed in late May. Plant potted plants in late May to early June.

WHERE TO PLANT

The tall varieties can be used at the back of the border. They are an excellent fresh cut flower and so can join your other favorites in the cutflower garden. Smaller varieties can be used in mixed borders, rock gardens, and containers. Strawflowers will tolerate poor soils and are a great choice for planting at the shore.

HOW TO PLANT

Sow seed on the soil surface. Provide light and maintain temperatures at 65 to 75 degrees Fahrenheit. Germination will take place in 5 to 20 days. Strawflowers are not fussy about soils and will do fine in average sandy soil. Since they prefer a pH of 6 to 7, be sure to add lime to the soil. Plant small varieties 8 to 10 in. apart and tall ones up to 18 in. apart.

CARE AND MAINTENANCE

If you would like larger blooms, remove all but one of the developing flower buds per plant. Strawflowers are very drought tolerant so you should not have to water. If you leave the plants in the garden, they will probably return from seed the following year, though this is not guaranteed. They seem more inclined to make a return visit if growing in sandy soil.

ADDITIONAL INFORMATION

I recently visited a farm in Bergen County where the farmer grew a field of cut flowers for his farm stand. He had an enormous bed of strawflowers in wonderful rich shades of yellow, orange, gold, and red. I stood in the field as the sun streamed through the beautiful patch of strawflowers. When I looked through the flowers I could clearly see the New York skyline. It was breathtaking.

ADDITIONAL SPECIES, CULTIVARS, OR VARIETIES

'Monstrosum' reaches 3 or 4 ft. and has larger flowers. You can purchase colors separately. Try 'Monstrosum Golden' or 'Monstrosum Rose'. 'Tanner's Pride' is much like a white daisy with a yellow center. 'Dwarf Hot Bikini' is a dwarf mixture in very bright colors. There are many others available.

Sunflower

Helianthus annuus

> **Height:** Up to 12 ft.
> **Spread:** 3 to 4 ft.
> **Flowers:** 4 to 18 in. daisylike flower head with a central disc and yellow petals; sometimes white or dark red
> **Bloom Period:** Late summer
>
> **Light Requirement:**

*E*veryone loves sunflowers. They are gentle giants that bring feelings of well-being when they bloom. There is tremendous satisfaction in producing such spectacular results in a single gardening season. It touches that "Jack-and-the-Beanstalk" magical place in the hearts of all gardeners, but especially in children. There is no plant that better teaches the wonder of tending a garden. The flowers are beautiful and the selection is astounding. While classic yellow reigns supreme, varieties are available in dark red, orange, cream, bicolors, and semi-doubles. Full doubles look like giant pompons. Branching types make sensational cut flowers. In addition to being spectacular garden flowers, these North American natives are one of the most useful plants known to man. Every part has value. The seeds are favorites of birds and when toasted are a popular snack for humans. Oils are pressed from the seeds and commonly used for cooking and to make margarine, but also as lamp oil, lubricant, in soaps, for candle making, and in the manufacture of paints. Flower buds can be boiled or roasted and are supposed to be quite tasty. The seeds are roasted to make sunflower coffee and powdered to use as a thickening agent for soups. Dried leaves are used as tobacco. American Indians used sunflowers for everything from dye to medicine to soup. The inner part of the stalks is the lightest natural substance known to man; almost 90 percent lighter than cork. It has been used to stuff life preservers. Sunflowers do all this, and they are incredibly easy to grow, too.

WHEN TO PLANT

Direct seed in late May.

WHERE TO PLANT

Plant in a sunny location. The shorter, branching types work in the back of a border or cutflower garden, but those that reach 8 or 12 ft. may be difficult to mix with other flowers. A single plant anywhere becomes a focal point. Plant along the road for drive-by impact or to hide an ugly fence, or group sunflowers in a bed by themselves.

HOW TO PLANT

Starting seed indoors doesn't offer much advantage. The seeds will sprout and grow but will be set back after transplanting. Direct-seeded plants get a later start but catch up quickly. If you have volunteers that you would like to move, do it while the plants are about 8 in. tall and make sure to take a ball of earth with them. Cover seeds with 1/4 in. of soil. They grow almost anywhere, but a deep, rich, well-drained soil gives the best results. Sunflowers tolerate a pH range of 5 to 7, so lime is probably not necessary. Seedlings will pop up in 10 to 14 days. Thin seedlings to 12 in. for smaller varieties and 24 to 36 in. for the tall ones.

CARE AND MAINTENANCE

Keep sunflowers well watered. Pinch branching varieties to encourage bushiness. Fertilize at planting time and again later in the season. To save the seed, wait until all the disc flowers have been pollinated. You can observe bees working from the center of the disc in a spiral until they have pollinated all the flowers. The seeds mature from the center out. Cover the heads with a paper bag and tie around the stem. After the seeds develop, cut the head. Remove the seeds for storage or keep intact. Smear peanut butter all over the surface and hang it in the trees as an extra winter treat for the birds.

ADDITIONAL INFORMATION

Squirrels like sunflower seeds almost as much as birds do. I once saw a very large sunflower with its head completely bent over from the weight of the seeds. A squirrel hung by its toes from the edge of the flower head. It did repeated stomach curls to reach up and grab the seeds, which it ate while dangling upside down. The squirrel did not seem the least inconvenienced by its strange position.

ADDITIONAL SPECIES, CULTIVARS, OR VARIETIES

Try 'Paul Bunyan' or 'Russian Mammoth' for the biggest sunflower. 'Lion's Mane' grows to 6 ft. and 'Teddy Bear' reaches only 2 ft.— both have double flowers. 'Chianti Hybrid' is a very deep red. 'Italian White' and 'Vanilla Ice' are both ivory. There are many more selections available.

Verbena

Verbena × hybrida

Other Names: Vervain, Sweet Verbena, Rose Verbena, *V. hortensis*
Height: 6 to 12 in.
Spread: 12 to 18 in.
Flowers: Small, brightly colored flowers in flat clusters up to 3 in. across
Bloom Period: Summer

Light Requirement:

Verbena is one of those less common garden flowers that warrants more appreciation than it generally gets. The flowers are vivid and the plants bloom all summer with little complaint in the hottest, driest weather. The individual flowers are five petaled stars. Those with a contrasting white eye are very flashy; the solids create rich mats of color. Though the plants stay low to the ground, the stems get long as they spread out. Verbena makes a surprisingly effective cut flower. The leaves are opposite, 2 to 4 in. long, and relatively narrow. They are coarsely toothed and tend towards a grayish green. They tend to be lost in the layers of sprawling branches, especially when verbena's brilliant flowers attract all the attention. Verbena can be used as a summer groundcover. If you direct the branches to bare spots and pin them to the soil, they will root and fill in any gaps. Verbena is almost as tolerant of brutal growing conditions as portulaca. Try using these two plants in the same spot in alternate years for a little diversity.

WHEN TO PLANT

In late March, refrigerate seeds in a plastic bag with damp peat moss. Sow seeds 2 weeks later. Plant out potted plants in late May. Do not direct seed.

WHERE TO PLANT

Plant verbena in any sunny spot, but take advantage of its heat tolerance and plant in the hot, dry places where other plants struggle. It can be particularly lovely flowing over a wall or wandering hither and yon in a rock garden. When used as edging, the plants may need a bit more room to spread than does the classic edging plant, but it can be lovely when used to soften railroad ties, bricks, or even the edges of sidewalks. Verbena is an excellent container plant. It is successful by itself, or you can mix it with other flowers such as salvia, petunias, or dwarf marigolds.

HOW TO PLANT

Think carefully before growing verbena from seed. The germination rate is never great and sometimes very poor. Germination is sporadic with seeds taking up to 3 months to pop. If you are determined to try, sow seeds after 2 weeks of refrigeration in damp peat moss and cover lightly with soil. Keep them dark and at 65 to 75 degrees Fahrenheit. While verbena is tolerant of dry sandy soils, it will give its best performance in better soils. Verbena requires a pH of 6 to 7; applying lime to the soil is recommended. Spacing is variety dependent, but 12 in. apart is suitable for most garden varieties.

CARE AND MAINTENANCE

Pinch young plants to make them branch and become bushy. Regular removal of dead flower clusters will keep flower production enthusiastic. Verbena tolerates drought but will be happier with an occasional deep watering in hot weather, especially if it is planted in a container. Spider mites and leaf miners can both be a problem which gets worse in hot weather.

ADDITIONAL INFORMATION

Verbena is an old fashioned flower and was considered a favorite in Victorian gardens. As with many flowers during that time, it was assigned a meaning in the contemporary language of flowers. A white verbena means "pure and guileless." A scarlet verbena means "sensibility."

ADDITIONAL SPECIES, CULTIVARS, OR VARIETIES

'Imagination' is violet blue. 'Peaches and Cream' comes in shades of apricot and salmon. 'Romance Lavender' is a dwarf plant with soft lavender pink flowers. 'Blaze' is scarlet. There are many more available.

Wishbone Flower

Torenia fournieri

Other Names: Blue Torenia, Blue Wings
Height: 12 in.
Spread: 6 in.
Flowers: Two-lipped tubular flowers, usually
   violet with a yellow throat
Bloom Period: Summer

Light Requirement:

---

*T*his shade loving plant provides an alternative to the workhorse shade plants, impatiens and begonias. The flower are not as bright and showy, but they are lovely little flowers that will bloom in large numbers all summer. In the fall, *Torenia* can be brought indoors as a potted plant. Place it in a sunny window and it will add color well into winter. Wishbone flower gets its name from the arrangement of stamens within the flower. Stamens, the male flower parts, consist of threadlike wisps with bulbous anthers at the tips. Two stamens bow out and up, forming a shape that looks just like a tiny wishbone. The flower itself resembles a smaller version of the snapdragon flower. The petals are variegated; often the upper lip is one color and the lower lip is a darker shade, or a different color altogether, with a yellow throat. Wishbone flower blooms profusely. New varieties have larger, showier flowers.

WHEN TO PLANT

Sow seed indoors in early April or outdoors in late May. Plant potted plants in late May.

WHERE TO PLANT

Plant *Torenia* in a cool, shady spot. Its compact size makes it a good choice for shaded rock gardens. In a woodland setting, it will mix well with ferns and hostas. Use it to edge a shady path or in the front of a mixed border, or tuck it under azaleas and rhododendrons. Plant under shade trees or in any shady nook that needs a touch of color. Wishbone flower makes a great container plant for a shady spot in the summer or a sunny window in wintertime.

HOW TO PLANT
Seed requires light to germinate; sow on the soil surface. Keep at 70 to 75 degrees Fahrenheit. Germination time varies. You may see tiny leaves in anywhere from 7 to 30 days. In the garden, be sure to add plenty of organic matter when you prepare the bed for planting. *Torenia* needs moist, well-drained soil. Space plants 6 to 8 in. apart.

CARE AND MAINTENANCE
Pinch young plants to encourage bushiness. Keep well watered during hot weather. Spent flowers drop on their own. They have no serious insect or disease problems. Pot up a few garden plants in early September. This will give them a chance to get acclimated before you bring them indoors in early October. They will bloom for months before their season ends.

ADDITIONAL INFORMATION
Torenia is native to Vietnam. I thought that its introduction to North American gardens could perhaps be traced to the time of the Vietnam War—a relatively recent availability would explain its scarcity in home gardens. I checked a 1937 Inter-State Nursery catalog to find the little blue flower listed among the annuals for the bargain price of 10 cents a pack. So much for that theory! Mel, at Livingston Park Nursery in North Brunswick, believes he sells so few of these flowers because they don't start blooming until the weather warms up. Most home owners will only buy what is blooming in the trays, so they walk right past this little beauty. If you have read this far, you now know that wishbone flower should not be passed by. Plant some in the shady nooks of your yard. You will be delighted with the results.

ADDITIONAL SPECIES, CULTIVARS, OR VARIETIES
'Clown Mix' has larger flowers with new colors in the mix. 'Susie Wong' has 1¹/₂ in. yellow blooms with almost black throats. Burpee's offers 'Happy Faces Hybrid Mix' which offers some unusual bicolors.

Zinnia

Zinnia elegans

Other Name: Youth and Old Age
Height: Up to 3 ft.
Spread: 1 to 2 ft.
Flowers: A large single or double daisylike flower in several different flower types and many colors
Bloom Period: Summer

Light Requirement:

---

innias are, well, zinnias. If you had nothing else in your garden but zinnias you would have a full plate. They come in many sizes and in perhaps the most wonderful selection of colors available for any flower. It seems appropriate that the last flower in the last chapter of this book should be zinnias. They are essential, dependable, and magnificent, like the air and the sun and the rain. The stiff plants have paired leaves that are pointed but broad. The flowers, the wonderful smile generating flowers, are what makes them treasures. Zinnias are one of the easiest flowering plants to grow and are great for beginning gardeners, especially children. Yet gardeners who have come to know Mother Nature on a first name basis plant zinnias for the pure joy they bring. In even the worst of seasons zinnias will sing happily and provide generous armfuls of flowers. This remarkable plant is a native American. It can be found from Colorado down to Mexico. More colorful versions come from South America. The Aztec Indians had long been cultivating the flowers by the time the Spanish came upon them. Zinnias traveled to Europe in the 1700s, where breeders began to develop the almost limitless number of varieties we have today. Crossing and crisscrossing continues, and in recent years even green flowers have appeared. Zinnia flowers can be anywhere from 3 ft. tall and 6 in. across to 6 in. tall and 1 in. across. There are small flowers on tall stems and large flowers on compact plants. Singles, doubles, wavy-petaled cactus types, and pompons add more fun. The flowers can be pastel, vibrant, or bicolored.

WHEN TO PLANT

Start seed indoors in early April. Plant out potted plants or direct-seed in late May.

WHERE TO PLANT

Plant zinnias in any sunny spot. Use tiny varieties as edging and in containers. Intermediate zinnias will do well almost anywhere: a mixed border, cutflower garden, larger containers, in front of larger foundation plantings, along fences and buildings, or at the base of the mailbox. The tallest plants need to be in the back of a row or bed, but make sure you have clear access to them for cutting bouquets.

HOW TO PLANT

Barely cover seeds in the flats and keep at 70 to 80 degrees Fahrenheit. They should germinate in a week or less, though it may take up to 24 days. Direct seeding is usually just as effective. In the garden, zinnias will appreciate extra organic matter though they will grow in almost any soil. Adding lime is recommended since zinnias require a pH of 6 to 7. Spacing is variety dependent, but don't crowd the plants. Good air circulation is beneficial. Zinnias are stiff, which really only detracts from tall varieties as they age. Larger varieties will show to best advantage if something smaller with a looser habit grows around them. Petunias or dwarf snapdragons will work well.

CARE AND MAINTENANCE

Water regularly, but try not to get water on the leaves. Fertilize when plants start to bloom. Regular deadheading will keep the flowers blooming and the plants attractive. Watch out for powdery mildew, zinnia's one real problem. Spray at the first sign of white blotches on the leaves.

ADDITIONAL INFORMATION

There are two theories about the name "youth and old age." One is that the flowers are so long lived, early flowers are still lovely while new buds are opening. The other is that the ray petals around the edge begin to fade just as the true disc flowers open. (I must say that zinnias are really a summer favorite at our place. So much so, we named our Cairn terrier "Zinnia.")

ADDITIONAL SPECIES, CULTIVARS, OR VARIETIES

'Persian Carpet' is an old fashioned variety favored by butterflies. Park's 'Big Red' has enormous red flowers that are very mildew resistant. Many zinnia seeds and plants come in mixed colors. If you want a particular color, buy the seed and start it yourself. Choose varieties carefully. The selection is exhaustive.

MAPS
BIBLIOGRAPHY

Resources

Average Dates of First Killing Frost in Fall

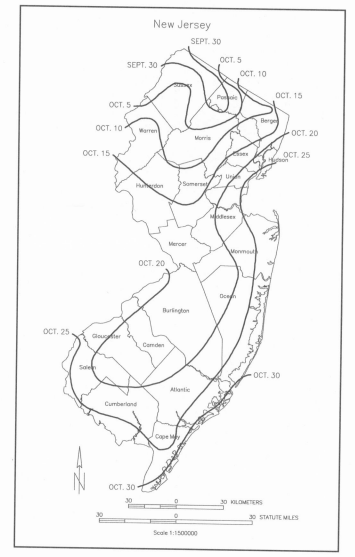

New Jersey

SEPT. 30

SEPT. 30

OCT. 5

OCT. 10

OCT. 15

OCT. 5

OCT. 10

OCT. 20

OCT. 15

OCT. 25

OCT. 20

OCT. 25

OCT. 30

N

OCT. 30

30   0   30 KILOMETERS

30   0   30 STATUTE MILES

Scale 1:1500000

Base Map: 1:250000 DLG USGS, 1990
Thematic Data: SCS Field Office Technical Guide
Originally compiled by USFS   Feb 1994

396

Resources

Average Dates of Last Killing Frost in Spring

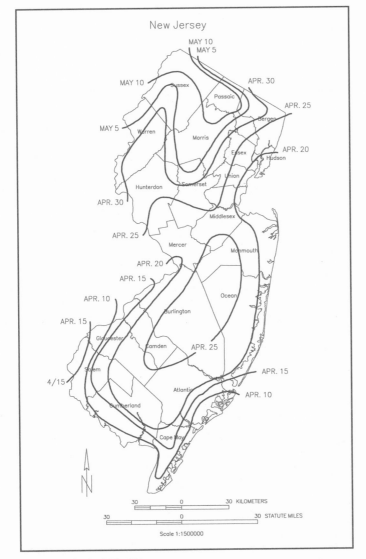

New Jersey

MAY 10
MAY 5
MAY 10
Sussex
APR. 30
Passaic
APR. 25
MAY 5
Warren
Bergen
Morris
APR. 20
Essex
Hudson
Union
Hunterdon
Somerset
APR. 30
Middlesex
APR. 25
Mercer
APR. 20
Monmouth
APR. 15
APR. 10
Ocean
APR. 15
Burlington
Gloucester
Camden
APR. 25
Salem
4/15
APR. 15
Atlantic
APR. 10
Cumberland
Cape May

| 30 | 0 | 30 KILOMETERS |
| 30 | 0 | 30 STATUTE MILES |

Scale 1:1500000

Base Map: 1:250000 DLG USGS, 1990
Thematic Data: SCS Field Office Technical Guide
Originally compiled by USFS   Feb 1994

397

Average Number of Days Without Killing Frost

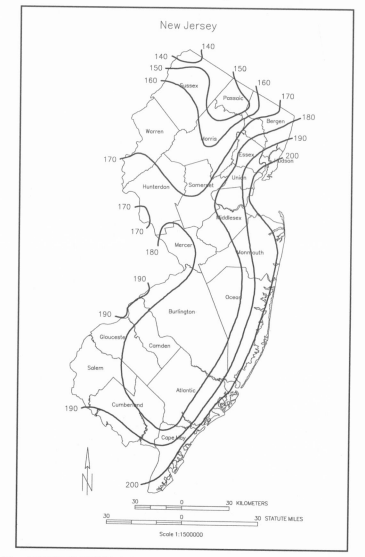

New Jersey

Base Map: 1:250000 DLG USGS, 1990
Thematic Data: SCS Field Office Technical Guide
Originally compiled by USFS   Feb 1994

Resources

Mean Daily Minimum January Temperature in Fahrenheit

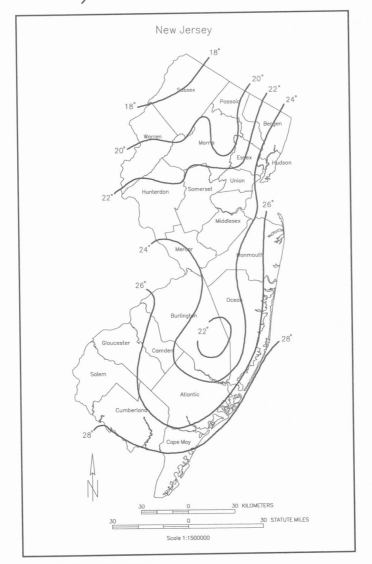

Base Map: 1:250000 DLG USGS, 1990
Thematic Data: SCS Field Office Technical Guide
Originally compiled by USFS   Feb 1994

399

Resources

Mean Daily Maximum July Temperature in Fahrenheit

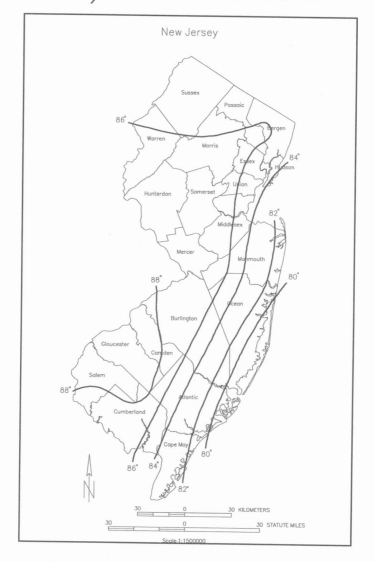

New Jersey

Sussex

Passaic

86°

Bergen

Warren

Morris

Essex

84°

Hudson

Union

Hunterdon

Somerset

82°

Middlesex

Mercer

Monmouth

88°

80°

Ocean

Burlington

Gloucester

Camden

Salem

88°

Atlantic

Cumberland

N

Cape May

80°

86° 84°

82°

30   0   30 KILOMETERS

30   0   30 STATUTE MILES

Scale 1:1500000

Base Map: 1:250000 DLG USGS, 1990
Thematic Data: SCS Field Office Technical Guide
Originally compiled by USFS   Feb 1994

400

Resources

Average Annual Precipitation (Inches)

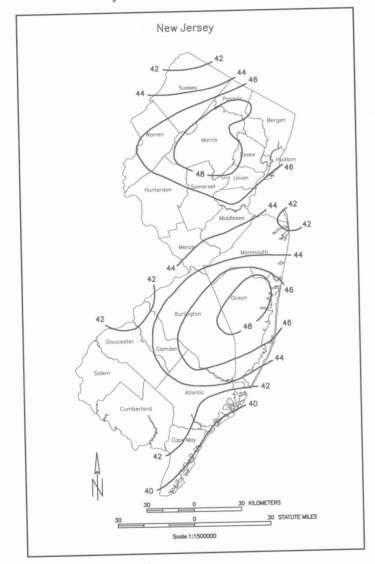

New Jersey

42
42
42
44
44
46
Sussex
Passaic
Bergen
Warren
Morris
Essex
Hudson
48
46
Union
Hunterdon
Somerset
Middlesex
44
42
42
Mercer
Monmouth
44
44
42
46
Ocean
Burlington
48
46
Gloucester
Camden
44
42
Salem
Atlantic
42
40
Cumberland
Cape May
42
40

N

| 30 | 0 | 30 KILOMETERS |
| 30 | 0 | 30 STATUTE MILES |

Scale 1:1500000

Base Map: 1:250000 DLG USGS, 1990
Thematic Data: SCS Field Office Technical Guide
Originally compiled by USFS   Feb 1994

401

ℬibliography

Anglade, Pierre, ed. *Larousse Gardening and Gardens*. New York, NY: Facts on File, Inc., 1990.

Bailey, L.H. *The Standard Cyclopedia of Horticulture*. New York, NY: The MacMillan Company, MacMillan & Co., Ltd., 1922.

Barton, Barbara J. *Gardening by Mail*. Boston, MA: Houghton Mifflin Company, Tucker Press, 1997.

Beales, Peter. *Classic Roses*. New York, NY: Holt, Rinehart and Winston, 1985.

Bradley, Fern Marshall, and Barbara W. Ellis, eds. *Rodale's All-New Encyclopedia of Organic Gardening*. Emmaus, PA: Rodale Press, 1992.

Bubel, Nancy. *The New Seed Starter's Handbook*. Emmaus, PA: Rodale Press, 1988.

Burrell, C. Colston, et. al. *Treasury of Gardening*. Lincolnwood, IL: Publications International, Ltd., 1994.

Clausen, Ruth Rogers, and Nicolas H. Ekstrom. *Perennials for American Gardens*. New York, NY: Random House, 1989.

Coon, Nelson. *Using Wild and Wayside Plants*. New York, NY: Dover Publications, Inc., 1980.

Cox, Jeff, and Marilyn Cox. *The Perennial Garden*. Emmaus, PA: Rodale Press, 1985.

Crockett, James Underwood, and the editors of Time-Life Books. *Annuals*. New York, NY: Henry Holt and Company, 1971.

—. *Bulbs*. New York, NY: Henry Holt and Company, 1971.

Crockett, James Underwood, Oliver E. Allen, and the editors of Time-Life Books. *Wildflower Gardening*. New York, NY: Henry Holt and Company, 1977.

Cutler, Sandra McLean. *Dwarf & Unusual Conifers Coming of Age*. North Olmsted, OH: Barton-Bradley Crossroads Pub. Co., 1997.

Dirr, Michael. *Manual of Woody Landscape Plants*. Champaign, IL: Stipes Publishing Co., 1983.

Dobelis, Inge N., ed. *Reader's Digest Magic and Medicine of Plants*. Pleasantville, NY: The Reader's Digest Association, Inc., 1986.

Durant, Mary. *Who Named the Daisy*. New York, NY: Congdon & Weed, Inc., 1976.

Elias, Thomas S. *The Complete Trees of North America*. New York, NY: Times Mirror Magazines, Inc., Book Division, Van Nostrand Reinhold Company, 1980.

Ernst, Ruth Shaw. *The Naturalist's Garden*. Emmaus, PA: Rodale Press, 1987.

Resources

Gardner, JoAnn. *The Heirloom Garden*. Pownal, VT: Storey Communications, Inc., 1992.

Harlow, William M., and Ellwood S. Harrar. *Textbook of Dendrology*. New York, NY: McGraw-Hill Book Company, 1958.

Heriteau, Jacqueline. *The National Arboretum Book of Outstanding Garden Plants*. New York, NY: Simon and Schuster, The Stonestrong Press, Inc., 1990.

Hertzberg, Ruth, Beatrice Vaughan, and Janet Green. *The New Putting Food By*. Lexington, MA: The Stephen Greene Press, 1984.

Holmes, Roger, and Frances Tenenbaum, eds. *Taylor's Guide to Container Gardening*. Boston, MA: Houghton Mifflin Company, 1995.

Jimerson, Douglas A., ed. *Successful Rose Gardening*. Des Moines, IA: Better Homes and Gardens Books, Meredith Books, 1993.

Kelly, John, ed. *Reader's Digest A Garden for all Seasons*. Pleasantville, NY: The Reader's Digest Association, Inc., 1991.

Kowalchik, Claire, and William H. Hylton, eds. *Rodale's Illustrated Encyclopedia of Herbs*. Emmaus, PA: Rodale Press, 1987.

Liberty Hyde Bailey Hortorium (staff). *Hortus Third*. New York, NY: MacMillan Publishing Company, Collier MacMillan Publishers, 1976.

Loewer, Peter. *The Annual Garden*. Emmaus, PA: Rodale Press, 1988.

Ortho Books (editors). *Enjoying Roses*. San Ramon, CA: Ortho Books, 1992.

Ortho Books (editors). *The Ortho Home Gardener's Problem Solver*. San Ramon, CA: Ortho Books, 1993.

Phillips, Roger. *Trees of North America and Europe*. New York, NY: Random House, 1978.

Pickles, Sheila, ed. *The Language of Flowers*. New York, NY: Harmony Books, 1990.

—, ed. *A Victorian Posy*. New York, NY: Harmony Books, 1987.

Pickston, Margaret. *The Language of Flowers*. London: Michael Joseph Ltd., 1968.

Powell, Eileen. *From Seed to Bloom*. Pownal, VT: Storey Communications, Inc., 1995.

Riotte, Louise. *Sleeping With A Sunflower*. Pownal, VT: Storey Communications, Inc., 1987.

Rossi, Rosella. *Simon & Schuster's Guide to Bulbs*. New York, NY: Simon & Schuster Inc., 1989.

Resources

Sanders, Jack. *Hedgemaids and Fairy Candles*. Camden, ME: Ragged Mountain Press, 1993.

Schenk, George. *The Complete Shade Gardener*. Boston, MA: Houghton Mifflin Company, 1984.

Schuler, Stanley. *How To Grow Almost Everything*. New York, NY: M. Evans and Company, Inc., 1965.

Sunset Books and Sunset Magazine (editors). *Sunset National Garden Book*. Menlo Park, CA: Sunset Books, Inc., 1997.

Taylor, Norman. *Taylor's Guide to Annuals*. Gordon P. DeWolf, Jr., ed. Boston, MA: Houghton Mifflin Company, Chanticleer Press, 1961.

—. *Taylor's Guide to Bulbs*. Gordon P. DeWolf, Jr., ed. Boston, MA: Houghton Mifflin Company, Chanticleer Press, 1961.

—. *Taylor's Guide to Ground Covers, Vines & Grasses*. Gordon P. DeWolf, Jr., ed. Boston, MA: Houghton Mifflin Company, Chanticleer Press, 1961.

—. *Taylor's Guide to Ornamental Grasses*. Gordon P. DeWolf, Jr., ed. Boston, MA: Houghton Mifflin Company, Chanticleer Press, 1961.

—. *Taylor's Guide to Perennials*. Gordon P. DeWolf, Jr., ed. Boston, MA: Houghton Mifflin Company, Chanticleer Press, 1961.

—. *Taylor's Guide to Roses*. Gordon P. DeWolf, Jr., ed. Boston, MA: Houghton Mifflin Company, Chanticleer Press, 1961.

—. *Taylor's Guide to Shrubs*. Gordon P. DeWolf, Jr., ed. Boston, MA: Houghton Mifflin Company, Chanticleer Press, 1961.

—. *Taylor's Guide to Water-Saving Gardening*. Boston, MA: Houghton Mifflin Company, Chanticleer Press, 1990.

Tenenbaum, Frances, ed. *Taylor's Guide to Seashore Gardening*. Boston, MA: Houghton Mifflin Company, 1996.

—, ed. *Taylor's Master Guide to Gardening*. Boston, MA: Houghton Mifflin Company, 1994.

Van Hazinga, Cynthia. *Flower Gardening Secrets*. New York, NY: Time-Life Books, Inc., 1997.

Venning, Frank D. *Wildflowers of North America*. New York, NY: Golden Press, Western Publishing Company, 1984.

Wister, John C. *Bulbs for Home Gardens*. New York, NY: Oxford University Press, 1948.

Wyman, Donald. *Wyman's Gardening Encyclopedia*. New York, NY: MacMillan Publishing Co., 1986.

Zucker, Isabel. *Flowering Shrubs & Small Trees*. New York, NY: Michael Friedman Publishing Group, Inc., Grove Weidenfeld, 1990.

INDEX

Index

Index

Index

Index

Index

Index

Index

412

Index

Index

ABOUT THE AUTHOR

*P*EGI BALLISTER-HOWELLS is well suited to write about New Jersey ornamental gardening. She received her bachelor's degree in Biology from Rutgers College and master's degree in Horticulture from Rutgers University. She has worked with numerous organizations in the horticulture field, including the New Jersey Farm Bureau as marketing consultant since 1993, Herb Tech of New Jersey as regional manager since 1996, and the Rutgers University Cooperative Extension as an assistant professor and county agricultural agent. She is a member of the Board of Trustees for the New Jersey Museum of Agriculture, and takes agricultural photographs across the state.

The author is well known through her weekly columns, "Garden Chores" and "Speaking of Gardens" in New Brunswick's *Home News and Tribune*. Her expertise is also shared through hosting the popular call-in radio program, "The Garden Show," on WCTC-AM 1450 in New Brunswick. Additionally, she conducts gardening spots for Comcast Cable.

The writing of Pegi Ballister-Howells has appeared in many periodicals, including *Garden State Home and Garden, The Star Ledger, The Courier News, Rutgers Magazine, Heresies, New Jersey Living,* and *The Plant Press*, a quarterly newsletter for the nursery industry. Pegi, her husband, family, and assorted pets live on a ten-acre working farm, Blooming Acres, where they do extensive ornamental and vegetable gardening.

NEW JERSEY GARDENING
ONLINE